Health Care Terms

Health Care Terms

Second Edition

Vergil N. Slee, MD
Debora A. Slee, JD

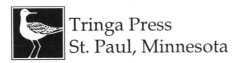

Tringa Press
St. Paul, Minnesota

To the people who persuaded us this book was needed:

The Spouses of the Estes Park Institute
Board of Directors and the Conference Faculty

and

The Spouses of the Estes Park Institute Conference Participants

Tringa Press
P.O. Box 8181
St. Paul, MN 55108

Printed in the United States of America on recycled paper.
95 94 93 92 91   10 9 8 7 6 5 4 3 2 1

Library of Congress Cataloging in Publication Data

Slee, Vergil N., 1917-
    Health care terms / Vergil N. Slee, Debora A. Slee. — 2nd ed.
        p.   cm.
    ISBN 0-9615255-1-7 (pbk. : alk. paper)
    1. Medical care—Dictionaries. 2. Public health—Dictionaries.
3. Medical laws and legislation—Dictionaries. 4. Medicine—
Dictionaries.   I. Slee, Debora A.   II. Title.
    [DNLM: 1. Delivery of Health Care—terminology. 2. Health
Planning—terminology. 3. Health Services—organization &
administration—terminology.   W 15 S632h]
RA423.S55   1991
613'.03—dc20   90-28543

Preface

Origin of *Health Care Terms*

This book was stimulated by the spouses of both the faculty and the participants of the Hospital Medical Staff and Trustee Conferences conducted by Estes Park Institute (EPI). Estes Park Institute holds these educational sessions nationally for physicians in leadership positions, hospital and other health care administrators, and trustees of health care institutions. EPI's primary purpose is to identify and treat the emerging issues in health care. During the conference sessions, the faculty of EPI and their spouses conduct a concurrent program for the participants' spouses. The spouses' program, designed in response to feedback from the group, is intended not merely to entertain, but primarily to inform about the changing world of health care. It is, in fact, called the Healthcare Seminar for Spouses.

Early on, the spouses let it be known that one of the greatest barriers to their understanding the current health care scene and its problems and stresses is the language used. Different terms are often applied to the same thing, and many of the terms have multiple meanings (a "sanction," for example, can be either a punishment or a support). In addition, new terms are appearing daily in health care circles, some dealing with new technology, some with new forms of organization, and some with legal and financing developments. Many terms are part of the jargon and slang which are the natural means of communication among insiders. Among the most irritating impediments to the "outsiders," the spouses, are the abbreviations and acronyms; an unwritten rule seems to be that if there are three or more words in a

i

phrase, they will be replaced in conversation (and writing) by the first letters of the words (and bureaucratic jargon lends itself beautifully to this game).

Unless this language barrier could be surmounted, there was little chance for the Healthcare Seminar for Spouses to achieve its goal of complementing the programs presented to the professionals in the Conference: a glossary was clearly needed. Finding no glossary which covered the breadth of the field with which the health care professional now deals (it's far more than hospitals today), the senior author in 1984 drafted the precursor to this volume. *Health Care Terms, First Edition*, was the outgrowth of that experience, and owed much to the helpful comments of the participants in both the Conferences and the Seminars.

Once the idea of a glossary was discussed, it was apparent that there was almost as much demand for one by the trustees, administrators, and physicians. Each group had been suffering in silence while the others used terms that "everybody understood." In fact, many terms used within one group (physicians or administrators, for example) are not familiar to members of another group; and, in the case of new terminology, often no one really knows what it means.

The most pressing need appeared to be in the areas of health care regulation, administration, organization, financing, and the law. But it was soon found that other areas had to be included. For example, some clinical terms, particularly those dealing with new technology (lithotripsy, for instance), couldn't be looked up handily by trustees and concerned citizens. Nor could many terms dealing with medical and other professional education—on which trustees must now increasingly focus because of problems of financing education under prospective payment, and because of changing governmental attitudes—easily be found. Organizational development and human resources development have languages all their own. So the vocabulary continues to grow as the hospital is more and more integrated "horizontally" with other similar institutions, and "vertically" into more complete and comprehensive health care systems, and as "alternative" methods of organization, financing, and practice appear.

Most of the new terms coming into play, or old terms taking on new usage, do so innocently; a new thing can't carry the same label as something else, and it is the nature of language for meanings to change over time. But in health care, as in other fields, some of the changes are mischievous. As J. M. Juran states in "A Wistful Postscript on Terminology" in his *Quality Control Handbook* (McGraw-Hill, 1974), some are the products of

> . . . deliberate efforts of human beings to create and use terminology to secure benefits for their organizations and for themselves. . . . The prime need is to discover the realities under the labels, i.e., the deeds, activities, or things which the other fellow is talking about. Once these are understood, accurate communication can take place whether the labels are agreed upon or not. In contrast, if communication is purely through labels, it is easy to be deluded into believing there is an understanding despite the fact that each of the parties literally does not know what the other fellow is talking about.

This book is intended to help us understand what the other person is talking about.

The *Second Edition*

Since publication of the First Edition five years ago, many new terms have come into usage in the health care field which reflect current events, technological developments, new legislation, and so forth. These, to the extent possible, have been included in the Second Edition of *Health Care Terms*. In addition, the authors have expanded both the scope and content of the book to make it more useful to the wide audience it serves. The Second Edition contains over three times as many terms as the First. In addition, some previous definitions have been expanded, or changed to reflect changes in usage of a term.

As in the First Edition, each definition is intended to present a concept and show how that concept relates to the health care field, and at the same time serve as a quick reference (reminder) for those already familiar with the concept. The emphasis of the work is on breadth, not depth. In certain instances, however, some depth is necessary to explain the term (coding, for example); in others, such as with the highly technical (and changing) computations used in the Medicare payment system, no attempt has been made to give detail. Technical terms, such as those from the fields of law, medicine, and accounting, are defined simply; they are not intended to be authoritative or to take the place of professional advice.

Explanatory Notes

Where there are a number of types of persons, processes, or things—such as "nurses," "admissions," "hospitals," and "reviews"—they have been, for the most part, grouped together under those headings, in order to facilitate the comparison of the various kinds of processes or things. Occasionally such terms may be listed in two places to make finding them easier. Where a term is commonly abbreviated, it can be located under the abbreviation or acronym. For example, "registered nurse," "scrub nurse," and "visiting nurse" will be found under the term "nurse." "RN," however, will be found under "RN" as well as under "nurse," since the reader may not necessarily know that an RN is a kind of nurse.

A word or phrase used in a definition may be italicized to show that the word or phrase itself is defined elsewhere in the glossary. Italics are used for such cross-references only when the meaning of the italicized word or phrase is necessary to an understanding of the term being defined. Common terms—such as hospital, physician, and Medicare—are not italicized even though they are defined in the glossary.

The word "hospital" is often used in a context which would clearly apply to other types of health care institutions as well. The purpose is to keep the definitions, as much as possible, simple and clear. Thus, "hospital" is used to represent all health care institutions in these instances. Similarly, "physician" or "nurse" might be used to denote health care professionals generally.

In an effort to make the glossary gender-neutral, yet not cumbersome, the choice was made to alternate the feminine and masculine pronouns from letter to letter (for example, a is masculine, b feminine, etc.).

Many words in the glossary have more than one meaning. In most cases, only the meaning relating to health care is given. For example, "acute" may mean sharp or urgent; the definition given in *Health Care Terms* is that relating to disease, meaning one with a short, relatively severe course. In some instances, a word or phrase has more than one meaning of interest to those in health care. For example, "agent" has both a clinical and a legal meaning. In these cases, the multiple definitions are listed separately and designated as follows:

agent (1): A chemical or biological substance.

agent (2): A person who acts for another person.

A note regarding comprehensiveness. The number of terms used in healthcare is very large, and growing constantly. The authors have attempted thoroughness in this volume, but are aware that not all terms have been included. Therefore, the exclusion of a specialty, professional, institution, or any other term should not be taken as a diminution of the importance of that term. Rather, it should be taken as either an editorial decision (excluding very commonly understood terms, for example) or an oversight by the authors. Readers are urged to bring to the authors' attention any terms which the reader believes should be included, and any comments regarding the definitions.

Acknowledgments

This book was the result of the efforts of many. The idea (as discussed in the Preface) grew out of the Estes Park Institute (EPI) Health Care Seminars for Spouses. The spouses of the EPI faculty, the spouses of the conference participants, and the faculty and participants themselves, all contributed to the concept of a glossary. They suggested terms in need of explanation and provided feedback on preliminary definitions. One spouse in particular—Beth E. Slee—gave exceptional support, provided insight to the needs of the spouses, and contributed much patience during the execution of the idea.

The authors are also indebted to their colleagues: C. Wesley Eisele, MD, who encouraged the compilation of the original glossary; Kenneth J. Williams, MD, who encouraged the publication of a more comprehensive book, suggested terms and definitions, and provided feedback and support; and John A. Lowe, MD, and Mary Ann Lowe, RN, ART, who contributed terms and definitions concerning long-term care. Terms, definitions, and comments were also provided by Richard Ament, Samuel P. Asper, MD, Richard C. Bates, MD, Barbara Bruns, ARM, CPCU, William R. Fifer, MD, U. Beate Krinke, MPH, RD, Charles F. Petet, Bobbi Ryan, Fay Coker Walker, MSW, E. Eugene Weaver, Barbara Wilcox, RN, and Toma C. Wilson.

Able assistance in editing was provided by Paul A. Ruschmann, JD, whose thoroughness and skill has caused those who know him to term his work "ruschmannizing" (unusually fine editing).

This book would not have come into being without the benefits of modern technology—the computer—and people who know how to make it all work. H. Joachim ("HJ") Schmidt, JD, was responsible for production (for details, see "Production Notes" at the back of the book). HJ provided numerous technical services to the authors: recommending equipment, teaching how to use it, writing software, fixing hardware, transferring data between distant contributors, and troubleshooting. HJ also contributed most of the computer definitions in the book.

The authors also wish to thank Peter J. Schmidt, whose birth coincided with that of this book, and who continues to provide both inspiration and joy.

About the Authors

Vergil N. Slee, MD, is President Emeritus of the Commission on Professional and Hospital Activities (CPHA). He received his BA from Albion College in Michigan, his MD from Washington University in St. Louis, and his MPH from the University of Michigan. Dr. Slee pioneered the Professional Activity Study (PAS) and founded CPHA, and was president of the Council on Clinical Classifications which, with the National Center for Health Statistics, created the *Clinical Modification* of the *International Classification of Diseases, Ninth Revision (ICD-9-CM)*. He has served for over twenty-five years as a member of the faculty of Estes Park Institute (EPI), which presents conferences for hospital trustees, administrators, and medical staff officers, and their spouses. He is a Fellow of the American College of Physicians, a Fellow of the American Public Health Association, and an Honorary Fellow of the American College of Healthcare Executives.

Debora A. Slee, JD, is an attorney with experience in health care law and quality management. She received her BA from the University of Michigan and her JD from William Mitchell College of Law in St. Paul. She is a member of the Minnesota State Bar Association, the Minnesota Society of Hospital Attorneys, and the American Society of Law and Medicine. She is contributing author to *The Law of Hospital and Health Care Administration, Second Edition*, by Arthur F. Southwick.

A

A-EMT: Advanced emergency medical technician. See *emergency medical technician-intermediate* under *emergency medical technician*.

AA: See *anesthesiologist's assistant*.

AAA: See *American Academy of Addictionology*.

AACN (1): See *American Association of Colleges of Nursing*.

AACN (2): See *American Association of Critical-Care Nurses*.

AAHA (1): American Academy of Hospital Attorneys, affiliated with the American Hospital Association (AHA).

AAHA (2): See *American Association of Homes for the Aging*.

AAHC: American Association of Healthcare Consultants.

AAMC: Association of American Medical Colleges.

AAMD: See *American Academy of Medical Directors*.

AAMSI: See *American Association for Medical Systems and Informatics*.

AAN: See *American Academy of Nursing*.

A

AAP (1):   See *Association of American Physicians*.

AAP (2):   American Academy of Pediatrics.

AARP: See *American Association of Retired Persons*.

abandonment: A *tort* in which the wrongdoing consists of leaving a patient without treatment when there is still a doctor-patient relationship requiring the physician to continue treatment.

ABIM: See *American Board of Internal Medicine*.

ABMM: See *American Board of Medical Management*.

abortion: Giving birth to an *embryo* or *fetus* before the fetus is capable of independent life (about the 20th week of gestation or after reaching about 500 grams (1 pound, 2 ounces) in weight). (A *premature birth* is one which occurs after the infant is generally capable of independent life.)

An abortion may be either "spontaneous" (without outside assistance) or "induced" (the result of efforts to cause the abortion).

abortus: The *fetus* out of the uterus (ex utero), whether alive or dead, *viable* or *nonviable*, after an *abortion*.

ABS: See *American Board of Surgery*.

abstracter: See *medical record abstracter*.

abstracting: The process of extracting information from a document in order to create a summary, called an abstract, of that document. The process of abstracting should not introduce the abstracter's judgment, that is, the resulting abstract must carry exactly the same information as in the original document for those items which have been extracted.

abuse: The improper use of health care products and *services (1)*. Abuse may result from excessive (unnecessary) use of diagnostic tests, unnecessary surgical and other procedures, and so forth. Abuse may be either intentional or unintentional, and may or may not be illegal.

The laws governing Medicare, for example, make certain referral arrangements illegal because they create opportunity for abuse, even though there may be no actual abuse or intent to abuse. See *fraud and abuse*.

abuse of process: A *tort* where the wrongdoing consists of using the legal system for an improper purpose. For example, initiating *involuntary commitment* proceedings to hospitalize a person to stop him from doing something (such as leaving town), rather than because he legitimately needs treatment, is abuse of process. Unlike a lawsuit for *malicious prosecution*, a plaintiff alleging abuse of process does not need to win the improper suit, nor prove a lack of probable cause for that suit.

acceptable daily intake (ADI): A measure, derived from animal studies, of the level of contamination in a soil below which there is hazard to humans.

ACCME: See *Accreditation Council for Continuing Medical Education*.

accountability: The obligation to provide, to all concerned, the evidence needed to: (1) establish confidence that the task or duty for which one is responsible is being or has been performed; and (2) describe the manner in which that task is being or has been carried out. When accountability has been fulfilled, the authority which delegated the responsibility can be satisfied by evidence (rather than simply assertion) that the duties or tasks which have been delegated are being or have been adequately performed.

Accountability must be defined in conjunction with responsibility. An individual or organization has responsibility (that is to say, an obligation) because some individual or body with authority has granted or delegated that responsibility. Failure to carry out the responsibility carries with it liability. A responsible party is entitled to delegate duties, that is, to get help in carrying out the obligation, but not to delegate the responsibility itself. The responsible party, therefore, must have reasonable ground on which he can render account (be accountable) for the duties which have been delegated. So the delegation of duties, as a matter of law, carries with it the requirement of accountability to the source of the delegation of the duties.

A

A hospital, for example, is delegated certain duties by "society," by government. For this purpose, the hospital's responsibility is accepted and held by its *governing body*. The governing body must render account for its performance (it holds accountability) to society, through specific reporting mechanisms, voluntary efforts to provide society evidence of its performance, and defending itself against liability suits. In turn the governing body delegates tasks to the *chief executive officer (CEO)* and demands accounting from that individual; the CEO, in turn, delegates tasks to departmental heads and demands accountability from them.

Similarly, the governing body gives the *medical staff organization (MSO)* duties, for example, with respect to examination of *credentials* of applicants for medical staff membership. The MSO incurs, along with the duty, the obligation of accountability—it must provide the evidence needed to establish the governing body's confidence that it, the MSO, has indeed performed the task, and the evidence must be presented in enough detail to permit the governing body to assess the quality of performance of the duty.

accounting period: The time, usually a month, a quarter, or a year, covered by a financial statement.

accounts payable (AP): Amounts on *open account* owed to *creditors* for goods and services.

accounts receivable (AR): Amounts owed by others on *open account* for goods or services.

accreditation: A process of: (1) evaluation of an institution or education program to determine whether it meets the standards set up by an accrediting body, and (2) if the institution or program meets the standards, granting recognition of the fact. Accreditation is a process performed by a non-governmental agency at the request of the institution or education program. Although governmental agencies carry out evaluation and recognition processes on a mandatory basis for licensure purposes, these processes are not accreditation.

Health care institutions are accredited by the Joint Commission on the Accreditation of Healthcare Organizations (JCAHO) in the United States and by the Canadian Council on Health Facilities

Accreditation (CCHFA) in Canada. Health care education programs are accredited by other bodies.

Accreditation Council for Continuing Medical Education (ACCME): A nonprofit organization that provides a method for *accreditation* of *continuing medical education (CME)*. See *medical education*.

Accreditation Council for Graduate Medical Education (ACGME): A nonprofit organization that provides *accreditation* for clinical training programs (usually residencies) in United States medical centers, upon submission of reports from *Residency Review Committees*. See *residency, medical education*.

accreditation decision grid: A numerical summary of an institution's *survey* scores and findings which the institution may obtain from the *Joint Commission on Accreditation of Healthcare Organizations (JCAHO)* on request. Its purpose is to provide a view of the institution's performance. JCAHO also offers a "standards compliance summary report," which is a prose counterpart of the accreditation decision grid.

Accreditation Manual for Hospitals (AMH): The annual publication of the *Joint Commission on the Accreditation of Healthcare Organizations (JCAHO)* which gives the *standards* that hospitals are expected to meet if they are to be *accredited* by the JCAHO after examination by the JCAHO surveyors. For each standard, the *AMH* spells out a number of "required characteristics." The 1990 *AMH* contains the following chapters (given along with their *AMH* abbreviation):

> Alcoholism and Other Drug Dependence Services (AL)
> Diagnostic Radiology Services (DR)
> Dietetic Services (DT)
> Emergency Services (ER)
> Governing Body (GB)
> Hospital-Sponsored Ambulatory Care Services (HO)
> Infection Control (IC)
> Management and Administrative Services (MA)
> Medical Record Services (MR)
> Medical Staff (MS)

Nuclear Medicine Services (NM)
Nursing Services (NR)
Pathology and Medical Laboratory Services (PA)
Pharmaceutical Services (PH)
Physical Rehabilitation Services (RH)
Plant, Technology, and Safety Management (PL)
Professional Library Services (PR)
Quality Assurance (QA)
Radiation Oncology Services (RA)
Respiratory Care Services (RP)
Social Work Services (SO)
Special Care Units (SP)
Surgical and Anesthesia Services (SA)
Utilization Review (UR)

Each chapter starts with a statement of the principle or rationale behind the standards for that chapter, followed by from four or five to perhaps 20 standards, for each of which explanatory material is provided under headings of "interpretation" or "required characteristics."

Accreditation Review Council for Educational Programs in Surgical Technology (ARC-ST): The body which reviews educational programs in surgical technology, using standards found in *Essentials and Guidelines of an Accredited Educational Program for the Surgical Technologist (Essentials)*, which were adopted by the American College of Surgeons (ACS), the American Hospital Association (AHA), the American Medical Association (AMA), and the Association of Surgical Technologists (AST). The results of the reviews are reported to the AMA's Committee on Allied Health Education and Accreditation (CAHEA) for *accreditation* of the programs.

accreditation survey: The on-site examination of an institution by *surveyors* of the *Joint Commission on the Accreditation of Healthcare Organizations (JCAHO)* for the purpose of determining its compliance with the relevant *JCAHO standards* and its eligibility for *accreditation*.

accredited: Formally recognized by an accrediting body as meeting its standards for *accreditation*. The accrediting body for hospitals and certain other health care institutions in the United States is the

Joint Commission on the Accreditation of Healthcare Organizations (JCAHO); in Canada, the counterpart organization is the Canadian Council on Health Facilities Accreditation (CCHFA).

Accredited Record Technician (ART): A *medical record technician* who has passed a *credential examination* of the *American Medical Record Association (AMRA)*. A medical record technician is a person who carries out certain technical duties with respect to *medical records*. The formal training of an ART is somewhat less than that of the *medical record administrator (MRA)*.

ACE: See *angiotensin-converting enzyme*.

ACEP: American College of Emergency Physicians.

ACGME: See *Accreditation Council for Graduate Medical Education*.

ACHA: See *American College of Hospital Administrators*.

ACHE: See *American College of Healthcare Executives*.

ACNM: See *American College of Nurse Midwives*.

ACOG: American College of Obstetricians and Gynecologists.

ACP: See *American College of Physicians*.

ACPE: See *American College of Physician Executives*.

acquired immunodeficiency syndrome (AIDS): The disease caused by the *human immunodeficiency virus (HIV)*.

ACS (1): See *American College of Surgeons*.

ACS (2): American Cancer Society.

activities director: The individual responsible for providing activities to patients in a *long term care facility (LTCF)* in order to promote continuing involvement in *activities of daily living (ADL)* and to retard or prevent disabilities.

activities of daily living (ADL): Functions which are ordinarily done for oneself, such as combing hair, brushing teeth, eating, dressing, and taking care of bodily functions. In the case of bedfast and paralyzed persons, the definition is restricted to activities which do not require mobility, such as combing hair and brushing teeth. See also *Instrumental Activities of Daily Living (IADL) scale*.

activities therapist: See *therapeutic recreation specialist*.

ACTS: See *American College Testing Service*.

actuarial analysis: A forecast developed by specialized actuarial methods, giving the probability of future events for a given population, such as life expectancy, frequency of hospitalization, or probability of loss from fire. A common use of such forecasts is the calculation of insurance premiums and, for the insurer, the necessary reserves.

acuity: Acuteness, as of an illness. The term is used a great deal in reference to nursing needs and demands for other health care resources: the greater the acuity, the more nursing care or other services are needed.

ACURP: See *American College of Utilization Review Physicians*.

acute: With respect to an illness, having a short course, which often is relatively severe. The term is also used for the portion or portions of an illness, ordinarily in its early stages, in which symptoms are most severe and the patient may be at greatest risk. The period following acute is referred to as "postacute."

acute care: Care for *short-term* patients.

AD: See *associate degree*.

ad damnum clause: The part of a legal complaint (the document which initiates a lawsuit) which states the amount of money (*damages*) the *plaintiff* demands. Some states prohibit a plaintiff from demanding any specific dollar amount other than that required for the court's jurisdiction (for example, "a sum greater than ten thousand dollars"). This requirement helps avoid tabloid headlines such as, "Patient Sues Physician for Ten Billion Dollars Over Hangnail."

ad hoc: For this. An ad hoc committee is one formed for a particular purpose, usually limited in duration until the purpose is completed. This is in contrast to a standing committee, which purportedly remains active over time.

ADA: See *American Dietetic Association*.

ADAMHA: See *Alcohol, Drug Abuse, and Mental Health Administration*.

ADC: See *Aid to Families with Dependent Children*.

addiction: Psychological and or physical dependence on a given substance or practice.

addictionologist: An individual, usually a physician, who specializes in the study and treatment of *alcoholism* and *drug dependency*.

addictionology: The study of *alcoholism* and *drug dependency*.

addictive: A drug or practice which results in psychological and/or physical dependence on the drug or practice by most individuals exposed to it.

ADFS: See *alternative delivery and financing system*.

ADI: See *acceptable daily intake*.

adjustment: A statistical term referring to a procedure for correcting for differences in the composition of two or more populations. The correction is made, for example, so that valid comparisons can be made between populations. The factors most commonly adjusted for are age and sex. Such adjustments are essential if the *rates (2)* of occurrence of a disease, for example, are to be compared without distortion. Adjustments are used in a specific procedure called *standardization.*

adjuvant: A *drug* which, when given in conjunction with another ("main") drug (usually by incorporating the adjuvant in the formulation), changes the action of the main drug in a predictable manner.

ADL: See *activities of daily living.*

administrative adjustment: A bookkeeping entry to a patient's bill to account for services rendered but not billed to the patient's account for some reason, such as in settlement of a disagreement between hospital and patient.

administrative agency: See *agency (1).*

administrative engineer: A hospital engineer who has administrative (planning or management) responsibility. Typically there is one person with this title, the highest rank among the engineers of the institution. Synonym(s): director of buildings and grounds, chief engineer, plant engineer.

administrative law: The body of law which governs the powers of administrative agencies (see *agency (1)*), the process of agency decision-making, and the procedures by which a party can challenge an adverse decision of an agency.

administrative process: The process by which an administrative agency (*agency (1)*) makes a decision. In the context of hospitals, an example would be the procedure for obtaining a *certificate of need (CON)*. This would include a petition for the certificate, setting of a hearing date and notice to all interested parties, the hearing itself (which is normally less formal than a court hearing), and a decision by the agency. The decision may be appealed within the administrative agency. After the complete administrative process is "exhausted," meaning that all avenues have been tried, a party dissatisfied with the result can go to the courts to challenge the decision.

administrative residency: See *residency*.

administrator: The individual responsible for carrying out policies established by the organization or agency for which he is employed. An administrator is a line official, that is, an employee with authority over others. When the authority is over the entire hospital, the individual is *the* administrator, and current usage is to call this person the "chief executive officer" (CEO). When a person is referred to as "the administrator," it usually means the CEO.

admissible: A legal term referring to whether evidence (such as a witness' testimony, medical record entry, or blood test result) will be allowed to be presented to the judge or jury to prove a legal *case (2)*. There are specific rules of evidence governing admissibility. For example, even though a plaintiff obtains a medical record during *discovery*, portions of the record may not be admissible in court because they are irrelevant to the plaintiff's case, protected by law (*privileged*), not properly *authenticated*, or for other reasons.

admission (1): Formal acceptance of a patient by a hospital or other health care institution in order to provide care. Such admission may be of a number of kinds:

clinic outpatient admission: Admission of a patient to a hospital *outpatient clinic*. This is a specific kind of *outpatient admission*.

elective admission: An admission that can be scheduled in advance because the illness or injury is not life-threatening.

emergency admission: An admission that must take place immediately, or else death or serious disability is likely to result.

emergency department admission: Admission of a patient, who needs prompt attention, to an *emergency department (ED)*, a department or facility which gives care for a single encounter. By definition, patients may not become continuing patients of an emergency department; the entire episode of emergency care is one *visit*. Also called an emergency outpatient admission.

inpatient admission: Admission to an institution which provides lodging and continuous *nursing services*.

newborn admission: Admission by virtue of being born in a hospital. Only a baby born in a given hospital can be a newborn admission to that hospital. A newborn delivered elsewhere (even on the way to the hospital or in its *emergency department (ED)*) is a *pediatric admission* or a *transfer*. Synonym(s): newborn inpatient admission.

newborn inpatient admission: See *newborn admission*.

outpatient admission (OP admission): Admission to a facility of the hospital which gives care but does not provide lodging. An *outpatient facility* is ready to furnish a series of *services (1)* to the same patient over a period of time (as contrasted with the *emergency department*, which can give a patient service only once for one *episode*).

pediatric admission: Admission of a child, with the upper age defined by the hospital (perhaps 15 to 20 years of age, depending on the clinical problem), except for infants born in the hospital (who are *newborn admissions*).

referred outpatient admission: A special kind of *outpatient admission* in which the patient is to receive only the *diagnostic procedures* or *treatments* specified by the *referring physician* or institution.

transfer admission: Admission of a patient by *transfer*: (1) from another institution where the individual was also a patient; or (2) from another division of the hospital, as when a newborn remains after discharge of the mother and becomes a "transfer admission" from the newborn service to the pediatric service of the hospital.

urgent admission: An admission of a patient whose condition is less *critical* than *emergency* (less life- or serious-disability threatening), but more critical than *elective*. An "urgent admission" stands between these two in priority.

admission (2): A statement made by a party to a lawsuit, which affirms or denies a material fact concerning the lawsuit. A "material fact" is one which is essential to the plaintiff's or defendant's case. Admissions are used to streamline the legal process, so that time is not wasted in court proving facts about which the parties do not disagree, such as the parties' names and addresses, whether the plaintiff was in fact a patient at the hospital, and so forth. If a party denies such a fact in bad faith, and the other party has to prove it at trial, the party acting in bad faith is penalized.

admission pattern monitoring (APM): The *monitoring* of the distribution of kinds of patients admitted to a hospital (that is, of the admission *case mix*) in order to detect changing needs for services, displacement of patients to other institutions, or other changes.

admitting department: The hospital department which carries out the administrative tasks connected with *admission, discharge,* and *transfer* of patients.

admitting manager: See *admitting officer.*

admitting officer: A hospital official, usually not a physician, who is responsible for the processes of *admission* and *discharge* of patients, and who is in charge of the *admitting department.* Synonym(s): admitting manager, registrar (2).

ADS: See *alternative delivery system (1)* and *(2).*

adult day care: Care, provided during the day, which will permit a patient to function in the home. The care may include a wide range of services—medical, social, nutritional, psychological, and the like.

adult day health services: Medical and other health care services provided to patients whose condition permits them to return home or to another facility at night. When such care is regularly scheduled, it may be termed *partial hospitalization.* Synonym(s): day health care services.

adult foster home: See *family care home.*

advanced emergency medical procedures: A term sometimes applied to *procedures* which an *emergency medical technician-paramedic (EMT-P)* (the highest level of EMT) may perform, but which lower levels of EMTs may not perform. Such procedures may include, for example, insertion of a tube in the patient's airway for assistance in breathing, and administration of certain drugs. State statutes typically govern the designation of levels of EMTs, and the procedures authorized for each.

advanced emergency medical technician (A-EMT): See *emergency medical technician-intermediate* under *emergency medical technician.*

advanced life support (ALS): A term used in emergency medical services which usually refers to the administration of *intravenous* medications and the use of *defibrillation* (heart starting) equipment. This term may have a specific definition in a state's statutes or regulations governing emergency medical care.

adverse patient occurrence (APO): An event which meets one or more criteria, such as the following: (1) a patient is injured, whether or not the hospital may be liable; (2) the admission was the result of an adverse result of outpatient care; (3) the patient was readmitted because of complications or incomplete care in the previous admission; (4) there were deficiencies in documentation, such as in *informed consent* procedures or in the *medical record*; (5) unplanned surgery was done; (6) procedures were employed which did not meet the hospital's criteria for appropriateness; (7) a problem occurred with use of blood or blood components; (8) a nosocomial (hospital-acquired) infection occurred; (9) drug usage was inappropriate; (10) cardiac or respiratory arrest or death occurred; (11) there was an incident (such as a patient fall); (12) abnormal laboratory or X-ray findings were not followed up; (13) the stay was unusually short or long for the condition; (14) there were problems in obtaining services; or (15) there was patient or family dissatisfaction. These criteria are paraphrased from the *Medical Management Analysis (MMA)* system for review of care, which depends heavily on screening for and reporting of APOs.

Sometimes an APO is called an *incident,* but these terms are not necessarily synonymous. "Incident" is sometimes more narrowly used to refer only to accidents (such as falls) or behavioral problems.

adverse selection: A situation in which patients with greater than average need for medical and hospital care enroll in a *prepaid health plan* in greater numbers than they occur in a cross-section of the population. A plan which somehow encouraged or allowed people to sign up when they were already ill would suffer from adverse selection.

aerospace medicine: The branch of *preventive medicine* which deals with the special problems of flying, both within and outside the atmosphere. One of the medical specialties for which *residency* programs have been approved by the Accreditation Council for Graduate Medical Education (ACGME). See *specialty*.

AFCR: See *American Federation for Clinical Research*.

AFDC: See *Aid to Families with Dependent Children*.

affirmative action: Steps taken to remedy inequalities which have resulted from past acts of discrimination. Federal law prohibits discrimination based on race and sex, and discrimination against handicapped persons and Vietnam-era and other disabled veterans. Anyone contracting with the federal government for more than $10,000 a year is required to have an affirmative action program.

AFS: See *alternative financing system*.

after care: Care during the period of *convalescence* following hospitalization.

against medical advice (AMA): A type of *discharge* which occurs when the patient, contrary to the advice of the attending physician, refuses treatment and "signs himself out," thus releasing the hospital from *liability* for subsequent events.

agency (1): Administrative agency. A part of state or federal government, created by the legislature, which has specific administrative duties and functions, often including regulation of a profession or industry. A state board of medical examiners, for example, is an administrative agency. There is a body of law (administrative law) which governs the powers of administrative agencies, the process of agency decision-making, and the procedures by which a party dissatisfied with a decision of an agency can challenge it. Ordinarily, any person who wishes to contest an administrative agency decision must go through all of the channels of appeal within the agency before challenging the decision in the courts.

agency (2): A legal relationship in which one person acts on behalf of another. A written agency agreement is called a *power of attorney*.

agency (3): An organization set up to carry out services such as home health care, "meals on wheels," or *registration (2)* of tumor patients. In this usage, the agency may be part of either the public sector or the private sector. If the agency is private, it may be either nonprofit or for-profit.

agent (1): A *chemical* or *biological* substance or an organism capable of producing an effect, for example, a "therapeutic agent," an "infectious agent," or a "noxious agent."

infectious agent: A microorganism (a germ, virus, or other living microscopic organism) which can cause a disease by invading the tissues and multiplying within the body. It is contrasted with other agents, such as chemicals, which can cause disease, but are not live and therefore are not capable of multiplying within the body.

agent (2): A person who acts for another person, who is called the *principal*. An agent can legally bind the principal. An agent may or may not be an employee, but an employee is always an agent of the employer.

actual agent: A person who has been authorized by another (the *principal*) to act for that other person. The term "actual" is used to describe the fact that the principal has, in fact, authorized the agent. Usually the nature and limits of the agent's authority are specific. In some circumstances, the law will impose liability on a principal even though the agent was not actually authorized; see *apparent agent*.

apparent agent: A person who has not been authorized to act on behalf of another (the *principal*), but who appears, to other people, to have such authority. In cases where the principal is responsible (or partly responsible) for this appearance, the principal may be held legally responsible for the acts of the apparent agent. See also *actual agent*.

A

agent (3): An instrument or means by which something is done. Often used to describe a person working within an organization:

change agent: A person whose efforts, by design or not, facilitate change in an organization. Such a person may not even be aware of causing change.

energy agent: A term which more accurately describes the role of an individual who provides leadership, from within the organization or outside it, to enhance the productivity and satisfaction of individuals. For many years the emphasis has been on *"change agents"*; however, at least as much effort must be employed for *entropy prevention* as for change. The term "energy agent" covers both of these tasks of management (as well as individuals who are effective in creating and maintaining an organization's enthusiasm and productivity).

AHA: See *American Hospital Association*.

AHA Guide: See *Guide to the Health Care Field*.

AHA/National Hospital Panel Survey: See *National Hospital Panel Survey*.

AI: See *artificial intelligence*.

AICPA: See *American Institute of Certified Public Accountants*.

AID: See *artificial insemination by donor*.

Aid to Families with Dependent Children (ADC, AFDC): A federally financed program for single-parent families, designed to provide welfare for single parents who cannot, without this assistance, take proper care of the children.

aide: An assistant without professional *credentials*. An aide is one who assists, usually without formal training, or with less training than the person assisted. An aide may also work under the supervision of an *agency (3)*, as in the case of a *home health aide* (homemaker). Usually, "aide" is preceded by an adjective, such as "nurse's aide" or "physical therapy aide."

A

AIDS: See *acquired immunodeficiency syndrome.*

AIDS-related complex (ARC): A term applied in the past to a variety of *symptom complexes* which are today considered to represent different degrees of severity or progression of acquired immunodeficiency syndrome (AIDS), the disease caused by the human immunodeficiency virus (HIV). Synonym(s): pre-AIDS.

AIDS-related virus (ARV): See *human immunodeficiency virus (HIV).*

AIH: See *artificial insemination by husband.*

airway: Either (1) the passage between a person's mouth and lungs, or (2) a device which can be inserted in the passage or replace a portion of it.

AL: See *Alcoholism and Other Drug Dependence Services.*

Alcohol, Drug Abuse, and Mental Health Administration (ADAMHA): An administration within the *Department of Health and Human Services (DHHS)* of the executive branch of the federal government. In the federal bureaucracy, a "department" consists of one or more "administrations."

alcoholism: Chronic dependence on the use of alcohol which leads to interference with health and to social and economic problems. Withdrawal of alcohol from a person with alcoholism leads to psychological and physical symptoms.

Alcoholism and Other Drug Dependence Services (AL): The chapter giving the *standards* for this component of the hospital in the 1990 *Accreditation Manual for Hospitals (AMH)* of the *Joint Commission on the Accreditation of Healthcare Organizations (JCAHO).*

alcoholism rehabilitation: A *service (6)* that includes services to enable the alcoholic patient to return to normal functioning. It is contrasted with *alcoholism treatment*, which confines itself to the acute episode of intoxication.

alcoholism treatment: A *service (6)* restricted to the diagnosis and treatment of alcoholic patients. It does not include rehabilitation services.

algorithm: A set of rules for carrying out a process, such as the care of a patient with a given set of problems, or the calculation of a statistic. The rules are such that a specific set of steps is required in sequence, with each step dependent on the preceding step.

alien FMG: See *foreign medical graduate (FMG)*.

all-payer plan: A payment policy under which the same payment method is applied to patients of all *payers*. Today, the term "all-payer plan" really means applying the *prospective payment system (PPS)* to all patients, rather than Medicare patients only. (Medicare patients are the only patients to which the PPS applies under the present federal regulations.)

allergist: A physician specializing in the diagnosis and treatment of patients with disorders due to *allergy*. This is a branch of *internal medicine*.

allergy: An acquired condition of the body so that it reacts abnormally to a chemical substance or physical *agent (1)*, such as cold. The term is also applied to the branch (*specialty*) of *internal medicine* dealing with the study, diagnosis, and treatment of allergic disorders.

allergy and immunology: That branch of medicine which deals with disorders due to allergy and diseases of the immune system. One of the medical specialties for which *residency* programs have been approved by the Accreditation Council for Graduate Medical Education (ACGME). See *specialty*.

allied health personnel: See *allied health professional*.

allied health professional: A person who is not a physician, nurse, or pharmacist, and who works in the health field. An allied health professional may, for example, be a dietitian, an emergency medical technician, or an aide. Allied health professionals are sometimes called paraprofessionals or paramedical personnel. There are some 26 allied health professions for which educational standards have been developed. For a list of occupations for which programs have been accredited by the *Committee on Allied Health Education and Accreditation (CAHEA)*, see that listing. Synonym(s): allied health personnel.

allograft: An *organ* or *tissue* transplanted (grafted) from one individual to another, both of the same species. Most organ transplants today are allografts. Synonym(s): homograft.

allopathy: See *medicine (4)*

ALOS: Average length of stay. See *length of stay*.

ALS: See *advanced life support*.

alternative: One of two or more feasible ways of doing something. Often the term is used to mean new or different from what has been done before. The term is being used increasingly in health care, for example, in connection with financing methods and the organization of services.

alternative delivery and financing system (ADFS): A general term which covers any kind of *alternative* organizational arrangement for the delivery of health care, such as a *health maintenance organization (HMO)*, in which payment for physician services is other than *fee-for-service (FFS)*. Thus, an ADFS is a combination of an *alternative delivery system (ADS) (2)* and an *alternative financing system (AFS)*.

alternative delivery mode: See *alternative delivery system (ADS)*.

alternative delivery system (1) (ADS): An *alternative* to traditional inpatient care, such as substitution of *ambulatory care, home health care, hospice*, or *same-day surgery*. Synonym(s): alternative delivery mode.

alternative delivery system (2) (ADS): An *alternative* to the traditional arrangements of health care providers into solo practice or group practice. Examples include the *independent physician associa-tion (IPA), preferred provider organization (PPO), health maintenance organization (HMO)*, and *health care organization (HCO)*. The method of purchase of service or payment of physicians (*fee-for-service (FFS)* or *capitation*, for example) does not govern the term in this usage.

alternative financing system (AFS):   An *alternative* to the *fee-for-service (FFS)* payment system, such as a *health care organization (HCO), health maintenance organization (HMO)*, or *competitive medical plan (CMP)* in which some other mechanism, usually *capitation*, is the method of payment to the organization and sometimes to the physician.

AMA (1):   Against medical advice. See *discharge*.

AMA (2):   See *American Management Association*.

AMA (3):   See *American Medical Association*.

ambulatory: A term which specifically means "able to walk," but which in health care refers to a person who is not bedridden. Thus a person who requires a wheel chair is ambulatory, and can come in for treatment and return home.

ambulatory care: Care provided to a patient without *hospitalization*.

ambulatory care center: A facility which provides health and allied services to patients who do not require overnight lodging in an inpatient facility. To be designated an ambulatory care center, the facility is expected to have an *organized professional staff*.

Ambulatory care centers are either freestanding or hospital-based. Those that are freestanding seem to be classified into several levels, while hospital-based centers are not. Freestanding ambulatory care centers of the highest level are stated to be able to provide *emergency* care; those of a lower level, *urgent* care; and those at the lowest level, *primary care*. Hospital-based ambulatory care centers, on the other hand, do not seem to be divided into these categories. No doubt the usage will be clarified with time.

A

ambulatory care system: Although people use this phrase, such as in "the United States ambulatory care system," it has no specific meaning.

ambulatory surgery: Surgery performed on an *outpatient*, with arrival and departure on the same day. If the patient has to be kept over night, he is admitted and then discharged the next day. Same as outpatient surgery and same-day surgery.

ambulatory visit group (AVG): A counterpart of the *Diagnosis Related Group (DRG) classification (1)*, but designed for use for *ambulatory care* rather than hospital care. Patients, as in DRGs, undergo *classification (2)* into diagnosis groups (in this case, AVGs rather than DRGs) for which a predetermined or prenegotiated fee can be established.

American Academy of Addictionology (AAA): A medical organization encouraging specialization in the diagnosis and treatment of *alcoholism* and *drug dependency*.

American Academy of Medical Directors (AAMD): The previous name of the *American College of Physician Executives (ACPE)*. The ACPE is a national medical *specialty society* whose members are physicians with leadership, management, or administrative responsibilities.

American Academy of Nursing (AAN): A body organized in 1973 with 36 Charter *Fellows* designated by the *American Nurses' Association (ANA)* board of directors. The objectives of the AAN include advancing new concepts in nursing and health care, and exploring issues in health, the nursing profession, and society, as they affect and are affected by nurses and nursing. AAN members are authorized to use the credential "Fellow of the American Academy of Nursing" (FAAN).

American Association for Medical Systems and Informatics (AAMSI): A national organization interested in the application of computers to medical problems.

American Association of Colleges of Nursing (AACN): An organization of institutions offering baccalaureate and higher degree programs in nursing. The purpose of the AACN is to provide its members with a framework through which to advance the quality of baccalaureate and graduate programs, promote research, and develop academic leaders.

American Association of Critical-Care Nurses (AACN): The professional association of *registered nurses (RNs)*, primarily those who give specialized care to critically ill patients.

American Association of Homes for the Aging (AAHA): A non-profit national organization representing the housing-for-the-elderly industry.

American Association of Retired Persons (AARP): An organization often referred to in current health care literature (sometimes only by its acronym) because of its intense activity in regard to health legislation, health care financing, access, and quality.

American Board of Internal Medicine (ABIM): The specialty organization which examines candidates for *certification* in *internal medicine* and grants *credentials* to successful candidates.

American Board of Medical Management (ABMM): The *specialty board* for physicians specializing in medical management.

American Board of Surgery (ABS): The specialty organization which examines candidates for *certification* in *general surgery* and grants *credentials* to successful candidates.

American College of Healthcare Executives (ACHE): The new name (1985) for the association of professionals in health care administration, formerly called the American College of Hospital Administrators (ACHA).

American College of Hospital Administrators (ACHA): The former name (until 1985) of the American College of Healthcare Executives (ACHE), an association of professionals in health care administration.

A

American College of Nurse Midwives (ACNM): A voluntary organization which, among other activities, provides *credentials* for *nurse midwives* by *certifying* them.

American College of Physician Executives (ACPE): The national professional association which *accredits*, serves, recognizes, and *certifies* physician executives. Individuals who are certified by the ACPE may be granted *fellowship* in the ACPE and may then use the designation FACPE (Fellow of the American College of Physician Executives) after their names as a *credential*. Formerly, ACPE was known as the American Academy of Medical Directors (AAMD).

American College of Physicians (ACP): The national organization of physicians (other than *family practitioners* and *surgeons*). All physicians may join if they meet membership and professional eligibility requirements.

American College of Surgeons (ACS): The national organization of surgeons, with headquarters in Chicago, Illinois, to which all *surgeons* meeting professional eligibility and membership requirements may belong.

American College of Utilization Review Physicians (ACURP): A nonprofit group that educates physicians and other health care professionals concerning *cost containment, utilization review, quality assurance,* and *risk management,* among other topics.

American College Testing Service (ACTS): An organization which administers tests, among them the *Medical College Admission Test (MCAT)*.

American Dietetic Association (ADA): The primary professional association for registered dietitians in the United States.

American Federation for Clinical Research (AFCR): An association of selected *clinical investigators* under age 41 who have published meritorious investigation in clinical medicine or allied sciences.

American Hospital Association (AHA): The national association of hospitals in the United States, with headquarters in Chicago, Illinois. Other health care organizations and individuals may also hold membership. In addition to membership activities, it maintains a major reference library of hospital literature, and publishes a number of titles, including the magazine, *Hospitals*, and two standard annual reference volumes, *Hospital Statistics* and *Guide to the Health Care Field*.

American Hospital System: Although this term is often used, there really is no such thing as the "American Hospital System," except that the nation's hospitals and other health care facilities, along with health professionals and allied health professionals, do make up an informal network across the country through which care is provided. The "American Hospital System" simply means what actually exists—community hospitals, university hospitals, nonprofit hospitals, investor-owned hospitals, government hospitals, and the like.

American Institute of Certified Public Accountants (AICPA): The national professional association of practicing *Certified Public Accountants (CPAs)*.

American Management Association (AMA): A national organization of business management personnel.

American Medical Association (AMA): The major national association of physicians in the United States. All physicians who are *doctors of medicine (MDs)* are eligible for membership.

American Medical Record Association (AMRA): The national association for professionals in *medical record* science.

American Medical Society on Alcoholism and Other Drug Dependencies (AMSAODD): A medical association concerned with *alcoholism* and *drug dependencies*. Upon successful completion of its *certification examination*, a physician is granted the *credential* of certification by the society.

American Nurses' Association (ANA): The professional association for registered nurses in the United States, made up of constituent nurses' associations in the states, the District of Columbia, Guam, and the Virgin Islands. The ANA works for better health standards and nursing services, high standards of nursing, and the professional development and economic and general welfare of nurses. It is concerned with nursing ethics and serves as spokesperson for nursing, nationally and internationally.

ANA also certifies nurses and nurse midwives who meet necessary eligibility requirements and pass examinations qualifying them as specialists. For a list of specialty areas, see *certified nurse* under *nurse*.

The *National League for Nursing (NLN)* is the other national organization concerned with all of nursing, but its primary interest is nursing education. NLN concentrates more on nursing than on nurses.

American Organization of Nurse Executives (AONE): An independent organization of directors of nursing services. The AONE is not affiliated with the *American Nurses' Association (ANA)* or the *National League for Nursing (NLN)*.

American Public Health Association (APHA): The national association which embraces all public health professionals.

American Society for Bariatric (Obesity) Surgery (ASBS): The national society for surgeons specializing in surgery for the treatment of obesity.

American Society for Testing and Materials (ASTM): An organization originally concerned with developing standards for and testing industrial materials, but which has more recently been doing similar work with computer systems, many of them in the medical field.

American Society of Clinical Investigation (ASCI): An association with active membership restricted to *clinical investigators* under age 45. Membership in ASCI is by invitation.

AMH: See *Accreditation Manual for Hospitals*.

amniocentesis: An established *diagnostic* technique for detecting *genetic* abnormalities in the fetus. A sample of fluid is removed by means of a hollow needle which is inserted through the abdominal wall into the amniotic sac (bag of waters) containing the fetus. Cells floating in the fluid are grown in laboratory culture for about two weeks, and then examined under the microscope. The procedure gives information at about the fifteenth week of pregnancy. Another procedure under investigation, *chorionic villus sampling (CVS)*, may be employed earlier in pregnancy, but both procedures have their unique values.

AMRA: See *American Medical Record Association*.

AMSAODD: See *American Medical Society on Alcoholism and Other Drug Dependencies*.

ANA: See *American Nurses' Association*.

analog: A term which, when used to describe information (data), means that the information relates to a point on a continuum, such as a person's body temperature. Those using analog information typically "round off" the information, such as using 98.6 instead of 98.596745. "Analog" is distinguished from "digital," which describes information relating to discrete steps, such as counting the fingers on one's hand. See *digital* for how these terms relate to modern devices such as computers.

anatomy: The structure of *organs* and *tissues*, rather than their activities (*physiology*).

ancillary personnel: Personnel other than physicians and nurses.

ancillary services: Hospital *services (1)* other than room and board. In a hospital, nursing services are included as part of "room and board"; since normal nursing services are not billed for separately, they are not ancillary services.

andrologist: A physician specializing in diseases of the male sex.

anesthesia: The condition of having lost feeling or sensation. This condition may arise because of the administration of a drug, the use of another *agent (1)* or method (cold, for example) which

A

depresses sensation, or neurological (nervous system) impairment. Words such as "ether" and "spinal" are commonly used to modify "anesthesia"; they refer to the *anesthetic* used, the route of administration, the area involved in the anesthesia, and the like.

anesthesiologist: A physician specializing in *anesthesiology* which, in modern hospitals, includes consultation in *cardiopulmonary resuscitation (CPR)*, *respiratory therapy (RT)*, and special problems in the relief of pain. Note that a physician may be called an "anesthetist," but only a physician may be called an "anesthesiologist."

anesthesiologist's assistant (AA): One of the 26 *allied health professionals* for whom the American Medical Association's *Committee on Allied Health Education and Accreditation (CAHEA)* has accredited education programs.

anesthesiology: The *medical specialty* concerned with *anesthesia*, including its *pharmacology* and *physiology*, and with related fields, such as *respiratory therapy, resuscitation*, and the relief of *chronic* pain. One of the medical specialties for which *residency* programs have been approved by the Accreditation Council for Graduate Medical Education (ACGME). See *specialty*.

anesthetic: A drug or other *agent (1)* which depresses feeling or the sensation of pain.

inhalation anesthetic: An *anesthetic agent (1)* administered as a gas, by breathing.

anesthetist: A person who administers *anesthesia*. An anesthetist may be a nurse, dentist, physician, or other individual. A *nurse anesthetist* is usually qualified by special training to administer anesthesia under the supervision of a physician (or dentist).

certified registered nurse anesthetist (CRNA): A *nurse anesthetist* who has met the *certification* requirements of the Council on Certification/Council on Recertification of Nurse Anesthetists (a voluntary body).

anesthetizing location: The area of the building designated to be used for administering *inhalation anesthetics*.

angiotensin-converting enzyme (ACE): A class of blood pressure reducing drugs. ACEs are thought to act by suppressing the renin-angiotensin-aldosterone system, but they are also effective at times in patients with low-renin hypertension. Synonym(s): kininase.

animal rights movement: The name adopted by the current movement to stop experimentation on animals in the course of medical and veterinary research. The movement threatens essential progress in a number of areas of medicine, particularly senile dementia, stroke, and cancer, in which other techniques, such as *computer modeling*, are not applicable. Synonym(s): antivivisectionism.

anthropometric assessment: Measurement of an individual's height, weight, skin fat folds, arm circumference, elbow breadth, or other body measures for the purpose of assessing nutritional status, growth, and development. Synonym(s): anthropometry.

antikickback law: Sometimes used to refer to the Medicare fraud and abuse laws, which prohibit, among other things, paying or receiving "kickbacks" for referral of Medicare patients. See *fraud and abuse.*

antitrust: That branch of law which seeks to prevent monopolies and unfair competition. A "trust" was originally a combination of several corporations (each maintaining its separate identity) to eliminate competition, control prices, and the like. The term "antitrust" now broadly covers any activity (or conspiracy) to eliminate competition and control the marketplace. It includes actions which unreasonably restrain trade. Such activities are illegal, and severe penalties are imposed by antitrust laws. For example, the trust may be broken up (see *divestiture*), and anyone who suffers injury to his business or property as a result of the combination or conspiracy may collect *treble damages*. Federal antitrust laws (principally the Sherman Act of 1890, the Clayton Act of 1914, and the Federal Trade Commission Act of 1914) apply to companies doing business in interstate commerce. Many states also have antitrust laws.

Antitrust problems may arise for hospitals when they place limitations on *medical staff* membership, for example, or when several hospitals seek to combine services. Careful legal guidance

A

is required in any area in which a hospital's actions may affect competition or regulate prices. See also *Clayton Act, Patrick case, per se, Robinson-Patman Act, Rule of Reason, Sherman Act.*

antivivisectionism: See *animal rights movement.*

AONE: See *American Organization of Nurse Executives.*

AORN: Association of Operating Room Nurses.

AOTA: American Occupational Therapy Association.

AP: See *accounts payable.*

APA: American Psychiatric Association.

Apache II: A severity index originally developed to measure the *severity of illness* of *intensive care unit (ICU)* patients, and now being used for hospitalized patients. Patients are classified as to severity on the basis of a physiological score based on 12 variables. The variables include vital signs, results of certain blood tests, and age. Note that these variables are objective items of information, rather than subjective, that is, they are not the judgments of a physician or nurse. This severity measure is in no way dependent on the disease. This measure can be applied on admission of the patient, or at any other time. A computer program is available from George Washington University for applying the measure in the ICU setting.

Apgar score: A method devised by Virginia Apgar, an American anesthesiologist, for giving a numerical score to the physical condition of a newborn infant. Points are given for the infant's color, heart rate, respiratory effort, muscle tone, and response to stimulation. Ten is the highest score possible.

APHA: See *American Public Health Association.*

APM: See *admission pattern monitoring.*

APO: See *adverse patient occurrence.*

appliance: A device which is used to provide function to a part of the body or for treatment. The term is used most commonly in *orthodontics*.

application: A term which, when used to describe computer software, refers to a program designed to accomplish a given task not related to the computer itself. Examples of applications include word processing, accounting, inventory control, and laboratory reporting. Accounting itself can be divided into such applications as accounts receivable, accounts payable, and general ledger. Application software is distinguished from utility programs, languages, and the like.

appropriateness: A term used in connection with review of care to indicate whether the measures taken were proper under the circumstances, and whether it would have been proper to have taken other measures under the circumstances.

AR: See *accounts receivable.*

arbitrage: The process of selling overvalued *assets* and buying undervalued assets to bring about an equilibrium where all assets are properly valued. One who engages in arbitrage is an arbitrager.

arbitrager: One who engages in arbitrage—the selling of overvalued *assets* and buying of undervalued assets—in order to bring about an equilibrium where all assets are properly valued.

arbitration: A method of resolving disputes without use of the courts. A single *arbitrator* or panel of arbitrators is chosen by the parties to hear the case, and the parties agree to be bound by the arbitrators' decision. The arbitrator's decision is usually final; a court will not overrule it unless there was fraud or partiality involved.

arbitrator: A person chosen by the parties to a dispute to make a final, binding decision concerning the dispute.

ARC: See *AIDS-related complex.*

A

ARC-ST: See *Accreditation Review Council for Educational Programs in Surgical Technology*.

area wage adjustment: A component of the payment formula under the *prospective payment system (PPS)* to allow for differences in wage scales in different parts of the country.

arithmetic mean: The ordinary average. It is the sum of a set of quantities, divided by the number of quantities in the set. (In this term, the first and third syllables of "arithmetic" are accented.)

arm's-length transaction: A transaction (such as a sale or purchase) in which both parties have approximately equal bargaining power, and which is not influenced by any *conflict of interest*.

ART: See *Accredited Record Technician*.

artificial: Produced by humans; "man-made."

artificial insemination by donor (AID): Introduction of semen (sperm) from a donor (a man other than the husband) into the genital tract of a woman by means other than sexual intercourse. This procedure is carried out in certain cases of infertility as a method of *noncoital reproduction*.

artificial insemination by husband (AIH): The introduction of a husband's semen (sperm) into the genital tract of his wife by means other than sexual intercourse. This procedure is carried out in certain cases of infertility as a method of *noncoital reproduction*.

artificial intelligence (AI): A term used to describe a type of system in which the computer appears to be "thinking," and thus exhibits intelligence. Although the system appears to "think," it really does not; rather, it has been given a number of "rules" to follow. A simple example would be a billing system which follows the rule: "if there has been no payment within 30 days, send letter "A"; if there has been no payment within 60 days, send letter "B." Another example would be a program which looks up "unfamiliar" words (those not in its memory): if the word is a synonym for or similar to a word to which the system should respond and take action, it will either go ahead with the action or ask a human to confirm its "decision." There is some tendency for computer salespeople to overuse the term "artificial intelligence" to gain a sales advantage; this leads the customer to believe that AI systems are invariably better for every task than other systems.

artificial neural system: See *neurocomputer*.

artificial respiration: The forcing of an exchange of gases (primarily air) between the lungs and the outside atmosphere by the application of pressure (or, sometimes, vacuum), either to the chest of the individual or to the gases themselves. Synonym(s): artificial ventilation.

artificial ventilation: See *artificial respiration*.

ARV: AIDS-related virus. See *human immunodeficiency virus (HIV)*.

AS-SCORE index: One of the methods devised for classifying patients as to *severity of illness*. It uses five factors: age, *stage* of disease, physiological systems involved, *complications*, and response to therapy.

ASBS: See *American Society for Bariatric (Obesity) Surgery*.

ASCI: See *American Society of Clinical Investigation*.

ASCII: Acronym for American Standard Code for Information Interchange. Also a name for a code list in which printable characters (such as A-Z, 1-0, etc.) as well as non-printing characters (such as tabs, carriage returns, etc.) are assigned standard reference numbers from 0 to 255. For example, "A" is 65, "a" is 97, "!" is 33.

Most frequently this term now comes up in microcomputer usage where it might be used to distinguish a human-readable "ASCII text file" from a file containing characters which only make sense to the computer.

aseptic: See *sterile*.

ASHCRM: See *American Society of Health Care Risk Managers*.

A

asset: An object (property or money, for example), a right (to royalties, for example), or a claim (a title to a debt, for example) which its owners consider to be of benefit to them.   Assets in hospitals include property and equipment (which may have less value than their original cost because of *depreciation*), investments, accounts receivable (claims to money owed to the institution), and the other items which are listed as "assets" on the *balance sheet* of the institution.   The term asset is often modified to indicate assets of specific kinds:

capital asset: An asset with a life of more than one year that is not bought and sold in the ordinary course of business.

current asset: An asset with a life of less than one year, such as inventory.

fixed asset: Long-term assets that are not bought or sold in the normal course of business.   Typically, fixed assets are land, equipment, and buildings.

intangible asset: An asset which is not physical.   Examples include goodwill and patents.

noncurrent asset: An asset with a life of more than one year.

tangible asset: An asset which is physical, such as a building and equipment.

assignment (of benefits):   A voluntary decision by the *beneficiary* to have insurance *benefits* paid directly to the *provider* rather than to the beneficiary himself.   The act requires the signing of a form for the purpose.   The provider is not obligated to accept an assignment of benefits; it may refuse and instead require the beneficiary to handle the collection procedure.   Conversely, the provider may insist on assignment in order to protect its revenue; if the provider accepts the assignment, it ordinarily assumes responsibility for the collection paperwork.

associate degree (AD):   A degree given by an two-year community college upon successful completion of a program in a given field.   The recipient is entitled to use the initials "AD" as a *credential*.

associate degree in nursing: An academic degree (*associate degree (AD)*) awarded by a community or junior college, usually after a two-year program. The holder of this degree is eligible to become a *registered nurse (RN)*. The degree is not offered in Canada.

Association of American Physicians (AAP): An association of physician scholars established in 1885. Membership in the AAP is by invitation.

assumption of risk: A legal defense to a lawsuit when the lawsuit is based on *negligence*. If a person knowingly and voluntarily exposes himself to a risk of harm, he is said to "assume the risk" meaning that he has agreed to accept it. This may release the *defendant* from *liability (1)*. This defense is not usually successful in *malpractice* suits, because courts do not consider that the patient has "consented" to malpractice, even though he may have consented to the treatment (surgery, for example).

AST: Association of Surgical Technologists.

Astler-Coller system: A method of *staging tumors*.

ASTM: See *American Society for Testing and Materials*.

at risk: See *risk (1)* and *(3)*.

atom: The smallest particle of an *element* which can enter into a chemical combination. The term "atom" was used in this sense before it was known that an atom consisted of a nucleus and electrons, and before it was known that for most elements the atoms did not all have the same mass (weight).

A simplified picture describes an atom as a nucleus containing a number of protons (Z) and neutrons (N), surrounded by the number of electrons (E) equal to the number of protons. Protons are particles which have mass *and* electrical charge; neutrons have mass but *no* electrical charge. The symbol "Z" indicates the number of protons in the nucleus, and the symbol "N" indicates the number of neutrons. Thus, N + Z = A, the mass number of the atom. Z also represents the atomic number of the element.

For example, carbon (C) has atomic number 6, meaning that it has six protons in its nucleus, that is, Z = 6. If a given atom of carbon also has six neutrons, its mass number is 12 (6 + 6), and modern notation would label it as $^{12}_{6}C$.

A

The small mass differences among atoms occur when their nuclei have different numbers of neutrons. For example, another carbon atom could have eight neutrons, and thus would have an atomic mass of 14 (6 + 8) and would be shown as $^{14}_{6}C$. This atom is sometimes referred to as "carbon-14." These two carbon atoms are called *isotopes* of carbon since they have the same number of protons (thus both are carbon) and differ only in the numbers of neutrons and mass numbers. The chemical properties of these carbon atoms are the same; the small mass differences among them do not affect the way they enter into chemical combination.

In nuclear science, the important particle is the nucleus; thus a new word, *nuclide,* was coined to indicate a nucleus with a specific mass. This term allows one to describe the different atoms of carbon which have different atomic masses. See *nuclide* for more information.

atomic notation: See *nuclide.*

atomic number: See *nuclide.*

audiologist: A person with a master's degree in *audiology* who examines, evaluates, and provides treatment for persons with hearing defects.

audiology: The science of hearing. The practice of audiology involves examination, diagnosis, evaluation, and therapy for persons with hearing defects.

audiometrician: A person who administers hearing tests.

audit: A term which usually means a financial audit, in which the organization's financial statement, and the degree to which the statement reflects the actual affairs of the organization, are examined. An audit also includes a review of the procedures used to keep records, prevent losses of funds and equipment, and the like. An audit may be an *internal audit* or an *external audit*. When the term is used without a modifier, "audit" refers to an external audit by a *public accountant.*

An audit may also made of the organization's compliance with its own policies and with grant and contract obligations, of its management efficiency, or of its *quality management*. See also *patient care audit*.

external audit: An audit carried out by an independent *public accountant*. "Independent" means that the auditor is not an employee of the audited organization, and does not have certain other forbidden connections with the organization.

fiscal audit: An audit of the financial (fiscal) affairs of the institution. The fiscal audit has been developed over many years by the accounting profession, and standards for its conduct are well established.

internal audit: An administrative process carried out in organizations, by the organization's own employees, in an effort to determine the extent to which the organization's internal operations conform with its own intended procedures and practices. When a similar review is done by an outside group, it is called an *external audit*.

quality management audit: An audit of the *quality management* of an institution, similar in intent and conduct to a *fiscal audit*, but addressed at the *quality function* rather than the *fiscal function*.

authenticate: To provide evidence which can be used to prove (in the legal sense) the authorship of a written record. Forms of authentication include, for example, a written signature, initials, symbol, and computer keys. The Joint Commission on the Accreditation of Healthcare Organizations (JCAHO) permits authentication of a *medical record entry* by the use of a rubber-stamp signature if certain requirements are met as to possession and use of the stamp.

autograft: An *organ* or *tissue* transplanted (grafted) from one location to another in the same individual.

autologous: Related to the self. The term is found most frequently in *autologous blood transfusion*, a transfusion using the person's own blood which was stored in advance for that purpose. Often such blood is stored in the frozen state in an *autologous frozen blood program*.

A

autologous blood transfusion: A transfusion of an individual using his own blood, which was drawn previously and stored for later use, typically in *elective surgery*. This procedure, although used for many years primarily to avoid transfusion reactions (an individual does not react against his own blood), is gaining adherents because of the threat of acquired immunodeficiency syndrome (AIDS) and other diseases which may be transmitted by transfusion.

autologous frozen blood program: A program in which an individual may deposit one or more units of his own blood to be kept in the frozen state in a special *blood bank* under close supervision for his later use in case of elective surgery or emergency. Such programs are typically operated by private corporations, which charge a fee (1986) of roughly $150 per unit of blood for long-term storage, and about one third that amount for short-term storage. Autologous frozen blood programs are gaining adherents because of the threat of transmission of acquired immunodeficiency syndrome (AIDS), as well as other diseases, by transfusion.

autonomous: Independent; self-governing; not under the control of others.

autopsy: A post mortem (after death) examination of a body; also called a necropsy, postmortem, or PM. An autopsy is usually performed by an anatomical pathologist, a physician trained in this specialty. While hospital or other policy may require that an anatomical pathologist perform autopsies, the law does not impose such a requirement; another physician or even a non-physician may perform the examination, and it will still be called an autopsy.

Usually the consent of the deceased person's next of kin or legal representative is required for an autopsy. However, under certain circumstances prescribed by state law, an autopsy must be performed, usually by the state or county *medical examiner* (coroner). These circumstances may include death by homicide (murder), death in an automobile accident, death under suspicious circumstances, unexpected death of a younger person, or a suspected Sudden Infant Death Syndrome (SIDS) death.

epidemiologic autopsy: The use of data from autopsies for epidemiologic studies. A method has been described for carrying out such studies by using only "surprise" findings, that is, evidences of disease other than that for which the patient was treated, and which the physician did not know the patient had. Suitable statistical *adjustments* are made so that the findings are deemed applicable to the general or a specific population.

hospital autopsy: An autopsy performed on the body of a patient who dies in the hospital, or who has been a patient of the hospital. There seems to be no requirement as to how recent the hospitalization must have been in order for an autopsy to be called a "hospital autopsy." The issue of defining an autopsy as a hospital autopsy arises because hospitals are expected to attempt to obtain autopsies whenever they can: "...in all deaths, particularly in cases of unusual deaths and cases of medicolegal and educational interest, unless otherwise provided by law" (JCAHO Standard, 1988). It naturally follows that hospitals compute autopsy rates using hospital autopsies as here defined as the numerator and "hospital deaths" (deaths in the hospital) as the denominator. See *autopsy rate* under *rate (2)*.

auxilian: A member of a *hospital auxiliary*.

auxiliary: See *hospital auxiliary*.

average: A mathematical term which, unless otherwise stated, means the "*arithmetic mean*." The average is the result of adding together two or more quantities, and then dividing the sum by the number of quantities. For example, the average length of stay (ALOS) for four people, who stay in the hospital for periods of one, four, five, and eight days, is 4.5 days ($1 + 4 + 5 + 8 = 18$ divided by 4). See also *median*. Synonym(s): mean.

average daily census: The average number of *inpatients* in a hospital (or a unit of the hospital, such as a *patient care unit*) each day for a given period of time. Newborns (born in the hospital) are not included in the inpatient count for calculation of this statistic.

average length of stay (ALOS): See *length of stay*.

AVG: See *ambulatory visit group*.

azidothymidine (AZT): See *retrovir*.

B

Baby Doe case: A legal case involving an infant born with Down's syndrome and with esophageal atresia, a condition which prevented him from eating normally but which was surgically correctable. His parents decided not to consent to the corrective surgery nor to intravenous feeding. The hospital administration sought a court order to override the parents' decision. The court ruled that the parents had the right to withhold consent. Before an attempted appeal could be processed, the baby died. The case raised the public consciousness about the issues surrounding the withholding of treatment from seriously ill newborns, and legislatures acted to protect newborns from medical neglect. Among the resulting laws were the federal *Baby Doe regulations* and *Child Abuse Amendments*, and numerous state laws making medical neglect one form of child abuse and neglect. *Indiana ex rel. Infant Doe v. Monroe Cir. Ct.*, No. 482S140 (Ind. Sup. Ct. Apr. 16, 1982).

Baby Doe Law: See *Child Abuse Amendments*.

Baby Doe regulations: Regulations promulgated by the federal government in 1985 aimed at preventing the withholding of medically indicated treatment from a seriously ill infant ("Baby Doe") with a life-threatening condition, except under certain specific circumstances where treatment would be futile. These regulations were ruled invalid, but the federal *Child Abuse Amendments* of 1984 (also passed in response to *Baby Doe*) made such withholding of treatment a form of child neglect, and thus provided an avenue of legal recourse for health professionals or other interested persons who believe that medical decisions concerning seriously ill newborns are not being made appropriately.

Baby Fae case: The case of the infant whose life was sustained for a short time, in 1984, by the *implantation* of a heart from a baboon.

Baby M case: See *surrogate mother.*

baccalaureate program in nursing: A nursing education program offered by a college or university which leads to a baccalaureate degree with a major in nursing. This degree provides eligibility for licensure as a *registered nurse (RN).*

Bachelor of Science in Nursing (BSN): The degree awarded by a college or university with a *baccalaureate program in nursing.*

bacteria: One celled microscopic organisms of a particular class (Schizomycetes). Some bacteria (pathogenic bacteria) are able to cause disease in animals. The singular is "bacterium."

bacteriologist: A person who is specially trained in the study of bacteria.

bacteriology: The study of bacteria.

balance billing: The practice of physicians to charge some patients more than other patients for the same *service (1)* in order to maintain a desired average fee for that service. For example, when an insurance program, or Medicare, will pay the physician only 80 percent of her usual fee for a given service, she sometimes "balance bills" other patients to compensate for this loss. Some states have enacted statutes to prevent this practice.

balance sheet: One of the two standard components of a financial statement, on which are shown the *assets* (what is owned) and the *liabilities* (what is owed) by the organization. An organization is most unlikely to find the assets and the liabilities exactly equal, so a third category of entry makes the sheet "balance": a line entitled "profit" or "loss." When assets exceed liabilities, the line shows a profit; when liabilities exceed assets, the line shows a loss.

Since most hospitals are nonprofit, a line called "profit" would be inappropriate (although even a hospital could not survive if, over time, it owed more than it owned). Thus, most nonprofit

B

organizations long ago abandoned the term "profit" and in its place adopted a euphemism such as "fund balance." A profit, then, would be called a "positive fund balance"; a loss would be called a "negative fund balance."

The other standard component of a financial statement is an *income and expense statement* (also called a profit and loss statement or operating statement).

balloon angioplasty: See *percutaneous transluminal coronary angioplasty (PTCA)*.

bar code system: A computer-readable *coding* system which uses a pattern of bars and empty spaces to convey a specific meaning. The system is commonly encountered in grocery stores and other retail establishments, where a computer terminal reads the bar code with a scanning device. The system usually calculates the bill, corrects the inventory of the item, and carries out other management and accounting functions. Bar codes are being standardized in the hospital industry for such purposes as recording the receipt of materials and supplies purchased by the hospital, maintaining their inventory, and making charges for them. Other hospital applications include recording *services (1)* (such as in the laboratory or emergency department), posting the charges to the patient bills and to the appropriate revenue and expense accounts, and inventory control. When so used, the bar code is an input device for a *point of sale* system.

bariatrics: The branch of medicine dealing with obesity and related diseases.

barium enema: An X-ray examination in which a *radiopaque* substance, namely a barium compound, is introduced into the bowel by enema, and in which a physician examines the bowel "in action" through a *fluoroscope* and also makes permanent records by taking X-ray films at appropriate times.

base (1): A statistical term referring to the "per" number in a given *rate (2)*. A *ratio* or *proportion* is often expressed as a percentage (per 100), but it may also be expressed per 1,000, per 10,000, per 100,000, or even per million. These "per" numbers are called the "base." Thus a percentage is said to have 100 as the base. The base chosen is usually large enough to ensure that the rate will be expressed in whole numbers; the more rare the event, the larger the base used. For example, a death rate of 7 per 10,000 simply is easier to understand than a rate of 0.07 percent, although both actually give the same information.

base (2): A reference quantity or reference time, often a given year. For example, the data used in calculating a *consumer price index* include base prices, which are prices found in the year chosen as the base.

base unit: A *procedure* or *service (1)* used in developing a *relative value scale (RVS)*. The cost of the unit selected as the base unit is given a value of 1.0, and the relative values of all other units are expressed as multiples of the cost of the base unit. Consider, for example, this imaginary illustration. The developer of an RVS for laboratory work might decide to use the cost of a red blood count as the base unit. Its actual cost might be $5.00 but, as the base, its *relative value unit (RVU)* would arbitrarily be set at 1.0. If a blood sugar determination, then, actually cost $25.00, it would have an RVU value of 5.0 ($25.00 divided by $5.00).

base year Medicare costs: A hospital's costs for the *base (2)* year from which computations are made in the Medicare payment formula. The base year is, by definition, always several years behind the present, and its costs are those as determined according to the federal regulations for cost allocations.

basic nursing care: See *intermediate care*.

bassinet: A bed for a newborn. The term may be substituted for "newborn bed" in stating the hospital's *bed count*.

bassinet count: Same as *newborn bed count*; see *bed count*.

battery: A *tort* in which the wrongdoing is the physical touching of another person without that person's consent. The threat of such touching is called an assault. There does not have to be any physical harm for a battery to result in legal *liability (1)*. Treating or performing surgery upon a patient without the patient's consent, or going beyond the scope of the patient's consent, is a battery.

B

BC: See *Blue Cross.*

BC/BS: See *Blue Cross and Blue Shield.*

BCBSA: See *Blue Cross and Blue Shield Association.*

BEC: See *behavioral emergency committee.*

bed: A bed for an *inpatient* in a hospital or other health care facility. Types of bed include:

adult bed: A bed maintained for an adult patient (not for a child or a newborn). Sometimes a hospital's adult beds are subdivided into two categories:

adult inpatient bed: A bed maintained for an adult patient who needs round-the-clock inpatient care.

adult outpatient bed: A bed maintained for an adult patient who does not require round-the-clock inpatient care.

bassinet: See *newborn bed.*

day bed: A bed maintained for use by *partial hospitalization* patients who need a bed during daytime periods. A bed used similarly during the night is called a *night bed.*

hospital bed: When used by itself, that is, without other modifiers, this term implies not only the bed itself but also the routine accommodations for inpatients: board, lodging, and nursing and certain medical services.

incubator bed: A special bed (an incubator) maintained by a hospital for an infant who needs control of its environment: temperature, humidity, and breathing (such as supplementary oxygen). Such a bed also provides *isolation* for the infant. Incubators are used for *premature* infants and other infants with special problems, whether born in the hospital or elsewhere. Thus incubator beds are not part of the hospital's *newborn bed* (bassinet) count.

inpatient bed: A bed maintained by the hospital for *inpatient* use. When used alone, the term "inpatient bed" could mean a newborn, pediatric, or adult inpatient bed.

isolation bed: A bed maintained for a patient who requires *isolation*. For an infant, such isolation may be provided in an *incubator bed*. Isolation may be provided in a variety of regular beds by "setting up isolation" for beds when needed by the particular patients; techniques include using private rooms, instituting special nursing routines, using separate waste cans, and following other procedures appropriate to the case.

newborn bed: A bed (bassinet) maintained by a hospital for a child born in the hospital (a newborn admission). A newborn admission to a hospital, by definition, must have been born in that hospital; any other newborn infant is a *pediatric* patient, and occupies a *pediatric bed*.

night bed: A bed maintained for use by *partial hospitalization* patients during the night. The counterpart, for day use, is a *day bed*.

occupied bed: A bed which has a patient assigned to it.

partial hospitalization bed: A *day bed* or a *night bed*, used in *partial hospitalization*.

pediatric inpatient bed: A bed maintained for a child, other than a newborn admission (a newborn born in that hospital occupies a *newborn bed*).

resident bed: A bed for a *resident (2)*, that is, for a patient who does not require nursing and other hospital care, but who does need custodial and personal care.

specialty bed: Generally, a bed maintained by the hospital for patients receiving care within a specific medical or surgical *specialty*. For example, an "orthopedic bed" would be a specialty bed normally held ready for patients requiring orthopedic care.

swing bed: A bed which the hospital may, according to changing needs, assign to different kinds of patients. For example, beds may swing between obstetrics and gynecology, or between general surgery and gynecological surgery. More commonly today, the term refers to beds which swing between *acute care* and *long term care*. Often the swinging of beds must be approved by a regulatory agency, such as the state's hospital licensing authority.

B

temporary bed: A bed set up for emergency use, that is, for use when the number of patients temporarily exceeds the number for which beds are regularly maintained.

bed capacity: The number of patients a hospital can hold. A hospital may have different bed capacity figures depending on whether one refers to its *constructed beds*, its *licensed beds*, or its *regularly maintained beds*. Thus, a statement of capacity should always tell which is intended. It is possible, though, that bed capacity figures may all be the same for a given hospital at a given moment.

constructed beds: The number of beds the hospital was built to accommodate.

licensed beds: The number of beds which the state licensing agency authorizes the hospital to operate on a regular basis.

regularly maintained beds: The number of beds a hospital has set up for daily operation (in units of the hospital in use and staffed) on a regular basis. This number may change from time to time. It would ordinarily be a number smaller than the number of *licensed beds* or the number of *constructed beds*. The count is usually expressed in three segments: for adult inpatients, pediatric patients, and newborns. See *bed count*.

bed conversion: The reassignment of beds by the hospital from one use to another, for example, the reassignment of beds from *acute care* to *long term care* use. When such a conversion is done in both directions (when it is, depending on changing circumstances, reversible) the beds are usually called *swing beds*.

bed count: The number of beds a hospital maintains regularly for the use of inpatients. The count is usually given in segments:

adult inpatient bed count: The number of *adult inpatient beds* (beds exclusive of *newborn beds* and *pediatric inpatient beds*) which a hospital maintains in regular use, or which are available for use at the time of the count.

bassinet count: See *newborn bed*; a bassinet is a bed for a newborn.

child inpatient bed count: See *pediatric inpatient bed count*.

newborn bed count: The number of *newborn beds* a hospital maintains regularly in use, or which are available at the time of the count.

pediatric bed count: The number of *pediatric inpatient beds* a hospital maintains regularly in use. Synonym(s): child inpatient bed count.

bed day: See *day*.

bed pan mutual: A slang term for a physician-owned *professional liability* insurance company.

bed turnover rate: The average number of times during a given period of time, ordinarily a year, that a change of occupants occurs in a hospital bed which is normally in use. For example, if the average stay were five days, the bed would have a bed turnover rate of 73 (365 divided by 5).

behavioral emergency committee (BEC): A hospital committee concerned with incidents involving patients' violent or assaultive behavior toward other patients, employees, visitors, or property.

beltway bandits: A term used in Washington, D.C., referring to research corporations in the DC area (many of which are located near the "beltway" surrounding the city) and who survive on contracts from government agencies.

beneficiary: The person entitled to *benefits* from insurance or some other health care financing program, such as Medicare—the person "insured" as contrasted with the owner of the policy, for example.

benefits: The money, care, or other services to which an individual is entitled by virtue of insurance. In health care insurance, there are two basic kinds of benefits:

indemnity benefits: Insurance benefits provided in cash to the beneficiary rather than in *services (1)* (*service benefits*). Indemnity benefits are usual with commercial insurance.

service benefits: Insurance benefits which are the health care *services (1)* themselves, rather than money. Money benefits are called *"indemnity benefits."* Service benefits are traditional with Blue Cross/Blue Shield (BC/BS) and Medicare.

bereavement care: Care which assists with the physical, emotional, spiritual, psychological, social, financial, and legal needs of the survivor(s) of a person who has died.

bill: A statement from the *provider* of the charges for *services (1)*, drugs, *appliances*, use of facilities, and other items for a given patient's care, for example, for an emergency department admission or an inpatient episode of care.

biochemical: Relating to chemical elements or compounds (biochemicals) involved in living organisms.

biochemical assessment: The use of laboratory tests on urine, blood, blood fractions, and other tissue, to describe an individual's nutritional status. For example, sodium excretion (in urine) can be used to measure compliance with a low sodium diet in hypertensive patients.

biochemist: A person expert in the study of the class of chemicals known as biochemicals (chemicals involved in living organisms). Synonym(s): physiological chemist, clinical chemist.

biochemistry: The chemistry of living organisms.

bioengineer: An engineer who specializes in biological applications of engineering principles.

biological: Pertaining to life and to living matter.

biological substance: A substance produced by a living organism, as distinguished from a chemical substance, which is produced by chemistry. Both chemical and biological substances are used in diagnostic procedures and the treatment of disease.

biological waste: See *hazardous waste.*

biomedical engineer: An engineer trained in biological applications of engineering, and who specializes in medical problems. Usually this application involves both the bioengineer and the medical scientist.

biomedical engineering department: The hospital department responsible for medical instruments and equipment. The responsibility may involve testing of equipment being considered, recommendations regarding purchase, maintenance of equipment, training in its use, and, on occasion, the design and construction of equipment. The hospital's biomedical engineering staff is found in this department. There is some trend to rename this department the "clinical engineering department."

birth certificate: The official record of a person's birth, signed by the attending physician (if the delivery was assisted by a physician) or other authorized person. A record form designated by the state, which specifies the items of information to be included, must be used. The birth certificate is filed with the *registrar (1)* for the local unit of government, who in turn files a copy with the state office of *vital statistics*.

birth defect: A defect which is present at birth. A birth defect may be due to inheritance (hereditary), or due to some other cause, such as injury to the mother or infection.

birth room: See *birthing room*.

birthing center: See *childbirth center*.

birthing room: A "homelike" hospital room which is both a *labor room* and *delivery room*. Usually the father is permitted to be present for the delivery. Synonym(s): birth room.

bit: BInary digiT. The smallest unit of information with which a *digital* computer works. A bit is often compared to a simple light switch, which is either "on" or "off." The use of binary digits explains why powers of two (2, 4, 8, and so on) appear so frequently in computer jargon. See also *byte* for additional discussion.

B

block grant: A type of health grant from the federal government in which a "block" of money is provided, and the recipient is given relatively broad discretion in its use. Block grants are distinguished from "categorical grants," which are made for specific purposes, for example, the control of tuberculosis or the detection of cancer.

blood: Terms relating to blood include:

fractionation: The process of separation of the *blood components* of whole blood.

outdated blood: Whole blood which has been properly stored (under refrigeration at the proper temperature) but which has passed its expiration date, typically 21 days.

unprocessed whole blood: Blood which has been drawn for future use in transfusion, but which has not been grouped and typed or given the required tests for safety.

whole blood: Blood which has not been subjected to *fractionation*, that is, to the separation of the blood into *blood components*.

blood bank: A facility for provision of whole blood and its components for transfusion. Its functions include recruitment of donors for procurement of blood, drawing blood, processing (grouping and typing and testing for safety), storage, and distribution. A pathologist or other physician, or another qualified scientist, is ordinarily in charge of a blood bank. Blood banks may be characterized as of several types, depending on their auspices:

commercial blood bank: A blood bank operated as a money-making enterprise. Donors are paid for blood and the blood is sold to hospitals. The profit goes to the owners of the blood bank. Sometimes called a proprietary blood bank.

community blood bank: A nonprofit blood bank serving more than one hospital. Fees are charged to cover the costs of operation.

hospital blood bank: A blood bank operated by a hospital for the benefit of its own patients. Fees are charged to cover the operating costs.

blood bank technologist: A person who, under the supervision of a physician or other qualified scientist, carries out one or more of the functions necessary in a *blood bank*. The blood bank technologist typically is a *medical technologist* with special training and experience in the specific tasks involved with collecting, processing, storing, and distributing blood.

blood banking (1): The entire process of obtaining, drawing, processing, storing, and distributing blood and its components. See also *blood processing*.

blood banking (2): One of the medical specialties for which *residency* programs have been approved by the Accreditation Council for Graduate Medical Education (ACGME). See *specialty*.

blood chemistry: The determination of the quantities or levels of various chemicals in the blood. For each chemical, such as sugar (glucose) or cholesterol, there is a range of quantity (amount per unit of blood volume) which is found in the normal, well individual. Amounts of the chemical above or below the normal range are associated with various disease states and disturbances in *physiology*. Blood chemistry determinations are made in one portion of the *clinical laboratory*.

blood components: The components ("ingredients") of human blood, for example, red cells, white cells, plasma, and the antihemophilic fraction. Blood components can be separated out by a process called "fractionation." When whole blood is not needed, each blood component can be administered by itself, with greater benefit and safety to the patient than whole blood. Furthermore, each unit of whole blood "goes farther" (can be used to treat more patients) when it is distributed as blood components.

blood distribution: The issuance, sale, or exchange of blood (both *whole blood* and *blood components*) by a *blood bank*.

blood processing: The testing steps taken to determine the group and type of blood available for transfusion, and its safety, and to prepare it for distribution and use, both as *whole blood* and as *blood components*.

blood replacement deposit: A charge levied against the recipient of blood. It is called a deposit because the intent is to encourage the

B

replenishment of the blood supply of the *blood bank* rather than to obtain money. If the blood is replaced, the deposit is returned.

blood repository: A facility which carries out the storage and distribution functions for a *blood bank*.

Blue Cross (BC): The nonprofit hospital care *prepayment plan* which was developed and sponsored by hospitals, and which originally was restricted to furnishing hospital care. Many BC plans have linked with their counterpart *Blue Shield (BS)* plans, which are physician sponsored, and which deal with physician (medical) care. Some 77 plans of each type, BC and BS, are in existence across the United States, and state statutes typically govern their operation. While plans are similar in principle, each one is autonomous; there are differences in policies, benefit structure, and administration from plan to plan. When the local BC and BS plans have linked, they are typically referred to jointly as Blue Cross/Blue Shield (BC/BS).

Blue Cross and Blue Shield (BC/BS): The nonprofit health care *prepayment plans* (health insurance plans) which originated with hospitals and physicians, respectively. In many areas the Blue Cross (BC) and Blue Shield (BS) plans have merged. There are 77 of these health insurance plans linked by a national association, the Blue Cross and Blue Shield Association (BCBSA).

Blue Cross and Blue Shield Association (BCBSA): The national association of the nonprofit health care *prepayment plans*, originated by hospitals and physicians, respectively, called *Blue Cross (BC)* and *Blue Shield (BS)* plans. The original stimulus for the national association was to facilitate the BC and BS plans entering into "national" contracts, for example, with large corporations having plants or offices in the territories of several BC and BS plans, each of which has somewhat different policies and benefit structures.

Blue Shield (BS): The nonprofit medical (physician) care *prepayment plan* which was developed by and sponsored by physicians, and which originally was restricted to furnishing physician care. Many BS plans have linked with their counterpart *Blue Cross (BC)* plans, which are hospital sponsored, and which deal with hospital

B

care. Some 77 plans of each type, BC and BS, are in existence across the United States, and state statutes typically govern their operation. While plans are similar in principle, each one is autonomous; there are differences in policies, benefit structure, and administration among them from plan to plan. When the local BS and BC plans are linked, they are typically called jointly Blue Cross/Blue Shield (BC/BS).

BNDD: See *Bureau of Narcotics and Dangerous Drugs*.

BNDD number: The former name for the number assigned by the federal government indicating that an individual (a physician, pharmacist, hospital, pharmacy, or other qualified "business activity") registered with the former Bureau of Narcotics and Dangerous Drugs (BNDD) was authorized to prescribe or dispense *controlled substances*. The current agency with this authority is the Drug Enforcement Administration (DEA); the BNDD number is now called the DEA number.

board (1): A common term for the hospital's *governing body*, the body which is legally responsible for the hospital's policies, organization, management, and quality of care. "Board" is short for "board of trustees," "board of directors," or "board of governors." It is discussed further under *governing body*.

board (2): A *licensing* or other qualifying or *credential*-awarding body. See *boards*.

specialty board: A nongovernmental, voluntary body which *certifies* a physician or dentist as a specialist when that person has met the specialty board's requirements. Examples of specialty boards in medicine are the American Board of Internal Medicine (ABIM) and the American Board of Surgery (ABS). When the term "*specialty boards*" (plural) is used, it refers to the examinations.

board certified: The term applied to a physician (or other health professional) who has passed an examination by a *specialty board* and has been certified by that board as a specialist in the subject of expertise of the board. A specialty board is a nongovernmental, voluntary body which certifies an individual as a specialist when that individual has met the board's requirements. Examples of specialty boards for physicians are the American Board of Internal Medicine (ABIM) and the American Board of Surgery (ABS).

board eligible: The term applied to a physician (or other health professional) who has met or can meet the requirements of a *specialty board* for eligibility to take the examination required to become *board certified*. A specialty board is a nongovernmental, voluntary body which certifies a physician as a specialist when the physician has met the board's requirements.

board in residence: A term used to indicate the role of the executive committee and the *chief executive officer (CEO)* of an organization. When the full board (*governing body*) is not in session, but its executive committee is, the executive committee is "in residence" and has the authority of the full board in most matters. When the executive committee is not in session, the CEO has the authority of the full board in most matters (unless forbidden by specific board action), especially in response to emergencies.

board of directors: See *governing body*.

board of trustees: See *governing body*.

boarder: A person, other than a patient, physician, or employee, who is temporarily residing in a hospital or other health care facility. A patient's parent or spouse staying in the hospital would be a boarder.

boarder census: The number of *boarders* (non-patients residing temporarily) in a hospital.

boards: A term commonly used to describe examinations given by a *"board (2)"* to a physician (or medical student) or other health professional. When the term "board" is used in the singular, it refers to the certifying body. Successfully passing board examinations gives specific *credentials* to physicians, nurses, and others:

national boards: Examinations given by the *National Board of Medical Examiners (NBME)*. These are similar to *state board* examinations in scope and provide "portable" evidence (evidence acceptable in various states), which some states accept in lieu of their own state boards for awarding medical licensure. Part of the National Board examination can be taken by *undergraduate* medical students.

specialty boards: A short term for "specialty board examinations," examinations given by a voluntary *specialty board* to eligible professionals who wish to become *certified specialists*. A certified specialist is a person who has been given a statement by the *board* involved that he has met the qualifications for specialty "rating" in that specialty. Such a specialist is called "board certified." The term "specialty board" (singular) refers to the certifying body.

state boards: Examinations given by a state *board (2)* (of medicine or nursing, for example) to applicants who wish to be *licensed* to practice a profession or occupation. State boards must be passed by a graduate physician in order for that physician to become licensed to practice medicine in the examining state unless that state (1) accepts *national boards* in lieu of state boards or (2) grants licensing by *reciprocity* with another state in which the applicant is already licensed. Similarly, state boards are involved in the licensing of dentists, nurses, and those wishing to practice certain other professions and occupations.

boilerplate: Standard language in a contract, often in small print. Boilerplate may be distinguished from language which has been written specifically for a certain contract, and which reflects the specific intentions of the unique parties involved. Boilerplate may not always be enforced, especially if it conflicts with the specific, expressed intentions of the parties.

bond: A certificate sold by a corporation or government entity to raise funds. It is basically a form of "IOU" upon which the corporation or government entity will pay interest to the bondholder for a given period of time, and pay the bondholder the amount borrowed (the principal amount) at the end of that time. Some bonds qualify as "tax-exempt," meaning that the bondholder does not have to pay taxes on the interest earned.

rapid amortization bond: A bond with special provisions which permit the principal to be paid off without penalty (i.e., the bond may be retired) prior to its maturity date.

revenue bond: A bond payable solely from the *revenue* generated from the operation of the project being financed, for which the bond was sold. In the case of hospital revenue bond financing, the bonds are typically payable from the gross *receipts* of the hospital. Such bonds may only be sold by *municipalities* (or by quasi-municipal organizations, such as hospitals, under special legislation).

tax-exempt bond: A bond, the holder of which does not have to pay taxes on the interest she receives. Municipalities and, in some instances, nonprofit hospitals, are authorized to sell "tax-exempt" bonds.

bond indenture: The contract between a bondholder and the institution (for example, a hospital) issuing the *bond.*

break-even analysis: An analytical technique for studying the relation among *fixed costs, variable costs,* volume or level of activity (sales), and profits.

break-even chart: A chart graphically presenting the results of a *break-even analysis.*

break-even point: The volume of activity (for example, sales) where *revenues* and *expenses* are exactly equal, that is, the level of activity where there is neither a gain nor a loss from operations. Activity above the break-even point produces profits; activity below it results in losses.

BS: See *Blue Shield.*

BSN: See *Bachelor of Science in Nursing.*

budget neutrality: A term which came into use as part of the *prospective payment system (PPS)* to mean that the new payment system may not pay hospitals, in the aggregate, any more or less for Medicare patients than the hospitals would have been paid under the previous system. More generally, a budget may be said to be "neutral" if, in total, it is neither larger than nor smaller than the previous budget.

budget reconciliation: A part of the legislative budgeting process which defines federal programs in such a manner that program costs are consistent with Congress' decision as to how much money is to be spent for the program in question.

building codes: Regulations which owners must meet in the construction, use, and maintenance of buildings. Building codes are promulgated and enforced by government agencies and are designed to ensure that buildings are durable and safe. The National Fire Protection Association (NHPA) issues, and periodically revises, a standard called the "Life Safety Code" which covers both construction and operation of buildings in such a manner as to maximize fire safety. While not strictly a building code, compliance with this code is required of hospitals wishing accreditation by the Joint Commission on Accreditation of Healthcare Organizations (JCAHO).

Bureau of Narcotics and Dangerous Drugs (BNDD): The federal agency which was the predecessor to the *Drug Enforcement Administration (DEA)*.

burn care unit: A special unit of the hospital set up to give *intensive care* to burn patients. It is a specialized *intensive care unit*.

burn center: A highly specialized facility in a *tertiary care* center, set up with specially trained physicians, nurses, and allied health professionals, and with special equipment, to care for severely burned individuals. Only a handful of burn centers are found in the United States, and the practice is to transfer severely burned patients to them. Burn centers have proven superior to less specialized units in saving the lives of burn patients and restoring them to optimal function.

bylaws: A document adopted by a corporation or association which governs its business conduct and the rights and responsibilities of its members. Hospital bylaws, for example, cover such matters as how directors will be elected to the board of directors (*governing body*), their terms, how often they will meet, and so forth. *Medical staff bylaws* (which are part of the hospital bylaws) cover medical staff governance, membership, privileges, discipline, and the like. Bylaws may also authorize the separate issuance of *rules and regulations* to govern specific activities. The process for changing the rules and regulations is less cumbersome than that for changing the bylaws themselves.

bypass: To go around. In surgery the term is most frequently used in reference to blood vessels which are transplanted in order to provide a passage around an area where the blood vessels have been narrowed or closed due to disease or to hereditary malformation. For example, in the heart, coronary artery bypass grafts (CABG) are used to bypass closed or narrowed blood vessels.

byte: A group of eight *bits*, which is a common unit of information used by *digital* computers. A single byte, sometimes referred to as an eight-bit "word," can represent any one of 256 different values, since each bit can represent one of two values, and 2 taken to the power of 8 equals 256. Most computer users are familiar with the use of "byte," since it is the unit used to measure the amount of information stored in a computer file. Thus, a file containing 135Kb (kilobytes) would likely contain 135,000 characters, since each letter, space, or punctuation mark in a text file typically occupies one byte.

A much less commonly used term is the "nybble," which is four bits, or half a byte.

C

CABG: See *coronary artery bypass graft*.

cafeteria plan: See *Zero Balanced Reimbursement Account (ZEBRA)*.

CAHEA: See *Committee on Allied Health Education and Accreditation*.

calcium entry blockers (CEBs): A class of drugs which block the entry of calcium to certain tissues.

Canadian Council on Health Facilities Accreditation (CCHFA): The Canadian counterpart to the *Joint Commission on the Accreditation of Healthcare Organizations (JCAHO)* in the United States. It was formerly called the Canadian Council on Hospital Accreditation (CCHA). Both CCHFA and JCAHO are voluntary bodies concerned with the quality of hospitals and other health care facilities. Originally JCAH (JCAHO's former name) performed its functions for hospitals in both the United States and Canada, but in 1955 CCHA was formed for Canadian hospitals.

Canadian Council on Hospital Accreditation (CCHA): The former name of the *Canadian Council on Health Facilities Accreditation (CCHFA)*.

Canadian Hospital Association (CHA): The national association of hospitals in Canada, the counterpart of the American Hospital Association (AHA) in the United States.

C

cancer: A general term for any *tumor* (growth) which is malignant, that is, which is subject to unlimited growth and extension or dispersal within the body.

capital: Usually, the long-term *assets* of the organization which are not bought and sold in the course of its operation. These assets are primarily *fixed assets* such as land, equipment, and building.

  working capital: The difference between *current assets* and *current liabilities*.

capital budgeting: The process of planning expenditures on capital items, that is, *assets* whose useful life is expected to extend beyond one year: property, plant, and equipment.

capital cost: The cost of developing or acquiring new equipment, facilities, or services; that is, the investment cost to the institution of such growth.

capital expenditure: An expenditure (chargeable to an *asset* account) made to acquire an asset which has an estimated life in excess of one year and is not intended for sale in the ordinary course of business. It is also known as a capital expense. Expenses for operation (including maintenance) of the asset are not capital expenditures, but operating expenses.

capital expenditure review (CER): A process carried out by a state agency prior to granting permission to the hospital to incur a *capital expenditure*.

capital financing: Obtaining funds for building or renovation, that is, for additions to *capital*, as opposed to the financing of operations. For the most part, operations are financed by fees for services rendered.

capital leverage: See *financial leverage*.

capital pass-through: Costs, such as depreciation and interest, which are "passed through." In other words, these costs are not included in the *Diagnosis Related Group (DRG)* prices, but are paid directly to the hospital in the *prospective payment system (PPS)*.

capital rationing: A situation where a constraint is placed on the total size of *capital* investment during a particular period.

capital structure: The permanent long-term financing of an organization or institution represented by *long-term debt, preferred stock*, and *net worth*. Capital structure is distinguished from *financial structure*, which includes short-term debt plus all *reserve accounts*.

capitation: A method of payment in which a *provider* receives a fixed fee per person ("per capita") for a period of time, and the provider agrees to furnish to persons for whom the capitation payments are received all the care that may be required (within the contract limitations) without further fee. Capitation may, for example, pertain to virtually all medical and hospital services through a health care plan, or only to primary care services.

captive insurance company: An insurance company formed to underwrite (insure) the risks of its owner(s). Increasingly, hospitals and other health care providers are forming or buying their own insurance companies, either alone or with other providers.

cardiac: Referring to the heart. Words developed with this adjective usually take the form "cardio-," for example, *cardiology*. See also *coronary*.

cardiac arrest: The cessation of circulation with the disappearance of blood pressure. Cardiac arrest may be caused either by the heartbeat going from its normal rhythm to an abnormal, ineffective rhythm, or by the heart stopping its beat altogether.

cardiac care unit (CCU): A specialized kind of *intensive care unit* with cardiac monitoring abilities for inpatients having, or suspected of having, *acute* cardiac (heart) conditions. Synonym(s): coronary care unit, cardiac surveillance unit.

cardiac catheterization: The insertion of a tube (*catheter*) into the heart via an artery or vein for diagnostic purposes, for example, to measure the blood pressures in the heart, to take samples of blood for analysis, or to introduce radiopaque drugs (drugs which are visible by X-ray). Information can also be obtained by watching, via *fluoroscope,* the passage of the catheter as it is inserted.

cardiac rescue technician: An *emergency medical technician (EMT)* with special training in the care of cardiac (heart) emergencies, and authorization from the appropriate authority (such as a state agency), to use the title and carry out the measures required. Synonym(s): cardiac technician.

cardiac surveillance unit: See *cardiac care unit (CCU).*

cardiac technician: See *cardiac rescue technician.*

cardiologist: A physician specializing in diseases and disorders of the heart and circulatory system.

cardiology: The *specialty* of medicine dealing with diseases and disorders of the heart and the circulatory system.

cardiopulmonary resuscitation (CPR): The restoration of heart output and breathing after cardiac arrest (stopping of the heart) and stopping of breathing. The technique requires *artificial respiration* and *closed-chest cardiac massage.* More heroic measures to restore heart function and breathing are employed in hospitals and by trained and equipped emergency medical personnel. Synonym(s): resuscitation.

cardiovascular disease: A branch of *internal medicine.* One of the medical specialties for which *residency* programs have been approved by the Accreditation Council for Graduate Medical Education (ACGME). See *specialty.*

cardiovascular technologist (CVT): One of the 26 *allied health professionals* for whom the American Medical Association's *Committee on Allied Health Education and Accreditation (CAHEA)* has accredited education programs.

care: The treatment and other services provided to a patient. Care is often described according to the needs of the patient: for example, neonatal care describes the care given newborns;

respiratory care describes the care provided for patients with respiratory (breathing) difficulties. Care may also be described according to the "level" (intensity) or urgency of care, the health professional providing care, or the facility required. See also *level of care*.

Types of care defined in this book include acute, adult day, after, ambulatory, basic nursing, bereavement, critical, custodial, day, elder, elective, emergency, home health, home life, hospice, hospital nursing, inpatient, intensive, intermediate, intermittent, life, long-term, managed, medical, personal, primary, progressive patient, rehabilitative, rehabilitative nursing, respite, rest home, secondary, self, skilled nursing, secondary, terminal, tertiary, transitional, uncompensated, and urgent.

care plan: See *nursing care plan*.

caregiver: An individual who provides care for a disabled or ill friend or relative.

carrier (1): An organization which handles the claims for beneficiaries on behalf of certain kinds of health insurance. A carrier may be an insurance company, a prepayment plan, or a government agency. In general, a carrier is at some *risk (1)*. On the other hand, an intermediary, which is an agency in the Medicare system which has been selected to pay claims, and which is responsible only for taking care of the administration of the plan, is not at risk.

carrier (2): An individual who carries, and can transmit, a contagious disease without himself showing symptoms or signs of the disease.

case (1): A *patient* and his medical problem. Used alone, the term "patient" does not indicate whether the individual is ill or well. However, the term "case" denotes that the patient is ill, injured, or otherwise presents a problem to the health care provider. With a modifier or additional information, "case" describes the patient's problem, as, for example, a "case of influenza."

case (2): A controversy which is contested in a court of law. In common usage, a legal "case" refers to the particular facts of the

C

controversy and the legal theories, allegations, and defenses being applied to those facts.

case abstract: See *discharge abstract*.

case management (1): A traditional term for all the activities which a physician normally performs to insure the coordination of the medical services required by a patient. This is not the same function as that of the *gatekeeper* in *managed care*. Under ordinary circumstances, the American Medical Association (AMA) does not consider case management a separately reimbursable service.

case management (2): A term which, when used in connection with *managed care*, covers all the activities of evaluating the patient, planning treatment, referral, and followup, so that care is continuous and comprehensive and payment for the care is obtained.

case mix: The mix of cases, defined by age, sex, diagnoses, treatments, *severity of illness*, and so on, handled by a practitioner or hospital. Case mix is defined by: (1) grouping patients (*classification (1)*) according to these factors; and then (2) determining the *proportion* of the total falling into each group. At present, the most widely used classification for this purpose is the *Diagnosis Related Group (DRG)* system. Sometimes the term "case mix" is used, inaccurately, to mean the grouping system itself (DRG, for example).

In the Medicare *prospective payment system (PPS)*, which sets a price for each DRG, the total revenue for the hospital for its Medicare patients depends on how many "items" it "sells," and of what kind, that is, the number of patients cared for and the DRG of each. The revenue, therefore, is dependent upon the hospital's case mix.

case mix complexity: A phrase used to convey the idea that hospitals (and physicians) differ in the variety of patients they serve. A specialized hospital would have a less complex mix of patients than a general hospital. The complexity is sometimes described quantitatively by the use of a *case mix index*.

case mix index (CMI): A term used in the *prospective payment system (PPS)*. It is a measure of the "expected costliness," per patient, of treating a given hospital's mix of cases. CMI is scaled so that a hospital whose mix is like that in base data would have a CMI of 1.0. The base data for a CMI usually come from a broad sector of inpatients, often the Medicare patients, discharged from the nation's hospitals during a *base (2)* year.

For calculating CMIs, a *classification (1)* of patients is used, in which each *category* (class) is assigned a "weight" that is proportional to the average cost of treating a patient in that class. These weights are calculated from the base data. A hospital's CMI for a given time period may be calculated as follows: (1) for each patient, identify his class and note the associated weight; (2) take the average of these weights.

CMI may also be calculated by the following formula:

$$CMI = \sum_i p_i\, w_i$$

where i = patient class, p = the proportion of the hospital's patients falling into that class, and w = the weight assigned to that class.

case-mix management information system (case-mix MIS): See *management information system.*

case-mix MIS: Case-mix management information system. See *management information system.*

case-mix severity: A term referring, as yet without a single definition, to the degree of illness of a given group of patients. For example, one hospital's (or one time-period's) group of diabetes patients (or a specific *Diagnosis Related Group (DRG)*) may be much more severely ill than another's. Various *"severity of illness"* index methods are under development to quantify this fact.

case mix system: Usually, an information system in which clinical and financial data are merged, patient by patient, in such a manner that analyses can be made as to the profitability of a given type of patient (*Diagnosis Related Group (DRG)* category, for example), clinical department, physician, or other aspect of the hospital.

case shifting: See *dumping.*

C

case summary: A summary of the *medical record* of a patient, prepared by a physician, nurse, or other qualified individual, which condenses the essential elements of history, physical examination, other diagnostic findings, treatment, and recommendations. While similar to a *case abstract*, a case summary (1) reflects the individual case rather than carrying predefined *data elements*, uniform for all patients, (2) is written out rather than *coded*, as is the case abstract, and (3) may also contain the summarizer's interpretations, rather than being required to transfer the data exactly as recorded.

CAT: Computed axial tomography. See *computed tomography (CT)*.

CAT scanner: See *CT scanner*.

catastrophic illness: An illness which requires very costly treatment; one which is catastrophic to the patient's or family's finances. The illness may be either *acute* or *chronic,* and it may run its course quickly or over a protracted period.

catastrophic insurance: See *insurance*.

catchment area: See *service area*.

categorical grant: Federal funds which have been provided for specific purposes, for example, the treatment of cancer or the establishment of a burn center. This is in contrast to a "block grant," in which a "block" of federal funds is provided and the recipient is given much wider discretion in its use.

category: A pigeonhole ("class") of a *classification (1)*. For each category there is a definition and an explicit list of all the *entities* to be placed under (within) the category in question. The label of a category is called its rubric (although "rubric" sometimes is used interchangeably with "category"). For example, "pickup trucks" would be the rubric (label) for a category in a classification of motor vehicles. There would be a definition of what distinguishes a pickup truck from other vehicles, and a list of all the vehicles (for a given model year, for example) which were "officially" to be classified as pickup trucks.

A category may be designed to contain only a single item

(entity) and thus be a "single-entity category," or it may be designed to contain a variety of related entities.

single-diagnosis category: A category in a classification of *diagnoses*, such as *Diagnosis Related Groups (DRGs)* or the *International Classification of Diseases, 9th Revision, Clinical Modification (ICD-9-CM)*, which contains only one diagnosis.

category coding: Discussed under *coding*.

catheter: A thin tube to be inserted into the body, via a natural opening or an incision into a blood vessel or other structure, for the purpose of putting something into the body or taking something out. For example, *radiopaque* drugs used in *X-ray* examinations may be introduced, or blood or urine may be removed by catheter.

catheterization: Insertion of a tube into a body orifice or structure in order to put something in or take something out. Cardiac catheterization is the insertion of a tube into the heart, via a blood vessel, in order to permit chemical determinations on heart blood, or to introduce dyes or radioactive materials to be detected in diagnostic tests or *imaging*. More common catheterizations include insertion of a tube into a blood vessel to permit intravenous feeding, and insertion of a tube into the urinary tract to relieve an obstruction to the flow of urine or to obtain a clean specimen of urine.

cathode ray tube (CRT): An electronic device for the display of images in computers, computer terminals, *imaging* equipment, and television sets. CRTs may also be found in electronic instruments, such as cathode ray oscilloscopes.

cause of action: Legal grounds upon which to base a lawsuit. A cause of action may be based upon breach of a contract, commission of a *tort*, violation of a statute, or violation of a constitutional right.

CCC: See *Council on Clinical Classifications*.

CCHA: See *Canadian Council on Hospital Accreditation*.

C

CCHFA: See *Canadian Council on Health Facilities Accreditation.*

CCRC: See *continuing care retirement communities.*

CCRN: See *certified critical care nurse.*

CCU: See *cardiac care unit.*

CD: See *chemical dependency.*

CDC: See *Centers for Disease Control.*

CEBs: See *calcium entry blockers.*

cell: A small plant or animal structure which forms the building block (the structural unit) of a tissue. A cell contains two components known as nuclear material and cytoplasmic material, and is enclosed by a membrane. In the human body, all cells fall into one of five general types according to the tissues which they form: epithelial (surface and lining tissues), connective and supporting (bones and cartilages), muscle, nerve, and blood and lymph.

census: The number of patients in a hospital at a given time.

average daily census: The average number of *inpatients* in a hospital (or unit of the hospital, such as a *patient care unit*) each day for a given period of time. Newborns (born in the hospital) are not included in the inpatient count for calculation of this statistic.

boarder census: The number of *boarders* (non-patients residing temporarily) in a hospital.

Centers for Disease Control (CDC): A unit of the federal government, with headquarters in Atlanta, Georgia, responsible for monitoring and study of diseases which are controllable by public health measures. New diseases which appear to occur in epidemics are investigated, as are those due to environmental problems. Here, for example, is the government's center for monitoring and research on acquired immunity deficiency syndrome (AIDS), toxic shock syndrome, and Legionnaire's disease.

central processing: In hospital administration, a term which refers to the recycling of reusable items used in patient care (surgical instruments, for example), their collection, cleaning, sterilization, and repackaging. These are functions of the central service department (CS).

central service department (CS): The hospital department which provides *sterile* medical and surgical instruments and supplies. The pharmacy is not a part of CS. Synonym(s): central supply department.

central supply department: See *central service department (CS)*.

centralized services: *Services (4)* which are carried out from a single location, in an effort to improve efficiency, reduce cost, or both. The alternate is "decentralized services," the spreading out of the services in question to different locations. A given type of service usually is under a single management division in an institution, although, when decentralized, it may be under several managements.

CEO: See *chief executive officer*.

CER: See *capital expenditure review*.

certificate of insurance (COI): A document issued by an insurance company to verify that a particular person or institution is in fact insured for a certain type of *risk (2)*, during a specific period of time. The dollar limits of the insurance are shown. A hospital may require a COI from each medical staff member, for example, to assure that the member has adequate malpractice insurance coverage.

certificate of need (CON): A certificate, issued by a governmental or planning agency, which approves the hospital's contention that it needs a given facility or *service (6)* (for example, open heart surgery). A certificate of need is required under many regulatory situations in order to obtain approval to build or institute the service in question.

C

certification: The issuance of a "certificate" which gives evidence that its recipient (an individual, facility, or device) meets certain standards against which testing has been done by the certifying body. A certificate thus issued is a *credential*, and the recipient is said to be *certified*.

certification examination: An examination which is given for the purpose of determining the applicant's qualification for the *certification* sought.

certified: A term applied to an individual, facility, or device after a certifying body has conducted its testing, and declared that the subject has met the standards, and is entitled to *certification*. Being certified provides a *credential*.

Certified Professional in Quality Assurance (CPQA): An individual who has passed a *credential examination* given by the National Association of Quality Assurance Professionals (NAQAP). See *quality assurance professional (QAP (1))*.

Certified Public Accountant (CPA): An individual who has met the requirements of the American Institute of Certified Public Accountants (AICPA) which lead to the awarding of this *credential*.

certified registered nurse anesthetist (CRNA): A *nurse anesthetist* who has met the *certification* requirements of the Council on Certification/Council on Recertification of Nurse Anesthetists (a voluntary body).

certified surgical technologist (CST): An individual who has met the requirements of the Liaison Council on Certification for the Surgical Technologist (LCC), an autonomous board affiliated with the Association of Surgical Technologists (AST).

CFO: See *chief financial officer*.

CHA (1): See *Canadian Hospital Association*.

CHA (2): Formerly the Catholic Hospital Association. In the United States, the organization is now called the Catholic Health Association of the United States. There is a counterpart Canadian organization called the Catholic Health Association of Canada.

chain organization: See *multihospital system*.

chairman of service: See *chief of service*.

CHAMPUS: See *Civilian Health and Medical Program of the Uniformed Services*.

CHAMPVA: See *Civilian Health and Medical Program of the Veterans Administration*.

channel system: A term sometimes given to a computer network system in which computer terminals in a number of locations are tied into a central location and information system. An example of a channel system is an airline network serving travel agents who can use their terminals in the system to do scheduling, determine fares, and sell tickets, with the central computer and information system handling all the transactions and creating the data displays.

    Channel systems are being used in health care with the development of, for example, networks centered in a given hospital or health care system headquarters, with the remote terminals in physicians' offices, laboratories, and clinics. A number of tasks can be performed with this system. For example, a given physician's office can make appointments with other physicians and with hospitals. Such a system "channels" patients from the physicians who are in the network into other parts of the network rather than into other health care systems. The channel system is developed primarily to retain patients within the network, and to "feed" patients to the owner of the system, typically a hospital or other health care organization.

channeling: A term used in *long-term care* in which efforts are made to avoid institutionalization of patients by having them directed ("channeled") to community-based long-term care services. From 1980 to 1985, the *Health Care Financing Administration (HCFA)* and other federal agencies financed a demonstration of the concept, which used comprehensive *case management (2)*, but ended the demonstration when a study showed no lowering of cost. More recently, reports suggest that when a case manager participates in

C

the financial planning as well as the health care decisions, significant savings may be realized.

CHAP: See *Community Health Accreditation Program*.

chaplain: A member of the clergy whose duty is to provide pastoral services to patients and their families, and to the hospital staff.

charge: The dollar amount asked for a *service (1)* by a health care provider. It is contrasted with the *cost*, which is the dollar amount the provider incurs in furnishing the service. It is difficult to determine precise costs for many services, and in such cases charges are substituted for costs in many reimbursement and payment formulas (often with the stipulation that the hospital's bookkeeping follow certain rules).

allowable charge: See *covered charge*.

covered charge: An item of *service (1)* which, when billed to a *third party payer*, will be paid, since it is for a benefit provided under the contract. The charges for television and meals for visitors, for example, are not ordinarily covered charges. Synonym(s): allowable charge.

daily service charge: Same as "room rate"; see *rate (1)*.

charity allowance: A reduction of a *charge* (a discount) to a patient because that patient is *indigent* or *medically indigent*.

chart: See *medical record*.

CHC: See *community health center*.

CHD: See *coronary heart disease*.

chemical: A substance produced by chemistry, as distinguished from a biological substance, which is produced by a living organism. Both chemical and biological substances are used in diagnostic procedures and the treatment of disease.

chemical dependency (CD): The generic term covering *alcoholism* and addiction to other drugs, both legal drugs (prescribed by a physician or available over the counter) and illegal drugs.

chemical pathology: One of the medical specialties for which *residency* programs have been approved by the Accreditation Council for Graduate Medical Education (ACGME). See *specialty*.

chemistry technologist: A *medical technologist* who specializes in chemical analyses.

chief engineer: See *administrative engineer*.

chief executive officer (CEO): The person appointed by the *governing body* to direct the overall management of the hospital. The CEO is the *"board in residence."* Synonym(s): executive director.

chief financial officer (CFO): The corporate treasurer. Sometimes the term is also applied to the controller of the organization (the person in charge of the ongoing financial administration, including billing, accounting, budget management, and the like). Synonym(s): financial director.

chief information officer (CIO): The title often given to the person in charge of the organization's *management information system (MIS)*.

chief of nursing: See *nursing service administrator*.

chief of service: A *medical staff organization (MSO)* officer responsible for the management of a *clinical department*, such as internal medicine or surgery. Synonym(s): chairman of service.

chief of staff: The physician designated by the *governing body*, usually after nomination by the *medical staff organization (MSO)*, to be responsible for management of the MSO and for carrying out policy promulgated by the board. The term "chief of staff" or "president of the medical staff" usually refers to an unpaid person, while a paid physician with either of these same duties is likely to be called the "medical director," "vice president for medical af-

C

fairs," "director of medical affairs" (DMA), or some like title.

There is some ambiguity in the duties and titles, because there really are two duties involved "at the top of the medical staff": (1) to provide management for the MSO as a component of the hospital, and for this duty, the title "chief of staff" seems appropriate; and (2) to act as the "spokesperson" for the MSO members, and for this duty, the title "president" seems more apt.

Many hospitals have two separate positions: a president (often unpaid), elected by the MSO (and approved by the governing body) to represent the medical staff, and a director of medical affairs (or similar title), employed by the hospital, to manage medical staff affairs.

chief operating officer (COO): The person in charge of the internal operation of the organization, for example, a hospital. The *chief executive officer (CEO)*, while responsible for the internal operation of the organization, also has external responsibilities with the *governing body*, with the community, with other institutions, and so on. Often a single individual is made responsible for "inside" affairs, under the CEO. This person would be the COO, whether or not he is given that title.

Child Abuse Amendments: Amendments, enacted in 1984, to the federal Child Abuse Prevention and Treatment Act concerning medical treatment decisions for seriously ill newborns. The amendments added the term "withholding of medically indicated treatment" to the statutory definition of child neglect; this is now often referred to as "medical neglect." The law was passed in response to the *Baby Doe* case, and makes it a form of neglect to fail to treat correctable, life-threatening conditions in a child unless in the physician's "reasonable medical judgment" (1) the child is irreversably comatose, (2) treatment would be futile in saving the child's life, or (3) the treatment would be virtually futile and inhumane under the circumstances. States must require hospitals to report cases of suspected medical neglect to the child protective service agencies, and provide procedures for appropriate intervention. Synonym(s): Baby Doe Law.

child life specialist: A person with academic qualifications who is employed in a hospital to help children and their parents handle the stress of hospitalization.

child neurology: One of the medical specialties for which *residency* programs have been approved by the Accreditation Council for Graduate Medical Education (ACGME). See *specialty*.

child psychiatry: The branch of *psychiatry* dealing with children. One of the medical specialties for which *residency* programs have been approved by the Accreditation Council for Graduate Medical Education (ACGME). See *specialty*.

childbirth center: A facility, either a part of a hospital or free-standing, which provides *prenatal care* for the mother, delivery, and *postnatal* care. Typically a facility with this name involves the family rather than just the mother and baby; it permits the father's attendance at the delivery and his assistance in caring for the baby, and so on. Synonym(s): birthing center.

chiropody: See *podiatry*.

chiropractic: See *medicine (4)*.

chiropractor: A practitioner of *chiropractic* (see *medicine (4)*). In order to practice, the chiropractor must be *licensed* by the state. The chiropractor has the degree Doctor of Chiropractic (DC).

CHN: See *community health network*.

chorionic villus sampling (CVS): A diagnostic technique under investigation for early detection of certain genetic abnormalities in the fetus. A thin tube is inserted into the uterus as early as the ninth week of pregnancy (following ultrasound examination), and a few cells from the chorion (the tissue which develops into the placenta) are removed and examined immediately under the microscope. The procedure may be useful at least six weeks earlier than *amniocentesis*, which must be done later, and which requires several weeks of laboratory work.

CHP: See *comprehensive health planning*.

CHP agency: See *comprehensive health planning agency*.

C

chronic: An illness which lasts for a long time, and usually without prospect of immediate change either for the better or the worse. It is contrasted with *acute*, which refers to having a short course, which often is relatively severe. "Chronic" is also used for the portion or portions of an illness, ordinarily in its later stages, in which symptoms are less severe and the patient may be at relatively low risk.

chronobiology: The branch of biology dealing with circadian biological rhythms (rhythms in a cycle of about a day, about 24 hours). For example, shifting work hours, which require an individual to change his pattern of sleep and wakefulness, create serious health problems for many individuals; studies have shown increases in errors in performance, and in accidents, during the periods of the circadian rhythm when neural functions are at their lowest ebb—between 2 am and 7 am, and between 2 pm and 5 pm, for individuals "working the day shift."

chronohygiene: That branch of the science of health dealing with the problems associated with changes in the individual's sleep and wakefulness cycle, such as "jet lag" and the shifting of work hours for nurses.

churning: The practice of *discharge* of a patient and *readmission* of the same patient for what is really a single *episode of (hospital) care* in order to be able to charge for two or more hospitalizations. Only the last discharge is "real" from a medical standpoint—except for the financial benefit of being paid for two or more hospitalizations under the *prospective payment system (PPS)*, there would have been no intermediate discharges.

CIO: See *chief information officer*.

circadian: Pertaining to biological rhythms which occur in a cycle of about 24 hours, about a day.

Civilian Health and Medical Program of the Veterans Administration: The federal program, administered by the Defense Department for the Veterans Administration, which provides care for the dependents of totally-disabled veterans. Care is given by civilian providers.

Civilian Health and Medical Program of the Uniformed Services (CHAMPUS): A program that pays for medical care given by civilian providers to retired members of the uniformed services of the United States, and to the dependents of both active and retired members of these services. The program is administered by the Department of Defense. A similar program for dependents of totally disabled veterans, the Civilian Health and Medical Program of the Veterans Administration (CHMPVA), is also administered by the Department of Defense.

clade: A term which originally referred to a group of descendants from a single biological organism, that is, having a common ancestor. It has been suggested that the concept could be used to depict graphically the situation with human immunodeficiency virus (HIV) infections. The usual illustration is that HIV infections are like an iceberg, with the visible portion consisting of the proportion of the persons who are clinically ill with acquired immunodeficiency syndrome (AIDS), in contrast with the submerged portion consisting of the number who are infected, but clinically well at any given time. The iceberg analogy is flawed because an iceberg melts and disappears, while the clade (and HIV infection) is a constantly growing number. The HIV clade could be graphed with numbers of cases along the vertical axis, and time along the horizontal axis. Those above a straight horizontal line beginning at the first description of HIV infections would be living cases of AIDS; those below it would be the infected but clinically well. The graph would look like the letter "V" on its side, with the point of the "V" to the left and the open side growing larger with time.

claim (1): A request for payment of *insurance benefits* to be paid to or on behalf of a *beneficiary*.

claim (2): A demand for money or other property due or believed to be due. The term may be used to refer to an allegation of legal *liability (1)* and an accompanying demand for *damages* (money) or other rights due. The term is sometimes used in health care to refer to a medical *malpractice* lawsuit, or to the allegation of malpractice (which allegation may or may not result in a lawsuit).

open claim: A claim for *damages*, usually involving *professional liability*, in which a decision has not been reached, either by *settlement* out of court or by court decision.

C

When an individual believes that he has been injured by the hospital or a physician, a claim may be made for damages. The claim may eventually be withdrawn. Claims not withdrawn may be settled, either by negotiation or by court decision. Before the settlement, the claim is open (pending); after settlement it is *closed*.

closed claim: A claim for which the issues of *liability* and *damages* (who owes what to whom) have been decided, either by *settlement* out of court or by court decision.

Closed claims are discussed in health care because they are the basis for analysis of the liability (*malpractice*) "problem" (i.e. the costs in the health care industry of malpractice insurance, judgments, and settlements, and related costs both monetary and otherwise; for example, the practice of "*defensive medicine*"). But while closed claim studies may be carefully done, at best they only display a part of the liability picture. This is so because: (1) the only claims certain to be available for analysis are those closed claims in which a court decision has been rendered, since these are in the public domain; (2) claims may be pending for years, and pending claims are kept confidential; (3) claims settled by negotiation (out of court) need not be made public; and (4) while a number of institutions and insurance companies do contribute data on their settled claims to bona fide research institutions for confidential use in statistical analysis, not all closed claims are submitted, so published analyses of closed claims are always an understatement of the liability problem.

claim (3): The usage in which the word is employed to describe one form of *asset*.

claims filing service: A service offered by private entrepreneurs to Medicare beneficiaries and others with health insurance. The service offers to "file, follow-up, and manage" *claims (1)*. Often the service charges a "registration" fee plus monthly fees. Such a service, which costs perhaps $100 per beneficiary per year, adds to the cost of health care by that amount and, equally importantly, decreases the individual's benefits by that amount.

claims-made coverage: See *insurance coverage*.

claims processing: The procedure by which *claims (1)* for payment for *services (1)* are reviewed in order to determine whether they should be paid, and for what amount. The review includes verifying that an authorized provider is submitting the claim, that the person served is a *beneficiary*, that the services are medically reasonable and are for available *benefits*, and the amount to be paid.

class: See *category*.

classification (1): A scheme for grouping the entities (items) making up a universe into *categories*. A classification is a systematic scheme of organization of *information* in which a whole body of things—for example, automobiles, houses, hospitals, or procedures—have been grouped (classified) into categories (classes or "pigeonholes") so that the groups can be compared, studied, analyzed, or otherwise processed. Classifications are used in health care to organize patient (and patient care) information for such purposes as studying diseases, assessing quality of care, and determining charges to be made for health care services. Confusion results when the word classification (the whole schema) is used when "class" is intended.

The purpose of the classification determines its organization or grouping system. A classification to describe the body of hospitalized patients requires different groupings than one for general office practice. For example, patients with the common cold are so rarely hospitalized that, in a hospital diagnosis classification, the common cold is grouped with miscellaneous respiratory conditions, while in general office practice the common cold may be seen so frequently that it deserves a category of its own.

classification (2): Derived from the verb "to classify." The process of placing an entity (item) of a universe into its *category* (pigeonhole) within a *classification (1)*. This is a specialized function which requires a "judgment call" as to which category a given entity falls into in cases where the entity is described in a term or terms which are not found in the classification as printed (or its index). Classification requires expert knowledge of the universe of objects to be classified, in contrast to "coding," which is a clerical task. See *coding*.

classifier: A person who classifies, that is, who does *classification (2)*.

C

classifying: Making the decisions necessary for placing an entity (item) into a *category* of a *classification (1)*.

Clayton Act: One of the primary federal *antitrust* laws. The Clayton Act specifically prohibits price discrimination (selling to different buyers at different, discriminatory prices) (Section 2(a), as amended by the *Robinson-Patman Act*), *tying agreements, exclusive dealing,* and corporate expansion if these activities substantially lessen competition or create a monopoly. It also prohibits interlocking corporate directorships where the corporations are competitors; no individual may simultaneously serve on the boards of directors of two or more competing corporations, if one of the corporations has assets over one million dollars. 15 U.S.C. secs. 12 *et seq.* (1982).

clean room: A room (which may be a "room within a room") with environmental controls which prevent bacteria and dirt from coming in or going out. This is accomplished by using a filtered air supply and by providing methods for manipulating the patient without direct contact. Ports in the "room" permit persons wearing sleeved rubber gloves or using special devices to perform tasks within the room.

clinic (1): A facility for *ambulatory* patients.

clinic (2): An establishment or meeting for the purpose of providing instruction, such as a prenatal clinic, where expectant mothers are instructed in their own care and prepared for the care of their babies.

clinic (3): An instructional session, especially in medical education, where students are taught by demonstration with actual patients.

clinic (4): A group of physicians practicing together, either all of one specialty (single specialty) or with various specialties (multispecialty). Such a clinic may or may not have *inpatient* facilities.

clinic clerk: A person who carries out clerical functions in an *outpatient* (clinic) setting.

C

clinical: A term referring to direct contact with or information from patients and to the course of illness; "things" medical about a patient. Thus personal (bedside) contact with the patient is clinical contact, a laboratory which examines blood and other specimens from patients is a clinical laboratory, the patient's medical record is a clinical record, research involving patients is clinical research, a nurse taking care of patients is a clinical nurse.

clinical chemist: See *biochemist*.

clinical clerk: A student in a medical or dental school who carries out certain tasks with patients (*clinical* tasks) under supervision as part of his training. The training period is called a *clinical clerkship*.

clinical clerkship: A training experience, involving actual care and treatment of patients (*clinical* experience) under medical or dental supervision, provided by a hospital to a medical or dental student. The trainee is called a *clinical clerk*.

clinical engineer: A person who is involved with patient care equipment and instruments. The duties ordinarily include maintenance, instruction in use, and solving problems requiring adaptation to special situations.

clinical engineering department: See *biomedical engineering department*.

clinical investigator: A person who has been designated as the individual responsible for a specific piece of research involving patients, particularly under a research grant from the federal government or a drug company.

clinical medical librarian (CML): A specialized librarian in a *teaching hospital* who participates in teaching activities (including those at the bedside), making notes of questions, and then obtaining relevant literature.

clinical nurse specialist: See *nurse clinician*.

clinical practice plan: See *medical practice plan*.

C

clinical privileges (1): The term is usually applied to the types of diagnostic and therapeutic procedures which given *medical staff* members (chiefly physicians and dentists) are permitted by the hospital to carry out, and the types of patients they are permitted to treat. Other professionals, such as podiatrists, clinical psychologists, nurse practitioners, speech pathologists, and physical therapists may also be given individual clinical privileges. Discussed in greater detail under *privileges*.

clinical privileges (2): When used in the statement that a certain physician "has clinical privileges" in a given hospital, the term indicates that the physician has been granted membership in the *medical staff* of that hospital in a category which permits him to treat patients there.

clinical record: See *medical record*.

closed account: An arrangement between a buyer and a seller in which goods or services have changed hands and payment has been made; the account is thus "closed."

closed-chest cardiac massage: A technique for stimulating the heart (and producing some circulation of the blood) by compressing the heart between the spine and the breast bone. Pressure is applied by the hands pressing on the front of the chest with the patient lying on his back. The technique is a part of *cardiopulmonary resuscitation (CPR)*. Synonym(s): external cardiac massage.

closed medical staff: See *closed staff*.

closed staff: A *medical staff* in a hospital which has a formal plan describing its desired medical staff size and specialty needs. Such a hospital does not accept new applications for any category of medical staff membership unless a vacancy exists (or is anticipated) under its plan. The fact that a hospital has one or more "exclusive contracts" (contracts which give a physician or physician group the exclusive privilege of furnishing certain administrative or clinical services) does not make that hospital a "closed staff hospital."

CME: Continuing medical education. See *medical education*.

CMH Principles: See *Principles for Accreditation of Community Mental Health Service Programs.*

CMHC: Community mental health center. See *community mental health service program.*

CMI: See *case mix index.*

CML: See *clinical medical librarian.*

CMP: See *competitive medical plan.*

COB: See *coordination of benefits.*

cobalt therapy: The treatment of patients with malignancies (cancers) with radioactive cobalt. Cobalt therapy is a type of *radiation therapy.*

COBRA: See *Consolidated Omnibus Budget Reconciliation Act of 1985.*

codable diagnosis: See *diagnosis.*

code (1): A unique symbol (usually alphanumeric) having a one-to-one correspondence with a term or a *rubric.* Codes may be used on the patient's bill, for example, to indicate the *service (1)* for which the charge is shown. Diagnoses and procedures are commonly coded for ease of manipulation by computer (see *coding*).

code (2): A shorthand representation for something. Hospitals often use colors or numbers to indicate urgent situations. For example, "code blue" often is used to mean that a patient needs resuscitation; "code 2" may signal a disruptive (violent) patient or visitor; "Dr. Red" might mean a fire. A "code purple" in some hospitals means that a "VIP" (very important person) has arrived as an inpatient or at the emergency department (ED). The codes are spoken over the public address system, usually along with information about the location of the situation; for example, "code 7, ICU" (intensive care unit). These codes give the people who need to know (and respond) concise information, without unnecessarily upsetting patients and visitors. See also *code blue* and *coded (2)*.

show code: A situation where a *code blue* (call for resuscitation) is made on a patient whose heart has stopped, but where the health care providers really do not believe that resuscitation is appropriate. The "code" is thus for "show," since authentic resuscitation efforts are not made. Show codes were sometimes done in the past if no clear decision had been made regarding whether the patient should be resuscitated in case of cardiac arrest, or where a physician was uncertain whether to document the decision. These days, most hospitals require an actual resuscitation attempt unless a *do not resuscitate* order has been written on the patient's chart by the physician. Synonym(s): slow code, code gray, code pink.

slow code: See *show code*.

code blue: Perhaps the most common *code (2)* used in hospitals for signalling a cardiac (heart) emergency, meaning that someone is in need of *cardiopulmonary resuscitation* (other hospitals will have a similar code; for example, "Code 7" or "Code Yellow"). Those individuals who are expected to respond know who they are, what it means, and what their response is expected to be. It is sometimes said that a patient has been *"coded (2)"* when a code blue alarm has been sent. See also *show code* under *code (2)*.

code gray: See *show code* under *code (2)*.

code pink: See *show code* under *code (2)*.

coded (1): When data or information has been replaced by a *code (1)*, it is said to have been coded, i.e., the *coding* process has been carried out.

coded (2): Hospital jargon referring to a patient for whom a *code blue* signal has been sent, indicating the occurrence of a cardiac (heart) emergency. Similarly, when a *do not resuscitate (DNR) order* has been recorded for a patient, that patient, in hospital jargon, is "not to be coded" (resuscitated).

coder: A person who does *coding*.

C

coding: The process of substituting a symbol (*code (1)*), usually a number, for a term, such as a diagnosis or procedure. Coding ordinarily has three purposes: (1) to compress the information from a string of letters or words into a compact, usually uniform, space; (2) to facilitate handling the information by mechanical (computer) methods; and (3) to introduce precision (reduce ambiguity), since numbers are not subject to spelling errors and it is easier to make an exact check of a number than of a word. (Inventories are controlled, for example, by code numbers rather than narrative descriptions of their contents.)

Coding is a clerical function and should only require substituting a code for the term to be coded. However, in many circumstances, the term to be coded will not be found in the coder's reference material, and a judgment will have to be made. In this case, the coder must know both the meaning of the term and also the way the coding system works, so that proper coding can be done. Under such circumstances, the task is far from clerical, and is really one of *classification (2)* rather than coding.

There are two basic ways to code: (1) assigning to each individual entity (term) its own unique code (number); and (2) assigning to each term a code which represents a *category*, which category may include one or more individual entities (terms). The first technique is called *"entity coding"*; the second is *"category coding."* These are discussed further:

category coding: Coding in which each code (number) represents (the *rubric* of) a *category* rather than an individual term being coded. Category coding is designed to achieve grouping to established classification "pigeonholes" in a single step which combines coding and *classifying*.

Category coding is the method presently used by hospitals for coding diagnoses and procedures. This coding is done for the indexing of medical records for retrieval and research, and in the submission of case abstracts for billing. Each diagnosis and procedure is given the code for the category of diagnoses or procedures to which it belongs, rather than a unique code ("entity code") which represents the diagnosis or procedure itself.

Except for "single-diagnosis categories," the (diagnosis of the) case cannot be retrieved precisely because *decoding* retrieves the rubric (label) of the category rather than the specific diagnosis or procedure which was coded. For example, a specific new condition such as AIDS (acquired immune deficiency syndrome), which had not been foreseen and had no category or pigeonhole of its

C

own, for several years was placed into various categories, such as the "waste basket" category labelled "other immune deficiency disorders." Such a system makes it impossible, without going back to the original medical records, to determine the exact number of AIDS cases or to retrieve them by themselves; all cases of "other immune deficiency disorders" are counted and retrieved together.

In the coding system now in use in the United States, which is a category coding system (*ICD-9-CM*), over 100,000 diagnostic terms are forced into 11,000 groups or classes; further detail is lost when these categories, in turn, go into the 468 *DRGs*. It is worth noting that this system violates a basic purpose of coding, the achievement of precise information.

entity coding: Coding in which each code represents an individual "entity" (term) rather than a *category* (group) of terms. In entity coding, each entity (specific term) to be coded (for example, a diagnosis or procedure) is exchanged for a code (number) which, when *decoded*, yields exactly the same words (term) which were coded. No detail is lost as is the case in *category coding*; entity coding achieves one of the major purposes of coding, the elimination of ambiguity in the information in order to increase its precision, since numbers are not subject to spelling errors and it is easier to make an exact check of a number than of a word.

The principle behind entity coding is that *classification (2)* should be a two-step process: in the first step, information is coded so that it can be manipulated (usually by a computer); and, in the second step, the coded information is then classified according to the needs of the particular user or the demands of a particular *classification (1)* system. In entity coding, the integrity of the items of information remains intact, and the system can meet the needs of any number of classification systems. For example, a person investigating the frequency of office visits for various medical problems would need to have a discrete class for the common cold because of its frequency in that setting. Since common colds seldom require hospitalization, however, placing the cold in a category of "other respiratory diseases" or "other infectious diseases" might meet the needs of the hospital studying reasons for admission.

cognitive services: A term applied to all the activities of a physician (or other professional) other than the performance of *procedures*. The charges of physicians are relatively easy to explain in surgery and other instances where "something is done" to the patient. High charges for, say, diagnostic evaluations, patient and family counseling, and the care of patients with infectious diseases, are much harder to explain, and thus charges are considerably lower. "Cognitive services" require as much time and skill as surgery. However, much of this effort and skill is simply not seen by the patient or payer. Nonetheless, an education as long and arduous as the surgeon's may be required, as well as unseen time in the library and informal consultation with colleagues. Efforts to overcome the resulting perceived inequities in payment have led to the labeling of non-procedural services as cognitive (intellectual). No term for "non-cognitive" services seems to have appeared.

COI: See *certificate of insurance.*

coinsurance: A type of insurance which requires that part of the charges be paid by the *beneficiary*, the primary purpose being to discourage small claims and "over-use" of services.

collateral source rule: A legal rule of evidence which prohibits the jury from considering the fact that the *plaintiff* has been compensated from any source other than the *defendant*. The practical result is that a medical *malpractice* defendant may have to pay the full amount of the plaintiff patient's medical and other expenses, even if the patient has already received reimbursement for those expenses from another source, such as medical insurance.

collective bargaining: The process of negotiation regarding compensation, working conditions, benefits, and other matters, between an employer and an organization representing the employees. In collective bargaining, the employees may be represented by a union or by some other form of association.

collegial: The sharing of power or authority equally among a number of colleagues. In a truly collegial environment, no one individual can be held accountable since no one individual is in charge.

colon and rectal surgery: One of the medical specialties for which *residency* programs have been approved by the Accreditation Council for Graduate Medical Education (ACGME). See *specialty.*

C

combined billing: A billing in which the hospital and physician services and their *charges* are not separately identified. Certain payers, such as Medicare, will not accept such billing. See also *separate billing*.

Commission on Dietetic Registration: A body formed by the *American Dietetic Association* (ADA) for the purpose of examining applicants for the *credential registered dietitian (RD)* and granting that credential to successful applicants.

Commission on Professional and Hospital Activities (CPHA): An independent nonprofit organization based in Ann Arbor, Michigan, dedicated to the improvement of health care quality through the use of comparative data. It was formed in 1955 with the national sponsorship of the American College of Physicians (ACP), the American College of Surgeons (ACS), and the American Hospital Association (AHA). CPHA provides certain shared clinical and *management information services (MIS)* data processing, performs interpretive research services for hospitals and other health care institutions, and disseminates information to the health care field. Its largest and oldest program is the prototype *hospital discharge abstract system*, the *Professional Activity Study (PAS)*.

commitment: See *involuntary commitment*.

committee: A group of people set up for a specific purpose: to consider or investigate a matter, to report on a matter, or to carry out certain duties. Committees can be self-appointed, but in the health care setting, they are ordinarily appointed, and their scope and powers derive from the authority which appointed them. The term "committee" is more often applied to a standing body than it is to an *ad hoc* (one-time) body set up to carry out a specific task and then be dissolved. The latter is more appropriately termed a "task force."

A number of committees are typically found in a hospital. Certain *medical staff* committees are specified in the *Accreditation Manual for Hospitals (AMH)* of the Joint Commission on Accreditation of Healthcare Organizations (JCAHO).

committee of the incompetent: See *guardian*.

Committee on Allied Health Education and Accreditation (CAHEA): A committee of the American Medical Association (AMA) which *accredits* educational programs for *allied health professionals*. Occupations for which programs have been accredited are:

> anesthesiologist's assistant (AA)
> cardiovascular technologist (CVT)
> cytotechnologist (CYTO)
> diagnostic medical sonographer (DMS)
> electroneurodiagnostic techologist (ENDT)
> emergency medical technician—paramedic (EMT-P)
> histologic technician/technologist (HT)
> medical assistant (MA)
> medical illustrator (MI)
> medical laboratory technician—associate degree (MLT-AD)
> medical laboratory technician—certificate (MLT-C)
> medical record administrator (MRA)
> medical record technician (MRT)
> medical technologist (MT)
> nuclear medicine technologist (NMT)
> occupational therapist (OT)
> ophthalmologic medical technician/technologist (OMT)
> perfusionist (PERF)
> physician assistant (PA)
> radiation therapy technologist (RADTT)
> radiographer (RAD)
> respiratory therapist (REST)
> respiratory therapy technician (RESTT)
> specialist in blood bank technology (SBBT)
> surgeon assistant (SA)
> surgical technologist (ST)

common law: Law which has been created by the courts, through decisions of judges, rather than by the legislature (statutory law). Synonym(s): judicial law.

community-based planning: Planning in which the attempt is made to have the planning initiative in the local community rather than external to the community itself.

Community Health Accreditation Program (CHAP): A program of a subsidiary of the *National League for Nursing (NLN)* for evaluating

C

and elevating the quality of *home health care* programs, their management, and their outcomes. Those programs meeting the standards of CHAP are given *accreditation*. The standards pertain to planning, finance, service delivery, operations, human resources, evaluation, and outcomes of care.

community health center (CHC): A term sometimes used to mean a facility set up to provide health care for and to do social work with a population in an area where such services are otherwise difficult to obtain.

community health network (CHN): A term sometimes employed as a label for a municipally operated system of providing health care for the poor.

community health services: A term which encompasses preventive procedures, diagnosis, and treatment for residents of a community. It does not imply any organizational structure.

community living facility: See *halfway house*.

community mental health center (CMHC): See *community mental health service program*.

community mental health service program: An organization set up to provide *mental health* services to a defined community. Synonym(s): community mental health center (CMHC).

community residential facility: See *intermediate care facility for the mentally retarded*.

comorbidity: See *morbidity*.

compensable: Something for which the law allows money to be awarded to make amends or restore someone to their prior position. Not all types of injury (for example, mental distress suffered by an unusually sensitive person) are compensable. See *damages*.

In *workers' compensation* law, "compensable" describes an injury or illness which is work-related, and therefore covered by the workers' compensation system.

competent: A legal term describing a person whom the law considers capable of making decisions. Competency is relative, and standards of competency vary according to the type of decision to be made. This concept is discussed further under *incompetent (1)*.

competitive medical plan (CMP): A health care plan which has met requirements of the federal government and thus become qualified to accept Medicare *vouchers* from Medicare *beneficiaries*, and which in turn provides the beneficiaries with all Medicare *services (1)*. The Medicare vouchers are negotiable only with competitive medical plans which have met the eligibility requirements.

complication: As used in the *prospective payment system (PPS)*, a diagnosis occurring *during* hospitalization which is thought to extend the hospital stay at least one day for roughly 75 percent or more of the patients. The occurrence of a complication is determined in the PPS by the presence, as a secondary *ICD-9-CM* diagnosis code in the patient's bill, of a condition defined by PPS as a complication. See also *comorbidity*.

Comprehensive Drug Abuse Prevention and Control Act of 1970: The federal act which governs access to controlled substances, that is, narcotics and other dangerous drugs which can only be obtained legally by *licensed* individuals or institutions or through *prescriptions*.

comprehensive health care: *Services (1)* that are intended to meet all the health care needs of a patient: outpatient, inpatient, home care, and other.

comprehensive health care delivery system: A health care delivery system which includes both facilities and professionals, and which is set up to provide *comprehensive health care* to a defined population.

comprehensive health planning (CHP): Attempts to coordinate environmental measures, health education, health care, and occupational and other health efforts to achieve the greatest results in a community.

C

comprehensive health planning agency (CHP agency):   An *agency (1)* established in response to a federal health planning act in 1966, which was later replaced by a group of agencies established under federal legislation passed in 1974. The latter agencies were the Health Systems Agencies, State Health Planning and Development Agencies, and Statewide Health Coordinating Councils.

compression of morbidity: See *morbidity.*

comptroller: See *controller.*

computed axial tomography (CAT):   See *computed tomography (CT).*

computed tomography (CT):   An *imaging* technique carried out by using radiation (*X-rays*) and analyzing and displaying the absorption (or transmission) of the radiation by the tissues. The key to this technology is a *microcomputer* within the machine. CT was formerly called computed axial tomography (CAT). The machine which creates the image is a CT (or CAT) scanner.

computer: A machine, typically electronic, that is capable of performing computations on *data* that is fed into it. The computations performed are governed by instructions given to the computer. The physical machinery itself is generally referred to as hardware, while the instructions given to the computer are referred to as software, or programs.

Since the widespread appearance of microprocessor chips in the 1980's, a variety of medical devices now contain computers to increase their capabilities. Not just limited to the common notion of a big box with a keyboard and TV-type screen attached to it, computers now control consumer electronics, cars, power tools, and washing machines. See below for some common types of computers.

laptop computer: A type of computer that became popular in th late 1980's. It is typically a small *microcomputer* (PC) weighing between seven and fifteen pounds, having a fold-up liquid crystal display (LCD). In most cases, this computer can be operated for up to several hours on an internal battery pack.

mainframe computer: A computer with one or more central processing units (CPUs) designed to be used by many "users" at one time, and usually run by one or more "operators." Its processing and output facilities are accessed via *computer terminals*, and it is usually kept physically separate from users, typically in a climate controlled environment with restricted access and a sophisticated fire extinguishing system. A mainframe is distinguished from its smaller counterparts, the "mini" and "micro" (personal) computers, although the distinctions are becoming increasingly blurry.

microcomputer: A computer distinguishable from a *minicomputer* and a *mainframe computer* in that its "brain," the central processing unit (CPU), is a microprocessor chip. Microcomputers typically contain CPUs manufactured by Intel or Motorola, who have given these chips cryptic names such as 8088, 80386SX, or 68000. The lines distinguishing micro, mini, and mainframe computers continue to get blurrier, as today's small computers outperform yesterday's large computers. Synonym(s): PC, personal computer.

minicomputer: A computer that is more powerful than a *microcomputer* but less powerful than a *mainframe computer*. It can be distinguished from most microcomputers because it is usually designed to be used by more than one user at a time, who access its capabilities via *computer terminals*.

neural computer: See *neurocomputer*.

neurocomputer: A computer or computer program which performs in a similar manner to the network of nerve cells in the brain. Other computers work by taking steps serially, that is, one step after another. However, in a neurocomputer, a number of elements of the computer work simultaneously. A neurocomputer can "learn," it can program itself, and it is especially good at pattern recognition. Synonym(s): neural computer, neural network machine, artificial neural system, electronic neural network, parallel associative network, parallel distributed processor, sixth generation computer.

notebook computer: A small *microcomputer* which started to become very popular in 1990. Similar to a *laptop computer*, the notebook weighs less than seven pounds and fits into a typical briefcase. It should be noted that this classification is still evolving at the time of this writing in 1991, and is hardly "official." Most notebook computers now being released are capable of running the same software run on their larger microcomputer cousins.

C

personal computer (PC): See *microcomputer*.

sixth generation computer: See *neurocomputer*.

computer-assisted encoding: See *encoding*.

computer hardware: See *hardware*.

computer modeling: The use of computers to design and test real world structures and processes, relying on the computers' ability to process vast amounts of data and perform complex mathematical calculations. In AIDS research, for instance, computer modeling could be used to study the effect of the virus on a variety of genetic structures which might be impossible to produce in the laboratory.

computer terminal: A mechanical device used by persons to communicate with a computer. It typically has a keyboard and cathode ray tube (CRT) display. The terminal may be directly connected ("hardwired") to the "host" computer, or may use telephone lines via a *modem*. Increasingly, personal computers (PCs) are being used as terminals in addition to their other uses.

computerized severity index (CSI): A *severity of illness* measurement method which uses objective data specially abstracted from the medical record (in contrast with methods which use standard *discharge abstract* data). Such a method could be used at intervals during care in order to assess response to treatment or progression of the illness. At present each case is classified as to severity into one of four categories.

computerized thermography: An *imaging* technique in which computer image processing technology is used to display the distribution of temperatures on the skin surfaces of patients. This method has achieved recognition as useful in neurology, surgery, orthopedic surgery, physiotherapy, emergency and trauma medicine, dermatology, and oncology.

CON: See *certificate of need*.

conception: The event of conceiving; becoming pregnant.

concurrent review: See *review.*

condition: See *patient condition.*

condom: A sheath of rubber or other material designed to encase the penis during sexual intercourse to prevent transmission of venereal disease or sperm. Synonym(s): rubber.

confidentiality: The aura of protection given *medical records* and other patient care information to safekeep personal, private information about the patient and the patient's care. The ethics of the health care profession require that patient confidences not be disclosed except where necessary to treat the patient, or with the patient's permission. The law provides a privilege (legal protection) for patient information, and requires that such information not be disclosed without the patient's permission or a proper court order. Improper disclosure of confidential patient information can result in legal *liability.* See also *privileged communication.*

conflict of interest: A situation where a person (or organization) has two separate and distinct duties owed concerning, or interests in, the same thing, and therefore cannot act completely impartially with respect to that thing. It is like one servant trying to serve two masters. For example, a hospital trustee has a legal duty to act in the best interests of the hospital. If that trustee owns real estate that the hospital wishes to buy, the trustee has a personal interest in obtaining the highest price, but as a trustee he has an interest in obtaining the lowest price. Since such a conflict of interest may cloud his judgment, the trustee is obligated to inform the hospital board about his personal interest, and usually will excuse himself from participating in the purchase negotiations. Even if there is no real conflict, or if the trustee is capable of making the right decision for the hospital, he would be wise to excuse himself so that the transaction will not appear to be tainted with impropriety, and so that no one can challenge it as such. Most corporate *bylaws* address conflict of interest situations.

congenital: A condition or illness with which one is born. It may be due to infection or other disease in the mother; due to physical events, such as injury to the mother before or during delivery; hereditary (a condition which one or both parents transmitted

C

genetically (as part of the genes) to the offspring); or due to a mutation (change) in the genes of the fetus itself.

conscience clause: A law (or portion of a law) which allows individuals (or institutions) the right to refuse to do something which is contrary to their moral or religious beliefs. For example, some state laws regulating abortion specifically state that no hospital, physician, or hospital employee may be compelled to participate in an abortion. The employee would have to state the refusal in writing, and could not be disciplined or sued for refusing to participate.

consent: Legal permission, given by the patient (or person legally authorized to give the permission), to the health care provider to care for, treat, or perform surgery or other procedures upon the patient. The patient may give valid consent only if he is legally *competent* to do so.

deferred consent: Consent to continue with a therapy after administration of that therapy has already begun. The term was coined (and the concept developed) in connection with resuscitation research, in which an emergency exists (an emergency patient is comatose) and any therapy, to be effective, must be administered promptly, and no qualified person is available to give *informed consent*. Instead of using standard therapy, a therapy under investigation (which has neither proven advantage over standard therapy nor greater risk) may be administered. Then, at the earliest opportunity, the family members or *guardian* are given full information on the steps taken, and at that time given a choice of granting consent for continuing the therapy under investigation (deferred consent) or having it discontinued.

informed consent: A legal term referring to the patient's right to make his own treatment decisions, based upon knowledge of the relevant alternatives and the benefits and risks of each. An "informed consent" is the consent of the patient after he has been fully informed, by the physician proposing the treatment or procedure, of the risks, benefits, and alternatives. Failure to obtain informed consent prior to surgery or administration of treatment may result in legal *liability*. An exception is ordinarily made in case of an emergency where the patient is unable to consent (e.g. he is unconscious), in which case the law presumes that the patient would have consented to the emergency treatment required to protect his life or health.

Although it is wise for the physician and hospital to obtain the written consent of the patient prior to a treatment or procedure, the patient's signature should not be confused with the consent itself. That is, the piece of paper is evidence of the patient's consent, but the essence of the informed consent is the patient's voluntary agreement based upon the relevant facts which have been communicated to the patient by the physician. Thus, a patient groggy from anesthesia who is asked to "sign this" on the way into the operating suite has not given informed consent.

Special conditions apply in biomedical research and with respect to comatose patients (subjects). Here a limited class of exempt research has been defined; waivers are allowed under certain conditions, and the concepts of *"deferred consent"* and *"minimal differential risk"* have been developed.

conservator: See *guardian*.

Consolidated Omnibus Budget Reconciliation Act of 1985 (COBRA): A federal law which requires (among other things) that employers of 20 or more workers must continue former employees' health insurance coverage (at the former employee's expense) for up to three years for qualified *beneficiaries*. Qualified beneficiaries include widows and divorced and separated spouses of former employees, as well as their dependents (even dependents who lost their dependent status). The law amends the Internal Revenue Code of 1954.

Consolidated Standards Manual for Child, Adolescent, and Adult Psychiatric, Alcoholism, and Drug Abuse Facilities and Facilities Serving the Mentally Retarded/Developmentally Disabled (CSM): An annual publication of *accreditation standards* by the *Joint Commission on the Accreditation of Healthcare Organizations (JCAHO)*.

consolidation: The formal union of two or more corporations (such as hospitals) into a single corporation. In a consolidation, all of the corporations which unite cease to exist, and a new corporation is formed with its own new identity. A *merger* is similar to a consolidation, except that one of the original corporations retains its identity and continues to exist, while the other corporations are merged into it and lose their former identities. In either case, the

C

surviving or consolidated corporation acquires the assets and assumes the liabilities of the former corporations.

consortium (1): An alliance between two or more parties (for example, hospitals) to achieve a specific purpose.

consortium (2): The right of a husband or wife to the companionship, comfort, and aid—including sexual relationships—of his or her spouse. In a *malpractice* case, for example, if the husband has been injured, the wife may join as a *plaintiff* to recover for her loss of consortium.

conspiracy of silence: The supposed tacit agreement among physicians (or other professionals) not to testify against one another in *malpractice* lawsuits. It is sometimes said that malpractice *plaintiffs* are not able to obtain a fair trial of their cases because the only way to prove the case is by expert testimony, and because of the so-called "conspiracy of silence," it is difficult to find experts (namely, physicians) willing to testify.

constructed beds: The number of beds the hospital was built to accommodate. See *bed capacity*.

consultation (1): A review of a patient's *problem* by a second individual, namely a physician or other health care provider (for example, a clinical psychologist), and the rendering of an opinion and advice to the referring physician. The review in most instances involves the independent examination of the patient by the consultant. In a consultation some evidence, such as X-rays, may not need to be repeated if it is made available to the consultant. The consultant's opinion and advice are not binding on the referring physician. A "second opinion" is a special kind of consultation in which a second surgeon consults on the desirability of elective surgery which has been recommended by the first surgeon. (Elective surgery is surgery which is not stated to be necessary to preserve life or prevent serious disability.)

consultation (2): Advice from an expert, given after a study of a situation or problem presented by the individual obtaining the consultation. In the health care field, such consultation often concerns organization, management, strategic planning, personnel policies, and the like.

consumer price index (CPI): A statistic produced by the federal government to measure inflation. The CPI compares the price of a "market basket" of goods and services at a given date against the average price of the same market basket at a reference date (the *base (2)*).

contagious: Transmissible by direct contact with an infected person or fresh secretions or excretions.

contaminate: To transfer bacteria or other infectious agents or harmful substances.

contingency fee: A fee which is paid to an attorney only if the client wins. Contingency-fee arrangements are commonly used in *malpractice* cases, where the attorney receives a portion (usually about one-third) of the amount awarded the *plaintiff* by the court or in an out-of-court settlement. If the plaintiff receives nothing, the attorney receives nothing (except reimbursement of expenses).

contingent worker: A person who works less than 35 hours a week (or in some usages, less than 12 months a year). Such individuals typically have lower earnings, less job security, and fewer promotions than full-time employees. Contingent workers are often without health insurance. Synonym(s): peripheral workers, marginal workers.

continued stay review: See *review*.

continuing care retirement communities (CCRC): Retirement communities which offer lifetime independent living and various health care services to residents.

continuing medical education (CME): See *medical education*.

continuity of care: The degree to which the care of a patient from the onset of illness until its completion is continuous, that is, without interruption. Interruptions occur sometimes because the patient does not follow through, sometimes because the system has gaps, often because of lack of facilities or because of financial impediments (absence of *benefits*, for example, which cover certain *services (1)*). The term "continuity of care" is sometimes used to refer to a longer span of time than the single episode of illness, and to the patient's health care when he is both well and ill.

continuous quality improvement (CQI): See *quality improvement*.

contraceptive: Any *agent (1)* or procedure whose purpose is to prevent *conception*, that is, to prevent a pregnancy.

contract: An agreement between two or more parties which gives legally enforceable rights and obligations to both. A contract need not be in writing to be enforceable, unless it is a certain kind of agreement, such as one for the sale of real estate. A state law called the "Statute of Frauds" specifies which contracts must be supported by written evidence.

contract of adhesion: A contract which has not been negotiated, but rather has been entirely written by one party, and presented to the other on a "take it or leave it" basis. Usually, there is great inequality of bargaining power, and the contract of adhesion strongly favors its author, while strongly disfavoring the rights of the other party. Because of this disparity, courts will not always enforce adhesion contracts in their entirety.

exclusive contract: A term which, in the hospital, usually refers to a written agreement under which a given physician or physician group is given the exclusive right to furnish certain, specified administrative or clinical services in the hospital. During the life of the exclusive contract, other physicians are precluded from the same activities in that hospital. Exclusive contracts have raised *antitrust* issues for hospitals; see *Rule of Reason*.

indemnity contract: A health care insurance contract in which the benefits are money (cash) rather than *services (1)* (the latter would be a service contract).

service contract: A health care insurance contract in which the benefits are the actual *services (1)* rather than money (the latter would be an indemnity contract).

contract management: An arrangement under which an "employing" institution obtains ongoing management services from a "managing" organization under a contract. The employing institution retains full ownership of and final responsibility for the institution. The services to be rendered by the contracting organization are spelled out in the management contract.

If the contractual services are for department management, the contracting organization reports to the employing institution exactly as though its manager were the employing institution's own employee, that is, at the same point in the hierarchy. If the contractual services are for the management of the entire institution, the contracting organization furnishes a *chief executive officer (CEO)* who reports to the *governing body* of the employing institution as though he were employed by the governing body as its CEO.

Contract management is one variety of relationship found in some multihospital systems.

contract provider organization (CPO): See *preferred provider organization*.

contract service: A service purchased from a person or another organization. If a hospital does not operate its own laundry or laboratory, for example, these may be obtained as contract services. Similarly, the physician services for an emergency department may be obtained by contract with an organization set up to furnish such services.

contractual adjustment: A bookkeeping adjustment to remove as *accounts receivable* uncollectible amounts which appear when the charges for *services (1)* under a given contract are less than the charges for the same services to patients whose care is not provided under that contract; the contract stipulates that the hospital must be satisfied with a given schedule of charges even though it otherwise would charge more.

contraindication: A known reason for not using a given treatment, usually a drug. Some contraindications are *drug interactions,* and thus depend on the use of a conflicting drug. Some relate to foods which should be avoided. Others depend on the patient's condition; for example, nasal decongestants typically tend to raise the patient's blood pressure, and thus are contraindicated in a patient who already has high blood pressure. "High blood pressure" appears on the label in a warning statement that it is a contraindication to the use of the product.

control: The term used by the American Hospital Association (AHA) in its listing of hospitals in the *Guide to the Health Care Field (AHA Guide)* to indicate the kind of organization or institution responsible for operating the hospital. Some 24 categories are used. In the non-federal sector, the grouping is quite general, such as "church-operated" and "investor-owned (for-profit), partnership." In the federal sector, however, classification is much more specific; for example "Army" hospitals are separated from "Navy" hospitals.

controlled substances: Drugs listed as being subject to the *Comprehensive Drug Abuse Prevention and Control Act of 1970*. These require a *prescription*, and the physician needs a special license from the federal government to prescribe them.

controller: The person who is in charge of the hospital's ongoing financial administration, including billing, accounting, budget management, and the like. A controller may or may not be the *chief financial officer (CFO)* (treasurer). "Controller" is sometimes spelled "comptroller."

convalescence: The period of time after the acute phase of an illness before the patient is back to "normal."

COO: See *chief operating officer*.

cooperative services: See *shared services*.

coordination of benefits (COB): An insurance *claims review* process used when a beneficiary is insured by two or more carriers. The process determines the *liability* of each carrier in order to eliminate duplication of payments. For example, benefits to which an individual is entitled under *workers' compensation* are not permitted to be duplicated by ordinary health insurance, even though the injury or illness would be covered were the problem not work-related.

copayment: The share of the *charges* for a health care *service (1)* for which the *beneficiary* is responsible under a health insurance plan of the *coinsurance* type.

core service(s): Those services which must be provided by an institution if it is to be accepted by the *American Hospital Association (AHA)* as an institution elegible for registration with AHA and inclusion in the annual *AHA Guide*. These services include an organized medical staff, a nursing service with registered nurse (RN) supervision, food service, pharmacy, and maintenance of medical records.

coronary: "Crown-like" or "relating to a crown," or "encircling." In health care usage, "coronary" refers to the blood vessels of the heart, which encircle the heart and are called "coronary vessels." A *cardiac care unit* is often called a "coronary care unit," since most of the patients treated there suffer from problems of the circulation serving the heart muscle.

coronary artery bypass graft (CABG): A surgical procedure to *transplant* a blood vessel or blood vessels to the patient's heart so as to carry blood for the heart muscle around (bypass) portions of the heart's arteries which have been narrowed or closed by disease.

coronary care unit: See *cardiac care unit (CCU)*.

coronary heart disease (CHD): A disease of the arteries supplying blood to the heart.

corporate planning: The establishment of goals for the corporation, along with the policies and procedures to be used to attain those goals.

corporation: A legal entity which exists separately, for all legal purposes, from the people or organizations which own it. To take advantage of legal advantages (limitation of *liability (1)* and tax benefits, for example), a corporation must observe certain "formalities" required by law, such as meetings, minutes, and filing of annual reports and tax returns.

C

for-profit corporation: A corporation whose profits (excess of income over expenses) are distributed, as dividends, to shareholders who own the corporation (in contrast to a nonprofit corporation, in which the profits go to corporate purposes rather than to individual shareholders).

medical staff corporation: Sometimes a *medical staff organization (MSO)* incorporates itself, and the matters which are ordinarily the subject of the medical staff *bylaws* are then handled by contract between the medical staff corporation and the hospital corporation, much as an emergency services corporation could be contracted with to provide emergency department services.

nonprofit corporation: A corporation whose profits (excess of income over expenses) are used for corporate purposes rather than returned to shareholders (owners) as dividends. To qualify for tax exemption, no portion of the profits of the corporation may "inure" to the benefit of an individual. See *inurement*.

parent corporation: A corporation which owns at least a majority of the shares of (controls) one or more *subsidiary corporations*.

professional corporation (PC): A corporation in which all of the shareholders (owners) are members of a given profession, such as physicians. In some respects, a professional corporation is not the same as other corporations. One difference is that persons who are not members of the profession forming the corporation may not be shareholders (for example, physicians may not be shareholders of a legal PC). Another difference is that unlike a normal business corporation, the liability of a PC is not limited; in other words, its owners can be held personally liable for the PC's debts. A PC may also be called a "professional service corporation," "professional association," or "service corporation."

service corporation (SC): See *professional corporation*.

subsidiary corporation: A corporation of which another corporation (the "parent corporation") owns at least a majority of the shares.

cost: The expense incurred in providing a product or service. A number of modifiers are used with "cost":

allowable cost: Items of *service (1)* which are contractually included in the *benefits* of an insurance or payment plan, similar to

C

"covered charges." The charges for television and meals for visitors are not ordinarily allowable costs.

capital cost: The cost of developing or acquiring new equipment, facilities, or services; that is, the investment cost to the institution of such growth.

direct cost: A cost which can be identified directly with any part of the hospital organization which the hospital designates as a *cost center*. In fact, cost centers are defined as such because they are segments of the hospital, such as the operating rooms, to which direct costs can be assigned rather clearly. To the direct costs of each cost center are added, on the basis of some accounting formula, allocated proportions of the hospital's *indirect costs* (costs, such as for heat and housekeeping, which are not easily allocated to specific cost centers).

fixed cost: A cost which is entirely independent of the volume of activity. If no charges are made for individual local calls, the cost of local telephone service is a fixed cost; on the other hand, long distance service, which depends as it does on the number and length of calls made, is a *variable cost* (however, an unlimited WATS line would be a fixed cost).

indirect cost: There are two kinds of indirect costs in a hospital. The first kind is costs which must be incurred by any organization furnishing services, but which cannot be exactly identified with any specific service rendered or support department. For example, the cost of having a chief executive officer (CEO) is necessary, but it cannot be charged directly to, for example, the operating room as can the salaries of operating room nurses. The second kind of indirect costs is the costs of "support activities," the costs of which can be determined, but which do not produce revenue. Such activities (for example, a hospital's medical record department) have clear direct costs, and must bear their share of the indirect costs of the first type above. But, since these activities do not produce revenue, their costs—both direct and indirect—become indirect costs for the revenue-producing departments and services.

Accountants have developed a variety of formulas for "cost allocation." Cost allocation means assigning appropriate portions of the indirect costs to the various *cost centers* and then further allocating the costs of non-revenue-producing cost centers to the revenue-producing cost centers, where they influence the charges.

C

marginal cost: The addition to total cost resulting from the production of an additional unit of service or product. This cost varies with the volume of the operation. A hospital, for example, has a high cost for its first meal served. Subsequent meals have much lower costs each (marginal costs) until the volume is so large as to require changes in facilities, supervision, and the like. At this point the marginal cost will usually rise until a new equilibrium ("optimum output level") is established.

pass-through cost: A term with a specific definition in the *prospective payment system (PPS)*. It refers to hospital costs, such as for medical education, which are not incorporated in the *Diagnosis Related Group (DRG)* prices. Funds are provided to the hospital directly, that is, outside the per-case payments for patient care; the costs are simply passed through (or outside of) the DRG mechanism.

semi-variable cost: A cost which is partly a *variable cost* and partly a *fixed cost* in its behavior in response to changes in volume. Automobile rental is typically a semi-variable cost, with a fixed charge per day and a variable charge depending on miles driven.

variable cost: A cost which is entirely dependent on the volume of activity, as opposed to a *fixed cost*, which is not affected by volume. In a typical telephone billing system, for example, long distance calls represent a variable cost while local calls represent a fixed cost.

cost allocation: An accounting procedure by which costs that cannot be clearly identified with any specific *cost center* are distributed among cost centers, and by which the costs of support services are distributed among revenue-producing services so as to be recovered in the charges.

cost-benefit analysis: A technique for placing a numerical value on the benefits to be derived from using a piece of equipment or operating a program as compared with its costs. The goal is to develop a *cost-benefit ratio*. If the ratio is greater than 1.0, the benefits more than outweigh the costs; if the ratio is less than 1.0, the costs are greater than the benefits. This process is difficult to use in health care in many instances where the benefits are in *quality of life* rather than something readily measured in dollars.

cost-benefit ratio: A mathematical expression of the benefits of a given service or the use of certain equipment compared with its costs. To develop such a ratio, both costs and benefits must be expressed in dollars, a task much easier for costs than benefits in many health care situations (improved *quality of life* may truly be a benefit, but expressing it in dollars is, at best, difficult). A ratio of 1.0 means that the benefits and costs are equal; a ratio over 1.0 means that the benefits exceed the costs; and a ratio under 1.0 means that the costs exceed the benefits.

cost center: An area of activity of the hospital with which *direct costs* can be identified. Accounting practice is to assign direct costs to such cost centers, and to allocate to each cost center its proportionate share of *indirect costs,* in order to give management a tool for cost control (or pricing). When a cost center is also revenue-producing, that is, an area for which charges are made (for example, an operating room), the allocation of direct and indirect costs, along with data about the *services (1)* rendered, permits the charge for each service to be sufficient to cover the cost of that service.

Some other cost centers, over which management wants to maintain control, do not produce revenue. An example is the medical record department. The costs of such departments (direct plus indirect costs) are reallocated as indirect costs to the revenue-producing cost centers.

cost containment: Efforts to prevent increase in cost or to restrict its rate of increase. Cost containment is rarely addressed at reducing cost.

cost control: A term usually applied to an external constraint of costs (or charges), such as legislation or the actions of a regulatory agency.

cost-effective: Providing a service at a "reasonable" cost (which might not necessarily be the lowest cost).

cost-effectiveness analysis: The comparison of the *cost-benefit ratios* for the same service provided by different methods or with different equipment.

C

cost-per-case management: The method (philosophy) of hospital management in which hospitals try to control the costs for each kind of case so that the revenue for that case will cover the cost. Cost-per-case management is a new style of management which was developed when hospital revenue changed from reimbursement for *services (1)* rendered to prospectively determined prices for various kinds of services. This change in reimbursement, in turn, came from the adoption of the *prospective payment system (PPS)* in the Medicare program. Previously, hospitals simply had to ensure that the aggregate of income covered the aggregate of costs.

cost-plus contract: A type of agreement, often used in construction, in which the owner agrees to pay for all costs incurred by the contractor in executing the plans and specifications, "plus" an additional amount (fixed sum, percentage, or other arrangement) as a fee or profit.

Cost Quality Management System (CQMS): A system which merges clinical and financial data, patient-by-patient, in a hospital. The diagnosis and procedure data are standardized by use of the *International Classification of Diseases, 9th Revision, Clinical Modification (ICD-9-CM)*, while the financial data are standardized by use of the *International Classification of Clinical Services (ICCS)*. The system is intended to facilitate data display for the individual hospital and also to permit valid comparisons among institutions and services through reference to the data base maintained by the *Commission on Professional and Hospital Activities (CPHA)*. CQMS is a joint venture between CPHA and Arthur Andersen & Company.

cost-shifting: Increasing the charges to one group of patients (such as private pay patients, who presumably have the ability to pay) when the payment for another group of patients will not cover the costs for that group. If the government pays too little for its beneficiaries, for example, through the *prospective payment system (PPS)*, it is clear that the cost will be shifted to other payers.

cost-to-charge ratio: See *ratio*.

Council on Certification/Council on Recertification of Nurse Anesthetists: A voluntary body which provides the *credential* of *certification* for *nurse anesthetists* who meet its requirements.

Council on Clinical Classifications (CCC): A non-profit organization formed in 1975 with the sponsorship of the American Academy of Pediatrics (AAP), the American College of Obstetricians and Gynecologists (ACOG), the American College of Physicians (ACP), the American College of Surgeons (ACS), the American Psychiatric Association (APA), and the Commission on Professional and Hospital Activities (CPHA) to prepare the North American adaptation of the *International Classification of Diseases, 9th Revision (ICD-9)* (World Health Organization (WHO), Geneva, 1975). Its product was the *International Classification of Diseases, 9th Revision, Clinical Modification (ICD-9-CM)* (1978).

coverage: See *insurance coverage.*

CPA: See *Certified Public Accountant.*

CPHA: See *Commission on Professional and Hospital Activities.*

CPI: See *consumer price index.*

CPO: Contract provider organization. See *preferred provider organization.*

CPQA: See *Certified Professional in Quality Assurance.*

CPR (1): See *cardiopulmonary resuscitation.*

CPR (2): See *customary, prevailing, reasonable charge (or fee).*

CPT: *Current Procedural Terminology.* See *Physicians' Current Procedural Terminology.*

CPT-1991: *Current Procedural Terminology, 1991 Edition.* See *Physicians' Current Procedural Terminology.*

C

CQI: Continuous quality improvement. See *quality improvement*.

CQMS: See *Cost Quality Management System*.

credential: An individual's right to a certain claim, for example, as to education. Usually a credential is supported by an official document: the physician's medical school diploma, state license, and specialty certification certificate are examples. Credentials, once attained, tend to be fixed, although in some instances they expire, and renewal or recertification may be required. In other instances, credentials may be withdrawn by the issuing body. And, of course, the individual may acquire additional credentials.

credential examination: An examination which is given for the purpose of determining the applicant's qualification for the *credential* sought.

credentialing: A term used to describe the process of determining eligibility for hospital *medical staff* membership, and *privileges* to be granted, to physicians and other professionals in the light of their academic preparation, licensing, training, and performance. "Credentialing" is a peculiar term to apply to this process because *credentials*—such as the physician's medical school diploma, state license, and specialty certification—are relatively fixed.

One danger in the use of the term credentialing in this manner is that a physician could use the evidence of membership on the medical staff of a specified hospital, along with a statement of the privileges granted by that hospital, as a "credential" with other hospitals and patients and with the public. Such use could place a significant responsibility on the hospital in question. Not only could the hospital be liable for the acts of the physician within the hospital subject to the "credentials" granted (as it is today), but it might also be held responsible for inferences drawn from these "credentials" outside that hospital.

Privileges are granted by the hospital's *governing body*, ordinarily upon recommendation of the *medical staff organization (MSO)*, usually via the MSO's credentials committee. (The exact procedure for "credentialing" is delineated in the hospital or medical staff *bylaws*.) The governing body must first verify the physician's credentials and determine whether they are adequate for admission to the medical staff. The governing body must then decide the more difficult question of what privileges the individual shall be granted initially and, upon periodic review of the professional's credentials and performance, whether it is necessary to modify them.

Credentialing must be done carefully and responsibly, both to protect patients and to be fair to practitioners. See also *corporate liability* (under *liability (1)*), *Health Care Quality Improvement Act, Patrick case, privileges,* and *recredentialing.*

credentials committee: A committee of the *medical staff organization (MSO)* charged with reviewing the credentials and performance of physicians and making recommendations as to medical staff membership and clinical privileges to be granted or modified. See *credentialing* and *privileges.*

creditor: A business or individual to whom money is owed.

criteria: A term used by the *Joint Commission on the Accreditation of Healthcare Organizations (JCAHO)* for statements of explicit, objective, generally accepted measures of appropriateness and quality which are to be used in the evaluation of the institution's performance with respect to its *indicators.*

critical: A term which, when used to describe the condition of a patient, means that the condition is life-threatening. Of the terms commonly used to describe a patient's condition, "critical" indicates the greatest severity of illness.

critical care: A term applied to exceptionally *intensive care,* usually delivered in the *intensive care unit (ICU),* but on occasion in other settings, in cases of emergency.

critical care unit: See *intensive care unit (ICU).*

CRNA: See *certified registered nurse anesthetist.*

cross-section: Usually, an *image* of an object, such as a part of the body, which is at right angles to the long axis of the object. A cross-sectional image of the leg, for example, is one which shows the leg as though it had been cut across at that location, for

C

example, the middle of the thigh. Such views are made by special *imaging* techniques.

CRT: See *cathode ray tube*.

Cruzan case: The first *right-to-die* case to reach the United States Supreme Court. Nancy Cruzan was in her early twenties when a 1983 automobile accident deprived her of oxygen for perhaps 12 to 14 minutes (the best estimate), and left her in a persistent vegetative state. A gastrostomy feeding tube was surgically implanted about a month after the accident, and she was fed through the tube continuously after that. Unlike Karen *Quinlan*, Ms. Cruzan was not sustained by a mechanical respirator or other life-support machine.

Ms. Cruzan's parents, who were also her legal *guardians*, believed that Nancy would not have wanted her life sustained in this manner under these circumstances, and asked a court to approve termination of the artificial nutrition and hydration. The trial court granted this request, but the Supreme Court of Missouri reversed, ruling that the guardians did not have the authority to order withdrawal of nutrition and hydration, and that the evidence was not sufficient to prove that the patient would have wanted this to happen.

The parents appealed to the United States Supreme Court, which ruled that it was not unconstitutional for the State of Missouri to require "clear and convincing evidence" that an *incompetent (1)* patient would wish to have life-sustaining treatment withdrawn, prior to permitting the withdrawal. *Cruzan v. Director, Missouri Dept. of Health*, U.S. , 110 S.Ct. 2841 (1990).

"Clear and convincing evidence" is a legal term which describes a burden of proof somewhere in between a "preponderance," which makes one thing more likely than another (this is the usual standard in a civil case; a malpractice suit, for example), and "beyond a reasonable doubt," the highest standard of proof, which is required in a criminal trial.

After the Supreme Court's ruling, the Cruzans again asked the trial court to permit termination of treatment, and produced additional witnesses to testify concerning Nancy Cruzan's wishes under the circumstances. The trial court found that there was clear and convincing evidence that Nancy Cruzan would have wanted treatment terminated, and authorized the Cruzans to withdraw nutrition and hydration. Ms. Cruzan died about two weeks later.

One implication of the case is that *living wills* may become more important as evidence to clearly establish the wishes of individuals concerning life-sustaining treatment, in the event they become incompetent.

CS: See *central service department.*

CSI: See *computerized severity index.*

CSM: See *Consolidated Standards Manual for Child, Adolescent, and Adult Psychiatric, Alcoholism, and Drug Abuse Facilities and Facilities Serving the Mentally Retarded/Developmentally Disabled.*

CST: See *certified surgical technologist.*

CT: See *computed tomography.*

CT scanner: A machine which carries out computed tomography (CT)—a type of *imaging* done by using radiation (*X-rays*) and analyzing and displaying the absorption (or transmission) of the radiation by the tissues. The key to this technology is a *microcomputer* within the machine. A CT scanner is also called a "CAT scanner."

Current Procedural Terminology (CPT): See *Physicians' Current Procedural Terminology.*

current ratio: See *ratio.*

custodial: Pertains to watching over and protecting, rather than, in the health care field, attempting to provide *treatment.*

custodial care: See *rest home care.*

custodial care facility: See *rest home.*

customary fee: See *customary, prevailing, reasonable charge (or fee) (CPR).*

C

customary, prevailing, reasonable charge (or fee) (CPR): The *charge (1)* or "fee" (same as charge), usually of a physician, which has traditionally been defined as that charge which is the lowest of the following: the actual charge made for the *service (1)*; the physician or supplier's "customary" (usual) charge for the service; or the fee "prevailing" in the community for the service. Such fees vary according to *specialty*, geographic area, and the physician's charge system. Increases in such fees are typically limited by *economic indexes* imposed by the paying agency. The definition of "reasonable and customary charge (or fee)" is under scrutiny by the federal government with the idea that the fees should be "inherently" reasonable, that is, related to some real worth of the service rather than a comparison. The *Tax Equity and Fiscal Responsibility Act (TEFRA)* and Medicare *regulations* both give specific formulas for calculating the "reasonable charges" limitation on physician fees. Synonym(s): customary fee, prevailing fee.

CVS: See *chorionic villus sampling*.

CVT: See *cardiovascular technologist*.

CYTO: See *cytotechnologist*.

cytology: The study of the cell (cyto-): biology, chemistry, physiology, structure, and its diseases.

cytotechnologist (CYTO): One of the 26 *allied health professionals* for whom the American Medical Association's *Committee on Allied Health Education and Accreditation (CAHEA)* has accredited education programs.

D

daily service charge: Same as *room rate*; see *rate*.

damages: A legal term describing the money to be paid to a *plaintiff* by the *defendant* when the defendant is found to be liable (see *liability (1)*). Only certain kinds of damages, some of which are described below, are permitted. The term "damages" is sometimes used more restrictively to describe the monetary value of the plaintiff's injuries, property loss, and the like.

actual damages: Money paid to compensate actual loss by the plaintiff, such as medical expenses, loss of earnings (or value of services, such as homemaking), *pain and suffering*, and (rarely) *emotional distress*. Synonym(s): compensatory damages.

compensatory damages: See *actual damages*.

exemplary damages: See *punitive damages*.

liquidated damages: An amount of money decided on by the parties to a contract at the time of contracting, which will be paid to one party upon default of the other. Such damages are permitted only if the actual amount of damages is very difficult to ascertain, and if the amount is reasonable.

nominal damages: A token sum (usually one dollar) paid to the plaintiff where legal liability is proven but there are no *actual damages*.

punitive damages: Money which the defendant is ordered to pay to the plaintiff, the purpose of which is to punish the defendant and discourage the misconduct; these damages are not compensatory. Punitive damages are like the fine imposed for criminal

D

behavior, except that the money is paid to the plaintiff instead of the state. Synonym(s): exemplary damages.

treble damages: Three times the damages (monetary compensation) the plaintiff would otherwise be entitled to. Certain laws permit treble damages as a punitive measure, to discourage certain types of conduct and to encourage injured parties to enforce those laws as "private attorneys general." For example, federal antitrust laws provide for treble damages; the jury's (or judge's) award to a successful plaintiff is tripled. See *Patrick case*.

Darling case: A landmark hospital law case which established that the hospital is responsible for care provided to patients, and that the *medical staff* must be accountable to the hospital for the care provided by medical staff members. The case involved a young man named Darling who was brought to a hospital with a leg fracture suffered while playing football. Through a series of events (notably, lack of communication among nurses, doctors, and hospital, and failure by the hospital and medical staff to enforce their own *bylaws*) the patient's leg became gangrenous and was eventually lost. *Darling v. Charleston Community Memorial Hospital*, 33 Ill.2d 326, 211 N.E.2d 253 (1965), *cert. denied*, 383 U.S. 946 (1966).

data: Material, facts, or figures on which discussion is held or from which inferences are drawn or decisions made. A distinction is sometimes made between data and *information*; generally, data have to be somehow "digested" (manipulated, summarized, organized, or interpreted) in order to become information. No rigid standardization in terminology has appeared in this regard, although generally the term "information" is rarely applied to material which is "raw."

Data Bank: See *National Practitioner Data Bank*.

data base (1): A collection of basic data or information, usually a *statistical data base*.

clinical data base: The array of information (*data set*) about a patient which is collected by the physician and others caring for the patient in order to make a diagnosis and to be able to detect changes in the patient's condition during treatment.

D

statistical data base: A compilation of data about a number of events (illnesses, for example) or objects (patients, for example) which has as its purpose the description of the group of events or objects. For example, a statistical data base consisting of identical items of information about many patients who smoke gives a statistical description of smokers, and is used to estimate the risk of smoking, an element in *health risk appraisal*.

data base (2): A collection of *data records*, often kept in a computer and accessible through the computer. Sometimes the term "data base" is used improperly as shorthand for a *data base access system*.

data base access system: A system providing access for many users to a computer-stored *data base (2)*. Users gain access via their own computers (or terminals), using telephone lines to receive data. The Medical Literature Analysis and Retrieval System (MEDLARS), for example, is a data base access system providing computer access to the National Library of Medicine (NLM). Sometimes the term "data base" is used to mean both the data base itself and the system of access.

data base management system: A computer system (program) of a specific type which, in its simplest form, is a computerized filing system. In more elaborate forms, it relates information from different files together, on demand, to produce new files, reports, and analyses.

data element: In general usage, an "item of information." When used in connection with computers, a data element may be one part of a *data record* (a logically connected group of data elements). Synonym(s): field.

data processing department: The department responsible for providing whatever computer services the hospital provides "in house." Its services are often confined to administrative tasks (such as accounting, personnel, medical records, laboratory reporting, and clinic scheduling), with research computer applications handled in some other manner. This department is often run by a person known as the Manager of Information Systems (MIS).

D

data record: A group of items of information logically connected in some fashion. Data records are often subdivided into smaller units of data known as *data elements* or "fields." Conversely, a group of data records may be described as a *data base (2)*. For example, a telephone book is a data base (collection) of data records, each entry being one data record. Each data record in the telephone book might be subdivided into three data elements or fields: name, address, and telephone number. Synonym(s): data structure.

data set: A specified set of items of information. The data set for a person's address, for example, may be name, street address, city, state, and ZIP code. In the hospital, the term "data set" would be applied, for example, to a case abstract (a specified list of items of information from the patient's medical record) and to a patient's bill. In this illustration, the nucleus of both data sets is, at a minimum, the *Uniform Hospital Discharge Data Set (UHDDS)* specified by the federal government.

patient's data set: A computer record of selected data items about an *episode of care*, including identity of the patient, identity of the physician, dates of care, diagnoses, procedures, reference to the original medical record, and other information.

data structure: See *data record*.

DATTA: See *Diagnostic and Therapeutic Technology Assessment Program*.

day: The hospital compiles a number of statistics on "days." A number of modifiers are used to designate days of different kinds:

adjusted inpatient service days: See *inpatient day equivalents*.

bed day: See *inpatient service day*.

available bed days: The number of bed days which the hospital is set up to provide in a given time period. It is computed by multiplying the number of *regularly maintained beds* by the number of days in the time period. Available bed days are ordinarily expressed in three segments: available adult inpatient service days; available newborn bed days;

and available pediatric (child) inpatient bed days. See also *bed*, *bed capacity*, and *bed count*.

occupied bed day: The period of time between the taking of the hospital *census* on two successive days (the census is taken at the same hour each day). In counting the *length of stay (LOS)* of a patient, "the day of admission is an occupied bed day, the day of discharge is not." Application of this rule gives one day of stay to a patient who is admitted and discharged during a single occupied bed day.

charity care day: An *inpatient service day* for which the hospital makes no charge.

inpatient day equivalents: A term used in compiling hospital statistics. The total number of *inpatient service days*, plus the volume of outpatient services expressed as (converted to) an estimate of inpatient service days. This computation has to use some sort of *relative value unit (RVU)* approach to convert outpatient services into inpatient service days. Synonym(s): adjusted inpatient service days.

inpatient service day: A day of *inpatient care*; one person in the hospital one day is one inpatient service day. Synonym(s): bed day, patient day. See also *patient days*.

partial hospitalization day: The *services (1)* provided to a *partial hospitalization* patient in one 24-hour period.

patient day: See *inpatient service day*.

resident day: The *services (1)* to one *resident (2)* in a *long-term care* institution during one 24-hour period.

day care: Care, provided by an institution, which does not include an overnight stay; patients reside at night at home or in some other facility. This term is sometimes equated with *adult day care*, but the latter appears to have a more formal definition.

day health care services: See *adult day health services*.

DC: See *Doctor of Chiropractic*.

DCGs: See *diagnostic cost groups*.

D

DDS: See *Doctor of Dental Surgery (or Science).*

DEA: See *Drug Enforcement Administration.*

DEA number: The number assigned by the federal government indicating that an individual (a physician, a pharmacist, a hospital, a pharmacy, or some other qualified "business activity") registered with the *Drug Enforcement Administration (DEA)* is authorized to dispense (prescribe) *controlled substances.* The former agency with this authority was the Bureau of Narcotics and Dangerous Drugs (BNDD); the DEA number formerly was known as the BNDD number.

death: The cessation of life. Until recent years, death meant the cessation of respiration and circulation; however, with mechanical respirators and other medical devices, life as previously defined may be continued indefinitely. A new definition of death therefore became necessary so that decisions to terminate life support systems and to remove organs for transplant could be made appropriately. Thus death is defined in most states, for most purposes, as either the irreversible cessation of circulatory and respiratory function, or brain death (absence of all measurable or identifiable electrical or other brain functioning for more than 24 hours).

death certificate: The official record of a person's death. State law governs the death certificate's content, which includes the deceased person's name, age, sex, and the date, time, and cause of death. State law also specifies the person (for example, a physician, coroner, or medical examiner) who is authorized to sign a death certificate. The certificate is filed with the *registrar (1)* for the local unit of government, who in turn files a copy with the state office of *vital statistics.*

death rate: The number of deaths divided by the number of patients at risk. The death rate is usually multiplied by 100, so as to be expressed as a percent. One death in 100 patients undergoing gall bladder removal (cholecystectomy), for example, would be expressed as a "cholecystectomy death rate (mortality rate) of 1 percent." A death rate may be calculated for any group of patients (for example, all patients, for the hospital overall death rate; or newborns, for the hospital newborn mortality rate). Note that the terms "death" and "mortality" are used interchangeably. For rare events, the death rate may use a different *base (1)*, for example, per 10,000, and will be expressed not as a percent, but as "per 10,000." A number of commonly computed death rates are described below:

disease specific death rate: The number of deaths attributed to a given disease in a specified population, expressed as a *proportion*. This rate is more likely given per 100,000 than as a percentage. Also called disease specific mortality rate.

fetal death rate: The number of fetal deaths (deaths of babies before birth) as a proportion of total births, with total births defined as live births plus fetal deaths. The rate is usually expressed per 1,000 total births. When computed in a hospital, it should be called the "hospital fetal death rate" and refer only to births in the hospital. Also called fetal mortality rate and stillbirth rate.

> **hospital fetal death rate**: The number of fetal deaths in the hospital (deaths of babies before birth) as a proportion of total births in the hospital for the same time period, with total births defined as live births plus fetal deaths. The rate is usually expressed per 1,000 total births.

hospital death rate: The number of deaths in the hospital as a proportion of the number of discharges, both alive and by death, during the same time period. Newborn deaths are excluded from the numerator and babies born in the hospital are excluded from the denominator. The figure is usually given as a percent (per 100). Also called hospital mortality rate.

hospital obstetric death rate: The more accurate term for *hospital maternal death rate*.

infant death rate: The number of infant deaths (deaths of children under one year old) in a given time period as a proportion of the number of live births in the same population in the same time period. It is usually expressed per 1,000. Also called infant mortality rate.

maternal death rate: A vital statistic (a public health rather than hospital statistic; see *hospital maternal death rate*). For the computation, the number of "maternal deaths" (see *maternal death*) is the numerator, and the number of live births during the same time period (as a proxy for pregnant women) is the denominator. Since maternal deaths are relatively rare, the rate is usually expressed per 1,000 or per 100,000 live births. Also called maternal mortality rate.

hospital maternal death rate: A bad label for a statistic computed in hospitals as the number of deaths of *obstetric patients* in a hospital (patients in the hospital for the purpose of delivering a baby) in a given time period, as a proportion of the number of obstetric patients discharged from the hospital alive or by death during the same time period.

The hospital maternal death rate should not be confused with the public health term *"maternal death rate,"* which pertains to all deaths of pregnant women and women within a specified time period after delivery from whatever cause, and which uses live births as the denominator. A maternal death rate thus defined cannot be calculated from hospital data for a number of reasons; for example, hospital data do not have information about what happens to patients after discharge, nor would a hospital record as a "maternal death" the death of a pregnant woman if pregnancy were incidental to the patient's cause of hospitalization.

What is called here the "hospital maternal death rate" should be called the "hospital obstetric death rate."

neonatal death rate: A vital statistic (a public health rather than hospital statistic; see *hospital neonatal death rate*), calculated with the number of deaths within the first 28 days of life (the "neonatal" period) as the numerator and the number of live births in the same period, usually a year, as the denominator. It is usually expressed per 1,000 live births. Also called neonatal mortality rate.

hospital neonatal death rate: The number of newborn deaths in the first 28 days of life occurring in the hospital in a given period of time, as a proportion of the number of newborns discharged during that time period, both alive and by death. This rate is usually given as a percent (per 100). Also called hospital neonatal mortality rate.

The hospital neonatal death rate cannot be compared to the public health neonatal death rate because the hospital only counts those deaths which occur before the newborn is discharged; a baby may leave the hospital before it is 28 days old, and yet still die within the 28 days. The hospital has no way to count those neonatal deaths.

perinatal death rate: In vital (public health) statistics from developed countries, the numerator for computing this rate is deaths of *fetuses* after 28 weeks of gestation plus deaths within the first week after delivery; the denominator is these same deaths plus live births. For less developed countries, the denominator of the formula is different in that only live births are used in the denominator, on the basis that these countries do not keep adequate records of the late fetal deaths. This difference in definitions makes comparisons between the health conditions in the two types of areas invalid. The rate is usually expressed per 1,000. Also called perinatal mortality rate.

> **hospital perinatal death rate**: A statistic which can be calculated from hospital data, with the numerator being deaths in the hospital of fetuses after the 28th week of gestation plus those dying in the hospital within one week after delivery, and the denominator being these same deaths plus live births in the hospital in the same time period. The rate is usually expressed as per 1,000. Also called hospital perinatal mortality rate. As with the *hospital neonatal death rate* (see discussion above), the hospital has no way to count those newborns who leave the hospital before they are one week old, yet die within that week.

> **total death rate**: The number of deaths, of all ages, in a given population in a specified time period as a *proportion* of the population. The rate is usually expressed as per 1,000. Also called total mortality rate.

debenture: A bond or long-term loan (more than one year) that is not secured by a mortgage on specific property.

debt: An obligation to pay, whether in cash, services, in goods.

> **long-term debt**: Debt which does not have to be paid within one year.

> **short-term debt**: Debt to be paid within one year.

debt ratio: Total *debt* divided by total *assets*.

decentralized services: *Services (4)* which are carried out from several locations in an effort to improve efficiency, reduce cost, or

D

both. The alternative is *centralized services,* the carrying out of the services in question at or from a single location. A given type of service is usually under a single management division in an institution although, when decentralized, it may be under several managements.

decoding: The process of translating a *code (1)* (usually a number) back into the term which the code represents. With many coding systems used in health care, which are really *category coding* systems, the original term is not retrievable because the *categories* of the classification are designed to hold groups of similar things. For example, in category coding, hospitals are coded as to "church" or some other *"control."* When all one knows about a hospital is this code, all that can be retrieved about a given church hospital by *decoding* is the fact that it is a church hospital; whether the church is Catholic or Methodist cannot be determined by decoding from the category coding. See *coding.*

deductible: The amount of money an insured person must pay "at the front end" before the insurer will pay. In automobile collision insurance with a $100 deductible, the insured must pay any damage under $100 in its entirety, and the first $100 when the total is over that amount. The reason for introducing this concept into health care coverage is primarily to discourage "unnecessary" use of *services (1),* and also to reduce insurance premiums, since all claims have a "first $100" deductible and the insurer will be spared that amount on every claim. The term "deductible" is related to *copayment,* but the latter is a term used primarily in health insurance.

deemed status: A term used in the Medicare, Medicaid, and *Maternal and Child Health* programs to indicate that the hospital had been "deemed" by the former *Professional Standards Review Organization (PSRO)* to meet the requirements of those programs with respect to *admissions review, continued stay review,* and *medical care evaluation.* The determinations of "deemed hospitals" in these matters had to be regarded as final, and the hospitals' demands for payment had to be honored.

defamation: The publication of a statement which injures the reputation of another. "Publication" means that the statement is communicated to a third person (someone other than the "defamer" and the "defamed"); if no one else hears or reads the statement, it is not defamation. Written defamation is called "libel"; oral defamation is "slander." Both libel and slander are *torts* for which the defamer may face *liability (1)*.

Some kinds of statements are considered defamatory "per se" (by themselves); that is, if the *plaintiff* (person defamed) can prove the words were spoken or written to a third party, she does not have to prove actual injury. Criticizing another's professional knowledge, expertise, or performance is defamatory per se. Thus, if one physician criticizes the performance of another, the critical physician may be liable for defamation. That physician may be protected, however, in one of two ways: (1) truth is always a defense to a defamation action (in other words, a statement is not defamatory if it is true); and (2) there are now a number of laws granting immunity (legal protection from suit) to physicians evaluating quality of care who act in good faith (without malice or bad motive).

defendant: The person (or organization) against whom a lawsuit is brought. Commonly, the defendant in a lawsuit is the alleged wrongdoer who has injured the *plaintiff* (the person bringing the suit).

defensive medicine: The obtaining of *services (1)*, mainly diagnostic procedures, in anticipation of defending against a possible lawsuit by the person treated alleging *malpractice*. The primary reasons for obtaining the services is to avoid convincing the jury in a malpractice trial that omission of any test was good medical care, and to show the jury documented evidence that other possibilities were "ruled out" by the tests.

Ordinarily, diagnostic tests are obtained because the physician honestly needs the information they provide. In defensive medicine, however, the tests have little or no medical value to her. For example, a physician may be quite satisfied that a sprained ankle is just that; nevertheless, because of the threat of a malpractice suit, she will still obtain an X-ray in order to have evidence that she did not overlook a fracture.

defibrillation: Stopping the fibrillation (a certain type of abnormal contractions) of the heart muscle and restoring the normal heartbeat. The procedure usually is carried out by the use of an electrical shock.

degree program in nursing: A nursing education program operated by an educational institution which confers a degree (usually, Bachelor of Science in Nursing (BSN)) upon successful completion. The term is sometimes used in connection with a program which confers an *associate degree (AD)*. A degree program is contrasted with a *diploma program*, which is conducted by a hospital that confers a diploma rather than a degree.

deinstitutionalization: The *discharge* of mental patients from mental institutions, with continued care to be provided in the community. This movement was made possible by the development of psychotropic drugs, which modify a patient's behavior to such an extent that she is considered able to function within the community.

delivery: The actual passage of the baby from the mother into the outside world. Synonym(s): parturition.

delivery room: A room equipped for giving care to the obstetric patient during *delivery*, and for first care to the newborn infant.

demarketing: Efforts to persuade individuals not to buy, or to go elsewhere. A hospital has a serious problem when the price set for a given *Diagnosis Related Group (DRG)* under the *prospective payment system (PPS)* is lower than the lowest cost the hospital can achieve for care for a patient with that DRG and still maintain quality. Under those circumstances, the hospital may elect to discontinue caring for such patients (for example, pediatrics). Alternatively, it may develop some more subtle strategy to discourage patients with a *problem* which falls into the DRG from coming to that hospital, or to discourage physicians from bringing such patients. The latter efforts have been labelled "demarketing."

demographic information: The class of information about a person which includes such items as age, sex, race, income, marital status, and education. Demographic information is important for proper patient care, and is also used as the data with which to compile certain statistics (*demographics*) on a population, for example, in the study of the distribution of certain types of injuries and illnesses.

demographics: Descriptions of patient populations or *service area* populations in such terms as age, sex, race, educational level, income, family size, and ethnic background.

dental assistant: A person who assists a dentist in patient care, and may perform other functions in the dental office or laboratory. Most dental assistants are trained by the dentist.

dental hygienist: A person trained in a two or four year program at the college level and licensed to give certain dental services: oral prophylaxis, dental X-rays, apply medications, and educate in dental matters. The services are to be under the supervision of a dentist.

dental laboratory technician: A person who works in a dental laboratory and prepares dentures and other appliances, such as orthodontic devices and crowns, to dental prescriptions. Synonym(s): dental technician.

dental technician: See *dental laboratory technician.*

dentist: A person whose profession is the care of the teeth and surrounding tissues. A dentist requires a state license. The degree held by the practitioner is usually Doctor of Dental Surgery (or Science) (DDS).

dentistry: The healing art which is concerned with the diagnosis and treatment of diseases of the mouth, teeth, and associated structures, and with the restoration of function.

department: A term with two major meanings in the hospital. When the term "department" is used without a modifier, in some contexts it is impossible to tell which of the two following meanings is intended:

clinical department: A division of the *medical staff organization (MSO)* according to clinical specialty, such as surgery, specialties of surgery, internal medicine, specialties of internal medicine, obstetrics and gynecology, pediatrics, and the like. In some hospitals, clinical departments are called services; for example, the surgical service may mean the same thing as the surgical department. In other hospitals, a service may be a subdivision of a department; for example, in a given hospital the "orthopedics service" may be a part of the larger "department of surgery."

hospital department: A major organizational unit of the hospital, such as the nursing service, the pharmacy, housekeeping, dietary, and the like. The *medical staff organization (MSO)*, which in some respects functions as a department, is not classified as one. On the other hand, the radiology department and the emergency department, although both employ members of the medical staff, are both termed hospital departments. Sometimes called hospital service instead of department.

Department of Health and Human Services (DHHS): The department of the executive branch of the federal government responsible for the federal health programs in the civilian sector, and for Social Security. DHHS is the portion of the *Department of Health, Education, and Welfare (DHEW)* left after the establishment of the Department of Education as an separate department. DHHS is sometimes referred to as HHS.

Department of Health, Education, and Welfare (DHEW): The antecedent of the *Department of Health and Human Services (DHHS)* in the executive branch of the federal government. DHHS was formed when the separate Department of Education was established. DHEW was sometimes referred to as HEW.

Department of Justice (DOJ): The federal government department which enforces certain federal laws; for example, antitrust laws. The Department of Justice is headed by the United States Attorney General.

Department of Transportation (DOT): The department in the executive branch of the federal government which is concerned with transportation. One concern of DOT is emergency medical services.

deposition: During a lawsuit but outside of the courtroom, the questioning under oath of a party or witness by the attorney for the adverse party, with attorneys for both sides and a court reporter (stenographer) present. Although the deposition is used to obtain information for trial, part or all of it may itself be *admissible* (allowed as evidence) at the trial. The term "deposition" may refer either to the actual questioning, or to the written record which is produced by the court reporter.

depreciation: A technique used in accounting to recognize the fact that certain kinds of property (*assets*), such as equipment, depreciate (lose their value) over time; assets may wear out or be made obsolete by new inventions, or materials, or techniques. Depreciated property must be replaced with the same or more modern equipment, or be abandoned as items no longer needed. Money must be spent on replacement, and a variety of accounting techniques have been developed to determine how much to allow for this purpose each year for each item. Simply stated, the allowance is equal to the initial cost (or sometimes the future replacement cost) divided by the estimated life of the property. The total allowance for depreciation is shown on the *balance sheet* as a deduction from the initial value of the assets. This allowance may be "funded," that is, actually set aside in a savings account from which to draw to pay for replacement, or may be "unfunded," in which case no savings account is set up, and the organization must find the money elsewhere when it is needed. In either case, however, the depreciation entry is the same.

dermatologist: A physician specializing in diagnosis and treatment of disorders of the skin.

dermatology: One of the medical specialties for which *residency* programs have been approved by the Accreditation Council for Graduate Medical Education (ACGME). See *specialty*.

dermatopathology: One of the medical specialties for which *residency* programs have been approved by the Accreditation Council for Graduate Medical Education (ACGME). See *specialty*.

desmoteric: Prison-associated, of or pertaining to the prison. Similar to "nosocomial," meaning hospital-associated.

D

detoxification service: An immediate treatment *service (6)* for reducing the acute effects of alcohol or other drugs.

development: See *fund-raising*.

device: An apparatus or item used for diagnosis, treatment, or prevention of disease, which does not achieve its purpose through chemical action on or within the body (to distinguish it from a *drug*). Examples of devices include artificial heart valves, cardiac pacemakers, prostheses, hearing aids, crutches, and wheelchairs. The federal Food and Drug Administration (FDA) regulates devices to assure that they are safe and effective.

DHEW: See *Department of Health, Education, and Welfare*.

DHHS: See *Department of Health and Human Services*.

diagnose: To apply a series of procedures for examining and gathering data about a patient in order to make a *diagnosis*.

diagnosis: A complex of "symptoms" (disturbances of appearance or function or sensation of which the patient is aware), "signs" (disturbances which the physician or another individual can detect), and "findings" (disturbances detected by laboratory, X-ray, or other diagnostic procedures, or response to therapy).

Note that a given diagnosis may essentially dictate therapy, but that a therapy is never a diagnosis. The terms "diagnosis" and "therapy" are often used improperly. For example, "hysterectomy" (removal of the uterus), while sometimes called a "diagnosis," is never a diagnosis, but rather a surgical procedure (therapy) done for a wide range of diagnoses, including tumors, infections, and other disorders.

The term "diagnosis" may be modified by a term indicating the way the physician arrived at the diagnosis. For example, a "laboratory diagnosis" is one established by the laboratory findings; a "clinical diagnosis" is one established by the patient's signs and symptoms; and a "physical diagnosis" is one established by physical examination of the patient.

admitting diagnosis: The diagnosis provided by the physician at the time of the patient's *admission* to the hospital. At least one admitting diagnosis, that primarily responsible for the hospitalization, is expected. While as much precision as possible is desired of the physician at the time of admission, the physician must not be required to be more exact than his clinical data base justifies; complying with a rigid demand for a *"codable diagnosis"* at this time may, in fact, start the patient on an inappropriate course of treatment. Often the diagnosis recorded at the time of admission must be vague, since one of the functions of the hospitalization is to add to the physician's information on the patient (for example, through observation by the nursing staff and others, diagnostic procedures, and response to treatment). As a result, the *discharge diagnosis*, benefitting as it does from these data sources, is often quite different from the admitting diagnosis.

One of the physician's first decisions regarding a patient is whether hospitalization is needed; if the decision is "yes," details on why hospitalization is necessary are often in part developed in the course of the care.

codable diagnosis: A diagnosis for which a category has been provided in a given *classification (1)*. As ordinarily used, however, the term means a diagnosis expressed in terminology which permits a *coder* to find it in the appropriate *code (1)* book and affix its numeric code. In North America at this time, coding of hospital diagnoses is *category coding* to the *International Classification of Disease, Ninth Revision, Clinical Modification (ICD-9-CM)*.

Virtually all *discharge diagnoses* likely to be used, except new terms, will be found in *ICD-9-CM*; thus they are "codable" (actually "classifiable"). (With the use of "wastebasket categories," for example, "Other diseases of the nervous system," *all* diagnoses can be placed somewhere, although often improperly).

Admitting diagnoses may necessarily at times be uncodable except to the most inexact categories; the patient's condition may be so vague as to defy terms which fit into the more specific categories of the classification, or they may be stated as *"problems,"* many of which, due to the origin and purpose of *ICD-9-CM*, cannot be accommodated. *ICD-10*, due for publication in 1992, has a new chapter (actually an expansion of an earlier "supplementary classification") entitled "Factors Influencing Health Status and Contact with Health Services" which will accommodate many more such "problems."

discharge diagnosis: A diagnosis supplied by the *attending physician* at the time of the *discharge* of the patient from the hospital.

D

This diagnosis has the benefit of the clinical data base developed up to the time of discharge, and is more accurate and also more exact than the *admitting diagnosis*. The discharge diagnosis is likely to be the *principal diagnosis*, but *secondary diagnoses* should also be recorded as appropriate. In virtually every case, the discharge diagnosis is a *codable diagnosis*.

major diagnosis: A term sometimes used to designate the diagnosis which is most responsible for the length of a given stay or the resource consumption (*services (1)* provided) for a given patient's care.

principal diagnosis: A specific term in the *prospective payment system (PPS)*, defined as "the diagnosis established after study to be chiefly responsible for occasioning the hospitalization." *Case abstracts* and the *Uniform Hospital Discharge Data Set (UHDDS)* also call for the principal diagnosis, usually with the same definition. It should be noted that in the mechanism for payment in the PPS, the system actually deals with a *category* code, which much of the time represents a number of different principal diagnoses, rather than the exact principal diagnosis itself.

secondary diagnosis: A diagnosis other than the *principal diagnosis* (patients often have more than one diagnosis). In the *prospective payment system (PPS)*, the secondary diagnoses to be recorded are presumed to be those which affect the treatment rendered or the *length of stay (LOS)*. Usual clinical practice, however, is to record in the medical record the complete array of diagnoses, including those which have no bearing on a given hospitalization. In the PPS, all diagnoses are given only as *International Classification of Diseases, Ninth Revision, Clinical Modification (ICD-9-CM)* codes.

suspected diagnosis: A diagnosis which seems to the physician to be likely, but for which there is insufficient proof. Some of the usual signs, symptoms, or findings may not yet be present, or the patient may present evidence which is in conflict with that for the diagnosis suspected.

Diagnosis Related Group (DRG): A hospital patient *classification (1)* system developed under federal grants at Yale University. The current payment system for Medicare is based on the federal government's setting a predetermined price for the "package of care" in the hospital (exclusive of physician's fees) required for

132

each DRG. If the hospital can provide the care for less than the DRG price, it can keep the difference; if the care costs the hospital more than the price, the hospital has to absorb the difference.

Originally each DRG was intended to contain patients who were roughly the same kind of patients in a medical sense and who spent about the same amount of time in the hospital. The groupings were subsequently redefined so that, in addition to medical similarity, resource consumption (*ancillary services* as well as *bed days*) was approximately the same within a given group. There are now 468 DRGs identified on the basis of the following criteria: the *principal diagnosis* (the final diagnosis which, after study in the hospital, was determined to be chiefly responsible for the hospitalization); whether an *operating room procedure* was performed; the patient's age; *comorbidity*; and *complications*.

A number of efforts are underway to modify DRGs by the use of *severity of illness* measures, and to develop new DRGs for specific classes of patients, as in the case of pediatrics with development of *Pediatric-Modified Diagnosis Related Groups (PM-DRGs)*. See also *prospective payment system (PPS)*.

Pediatric-Modified Diagnosis Related Groups (PM-DRGs): Diagnosis Related Groups (DRGs) for the classification of pediatric medical conditions. PM-DRGs have been developed by the National Association of Children's Hospitals and Related Institutions, Inc. (NACHRI) in a research project funded by the Health Care Financing Administration (HCFA). They add about 100 DRGs to the current DRG system. PM-DRGs are for use when a *prospective payment system (PPS)* is to be used for pediatric patients, and also by hospitals in analysis of utilization-management activities, study of pediatric *case mix*, and pricing of *services (1)*.

diagnostic: Done for the purpose of assisting in the making of a *diagnosis*.

Diagnostic and Therapeutic Technology Assessment (DATTA) Program: A program of the American Medical Association (AMA) for assessing medical technology, with the purpose of providing authoritative information to physicians on the appropriate use of specific medical technology.

diagnostic cost groups (DCGs): A system for paying for hospital care being tried by the *Health Care Financing Administration (HCFA)* for patients of Medicare *health maintenance organizations (HMOs)*. In this system, a patient's prior hospitalization history during the preceding 15 months is used to predict future costs. Prior utilization is expected to reflect the patient's health status and the physician's practice patterns. Each patient is placed in one of eight DCGs, depending on costliness, with the higher number DCGs reflecting higher expected costs to treat the patient. For each DCG, there is a set of cost weights that depend on the patient's age, sex, and welfare status. A formula results in the setting of the HMO's *capitation* rate.

diagnostic medical sonographer (DMS): One of the 26 *allied health professionals* for whom the American Medical Association's *Committee on Allied Health Education and Accreditation (CAHEA)* has accredited education programs.

diagnostic product: A chemical or other material which is used in diagnostic testing, either in the physician's office or by the patient, or in the hospital.

Diagnostic Radiology Services (DR): The chapter giving the *standards* for this component of the hospital in the 1990 *Accreditation Manual for Hospitals (AMH)* of the *Joint Commission on the Accreditation of Healthcare Organizations (JCAHO)*.

diagnostic screens: Batteries of diagnostic tests. See *screening (2)*.

diagnostic services: *Services (1)* aimed at determining the nature and cause of the patient's problem, rather than providing treatment. Diagnostic services include laboratory, X-ray, special testing such as stress testing, and the like.

dialysis: Selective filtering of chemicals in a solution through a membrane, such as the wall of a tube made of special material. This chemical property is used in *hemodialysis*, for example, in which blood is passed through a tube made of material which allows certain waste products to pass through, while other chemicals are retained in the blood. See also *renal dialysis* and *peritoneal dialysis*.

dialysis unit: See *hemodialysis unit*.

diener: A person who maintains a morgue and who assists in *autopsies*.

dietary assessment: See *nutrition assessment*.

dietary risk factors: Eating patterns which increase the likelihood for developing disease or other adverse health effects. Examples are: percentage of fat calories above 30 percent of total food calories increase one's risk for death from heart disease; being overweight is linked to heart disease, cancer, and diabetes; lack of adequate fluid intake puts many elderly persons at risk of dehydration.

dietary service: See *food service*.

Dietetic Services (DT): The chapter giving the *standards* for this component of the hospital in the 1990 *Accreditation Manual for Hospitals (AMH)* of the *Joint Commission on the Accreditation of Healthcare Organizations (JCAHO)*.

dietetic technician (DT): A graduate of an *American Dietetic Association (ADA)* approved academic and supervised practice program who assists registered dietitians in the provision of nutrition services.

dietetics: The science dealing with the relationships of foods and nutrition to human health.

dietitian: A specialist in food and nutrition science who assists the public in the modification and/or enhancement of its food-related behaviors.

clinical dietitian: A dietitian specializing in disease/nutrition relationships.

consulting dietitian: A dietitian who works with food services, agencies, clinics, industry, and the general public on a fee-for-service basis. Synonym(s): consultant dietitian.

licensed dietitian: A dietitian who is *licensed* by the state. Not all states require dietitians to be licensed.

D

registered dietitian (RD): A dietitian who has met the *registration* requirements of the *Commission on Dietetic Registration* of the *American Dietetic Association (ADA)*. The dietetian must have at least a bachelor's degree in food related science, passed a comprehensive registration examination, completed supervised field experience in dietetic practice, and must maintain a record of mandatory continuing professional education experiences.

digital: When used to describe information (data), "digital" means based on a system of discrete steps, such as counting the fingers on one's hand. Frequently, the term "digital" is associated with binary logic, where each *bit* of information can have one of two states (such as "on" or "off," or "true" or "false"). This term can also describe most computers in use today, which process information in this manner. "Digital" is distinguished from *"analog,"* which treats information as based on a continuum, such as body temperature. In order to convert analog information to digital information, one must arbitrarily select samples (steps) along the continuum, and discard the rest of the information.

diploma program in nursing: A nursing education program operated by a hospital school of nursing, which confers a diploma in nursing, rather than a degree. A degree in nursing is only awarded upon completion of a nursing program conducted by an educational institution.

direct care provider: An individual who is responsible for the care of an individual, as contrasted with a "consultant" who is responsible only for giving an opinion. However, the consultant may take over the care of the patient and become the direct care provider.

direction: As used by the *Joint Commission on the Accreditation of Healthcare Organizations (JCAHO)*, this term often occurs in the phrase "under the direction of" to mean under the "procedural guidance of."

director (1): A member of the *governing body* when the official term for that body is "board of directors." When the governing body is called the "board of trustees," its members are individually "trustees."

director (2): An operating officer. The title "director" is used by many institutions for their officers and executives. The *chief executive officer (CEO)* may be called *the* director, and various subordinates may carry titles such as "director of development," "director of nursing," and the like.

director of buildings and grounds: See *administrative engineer*.

director of education: An individual responsible for arranging and coordinating employee training (on-the-job and continuing), employee orientation, and, in some circumstances, community health education programs and patient education programs. The director of education is not responsible for *continuing medical education*; that person is the *director of medical education (DME)*. Synonym(s): inservice education coordinator.

director of medical affairs (DMA): The person designated by the *governing body* to be responsible for management of the *medical staff organization (MSO)* and for carrying out policy for the medical staff as promulgated by the board. Ordinarily the DMA is a physician, and may be nominated by the MSO. A physician with this title is ordinarily paid. This term is discussed further under *chief of staff*.

director of medical education (DME): The individual, ordinarily a physician, who is responsible for administering the educational program for physicians in training in the hospital. The actual training is provided by the *clinical departments* (surgery, medicine, and the like). However, the coordination of programs for both continuing and graduate medical education, such as collecting and giving primary review to applications for training, handling personnel matters for trainees (such as scheduling vacations), arranging conferences, and the like is done by the DME. The DME may be either a physician or an educator.

director of nursing: See *nursing service administrator*.

director of staff development: A title often given to the individual responsible for *inservice training* of hospital employees.

D

director of volunteers: A hospital employee who administers the hospital's *volunteer services department*. Her duties usually include the planning and coordination of *volunteer services*.

disability: The absence or loss of physical, mental, or emotional function and, sometimes, earning ability. May be temporary or permanent, total or partial. "Disability" will have a specific legal definition for a particular purpose; for example, Social Security or workers' compensation laws.

disaster drill: A formal attempt to simulate a disaster as realistically as possible and to test as many elements as possible of a *disaster preparedness plan* under practice conditions. Such drills are carried out periodically. The purposes of the disaster drill are: to train the personnel in execution of the plan; and to discover flaws in the plan so that it can be rewritten as an improved plan.

disaster plan: See *disaster preparedness plan*.

disaster preparedness plan: A formal plan for coping with a disaster. An *accredited hospital* is expected to have an *internal disaster plan* for dealing with disasters within the institution, and an *external disaster plan* for carrying out its functions in case of a community disaster. Often such plans have basic elements relating to any kind of disaster and dealing with such items as emergency communication, alerting of police and fire departments, mobilization of off-duty personnel, and the like. The basic plan also has supplements for various kinds of disasters; for example, a nuclear disaster would call for different procedures than a flood or a tornado. It is expected that the written plan will periodically be tested and modified on the basis of *disaster drills*. Synonym(s): disaster plan. See also *hazardous materials*.

external disaster plan: A formal disaster preparedness plan for coping with a disaster in the community, or for which the hospital may be expected to provide health care services.

internal disaster plan: A formal disaster preparedness plan for coping with a disaster, such as a fire, within the institution itself.

disbursement: Paying money to take care of an expense or a debt.

discharge: The formal release of a patient from a physician's care or from a hospital (in Canada, a hospital discharge is called a "separation"). Sometimes called "signing out" the patient. A discharge terminates certain responsibilities on the part of the *provider*. There are several kinds of discharge:

discharge against medical advice (discharge AMA): A type of discharge which occurs when the patient, contrary to the advice of the attending physician, refuses treatment and "signs herself out," thus releasing the hospital from *liability* for subsequent events.

discharge by death: A hospital discharge which occurs when a patient who has been admitted dies in the hospital. A patient who is "dead on arrival" cannot be a hospital discharge.

discharge by transfer: A discharge which occurs when the patient is *transferred* from one institution to another and responsibility for care is shifted to the receiving institution. Medicare has special rules for the payment to each of the two institutions for this kind of discharge.

inpatient discharge: The discharge of an inpatient by release from the hospital on a physician's order, *against medical advice (AMA)*, or by death. A special usage of this term occurs under Medicare, when *transfer* of the patient to another unit of the hospital for which Medicare does not provide benefits is also an "inpatient discharge."

outpatient discharge (OP discharge): The formal release of a patient receiving *outpatient* care; it occurs when the physician states that there is no need for the patient to return for more care.

discharge abstract: A *coded (1)* summary of selected data in the patient's hospital *medical record*, prepared after *discharge*. It contains a standardized set of items in a form ready for computer processing in order to provide statistics, medical record indexes, submission of bills, patient care quality review, and health care research. The core content is usually the *Uniform Hospital Discharge Data Set (UHDDS)* prescribed by the federal government. Synonym(s): case abstract.

discharge abstract system: See *hospital discharge abstract system*.

discharge coordinator: See *discharge planner*.

D

discharge planner: A person whose duties involve making arrangements so that patients who are being *discharged* have an place to go which is appropriate to their needs, with the necessary care available. These duties start early in hospitalization, so that discharge which is medically indicated will not be delayed because of the absence of needed medical or social resources. Synonym(s): discharge coordinator.

discharge planning: The process of making sure that arrangements are made outside the hospital to receive the patient upon *discharge* and to provide the necessary continuity of care.

discharge summary: A summary of the medical record, prepared at the end of hospitalization, giving the essentials of diagnosis, treatment, prognosis, and recommendations. Preparation of the discharge summary is the responsibility of the attending physician or dentist. A discharge summary must not be confused with a *discharge abstract*, which is different in content, and the preparation of which is not the responsibility of the attending physician or dentist.

discipline: A field of study, such as medicine or nursing.

discounting of accounts receivable: See *pledging of accounts receivable*.

discoverable: Information which may be legally obtained by a party to a lawsuit, from the adverse party. Not all such information is *admissible* during a trial, however; the rules concerning discoverable information are much broader than the rules of admissibility. Generally, information is discoverable if it may lead to admissible evidence.

discovery: The process during a lawsuit, before trial, by which each party obtains information from the other party which may be used as evidence, or may lead to useful evidence, at the trial. Common methods of discovery include *interrogatories* (written questions), requests for documents, requests for *admissions (2)*, and *depositions* (verbal questions).

discovery period (1): The period of time after expiration of an insurance policy during which the beneficiary of the policy may report an event which occurred during the life of the policy.

discovery period (2): The period of time during the life of a lawsuit, after the suit is filed and prior to the trial, during which both parties may use *discovery* to find out as much as possible about the other side's case. There is a specific date, set by court rules and/or ordered by the judge, by which discovery must be completed.

discovery rule: A provision in some states' *statutes of limitations* which requires a *plaintiff* to file certain types of lawsuits within a specific period of time after she discovers (or should have discovered) her injury, rather than when her injury actually occurred.

disease: An illness or disorder of the function of the body or of certain tissues, organs, or systems. Diseases differ from injuries in that injuries are the result of external physical or chemical *agents (1)*.

acute disease: A disease which normally is of short duration—a rule of thumb is 30 days or less—and which ordinarily is confined to a single *episode*. *Chronic diseases* typically violate one or both of these criteria, but the distinction is not hard and fast.

chronic disease: A disease which requires more than one *episode of care*, or is of long duration (more than 30 days, for example), or both. This is in contrast with an *acute* disease, which is of short duration and which normally is confined to a single episode.

disease staging: See *staging (1)*.

disincentive: An undesirable "reward" for undesired behavior. For example, as part of efforts to reduce hospital and physician costs, patients are sometimes required to pay the first dollars for *services (1)*; this payment is called a *deductible*. The deductibles are a "disincentive" (a negative incentive) to seek the care, and thus an *incentive* to be frugal.

dispense: See *drug dispensing*.

D

distribution system: In the hospital, a system for providing supplies such as linens, drugs, food, and equipment to patient care areas.

diversification: A term coming into use as hospitals enter lines of business other than care of the sick and injured in an effort to obtain revenue from a variety of sources and remain solvent. The hospital is typically restructured in the process of diversification, and foundations, holding companies, and the like may result. The new "businesses" may be other health care enterprises such as home care or neighborhood health centers; they may also be other activities, such as offering its collection or public relations services to other clients.

divestiture: Getting rid of something, for example, to comply with a court order breaking up a monopoly. A corporate sale of a *subsidiary* is said to be a divestiture.

dividend: The distribution of the earnings of a company to its shareholders in proportion to the shares of *stock* held by each shareholder.

DMA: See *director of medical affairs.*

DME (1): See *director of medical education.*

DME (2): See *durable medical equipment.*

DMS: See *diagnostic medical sonographer.*

DNAR: Do not attempt resuscitation. See *do not resuscitate order (DNR).*

DNR: See *do not resuscitate order.*

DO: See *Doctor of Osteopathic Medicine.*

do not attempt resuscitation (DNAR): See *do not resuscitate order (DNR).*

D

do not code: See *do not resuscitate order (DNR)*.

do not resuscitate order (DNR): An order by the physician, with respect to a specific patient, to the effect that, should *cardiac* or *respiratory arrest* occur, no attempt should be made to give *cardiopulmonary resuscitation (CPR)* to the patient (restart the heart or otherwise revive her). "Do not resuscitate" is sometimes translated into the jargon that the patient is "not to be coded," or "do not code this patient"; this means that a *code blue* signal should not be issued. A suggestion has been made that the term "do not resuscitate" be changed to "do not attempt resuscitation" (DNAR).

A DNR order may be issued for one or more of three reasons: (1) no medical benefit; (2) poor *quality of life* predicted after CPR; or (3) poor quality of life before CPR. Or, such an order may be issued because a *competent* adult patient has asked not to be resuscitated. There is controversy about the circumstances under which a DNR order may be issued for an *incompetent* patient. The conservative approach is to obtain the consent of the patient's legal representative for any DNR order; however, some believe that no consent is required where there is no medical benefit, since CPR would not be medically indicated under these circumstances. (For example, consent is not required to *not* perform an appendectomy, if an appendectomy is not medically indicated.) Synonym(s): not to be coded, do not code, no-code order, order not to resuscitate (ONTR), do not attempt resuscitation (DNAR).

doc-in-a-box: A disparaging term for any one of a growing variety of *ambulatory care* facilities: storefront physician's offices or clinics; walk-in outpatient facilities; or specialized offices for foot care, dietary advice, and the like. The term is less likely to be used for ambulatory surgical centers, sports medicine centers, and other similar facilities with more formal structure, and which offer *continuity of care*.

Doctor of Chiropractic (DC): The degree held by a chiropractor, a practitioner of chiropractic, which is a system of medicine based on the theory that disease is caused by malfunction of the nerve system, and that normal function can be restored by manipulation and other treatment of body structures, particularly the spinal column. State licensure is required if the chiropractor wishes to practice.

D

Doctor of Dental Surgery (or Science) (DDS): The graduate degree (doctorate) awarded to an individual on graduation from a school of dentistry.

Doctor of Medicine (MD): The graduate degree (doctorate) awarded to an individual upon graduation from a school of *allopathic medicine* (or, formerly, *homeopathic medicine*). See *medicine (4)*.

Doctor of Osteopathic Medicine (DO): The graduate degree (doctorate) awarded to an individual upon graduation from a school of *osteopathic medicine*. See *medicine (4)*. Note that "OD" refers to an *optometrist*, not to an osteopath.

doctor's order: See *order (1)*.

DOJ: See *Department of Justice*.

Dole Foundation for the Employment of People with Disabilities: A foundation based in Washington, DC, established by Senator Robert Dole, to make grants to community-based nonprofit organizations for innovative programs for job-skill training and job placement for people with disabilities.

donated services: The estimated monetary value of the services rendered by personnel who receive no monetary compensation or only partial monetary compensation for their services. The term is applied to services rendered by members of religious orders, societies, volunteers, and similar groups.

donor (1): The source, human or animal, of biological material, blood, organs, or tissues for *transplantation* to or *implantation* in a patient. The donor is labelled by the type of material for which it serves as a source:

blood donor: A person who permits the removal of her blood for transfusion or other medical use.

professional blood donor: A blood donor who is paid for the blood she donates to a *blood bank*. Professional blood donors are likely to be individuals with low incomes and economic levels, and who present a greater hazard with respect to the transmission of disease (such as hepatitis or acquired immunodeficiency syndrome (AIDS)) than *voluntary blood donors* who, generally speaking, come from a higher socio-economic level, are generally healthier, and are less likely to carry the diseases transmissible by transfusion.

replacement blood donor: A blood donor who gives her blood with the stipulation that it be used to replace the blood transfused to a specific individual. A *blood bank* typically levies charges for (a) the services it renders in processing, storing, and distributing blood, and (b) for the blood itself, with the understanding that for each unit of blood obtained on behalf of a given patient, the patient's charge for the blood itself will be offset one-for-one (one replacement unit would offset one unit transfused and its charge).

voluntary blood donor: A blood donor who is not paid for her blood donated to a *blood bank* for transfusion or other use. A *replacement blood donor* is typically a voluntary blood donor.

organ donor: An individual one or more of whose *organs* are used for transplantation to an individual needing those organs. The organ donor may himself donate the organ, for example, in the case of a kidney, or the donation may be made by the donor's survivors. At other times, the donation may be made on the basis of a prior agreement by the donor that his organs will be available after death; often such an agreement is obtained at the time of driver's license renewals and recorded on the individual's driver's license.

tissue donor: A person who donates a body *tissue*, other than blood or an entire organ, for transplantation into another human. A bone marrow donor would be a tissue donor, as would a donor from whom bone was obtained.

donor (2): A person or organization that provides a gift of money or other item of value, such as equipment or property, to an institution.

DOT: See *Department of Transportation*.

DPW: Department of Public Welfare.

DR: See *Diagnostic Radiology Services*.

D

DRG: See *Diagnosis Related Group.*

DRG coordinator: A hospital employee with duties regarding the *prospective payment system (PPS)*. The duties typically are to: determine at an early date (the first hospital day, if possible) the *Diagnosis Related Group (DRG)* of the patient; inform the attending physician of the normal *length of stay (LOS)* for that DRG and its price; assist in *discharge planning*; and provide feedback from the *case-mix management information system (case-mix MIS).*

DRG cost weight: A number, or weight, assigned to each *Diagnosis Related Group (DRG)* by the federal government. It reflects the DRG's use of resources in relation to the cost of the average Medicare patient as determined by the federal government. The average Medicare patient's cost, when multiplied by the DRG cost weight, gives the price for the DRG in question.

DRG creep: A change in the distribution of patients among *Diagnosis Related Groups (DRGs)* without a real change in the distribution of patients treated in the hospital. It is feared that hospitals and physicians will change their record-keeping and reporting so that more patients will appear in higher-priced DRGs, and thus hospital income will be increased without a corresponding increase in cost—the creep will be "upward," and will represent exploitation of the payment system. This term is sometimes inappropriately used when the fact of the matter is that the apparent creep simply represents a systematic improvement in record-keeping and coding. When this is the case, of course, there should be a one-time adjustment, which the PPS system should recognize as laudable.

DRG enhancer: A computer program that arranges the medical data for billing to Medicare so as to achieve the best *Diagnosis Related Group (DRG) classification (1)*, i.e., the one with the biggest price tag.

DRG payment system: Originally, slang for the *prospective payment system (PPS)* of Medicare. However, this term may now be appropriate usage when payment by other than the Medicare program (insurance plans, for example) is also based on *Diagnosis Related Groups (DRGs).*

DRG-specific price blending: See *price blending.*

drug: Any substance, other than food, used medicinally, that is, in the prevention, diagnosis, or treatment of disease. In health care, the term "medication" ("med" for short) is used to cover both *prescription drugs* and *nonprescription drugs.*

investigational new drug (IND): A drug not yet approved by the Food and Drug Administration (FDA) and so not yet available to the general public. Before the drug can be used on humans, the FDA must approve an IND application, which gives reports of animal toxicity tests with the drug, a description of proposed clinical trials, and a list of names and qualifications of the investigators conducting the studies. Once the IND application is approved, the drug may be used only experimentally, to determine its safety and effectiveness, and only authorized persons may prescribe it.

legend drug: See *prescription drug.*

nonprescription drug: A drug which may be purchased without a prescription from a physician, dentist, or other authorized professional. Synonym(s): over-the-counter (OTC) drug.

over-the-counter (OTC) drug: See *nonprescription drug.*

prescription drug: A drug which can only be provided to a patient on the *prescription* of a physician, dentist, or other authorized professional. Synonym(s): legend drug.

drug administration: The giving of a single dose of a drug to a patient. Also called "medication administration."

drug dependency: Dependence on the use of drugs or chemicals which leads to interference with health and to social and economic problems. Withdrawal of the drug from a drug-dependent person leads to psychological and physical symptoms. Alcoholism is a kind of drug dependency.

drug dispensing: A portion of the process of providing *prescription drugs* to patients. It involves the preparation (if not a pre-prepared product), packaging, labelling, recording, and delivery of the drug (one or more doses) to the patient, the patient's representative, or an agent of the hospital, such as a nurse.

D

Drug Enforcement Administration (DEA): The federal agency which has to do with licensing the physician, hospital, and others to handle *controlled substances*, such as narcotics. The predecessor agency was the Bureau of Narcotics and Dangerous Drugs (BNDD).

drug error: See *medication error*.

drug incompatibilities: The interference by certain *drugs* or foods with the actions of certain other drugs. See also *drug interaction*.

drug information service: The service of providing readily accessible information about drugs, such as their properties, effects, dosage, *contraindications*, and *drug interactions*.

drug interaction: The term applied to the effects (actions) of one or more of the drugs when two or more drugs are given simultaneously. If each drug acts as though no other drug were being administered, there is no interaction. However, if the action on the body of one or more of the drugs is different than if given by itself, there is a drug interaction. Such interactions are increasingly known, and watched for by physicians and pharmacists; computer systems are being introduced to check for interactions among the list of medications for a given patient. A known drug interaction may or may not be a *contraindication* to using a drug on a given patient, depending on whether the altered effect would be harmful.

An extension of the checking against interactions is a systematic check (often by computer) for other contraindications, that is, for problems of the patient which may make it inadvisable to give a certain drug, or for foods which should be avoided when a certain drug is used. These effects are called *drug incompatibilities*.

drug prescription: A written order, by a licensed physician, dentist, or other authorized individual, for a *prescription drug* to be dispensed by a pharmacy or given in a hospital to a specific patient. When such an order is given in a hospital for a drug to be given to an inpatient, it is called a "medication order" (medication orders are required for any drug to be given an inpatient, even if the drug is a *nonprescription drug*).

D

drug utilization: A term which usually refers to the patterns of use of drugs by individual physicians and in hospitals. The term "drug utilization" usually occurs in connection with the terms "drug utilization committee" or "drug utilization study," both of which have to do with efforts to determine whether certain drugs are used appropriately (for example, whether obsolete drugs are still being given, or whether certain drugs, such as antibiotics, are given for the correct indications).

DSRF: See *debt service reserve fund*.

DT (1): See *Dietetic Services*.

DT (2): See *dietetic technician*.

dual capacity doctrine: A legal doctrine used to permit an employee to sue her employer despite *workers' compensation* which ordinarily employs the *exclusive remedy* doctrine. It is used in circumstances where the employer has provided medical treatment for an employee's work-related injury, and has caused additional injury through negligent treatment. The employer may not be sued as an employer because of the exclusive remedy provision; however, some states allow the employer to be sued for *malpractice* in its second capacity, that of health care provider.

dual injury doctrine: A legal doctrine used to permit an employee to sue her employer despite *workers' compensation* which ordinarily employs the *exclusive remedy* doctrine. The dual injury doctrine is used in circumstances where the employer concealed the injury or illness from the employee, such as where the company physician detects asbestos poisoning but fails to tell the employee. The first injury is the poisoning, which falls under the exclusive remedy doctrine; the second injury is the aggravation of the first due to the concealment, which does not fall under the exclusive remedy doctrine.

due process: A fair, just method to determine a person's rights or obligations. The law defines two kinds of due process: "procedural" due process concerns fairness in the process by which rights are decided; "substantive" due process requires that laws not be arbitrary or unfairly discriminate among classes of persons. In

D

common usage, "due process" usually means procedural due process.

The Fourteenth Amendment to the United States Constitution states that no one shall be deprived of life, liberty, or property without due process of law. The kind and amount of process which is "due" depends on the nature of the rights and obligations to be determined, and upon who is doing the determination. The Constitution applies to actions of the federal or state government; however, the courts have, for various reasons, extended the principle to require fairness in a variety of previously private arenas. In addition, some federal and state laws prescribe due process requirements for specific actions.

Basic principles of procedural due process require that a person facing an allegation or adverse action be given reasonable notice of and an opportunity to challenge the allegation, and to present evidence on her own behalf. The law requires hospitals to provide a certain amount of due process to physicians who may have their medical staff *privileges* denied, reduced, or revoked. The *Health Care Quality Improvement Act* of 1986 (HCQIA) in particular describes minimum due process requirements that a hospital must meet in order to obtain the protections of the Act.

Duke's system: A method of *staging tumors*.

dumping: The denial or limitation of the provision of medical care to, or the transfer elsewhere of, patients who are not able to pay or for which the payment method (for example, the *prospective payment system (PPS)*) does not pay the hospital enough to cover its costs. Laws intended to prevent dumping typically prohibit the transfer of patients if the transfer cannot be justified by medical necessity. Synonym(s): patient dumping, case shifting.

durable medical equipment (DME): Medical equipment, such as a wheelchair, breathing equipment, home dialysis equipment, or other equipment, that is prescribed by the physician. The term is used most often when DME is used in the home.

Dx: Shorthand for (the patient's) *diagnosis*.

E

EAP: See *employee assistance program.*

Early and Periodic Screening Diagnosis and Treatment Program (EPSDT): A program required of states by Medicaid for children under age 21 in families receiving Aid to Families with Dependent Children (AFDC). EPSDT is designed to detect physical and mental defects and arrange treatment.

ECFMG: See *Educational Commission for Foreign Medical Graduates.*

ECG: See *electrocardiogram.*

economic index: A statistical measure of the economy. One such index is the *consumer price index.*

ED: See *emergency department.*

education department: The department of the institution responsible for arranging and coordinating education and training programs (both inservice and continuing education) for employees, employee orientation and, in some circumstances, community health education programs and patient education programs.

Educational Commission for Foreign Medical Graduates (ECFMG): A nonprofit organization responsible for examining *credentials*, testing medical knowledge and English-language competency, and granting *certification* to all foreign-educated (except

E

Canadian) physicians who seek to enter clinical training programs in United States medical centers. ECFMG is sponsored by the American Hospital Association, American Medical Association, American Board of Medical Specialties, National Medical Association, Federation of State Medical Boards of the United States, Association of American Medical Colleges, and Association for Hospital Medical Education.

EEG: See *electroencephalogram*.

effectiveness: The degree to which the effort expended, or the action taken, achieves the desired effect (result or objective). For example, one drug is more effective than another if it relieves certain symptoms to a greater extent, or in a higher proportion of patients.

Effectiveness is often confused with *efficiency*; efficiency is the relationship of the amount of work accomplished to the amount of effort expended. A given hospital's food service is more efficient than another hospital's in one measure if, for example, it can furnish meals to patients for a lower average cost per meal (assuming that the meals are of equal quality). Synonym(s): efficacy.

efficacy: See *effectiveness*.

efficiency: The relationship of the amount of work accomplished to the amount of effort required. A given hospital's food service is more efficient than another hospital's in one measure if, for example, it can furnish meals to patients for a lower average cost per meal (assuming that the meals are of equal quality). Although efficiency is usually thought of in terms of cost, it can equally well be measured in other ways, such as time; for example, the automobile racing crew which can change a set of tires in the shortest time is the most efficient.

Efficiency is often confused with *effectiveness*; effectiveness means the degree to which the effort expended, or the action taken, achieves the desired effect (result or objective). For example, one drug is more effective than another if it relieves certain symptoms to a greater extent, or in a higher proportion of patients.

EHL: See *electrohydraulic lithotripsy*.

EKG: See *electrocardiogram.*

elder care: Home care of the elderly by relatives. Tax relief for families who provide home health care for an elderly relative has been proposed. Relief has also been proposed for families who care for a dependent suffering from Alzheimer's disease.

elective (1): A term that refers to treatment which is medically advisable, but not critical. Elective care (such as hospitalization, treatment, or surgery) can be scheduled in advance, in contrast to *emergency care*, which must be rendered immediately to avoid death or serious disability. See *elective surgery.*

elective (2): A situation in which delay in response or care would not jeopardize health or life. Failure to carry out the care at all might, however, have serious effects, such as disability.

electrocardiogram (ECG, EKG): The recording made in the diagnostic procedure called *electrocardiography.* "EKG" is used interchangeably with "ECG" as an abbreviation.

electrocardiography: A diagnostic procedure which records, or shows on a screen, the electrical activity of the heart muscle as it contracts and relaxes with the heartbeat. The recording is called an electrocardiogram (ECG, EKG). While ECGs may be taken directly from the heart during surgery, ECGs are routinely taken for diagnostic purposes as well: it involves placing perhaps a dozen electrodes (small plates which conduct electricity) on the skin at various locations (leads), and connecting (leading) the plates with the recording instrument (electrocardiograph). This provides a variety of views, which appear as "tracings" on the screen or recording paper. A large body of experience has been developed which permits the translation of the patient's particular array of views into diagnostic information for the physician.

electroencephalogram (EEG): The record of the electrical activity of the brain obtained by *electroencephalography.*

electroencephalography: A diagnostic procedure for determining the electrical activity of the brain by the use of equipment which makes recordings (or video displays) from electrodes (electrical contacts) which pick up the electrical impulses. The electrodes are ordinarily placed on the scalp but may, during surgery, be placed on the surface of the brain or in its interior. The record obtained is called an electroencephalogram (EEG).

electrohydraulic lithotripsy (EHL): See *lithotripsy*.

electroneurodiagnostic technologist (ENDT): One of the 26 *allied health professionals* for whom the American Medical Association's *Committee on Allied Health Education and Accreditation (CAHEA)* has accredited education programs.

electronic neural network: See *neurocomputer*.

element: A substance which cannot be decomposed by the ordinary types of chemical change, or made by chemical union. An *atom* is the smallest particle of an element.
  A "data element" is, in general usage, an "item of information." When used in connection with computers, a data element may be one part of a *data record* (a logically connected group of data elements).

eligibility: A term usually used in health care with reference to whether an individual is entitled to *benefits* under a given insurance plan, governmental program, or other *health care plan*.

ELISA: See *enzyme-linked immunosorbent assay*.

embryo: An organism in the very early stages of development. From *fertilization* of the ovum until the eighth week of growth, a human is usually considered an embryo; thereafter it is called a fetus.

EMCRO: See *experimental medical care review organization*.

emergency: A situation requiring immediate attention in order to prevent death or severe disability. A situation less critical is *urgent*. The least critical level is *elective*. See *emergency surgery* under *surgery*.

emergency department (ED): A hospital department which gives care for patients who need prompt attention. By definition, patients may not become continuing patients of an emergency department; the entire episode of emergency care is one visit. Ordinarily, an emergency department is available 24 hours a day. Also called emergency room (ER).

emergency medical service system (EMS or EMSS): A system for providing *emergency medical services* within a designated geographic area. It includes personnel, transportation, communication, equipment, and sometimes facilities. Such systems are subject to regulation by federal, state, and local agencies with respect to personnel qualifications, equipment and its maintenance, and the like.

emergency medical services: A broad term covering all services required to care for patients in emergencies, at the sites of the emergencies, in transit, and at emergency facilities. It includes emergency medical treatment; transportation arrangements; communication among vehicles, personnel, and facilities; *triage* of patients prior to and following transportation; and mobilization of personnel and resources as necessary.

emergency medical services board: A term sometimes used for the state agency with responsibility for, among other things, licensing *emergency medical technicians (EMTs)*, approving ambulances and emergency medical facilities, and similar functions.

emergency medical technician (EMT): An *allied health professional* with special training in on-site and in-transit care of injured and emergency medical patients (victims), and also in providing *emergency* care in the hospital *emergency department (ED)* if requested to. State regulations typically govern the use of specific titles for EMTs, the training required for each of several levels, supplementary training needed for special procedures (such as the administration of *intravenous* fluids, the insertion of a tube into a patient's *airway* for assistance in breathing, the use of *cardiac defibrillation* equipment, and the like). In national usage, there are three levels of EMTs, depending on training:

emergency medical technician—ambulance (EMT-A): The basic level EMT, qualified by successful completion of the *Department of*

E

Transportation (DOT) 81-hour course and *certification* by the state's *emergency medical services board.*

emergency medical technician—intermediate (EMT-I): The second level of EMT, qualified as such by first attaining the *emergency medical technician—ambulance (EMT-A)* rating, followed by specific training programs for locally-determined procedures for *intermediate* and *advanced life support.* This person may also be called an "advanced emergency medical technician" (A-EMT). In some states *"cardiac technicians"* and *"cardiac rescue technicians"* are also classed as EMT-Is.

emergency medical technician—paramedic (EMT-P): The highest of the three levels of *emergency medical technician* (EMT). The EMT-P may perform *advanced emergency medical procedures* which lower levels of EMTs may not perform. Such procedures may include, for example, insertion of a tube in the patient's airway for assistance in breathing, and administration of certain drugs.

This title may be used by an individual who has been qualified by successful completion of the *Department of Transportation (DOT)* paramedical training (15-module) program or its equivalent. State regulations may also govern its usage. One of the 26 *allied health professionals* for whom the American Medical Association's *Committee on Allied Health Education and Accreditation (CAHEA)* has accredited education programs.

emergency medicine: One of the medical specialties for which *residency* programs have been approved by the Accreditation Council for Graduate Medical Education (ACGME). See *specialty.*

emergency room (ER): See *emergency department.*

Emergency Services (ER): The chapter giving the *standards* for this component of the hospital in the 1990 *Accreditation Manual for Hospitals (AMH)* of the *Joint Commission on the Accreditation of Healthcare Organizations (JCAHO).*

emotional distress: A legal term referring to a nonphysical injury caused by malpractice or other wrongdoing. "Emotional distress" is used in the context of deciding what kinds of injury are *compensable;* that is, the kinds of injury for which a *plaintiff* can recover money from the wrongdoer. Normally, money damages are awarded for actual economic loss, such as medical expenses and lost earnings, and for noneconomic loss such as the pain and suffering which accompanies physical injury. Although emotional distress is acknowledged by the courts to be very real, money *damages* for emotional distress alone are usually not allowed unless the wrongdoing that caused it was intentional or grossly reckless. Most medical *malpractice* cases do not involve the type of *malice* or recklessness required for the allowance of damages for emotional distress.

Emotional distress is most often claimed by a third party, that is, someone who was not physically injured by the malpractice, but was nevertheless terribly disturbed. An example of such a third party would be a mother who witnesses her newborn baby being dropped by a hospital attendant; although the baby is seriously injured, the mother herself is not put in danger by the act. Therefore, the mother cannot recover for her own emotional distress. Denying the mother damages for emotional distress is an example of the "line-drawing" which courts do to limit liability, especially for unintentional behavior. Emotional distress is also called mental distress.

employee: A person who works for and is paid by another (the employer), and who is under the control of the employer. An employee is to be distinguished from an *independent contractor*, who works for himself. The line between the two is often fuzzy, but the legal consequences are important. Different tests to determine whether someone is an employee or independent contractor are used for different purposes—taxes, *workers' compensation*, *liability (1)*, unemployment insurance, and so forth. The same person can easily be both an employee and an independent contractor, at the same time, for different purposes.

employee assistance program (EAP): An *occupational health* service program to help employees with substance abuse or physical or behavioral problems deal with these problems when they affect job performance. The assistance may be provided within the organization or by referral to outside resources.

employee health benefit plan: An organization's plan for health benefits for its employees and their dependents. The term generally refers to the "package" of benefits which are provided. Such

E

plans are among the "fringe benefits" of the employees, and thus are not part of the employee's salary. The employees may or may not contribute to paying the cost by deductions from their salaries.

employee health service: A service provided by an organization to examine persons prior to employment and to give certain health care (and, often, counseling) to employees.

employee stock ownership plan (ESOP): A qualified stock bonus or combination money purchase and stock bonus plan designed to invest primarily in employer securities. Specific Internal Revenue Service (IRS) requirements must be met for setting up such a plan.

employment at will: Employment of an individual without a personal or union contract. Notwithstanding the lack of an employment contract, however, termination of such an employee under certain circumstances may subject an employer to *liability (1)* for "wrongful discharge." Such circumstances include a discharge violating an implied contract, not carried out in "good faith and fair dealing," or against public policy. For example, firing an employee who reasonably refuses to do something dangerous may be against public policy.

emporiatrics: That branch of medicine which deals with the health of travelers.

EMS: See *emergency medical service system.*

EMSS: See *emergency medical service system.*

EMT: See *emergency medical technician.*

EMT-A: Emergency medical technician—ambulance. See *emergency medical technician.*

EMT-I: Emergency medical technician—intermediate. See *emergency medical technician.*

EMT-P: Emergency medical technician—paramedic. See *emergency medical technician.*

encoding: Converting information into *code (1)*.

computer-assisted encoding: A process in which a person (*coder*) is assisted by a computer in the process of *coding*. The coder, using a computer keyboard, enters the words of the diagnosis (or other item to be coded) and the computer identifies the correct code. The better systems are "interactive" in that they "prompt" the coder to enter more detailed information, more exact terminology, or additional information in order to find the most precise term and its code. When used for diagnosis or procedure coding in the hospital, the prompting insists on careful study of the medical record, and considerably improves precision over manual coding. For example, "myocardial infarction" is a valid term to label a disease process involving the heart; a more precise term tells which part of the heart is involved, for example, "anterior (front) myocardial infarction." Each of these two terms has its own code, but the more precise code is preferred; the interactive system prompts the coder to seek the detail (which almost certainly is in the record) needed to use the detailed term rather than the more general term.

encoder: Computer software (program) for assisting in the assignment of a *code (1)* to a word or phrase expressed in natural language (human language, such as English). Encoders are found in health care primarily in disease or procedure coding. A person types the diagnostic or procedure term from the medical record on a computer keyboard, and the software looks up the word or words entered. When the words are found in the computer memory, the code is supplied, usually on the computer monitor. More sophisticated (and helpful) encoders prompt the user to seek in the medical record all the information needed to find the most accurate (detailed) code.

encounter: The personal contact between the patient and a professional health care giver. This term is typically used only with respect to personnel involved in assessment or treatment, or providing social services, not with obtaining a prescription drug from a pharmacy, for example.

end-stage renal disease (ESRD): Renal (kidney) disease in which the kidneys no longer function enough to sustain life, a condition known as renal insufficiency. Life may be sustained by kidney *transplant* in some instances, or by *hemodialysis*. Specific benefits are available for patients with ESRD under Medicare, which is the primary source for paying for long-term hemodialysis, either in the hospital or in the home.

endocrine: A kind of *organ* which produces and secretes into the body itself, generally into the blood, chemical substances called hormones which have effects on one or more other organs. The pancreas, which secretes insulin (a hormone involved in the body's use of sugar, and in diabetes), is an endocrine organ.

endocrinology: The specialty of medicine which deals with the *organs* of internal secretion, that is, organs which produce chemicals essential to specific body functions. Such chemicals (and organs) include, for example, insulin (from the pancreas) and adrenalin (from the adrenal glands).

endocrinology and metabolism: A branch of *internal medicine*. One of the medical specialties for which *residency* programs have been approved by the Accreditation Council for Graduate Medical Education (ACGME). See *specialty*.

ENDT: See *electroneurodiagnostic technologist*.

energy agent: See *agent (3)*.

ENT: See *otorhinolaryngology*.

entity: One of the items making up a universe.

entity coding: See *coding*.

entrepreneur: A person who organizes a new venture and assumes the risk. This is in contrast with the new term "intrapreneur," meaning a person *within* an organization who creates a new venture or "product" for the organization.

entropy prevention: The set of management activities directed at maintaining quality and enthusiasm in the performance of established activities and duties which are not in need of change. Entropy is a term taken from physics for the tendency of any *system*

(2) to lose energy, to "run down," if no additional energy is provided. An appreciable amount of management energy is applied to change which, while resisted, is seen as "where the action is." However, an equal or even greater amount of management energy must be applied to keep ongoing activities (systems) interesting and exciting, and to prevent quality from declining and change from occurring.

environmental assessment: A technique used in planning in which influences and events external to the organization which are felt likely to present either problems or opportunities are listed. An attempt is then made to predict the effects of these factors on the organization, and to suggest the appropriate responses. It is to be contrasted with "environmental impact," in which the effects of actions of the organization on its environment are assessed.

environmental services: A term sometimes used to include some of the services in the institution which are involved in providing for the patients, employees, and visitors a "clean" environment. It may include housekeeping, laundry, and solid and liquid waste control; however, maintenance, radiation protection, and air conditioning, for example, are unlikely to be included in this term.

enzyme-linked immunosorbent assay (ELISA): A diagnostic test used to detect acquired immunodeficiency syndrome (AIDS).

EP: See *emergency physician*.

EPI: See *Estes Park Institute*.

epidemiologic autopsy: The use of data from *autopsies* for epidemiologic studies. A method has been described for carrying out such studies by using only "surprise" findings, that is, evidences of disease other than that for which the patient was treated, and which the physician did not know the patient had. Suitable statistical *adjustments* are made so that the findings are deemed applicable to the general or a specific population.

epidemiologist: A physician or other specialist who studies diseases or causes of disease in relationship to a population, such as a hospital or a community. An epidemiologist deals primarily with analysis of existing data rather than data collected prospectively in an experimental design.

hospital epidemiologist: The person who has charge of a hospital's *infection control program*. The hospital epidemiologist may be a qualified epidemiologist or a physician or other individual assigned to the task.

medical epidemiologist: An epidemiologist who is a physician.

nurse epidemiologist: An epidemiologist who is a nurse.

epidemiology: The study of diseases or causes of disease in relationship to a population, such as a hospital or a community. Epidemiology deals primarily with the analysis of existing data rather than data collected prospectively in an experimental design.

molecular epidemiology: The study of the specific strains of pathogenic organisms which are responsible for the production of disease and epidemics. Toxicity alone is apparently not enough; the organism must also be able to colonize and invade.

episode: A series of events which is distinct in itself. For example, a period of fever which disappears may be an episode of fever within a continuous process, such as a chronic illness.

episode of care: A continuous course of care by a hospital or physician for a specific medical *problem* or condition. Often the term has a specific definition under a federal or state statute.

EPO: See *exclusive provider organization*.

EPSDT: See *Early and Periodic Screening Diagnosis and Treatment Program*.

equity: *Assets* minus *liabilities*; also called "net worth."

equivalency: A term which means, in the *Joint Commission on Accreditation of Healthcare Organizations (JCAHO) Accreditation Manual for Hospitals (AMH)*, documented compliance with a JCAHO *standard* in a manner other than that specified in the standard.

ER (1):   Emergency room. See *emergency department*.

ER (2):   See *Emergency Services*.

ESOP: See *employee stock ownership plan*.

ESRD: See *end-stage renal disease*.

Essentials and Guidelines of an Accredited Educational Program for the Surgical Technologist: Standards for educational programs for surgical technologists which were adopted by the American College of Surgeons (ACS), the American Hospital Association (AHA), the American Medical Association (AMA), and the Association of Surgical Technologists (AST). Often referred to simply as *"Essentials."*

Estes Park Institute (EPI):   An independent nonprofit corporation providing education and other services for the health care community. EPI's main programs are national conferences for hospital *medical staff organization (MSO)* officers, hospital and other health care *administrators* and *trustees*, and their spouses. EPI is based in Englewood (Denver), Colorado.

ethics committee: A hospital committee, typically with a broad representation from the medical staff, hospital administration, nursing, the clergy, social services, and others, which is concerned with education of hospital personnel on biomedical ethical issues and decisionmaking processes, formulation of institutional policies on medical-ethical issues (for example, "do not resuscitate" policies), and with review of and consultation on cases presenting ethical problems. Such committees do not make decisions on the care of individual patients, but rather act, if consulted, in an advisory and educational capacity. The role of the ethics committee varies from hospital to hospital (or other health care institution).

Ethics in Patient Referrals Act of 1988:   See *Stark bill*.

E

etiology: In common usage, the cause of a disease or disorder. Technically, however, the term "etiology" means the study of causes.

eugenics: Efforts to control reproduction as a means of improving a race, either by eliminating traits which are thought undesirable (negative eugenics) or by enhancing the frequency of traits thought desirable (positive eugenics).

euthanasia: Permitting the death of a hopelessly ill or injured person (passive euthanasia), or causing the death of that individual in a reasonably painless manner (active euthanasia) as an act of mercy. The term "euthanasia" may be applied to the policy as well as to the act. The line between active and passive euthanasia is not always clear, and some believe that asserting the *right to die* (refusing or withdrawing life-sustaining treatment) on behalf of an incompetent individual is a form of euthanasia.

evaluation of care: Assessment of the degree to which care measures up to accepted standards. See also *quality management, quality of care*.

ex officio: Membership by virtue of holding a position or office. An ex officio member of a body (such as a board of directors or a committee) may or may not have authority to vote, depending on the *bylaws* of the body.

excess coverage: See *insurance coverage*.

exclusive contract: See *contract*.

exclusive dealing: An agreement between a seller and buyer, for the seller to sell only to the buyer (or the buyer to buy only from the seller). When such an arrangement unfavorably affects competition, it may violate the federal *antitrust* laws.

exclusive provider organization (EPO): An *alternative (health care) delivery system (ADS)* which is a cross between a *health maintenance organization (HMO)* and a *preferred provider organization (PPO)*. As in PPOs, the *providers* are paid on a *fee-for-service* basis and generally the providers are not at *risk (1)*. However, *beneficiaries* have less freedom in obtaining their care from providers outside the panel than they do in PPOs (where other providers may be employed by the patient, but at some financial penalty).

exclusive remedy: See *remedy*.

exculpatory clause: A clause in a contract which releases a party from liability for its acts. Such clauses are not always enforceable.

executive: An individual who is a high-level manager, and who has authority to make significant decisions. Similar authority is implied by use of the terms employed for corporate officers, such as "president" and "vice-president." The trend is to use these terms in health care organizations where formerly such persons might have been called "administrators," implying that the decisions came from elsewhere and the person simply carried them out.

executive director: See *chief executive officer (CEO)*.

expense: The using up of an *asset* (as in *depreciation*), or the cost of providing services or making a product, during an *accounting period*. The subtraction of expenses from *revenue* gives the net *income*.

experimental medical care review organization (EMCRO): Prior to the establishment of the *Professional Standards Review Organization (PSRO)* as part of the Medicare administration, several organizations were set up under federal grants to experiment with the concept of having a body composed of physicians, external to the hospital, review the medical necessity, appropriateness, and quality of *services (1)* provided to beneficiaries of the Medicare program. After experience was gained with their operation, the EMCROs were disbanded, and legislation was enacted which established the PSRO program on a nationwide basis. Later, PSROs were replaced by *Peer Review Organizations (PROs)*.

explicit: Specifically stated. For example, if there are conditions tied to one's income which state that nothing can be spent on travel, that is an "explicit" limitation. If there are no conditions, but the income will not permit both a vacation trip and painting the house, the necessity for choice (or establishing priorities) is *"implicit"*; it goes "naturally" with the idea of limited funds. In the case of financing medical and hospital care, in the face of limited funds choices must be made as to how to spend them. In the past, the rationing has been implicit, but currently, 1990, Oregon is proposing to ration its Medicaid funds by explicit methods: certain specific benefits to children, pregnant women, and caretaker relatives of children would be rationed, and the state would in return for the waiver provide specific, stated benefits (and presumably no others) to all uninsured residents with incomes below the federal poverty line.

extern: A person, usually in medicine or dentistry, who provides medical or dental care, under professional supervision, while still a student.

external cardiac massage: See *closed-chest cardiac massage.*

extracorporeal shock wave lithotripsy (ESWL): See *lithotripsy.*

extraordinary treatment: See *treatment.*

F

FA: See *functional administration*.

FAAN: See *Fellow of the American Academy of Nursing*.

FACEP: See *Fellow of the American College of Emergency Physicians*.

FACHA: See *Fellow of the American College of Hospital Administrators*.

FACHE: See *Fellow of the American College of Healthcare Executives*.

facility (1): A heading in the American Hospital Association (AHA) listing of hospitals in its annual *Guide to the Health Care Field*. In the 1990 edition, some 77 categories are provided, which cover a mixture of physical facilities (for example, birthing room/LRDP room), equipment (for example, CT scanner), activities (for example, genetic counseling/screening services), types of care (for example, psychiatric inpatient unit), and other hospital attributes. (In the 1989 *Guide*, only 54 categories were listed.) The facilities listed in the 1990 *Guide* are:

> Adult day care program
> AIDS/ARC unit
> Alcohol/chemical dependency inpatient unit
> Alcohol/chemical dependency outpatient services
> Alzheimer's diagnostic/assessment services
> Angioplasty
> Arthritis treatment center
> Birthing room/LDRP room
> Blood bank

F

Burn care unit
Cardiac catheterization laboratory
Cardiac intensive care unit
Chronic obstructive pulmonary disease services
Community health promotion
Comprehensive geriatric assessment
CT scanner
Diagnostic radioisotope facility
Emergency department
Emergency department social work services
Emergency response (geriatric)
Extracorporeal shock-wave lithotripter (ESWL)
Fitness center
General inpatient care for AIDS/ARC
Genetic counseling/screening services
Geriatric acute care unit
Geriatrics clinics
Hemodialysis
Histopathology laboratory
Home health services
Hospice
Hospital auxiliary
Magnetic resonance imaging (MRI)
Megavoltage radiation therapy
Medical surgical or other intensive care unit
Neonatal intensive care unit
Obstetrics unit
Occupational health services
Occupational therapy services
Open-heart surgery
Organ/tissue transplant
Organized outpatient services
Organized social work services
Orthopedic surgery
Outpatient social work services
Outpatient surgery services
Patient education
Patient representative services
Pediatric acute inpatient unit
Physical therapy services
Psychiatric child/adolescent services
Psychiatric consultation-liaison services
Psychiatric education services

Psychiatric emergency services
Psychiatric geriatric services
Psychiatric inpatient unit
Psychiatric outpatient services
Psychiatric partial hospitalization program
Radioactive implants
Recreational therapy services
Rehabilitation inpatient unit
Rehabilitation outpatient services
Reproductive health services
Respiratory therapy services
Respite care
Senior membership program
Skilled nursing or other long-term care unit
Social services
Specialized outpatient program for AIDS/ARC
Speech therapy services
Sports medicine clinic/services
Therapeutic radioisotope facility
Trauma center (certified)
Ultrasound
Volunteer services department
Women's health center/services
Worksite health promotion
X-ray radiation therapy

facility (2): An institution. In the health care field, "facility" means a health care facility, which is any institution organized to provide ambulatory, inpatient, residential, or other health care.

FACPE: See *Fellow of the American College of Physician Executives.*

factor: A term used in the *International Classification of Diseases (ICD)* referring to reasons (other than disease or injury) why people come into contact with the health care system. See *problem.*

faculty practice plan: See *medical practice plan.*

false imprisonment: A *tort* in which the wrongdoing consists of depriving a person of his freedom against his will, and without legal right.

F

false negative: A diagnostic test result indicating that the patient does *not* have the condition being tested for, when in fact the patient *does* have it. A false negative leads to failure to treat a patient who has the condition in question, and a false sense of security on the part of the patient.

false positive: A diagnostic test result indicating that the patient *has* the condition being tested for, when in fact the patient does *not*. A false positive could lead to unnecessary treatment and psychological trauma.

family birth center: A family-centered unit in the hospital where mothers with normal pregnancies may, if they wish, deliver their babies in a hospital, but in a homelike environment.

family care home (FCH): A family residence which provides *rest home care* to a limited number of persons. Usually the number of persons who can be cared for is stipulated by law or regulations as, for example, six or fewer (a greater number of persons turns the facility into a "rest home" and places it under rest home licensure and supervision requirements). May also be called "adult foster home."

family planning: Efforts to determine the number of children and their spacing in a family by the use of birth control methods.

family practice (FP): The specialty of medicine which deals with providing, supervising, and coordinating the continuing general medical care of patients of all ages, primarily in family groups. The care provided is *primary care*. One of the medical specialties for which *residency* programs have been approved by the Accreditation Council for Graduate Medical Education (ACGME). See *specialty*.

family-centered maternity/newborn care: An approach to maternity and newborn care which emphasizes the physical and social needs of the entire family— mother, baby, and the others.

FAS: See *fetal alcohol syndrome*.

FCH: See *family care home.*

FDA: See *Food and Drug Administration.*

FE: See *frozen embryo.*

FEC: See *free-standing emergency center.*

Federal Register: The daily publication of the United States government in which federal administrative agencies officially publish their rules (including proposed rules subject to public comment).

Federal Trade Commission (FTC): A federal agency which has jurisdiction over unfair and deceptive trade practices. Some such practices may violate the federal *antitrust* laws. The FTC was created in 1914 by the Federal Trade Commission Act (15 U.S.C. sec. 45 (1982)).

fee: A *charge* for a *service (1)* rendered.

fee-for-service (FFS): A method of paying physicians and other health care providers in which each *service (1)* (for example, a doctor's office visit or operation) carries a *fee.* The physician's income under this system is made up from the fees she collects for services. Alternative methods of income for physicians are: (1) a salary, such as one paid by a *health maintenance organization (HMO);* and (2) a *capitation* payment system, in which the physician is paid a predetermined amount for each patient for which she assumes responsibility (rather than each service she renders) during a given period of time. Note that the capitation method can be applied via some type of organization, for example, an HMO; in that case the capitation payment is made to the HMO, which in turn pays the physician in the manner decided by the HMO.

fee schedule: A list of *charges* (or allowances) for specific *procedures* and *services (1).*

fellow: A person who has been granted status (fellowship) higher than that of membership by an association, for example, the American College of Healthcare Executives (ACHE) or the

F

American College of Physicians (ACP). The status is usually given after the candidate has met strict requirements for education and performance.

The term "fellow" is also used for certain individuals whose positions are supported by special stipends for advanced study and research, such as a "fellow in cardiology."

Fellow of the American Academy of Nursing (FAAN): A member of a state nurses association which is a constituent member of the *American Nurses' Association (ANA)* who has been elected to membership in the *American Academy of Nursing (AAN)*. There are about 500 Fellows (1988). These individuals are authorized to use the *credential* "Fellow of the American Academy of Nursing (FAAN)."

Fellow of the American College of Emergency Physicians (FACEP): A *credential* awarded by the American College of Emergency Physicians (ACEP).

Fellow of the American College of Healthcare Executives (FACHE): A *credential* awarded by the *American College of Healthcare Executives (ACHE)* to members meeting its requirements for the rank of *Fellow*. Fellows of the American College of Hospital Administrators (FACHA), that is, those individuals holding the rank of Fellow when the organization was under its former (prior to 1985) name, the American College of Hospital Administrators (ACHA), were authorized to change their designation to FACHE.

Fellow of the American College of Hospital Administrators (FACHA): A *credential* awarded by the American College of Hospital Administrators (ACHA) to members meeting its requirements for the rank of *Fellow*. When ACHA in 1985 changed its name to the *American College of Healthcare Executives (ACHE)*, members holding fellowship were authorized to change their designation to Fellow of the American College of Healthcare Executives (FACHE).

Fellow of the American College of Physician Executives (FACPE): A physician who is a member of the *American College of Physician Executives (ACPE)*, who has met its requirements for *certification* as a *physician executive*, and to whom the College has granted the distinction (a *credential*) of Fellowship.

fertile: Capable of reproducing.

fertility drug: A drug which enhances the ability of an individual to reproduce.

fertilization: The process of uniting the components necessary for reproduction, for example, a sperm and an egg, and thus starting the development of a new individual.

fetal alcohol syndrome (FAS): A pattern of birth defects found in babies as a result of the consumption of alcohol by their mothers.

feticide: Killing of a *fetus*.

fetus: An unborn baby from the eighth week after conception until the moment of birth. Prior to the eighth week, it is called an embryo.

FFS: See *fee-for-service*.

fiduciary: A person who is in a special, legal relationship of trust with respect to something or someone. A fiduciary owes a higher duty of care than a person acting only for her own benefit. Guardians, trustees, directors, and executors of estates are fiduciaries. Also, a physician is a fiduciary with respect to her patients. The term does not mean "interested in money."

"Fiduciary" is also used as an adjective, to describe the duty of a fiduciary: a trustee has a fiduciary duty to protect the assets of the hospital.

field: See *data element*.

financial director: See *chief financial officer (CFO)*.

financial statement: A "picture" of the financial condition of an institution, which consists of a *"balance sheet"* and an *"income and expense statement."* See those listings.

financial structure: The portion of an organization's *balance sheet* which shows how its *assets* are financed.

F

financing (1): A method of obtaining money. Types available to hospitals include debt financing (borrowing money), equity financing (selling ownership—shares of stock—in the institution), tax-exempt bond financing (if available), and obtaining donations (of decreasing prominence at present).

debt financing: Obtaining money by borrowing.

equity financing: Obtaining money by selling ownership in the organization (usually shares of stock).

tax-exempt bond financing: The sale of *tax-exempt bonds* in order to raise money. In some instances, *nonprofit hospitals* are permitted to issue tax-exempt bonds (a privilege ordinarily held only by government entities) and thus may use this form of financing.

financing (2): A method of paying for health care ("health care financing").

finding: An item of information about a patient which can only be elicited by laboratory, X-ray, or other diagnostic procedure, or by observation of the patient's response to therapy. The physician relies on signs (disturbances of appearance or function which can be detected by the physician or another observer), symptoms (disturbances of appearance, function, or sensation of which the patient is or should be aware), and findings in making a diagnosis.

first year resident physician: See *physician*.

first-dollar coverage: See *insurance coverage*.

fiscal: Having to do with finance.

fiscal function: The sum of the activities, wherever performed, through which the hospital achieves fiscal (financial) soundness.

fiscal intermediary: An agency, usually a Blue Cross Plan or private insurance company, selected by health care providers to pay claims under Medicare. Sometimes referred to simply as "intermediary."

fiscal period: An accounting period. A fiscal period is usually a year, and is therefore called a *fiscal year (FY)*.

fiscal year (FY): An accounting period which covers exactly one year, at the end of which books are closed, and the year's financial situation summarized. The fiscal year may or may not be the calendar year.

fitness program: A program intended to achieve and maintain a state of physical well-being which permits optimal performance.

flexible spending account (FSA): A account managed by an employer that allows employees to set aside pretax funds for medical, dental, legal, and day-care services. FSAs may be components of "cafeteria plans" for providing health care which allow employees to choose among various levels of *benefit* coverage.

float pool: A pool (group) of nurses without regular assignment to a patient care unit who are kept in readiness to serve as float nurses, that is, to be assigned wherever needed to fill in for absences or to meet extraordinary workloads.

fluoroscope: A device by which *X-ray images* may be viewed directly as the X-rays pass through the patient. The X-rays are projected on a screen which responds to being hit by the rays in the same manner as a film does. The viewer can see in the fluoroscope the movement of the body organs, and the passage of *radiopaque* substances. The physician carrying out a *barium enema*, for example, can manipulate the abdomen and get a variety of views of the bowel (she also takes films for detailed study and permanent records).

FMC: See *foundation for medical care.*

FMG: See *foreign medical graduate.*

focus group: A group of individuals convened to give their thoughts on a given subject. Focus groups are being used, for example, in market research.

focused survey: See *survey.*

F

Food and Drug Administration (FDA): The agency of the federal government responsible for controlling the sale and use of *drugs*, including the licensing of new drugs for use in humans.

food service: Provision of meals and other nourishments to patients and personnel, and special nutritional services for patients, such as diet modification. Synonym(s): dietary service.

for-profit: See *for-profit corporation* under *corporation* and *for-profit hospital* under *hospital*.

foreign medical graduate (FMG): A graduate from a medical school outside the United States and Canada. In order to practice in the United States, an FMG must be certified by the *Educational Commission for Foreign Medical Graduates (ECFMG)*, have one or more years of *accredited residency* training, and meet other requirements of the *state medical board*. There are two kinds of FMGs:

alien FMG: A foreign medical graduate (FMG) who was not a United States citizen at the time of obtaining his medical education.

United States foreign medical graduate (USFMG): A foreign medical graduate (FMG) who was a United States citizen when he obtained the medical education in a foreign country.

forensic medicine: The branch of medicine which deals with legal questions, such as poisonings, causes of death and injury, and the like.

forms 1007 and 1008: Forms used in the Medicare *prospective payment system (PPS)* to calculate a hospital's adjustments to its *base year Medicare costs*.

formulary (1): A document containing recipes for the preparation (compounding) of medicinal drugs. An example of such a volume is the *National Formulary (NF)*, an official publication of the United States Pharmacopeia Convention (USPC). *Pharmacopeias*, issued by various nations, contain not only the recipes, but also standards as to the strengths and purity of drugs. In the United States, USPC also issues the *Pharmacopeia of the United States of America (USP)*, which is a legal standard.

formulary (2): Within the hospital, the term "formulary" is applied to the list of drugs which are routinely stocked by the hospital *pharmacy (2)* and which are available for immediate dispensing; drugs not in the formulary will have to be obtained by special order from other sources.

foster care home: A *facility (2)* that provides *custodial care* (housekeeping and meals) for individuals unable to do these things for themselves.

foundation for medical care (FMC): A nonprofit organization, usually of physicians, that provides *medical services review* or *utilization review* of a specific population under a *prepayment* contract for health care.

fourth party: A recent term in health care financing. The first two parties were the *patient* and the *provider*. The *third party* was a *payer* other than the patient, such as *Blue Cross and Blue Shield (BC/BS)*, *commercial insurance*, or government. The term "fourth party" is sometimes used to designate industry or business, which buys health care for its employees, with or without the services of a third party.

FP: See *family practice*.

fractionation: The process of separation of the *blood components* of whole blood.

fraud: Obtaining products, services, or reimbursement by intentional false statements. Fraud includes such acts as misrepresenting eligibility or need for services, and claiming reimbursement for services not rendered or for nonexistent patients. Fraud is illegal and may carry civil and criminal penalties. Medicare law specifically prohibits fraud; see *fraud and abuse*.

fraud and abuse: The criminal misuse of the Medicare system. The crime consists of such behavior as filing false claims for Medicare reimbursement (such as for nonexistent patients, or *services (1)* that were never performed), paying or receiving "kickbacks" for patient referral, and so forth. Fraud and abuse is a felony which may be punished by fines up to $25,000 or five years in prison, or

F

both, and automatic suspension from participation in Medicare and Medicaid. 42 U.S.C. sec. 1395nn(b). See also *abuse, safe harbor regulations,* and *Stark bill.*

free-standing ambulatory care center: A *free-standing facility* which provides health and allied services to patients who do not require overnight lodging in an inpatient facility. To be designated an "ambulatory care center," free-standing or not, the facility is expected to have an organized professional staff. Free-standing ambulatory care centers appear to be classified into several levels: those of the highest level can provide *emergency care;* those of a lower level, *urgent care;* those at the lowest level, *primary care.*

free-standing emergency center (FEC): A *free-standing facility,* separate from the hospital, which provides services to patients needing immediate care. Such a facility has X-ray and laboratory services, and has arrangements for transportation and hospitalization of patients who require it.

free-standing facility: A *facility (2)* which is not a physical part of a hospital or other health care facility. A free-standing facility may be a facility for carrying out ambulatory surgery, emergency care, or other care. "Free-standing" does not necessarily indicate separate ownership; a hospital may operate a free-standing facility or the facility may be owned by a separate organization.

free-standing urgent care center: A *free-standing facility,* separate from a hospital, for providing *urgent care.* Such a center is set up for problems less serious than those which require *emergency care.* It is generally stated that such a center must have certain laboratory and X-ray services, but that it must not hold itself out as ready for emergencies such as those brought by an ambulance, nor should it offer continuity of care.

frozen embryo (FE): An ovum (egg) which has been fertilized and then frozen prior to introduction into the uterus (womb). Such ova are obtained from women who are taking *fertility drugs* and as a result produce more than the normal one ovum per month. Fertilization is carried out *in vitro* (outside the body). Frozen embryos have been kept for as long as two years before implantation. The procedure is controversial, since it raises a number of ethical and legal issues. This is one technique used in *noncoital reproduction*.

FSA: See *flexible spending account*.

FSOP: Free-standing surgical outpatient facility.

FTC: See *Federal Trade Commission*.

FTE: See *full-time equivalent*.

full-time equivalent (FTE): A concept used in developing statistics on the size of a work force. The idea is to express a work force made up of both full- and part-time employees as the number of workers that would be employed if all were full time. It is computed by dividing the total hours worked by all employees in a given time period by the number of work hours in the time period. Thus an FTE would be, for example, one person working a normal work week, two people working half time, and so on.

functional administration (FA): The traditional type of administration of an organization. Other forms of organization of the same institution are *product administration (PA)* and *market administration (MA)*. In a hospital, FA focuses on the organization's functional components, such as nursing and pathology. PA focuses on services or programs, such as surgery and internal medicine; and MA focuses on the hospital's markets, such as the elderly, women, and specific payers.

fund (1): When used as a verb, means to set aside an asset for a specific purpose, e.g., to "fund depreciation" means to set aside money at a rate determined by estimating the time before a given piece of equipment will have to be replaced so that, at the end of that time, there will be enough money to replace it.

fund (2): An asset set aside for a given purpose, e.g., a building fund, which is to be used only for that purpose.

debt service fund: See *debt service reserve fund (DSRF)*.

debt service reserve fund (DSRF): A fund to account for accumulating and paying out the funds necessary to retire long term debt which is not to be paid from specific sources. The term is used especially in government accounting. Synonym(s): debt service fund.

endowment fund: A fund whose principal must be kept intact; only the interest income from the fund may be used. Sometimes called a permanent fund.

general fund: Money that can be used; that is, money that has not been set aside ("funded") for a specific purpose. In governmental usage, the "general fund" has the same meaning, that is, it has not been set aside for social security, for example. Synonym(s): unrestricted fund.

permanent fund: See *endowment fund*.

sinking fund: Usually refers to a fund in which money is set aside to pay off financial obligations, for example, to retire bonds.

specific-purpose fund: A fund the principal and interest from which can only be used for the purpose specified. The restriction may be imposed by the terms of a gift or by *governing body* action.

unrestricted fund: See *general fund*.

fund balance: A term often used by nonprofit organizations in their financial statements to indicate the difference between *assets* and *liabilities*. A positive fund balance is sometimes called a gain; in the profit sector, it would be called a *profit*. A negative fund balance is a *loss* in either sector. Nonprofit organizations may also refer to the fund balance as "revenues over (under) expenses."

fund-raising: Planned and coordinated activities by which the organization seeks gifts. Fund-raising goes under the term "development," and the fund-raising director is called "the director of development."

funds: Available money resources. A number of kinds of funds are discussed in connection with hospital finance:

board-designated funds: Funds which were *unrestricted funds* but were later set aside by action of the *governing body* for specific purposes or projects.

bond sinking funds: Funds in which *assets* are accumulated in order to liquidate *bonds* at or before their maturity dates.

restricted funds: Funds that can be expended only for the specific purpose for which they were obtained.

unrestricted funds: Funds which the *governing body* can use at its discretion, as contrasted with *restricted funds*, those which can only be used for the purpose for which they were given or obtained.

FY: See *fiscal year*.

G

gainsharing: Sharing with employees any increase in revenue which is the result of gains in *productivity*. Gainsharing is a form of incentive program or profit-sharing (the term "profit" is not used in the nonprofit environment).

gaming: Attempting to manipulate "the system" in an illegal or unethical manner. The terms "gaming" and "to game the system" are used, for example, in connection with efforts to bill under the *prospective payment system (PPS)* in such a way as to maximize income by giving as the *principal diagnosis* that diagnosis which places the patient in the highest-priced *Diagnosis Related Group (DRG)*, even though a lower-priced one more correctly reflects the patient's *problem* and the *services (1)* rendered.

GAO: See *General Accounting Office*.

gastroenterology (GI): The branch of *internal medicine* which deals with the digestive (gastrointestinal (GI)) system. One of the medical specialties for which *residency* programs have been approved by the Accreditation Council for Graduate Medical Education (ACGME). See *specialty*.

gatekeeper: The person who is responsible for determining the *services (1)* to be provided to a patient and coordinating the provision of the appropriate care. The purposes of the gatekeeper's function are: (1) to improve the quality of care by considering the whole patient, that is, all the patient's problems and other relevant factors; (2) to ensure that all necessary care is obtained; and (3) to reduce unnecessary care (and cost). When, as is often the case, the gatekeeper is a physician, she is a *primary care physician* and usually must, except in an emergency, give the first level of care to the patient before the patient is permitted to be seen by a *secondary care* physician (*specialist*). In fact, the gatekeeper must refer the patient for the secondary care. Also called "patient care manager."

GB: See *Governing Body*.

General Accounting Office (GAO): The agency of the federal government which is the auditing arm of the legislative branch and its financial consultant.

general practitioner (GP): A physician who does not hold *specialty* qualifications, and who does not restrict his practice to any particular field of medicine. Sometimes called a family practitioner. In recent years it has become possible for a physician to specialize in family medicine (become board certified in that specialty), and become a *family practice* (FP) specialist. General practitioners and family practice specialists, as well as certain other specialists, are primary care physicians in that they refer patients to other physician specialists when more in-depth knowledge and skill are required to care for a given patient's condition. See also *primary care physician*.

general surgery: That branch of surgery which is often defined as dealing with surgical problems of all kinds. However, general surgery does not include the more complex procedures of the *surgical specialties* such as orthopedic surgery, hand surgery, and vascular surgery.

generic: Relating to or characteristic of a whole group. The term is often used in connection with drugs, where the meaning is slightly different; in this usage, a drug is "generic" when it is dispensed under its chemical name rather than under the proprietary or trade name of a particular firm's brand of that chemical. When a drug is initially introduced it typically has been patented, and cannot be manufactured by other firms except under license or until expiration of the patent. When the patent expires, however, other firms may produce the drug under their own trade names. When the patent protection has been removed, the drug may be sold as a

G

generic equivalent (under its chemical name), usually at a lower price than under a brand name.

"Generic" is also used in this volume to describe a term which applies to a class of things, of which there are several types, each of which would be a specific rather than a generic type. For example, the term "steering committee" is described as "generic," while the term "building program steering committee" would be "specific."

generic equivalent: A drug sold under its chemical (*generic*) name when patent and trademark protection for the drug under a proprietary or trade name has expired. Generic equivalents are generally less costly than the trademarked product. In many states, substitution of a generic equivalent by a pharmacist is permitted (or required) unless the physician specifically orders that the trademarked product be dispensed. The physician who specifically describes a trademarked product may feel that the generic drug has some differences not detectable by simple chemical analysis; for example, he may believe that its ability to dissolve may not be as good as the brand name product, or that it is not produced with as good quality control as that of a major drug firm which he trusts. The physician's reasons for choosing a trademarked product over a generic one are often well-founded.

generic screening: See *screening (1)*.

genetic counseling: Counseling to potential parents as to the likelihood of their offspring having genetic (hereditary) defects or diseases.

geriatric: Pertaining to elderly people.

geriatric consultation team: An in-hospital team, typically consisting of a physician, a clinical nurse specialist, and a social worker, all specialized in *geriatric* medicine and the problems of the elderly. Such a team evaluates the needs of a geriatric patient on admission to the hospital and provides recommendations on the patient's care to the *direct care providers*.

geriatrician: A physician specializing in the diagnosis and treatment of problems and diseases of the elderly.

geriatrics: That branch of medicine which deals with elderly people. Also called geriatric medicine. One of the medical specialties for which *residency* programs have been approved by the Accreditation Council for Graduate Medical Education (ACGME). See *specialty*.

gerodentistry: Dentistry of geriatric (elderly) patients.

gerontology: The study of the diseases and problems of aging and the elderly.

   preventive gerontology: Preventive services for the elderly in order to avoid illness and disability.

GI: See *gastroenterology*.

GME: See *graduate medical education*.

GMENAC: Graduate Medical Education National Advisory Committee.

going bare: Slang for practicing without *professional liability insurance* coverage.

golden parachute: See *parachute*.

good faith: A legal term which means honest in fact, and describes the state of mind of someone acting without intent to defraud or injure, but with the intent of carrying out his legal and professional obligations honestly and fairly, without ulterior or dishonest motive.

Good Samaritan statute: A state law which protects a volunteer who stops at the scene of an accident and assists the victims, making that volunteer immune from suit as long as he did not act maliciously or recklessly. Most states have such a law.

governing board: See *governing body*.

G

governing body: The body which is legally responsible for the hospital's policies, organization, management, and quality of care. It is often called the "hospital board," "board of trustees," "governing board," or "board of directors." Individual members of the body are "trustees" or "directors," depending on the name of the body. The governing body is *accountable* in turn to the owner of the hospital, which may, for example, be a corporation, a unit of government, or the community. There is a growing tendency to call the governing body the "board of directors" in order to emphasize its role in establishing policy and directing the hospital toward goals. The term "board of trustees" is losing some favor because trusteeship may be equated with safeguarding rather than achieving. Synonym(s): hospital board, board of trustees, governing board, board of directors.

Governing Body (GB): The chapter giving the *standards* for this component of the hospital in the 1990 *Accreditation Manual for Hospitals (AMH)* of the *Joint Commission on the Accreditation of Healthcare Organizations (JCAHO)*.

GP: See *general practitioner*.

graduate: An individual who has attained a given academic degree or has been certified as completing an education program not leading to a degree.

graduate medical education (GME): Formal education in *residency* programs. Graduate medical education is only available to those holding Doctor of Medicine (MD) or Doctor of Osteopathy (DO) degrees.

graduate year one (GY-1): The term now applied to the *residency* position for a physician who has already had formal training in medicine, and who is now obtaining his first year of supervised practical training. This position may also be called a "first year residency," and the person may be called a "first year resident physician."

 The term "internship" was formerly given to this position, but "intern" is no longer restricted to physicians; the term is applied in many disciplines.

G

graft: See *transplant*.

group practice: A medical practice consisting of three or more physicians or dentists, associated to share offices, expenses, and income.

   multi-specialty group practice: Group practice offering more than one medical *specialty*.

   prepaid group practice: Group practice providing care for a defined population under a *prepayment* arrangement.

   single-specialty group practice: Group practice in which all members of the group practice the same *specialty*.

group purchasing: A *shared service* which combines the purchasing power of individual hospitals in order to obtain lower prices for equipment and supplies.

GROUPER: A specific computer program (logic) by which patient bills under Medicare are classified to their *Diagnosis Related Groups (DRGs)*, using the *Uniform Hospital Discharge Data Set (UHDDS)* which contains up to five *diagnoses* and four *procedures* coded by the *International Classification of Diseases, 9th Revision, Clinical Modification (ICD-9-CM)* along with other standardized information about the patient.

guardian: A person who has the legal responsibility, and the authority to make decisions, for an *incompetent (1)* person or a *minor*. A guardian is appointed by a court. Sometimes the guardian will only make decisions about money and property management, and the protected person may still make personal decisions. In other cases, the guardian may make personal decisions, such as those regarding health care. Some guardians have the authority to make both personal and property-management decisions. The written guardianship order specifically states the authority of the guardian. Synonym(s): committee of the incompetent, conservator.

   guardian ad litem: A guardian appointed by a court to represent the interests of a *minor* or *incompetent (1)* person during a lawsuit or other court proceeding. A guardian ad litem normally has no authority over the person or property of the ward.

G

guardian of the person: A guardian who has the authority to make personal decisions concerning the *incompetent (1)* person, such as those regarding health care. Usually, the guardian of the person does not control the finances of the incompetent person.

guest bed program: See *hotel-hospital.*

Guide to the Health Care Field (AHA Guide): An annual directory of hospitals, multihospital systems, health-related organizations, and *American Hospital Association (AHA)* members, published by AHA.

guidelines: Suggestions promulgated by an *administrative agency* as to procedure or interpretations of law. Guidelines are less binding than *regulations*, which have the force of law.

GY-1: See *graduate year one.*

gynecology: The branch of medicine dealing with disorders of the female reproductive system.

H

HAD: See *health care alternatives development.*

halfway house: A *facility (2)*, which includes living quarters, for persons who require continuing treatment for mental illness or substance abuse (including alcoholism), but who no longer need hospitalization. The *rehabilitation* services provided include guidance. Synonym(s): community living facility.

hand surgery: That branch of surgery which specializes in surgical treatment of diseases of and injuries to the hand. One of the medical specialties for which *residency* programs have been approved by the Accreditation Council for Graduate Medical Education (ACGME). See *specialty.*

hardware: The physical components of the computer (keyboard, *cathode ray tube*, disk drives, and so on), as contrasted with the computer programs, which are called "software." Synonym(s): computer hardware.

hazardous area: A term used in health care facilities usually to mean an area with a fire hazard greater than usual. Specific definition in this usage can be found in the *Life Safety Code.*

hazardous materials: Substances, such as radioactive or chemical materials, which are dangerous to humans and other living things. Many hospitals have "hazardous materials plans" which are similar to (and sometimes incorporated within) their *disaster preparedness plans* and which deal specifically with handling emergencies involving hazardous materials. In the event of a nuclear

H

or toxic chemical accident, the plan would go into effect.

For example, a special entrance to the hospital is required to permit control over incoming patients, so that they and their clothing may be decontaminated; hospital staff must be specially garmented; air flow must be controlled to prevent contamination of other areas of the hospital; and so on.

hazardous waste: Waste materials which are dangerous to living things, and so require special precautions for disposal. Hazardous waste includes radioactive materials, toxic chemicals, and biological waste (blood, tissue, etc.) which can transmit disease (also called "infectious waste"). In health care, items disposed of regularly include used hypodermic needles, surgical sponges, and other products containing blood and body fluids. A special concern is contaminated needles; a needlestick is one way in which *AIDS* and *hepatitus B* can be transmitted. Hospitals are taking great care to ensure proper disposal of hazardous waste; precautions include special, stick-proof containers for needles, colored bags to signal biological waste (red, for example), and other special handling.

HBV: Hepatitus B virus. See *hepatitus B.*

HCFA: See *Health Care Financing Administration.*

HCO: See *health care organization.*

HCPCS: HCFA (Health Care Financing Administration) Common Procedure Coding System.

HCPOTP: Health care professionals other than physicians.

HCQIA: See *Health Care Quality Improvement Act.*

health: As defined by the World Health Organization (WHO), "a state of complete physical, mental, and social well-being and not merely the absence of disease or infirmity." The most frequent criticism of the WHO's definition is its use of the word "complete." In common usage, "health" is much like the word "quality" in that it is modified by adjectives in such phrases as "poor health," "good health," or "failing health." In this context, the WHO definition would be that of, perhaps, "optimum health" or "maximum health." It is worth noting that increasing attention is being given to *quality of life*.

health advocacy: An allied health field which originated as "patient advocacy," that is, efforts to help resolve patients' complaints in relation to medical care and hospital and other health care services and with the protection of their rights. Thus health advocacy was originally the field of the patient advocate or patient representative, also known as an "ombudsperson."

Today, however, the person who serves as the advocate of an individual patient's interests is but one variety of "health advocate." Health advocacy is practiced not only by patient advocates, but also by advocates for groups of people in health programs, by program specialists in health foundations, by patient advocates for special populations or interest groups, and by legislative specialists in health. The current trend is for this broader advocacy to be a joint effort of consumers and professionals.

health advocate: See *patient advocate*.

health care: Services of health care professionals and their agents which are addressed at: (1) *health promotion*; (2) prevention of illness and injury; (3) monitoring of *health*; (4) maintenance of health; and (5) treatment of diseases, disorders, and injuries in order to obtain cure, or failing that, optimum comfort and function (*quality of life*).

health care administration: The profession dealing with the management of health care organizations.

health care alternatives development (HAD): A term that refers to the development of *alternative delivery systems (ADSs (1,2))* and *alternative financing systems (AFSs)*. One must seek the context of this term to understand just what is meant.

health care coalition: An organization working on broad health care concerns, ordinarily including hospital and health care costs, and typically with *provider*, business, and consumer participation. Often there is government participation as well.

business health care coalition: A health care coalition comprised of or organized by business firms concerned with health care problems, primarily those problems affecting employees of the member companies. Such a coalition is also likely to have *providers* and consumers as members.

health care consultant: A person who holds herself out as an *independent contractor* to provide professional advice and services to hospitals, often concerning management matters and planning. The American Association of Healthcare Consultants (AAHC) recognizes consultants in several specialties: Strategic Planning and Marketing; Organization and Management; Human Resource Management; Facilities Programming and Planning; Finance; Operations and Information Systems; and Health Specialist. Synonym(s): hospital consultant.

health care delivery: A term sometimes used as a synonym for "comprehensive health care delivery system." However, the term "health care delivery" applies to providing any of the wide array of *health care* services as well as to the totality.

health care delivery system: A term without specific definition, referring to all the facilities and services, along with methods for financing them, through which health care is provided.

Health Care Financing Administration (HCFA):   The division of the *Department of Health and Human Services (DHHS)* which administers the Medicare and Medicaid programs at the federal level.

health care institution: As commonly used, any institution dealing with health. Some definitions state that an institution, to qualify for this term, must have an *organized professional staff*. However, there are no regulations, such as standards for the licensure or registry of institutions, which currently restrict the use of this term.

health care management: The efforts of employers and labor unions, separately and jointly, to devise and carry out strategies for providing health care and controlling its quality and cost.

health care organization (HCO): An organizational form for health care delivery in which the financial *risk (1)* is assumed by the organization, rather than individuals.

health care plan: An organized service to provide stipulated medical, hospital, and related *services (1)* (*benefits*) to individuals under a *prepayment* contract. The plan may be offered by a *Blue Cross/Blue Shield (BC/BS)* plan, an insurance company, a *health maintenance organization (HMO)*, a *health care organization (HCO)*, or other organization.

health care professional: In general usage, an individual with special education or training in a health-related field, whether she is practicing her profession or not. A Doctor of Medicine (MD), for example, is a physician, and meets the definition of "health care professional," even though she may never have been certified by a professional organization and may not be licensed to practice. Some definitions of the term "health care professional" restrict its use to individuals who have been awarded *credentials* by a governmental agency or professional organization.

health care proxy: A document which authorizes a designated person to make health care decisions in the event that the signer is incapable of making those decisions. State law governs whether such a document is valid, how it must be created, and to what extent the proxy is authorized to make health care decisions. For example, a proxy may not be able to consent to electroconvulsive therapy or sterilization.

Health Care Quality Improvement Act (HCQIA): A federal act of 1986 which (1) gives certain protection from lawsuits to physicians and hospitals for *peer review* activities and (2) sets up a national clearinghouse of information on disciplinary and *malpractice* actions against physicians. 42 U.S.C. Secs. 11101- 11152.

The title of the section concerning peer review is "Encouraging Good Faith Professional Review Activities." Participants in peer review activities who comply with the law are protected from liability, except for violation of civil rights or government enforcement of antitrust or other laws. The peer review must be done in *good faith* (without malice or ulterior motive, such as driving a competitor out of business), and anyone providing information to a review committee must also provide it in good faith.

Hospitals under the Act also receive certain protections from liability for peer review activities and physician sanctions. To obtain the protection, the hospital must provide specified minimum *due process* procedures (basically, a fair hearing) to physicians prior to taking adverse action on privileges.

The second portion of the Act creates the *National Practitioners Data Bank*; for further discussion, see that term.

health economics: The branch of economics (a social science) which deals with the provision of health care services, their delivery, and their use, with special attention to quantifying the demands for such services, the costs of such services and of their delivery, and the benefits obtained.   More emphasis is given to the costs and benefits of health care to a population than to the individual.

health education: Education which is directed at increasing the information of individuals and populations, especially communities, about health and its maintenance and the prevention of disease and injury; bringing about modifications in the behavior of individuals so as to achieve better health; and changing social policy in the direction of a more healthful environment and practices.

health facility licensing agency: A state agency which sets standards and issues permits for the operation of health *facilities (2)*.

health fair: A type of community *health education* activity in which exhibits are the main method used and in which free diagnostic services such as chest X-rays and *multiphasic screening* are sometimes offered.

Health Insurance Association of America (HIAA):   An organization made up of companies writing health insurance.

Health Insurance for the Aged: See *Medicare*.

health IRA: See *individual health care account (IHCA)*.

health maintenance: All efforts carried out in order to preserve *health*. As used in the term *health maintenance organization (HMO)*, however, the term is not so inclusive, but rather simply includes those efforts which are required under the contract between the subscriber (person enrolled) and the HMO.

health maintenance organization (HMO): A health care providing organization which ordinarily has a closed group ("panel") of physicians (and sometimes other health care professionals), along with either its own hospital or allocated beds in one or more hospitals. Individuals (usually families) "join" an HMO, which agrees to provide "all" the medical and hospital care they need, for a fixed, predetermined fee. Actually, each subscriber (person enrolled) is under a contract stipulating the limits of the service (not "all" the care needed). Such a contract is called a *risk contract*, and the HMO is therefore called a "risk contractor."

open-ended health maintenance organization: See *point of service option (health care plan) (POS)*.

social/health maintenance organization (S/HMO): A newer type of *long-term care (LTC)* "alternative" organization under experimentation in which one provider, under a capitation payment (a fixed fee for each individual covered), furnishes both social and health care services for (currently) low income individuals.

health physicist: A physicist concerned primarily with *radiation*, its uses and dangers. She may be involved in research, environmental safety and control, *radiation therapy*, or other applications of her expertise. Synonym(s): radiation therapist.

health planning: Planning (a formal activity directed at determining goals, policies, and procedures) for a health care facility, a health program, a defined geographic area, or a population. Health planning may be carried out by the organization itself or by a planning agency. When it is carried out for an area, and the people in the area itself furnish the initiative, it is called "community-based planning."

health planning guidelines: A set of *guidelines*, issued by the United States *Department of Health and Human Services (DHHS)* in

H

response to 1974 federal legislation, to assist state and local health planning agencies with their activities and policies.

Health Policy Agenda for the American People (HPA): A program spearheaded by the American Medical Association (AMA) to develop a set of proposals for improving health and health care in America. Among organizations sending representatives to HPA were the American Association of Retired Persons (AARP), American Nurses Association (ANA), Blue Cross and Blue Shield Association (BC/BSA), Business Roundtable, Health Insurance Association of America (HIAA), United States Chamber of Commerce, and various state and national medical and specialty associations. Completion of the agenda development was accomplished in 1986. A summary giving the 195 recommendations was published in early 1987 in the *Journal of the American Medical Association (JAMA)*.

health promotion: Efforts to change peoples' behavior in order to promote healthy lives and, to the extent possible, prevent illnesses and accidents and to minimize their effects, rather than having people use the health care system for "repairs." A health promotion program may include *health risk appraisal* of the individuals, and may give attention to fitness, stress management, smoking, cholesterol reduction, weight control, nutrition, cancer screening, and other matters on the basis of the risks detected. Synonym(s): wellness program.

health record analyst (HRA): A person who analyzes *data* from *medical records* and other sources for hospital management and medical staff. An HRA may abstract data from the records for computer input; however, *analysis* and *abstracting* are distinctly different functions, ordinarily carried out by different people. Analysis requires interpretation, while abstracting is basically a clerical function. An HRA is the same as a medical record analyst (MRA).

health-related care institution: A *facility (2)* providing some kind of health care to inpatients who do not require full nursing services.

health-related services: A term apparently used to include everything in the health care field except *medical care* (physician services).

health resources: Personnel (both *professional* and supportive), *facilities (2)*, funds, and technology which are available or could be made available for health services.

health risk appraisal: A technique for determining for a given individual the factors most likely to result in illness, injury, or premature death. The determination is based on comparing a set of data about the individual (her database) with statistics on the likelihood of specific illnesses, injuries, and causes of death among large groups of persons for whom the same database has been collected and analyzed. Included in the database are the individual's age, sex, physical condition, genetic background, behavior, environment, and other factors, obtained by examination of the individual, laboratory tests, and information obtained from the person by a questionnaire.

   The purpose of the appraisal is preventive, that is, to be able to prescribe measures and programs to counter the risks detected. For example, elevated blood pressure would be a risk whenever it occurs; inability to swim would be an especially great risk factor in a child exposed to water sports; and driving a motor vehicle would be a risk factor when a patient requires certain drugs which interfere with the ability to drive. Synonym(s): health risk assessment.

health risk assessment: See *health risk appraisal.*

health service area: A specific geographic area considered in the governmental *health planning* process. The boundaries of health service areas were established in compliance with 1974 federal legislation on the basis of population, political subdivisions, geography, and other factors. The term "health service area" may also be used more loosely to mean *service area*, the area from which a facility or program actually draws its patients or clients, that is, its "catchment area."

health services: A term without specific definition which pertains to any services which are health-related.

H

health services research: Research pertaining to the *efficiency* and *effectiveness* of various organizational forms for health care delivery, administrative approaches, relationship to needs, and like matters.

health status: The state of *health* of an individual or population. A description of health status is usually given either in vague lay terms, for example, "good," or as a *health status index*, which may appear more *objective* and meaningful than it really is.

health status index: A statistic which attempts to quantify the *health status* of an individual or a population. Such indices are developed using *health status indicators*. Statements of health status have not been developed to the point that they have standard definitions; each publication using such indices should give full details on the indicators used, their aggregation into the indices themselves, and any other pertinent methodological detail, such as the *sampling* techniques used (in the case of health status indices for populations).

health status indicator: A measurement of some attribute of individual or community health which is considered to reflect *health status*. Each attribute is given a numerical value, and a score (a *health status index*) is calculated for the individual or community from the aggregate of these values.

To the extent possible, the indicators are objective, that is, they are facts for which various observers or investigators would each find the same value. In the case of a community, such statistics as *mortality* and *morbidity* rates are sometimes used. For health status of individuals (and thus of the group), data may be obtained by *sampling* (obtaining data on only a properly-selected portion of the population). Such facts may be obtained by examination of individuals or by questionnaires inquiring as to physical function, *quality of life, activities of daily living (ADL)*, emotional well-being, episodes of medical care, and the like.

Much study has been and is being given to developing indicators and indices of health status. No standard measures have appeared. Published data on health status should be "taken with a grain of salt" unless the reader can satisfy herself as to the methodological detail of obtaining data on the indicators and calculating the indices.

health survey: An investigation of an area or population in order to obtain information about some aspect of the *health* of its population (its health problems, its health resources, or anything else pertaining to health). Such a survey typically employs *sampling*, and may obtain information from direct observations, questionnaires, published data, or other sources.

health systems agency (HSA): A nonprofit organization or agency set up under federal law to perform health planning functions, develop a *health systems plan*, conduct *certificate of need (CON)* reviews, and review the use of certain federal funds.

health systems plan: A five-year plan prepared by a *health systems agency (HSA)*.

hearsay: A statement made out of the courtroom, which is offered into evidence during a trial to prove the substance of what was said. The "hearsay rule" makes hearsay not *admissible* as evidence; however, there are many exceptions. A notable exception for hospitals is the business record exception, which makes admissible written statements made in the ordinary course of business. The *medical record* is usually accepted as a business record; thus its contents are admissible in court unless excluded for other reasons (such as privilege or irrelevancy). See also *privileged communication*.

heart-lung machine: A machine through which a patient's blood is circulated, bypassing the patient's heart, during surgery on the heart. The machine supplies the heart's pumping function during the operation, and also acts as a lung, supplying oxygen to the blood.

hematology (1): The study of blood and blood-forming tissues: chemistry, structure, physiology, biology, and diseases.

hematology (2) (medicine): The branch of *internal medicine* dealing with the blood and blood-forming organs. One of the medical specialties for which *residency* programs have been approved by the Accreditation Council for Graduate Medical Education (ACGME). See *specialty*.

H

hematology (3) (pathology): The branch of *pathology* which deals with the blood and blood-forming organs. One of the medical specialties for which *residency* programs have been approved by the Accreditation Council for Graduate Medical Education (ACGME). See *specialty*.

hemodialysis: A therapeutic (treatment) technique in which blood (hemo-) is passed through a tube made of a special material which permits some of the contents of the blood, such as certain waste products, to pass through the walls of the tubing and be removed from the blood. Other contents of the blood, which cannot pass through the tubing walls, are retained and returned to the body. This selective filtering is called *"dialysis."* The technique is used in patients with kidney (renal) failure, and may be carried out in the hospital or, in certain circumstances, in the home.

home hemodialysis: The carrying out of hemodialysis in the home. Ordinarily, patients and their families are not trained in, nor is the home equipped for, this procedure except in cases of long term illness such as *end-stage renal disease (ESRD)*.

hemodialysis unit: A unit of the hospital set up to treat patients with certain renal (kidney) disorders by the use of *hemodialysis*. Synonym(s): renal dialysis unit, dialysis unit.

hepatitis B: Hepatitis (inflammation of the liver) caused by hepatitis B virus (HBV). The virus is most commonly transmitted by contaminated needles, blood, or blood products. However, hepatitis B may also be transmitted when bodily secretions such as saliva or semen are in contact with mucous membranes, particularly during sexual contacts; thus, hepatitis B is classed as a *sexually transmitted disease (STD)*. Synonym(s): serum hepatitis, transfusion hepatitis.

hereditary: Having to do with the transmission or characteristics, through the cellular structure of the individual, from parent to offspring.

heterogeneous: Composed of a mixture of things. For example, a *Diagnosis Related Group (DRG)* which is heterogeneous is one that is composed of patients with a variety of *diagnoses*, as contrasted

Slee, Health Care Terms 2d Ed

with a "homogeneous" or "single-diagnosis" group, in which all the patients have the same diagnosis.

heterograft: See *xenograft*.

HEW: A short abbreviation for the former federal *Department of Health, Education, and Welfare (DHEW)*.

HHA: See *home health agency*.

HHS: A short abbreviation for the *Department of Health and Human Services (DHHS)*.

HI: Hospital Insurance Program. See *Medicare, Part A*.

HIAA: See *Health Insurance Association of America*.

hierarchy: A system in which persons or things are in graded ranks. Authority in an organization is usually hierarchical; perhaps the best example is the military. In a hospital, "line authority" illustrates the principle: a floor nurse reports to a head nurse, who in turn reports to the chief or nursing, who in turn reports to the chief executive officer of the hospital who, finally, reports to the governing body. Only a person higher in this series is authorized to "give orders" to a person lower in the series.

Hill-Burton program: A 1946 federal program of financial assistance for the construction and renovation of hospitals and other health care facilities.

HIS: See *hospital information system*.

histologic technician/technologist (HT): One of the 26 *allied health professionals* for whom the American Medical Association's *Committee on Allied Health Education and Accreditation (CAHEA)* has accredited education programs.

histology: The study of body tissues as visible under the microscope. Anatomy, the study of the body, is divided into the general fields of "gross anatomy," the study of the body to the degree of

H

detail visible to the naked eye, and histology ("microscopic anatomy"). *Cytology* is a subdivision of histology, concentrating on the study of individual cells ("cyto-") and involving more detailed study under the microscope. Synonym(s): microscopic anatomy.

history: See *medical history* and *natural history*.

HIV: See *human immunodeficiency virus*.

HMD: See *hyaline membrane disease*.

HMO: See *health maintenance organization*.

HO: See *Hospital-Sponsored Ambulatory Care Services*.

holding company: A *corporation* organized for the purpose of owning the stock of another corporation or corporations; or any company which owns such a large portion of the stock of a corporation that it controls that corporation.

holistic health: See *wholistic health*.

home care: See *home health care*.

home care program: See *home health care program*.

home health agency (HHA): Essentially the same as a *home health care program* in that it provides medical and other health *services (1)* in the patient's home. Unlike the home care program, which provides services itself, the home health agency has the option of arranging the services by contracting with others. The term "home health agency" is applied to both nonprofit and proprietary bodies.

home health aide: A person who assists ill, elderly, or disabled persons in the home, carrying out personal care and housekeeping tasks. The service is usually provided under the supervision of an *agency (3)*. Synonym(s): homemaker.

home health care: Care at the levels of *skilled nursing care* and *intermediate care* provided in the patient's home through an agency which has the resources necessary to provide that care. The care is given under the prescription of a physician by professional nurses (*registered nurses (RNs)* and *licensed practical nurses (LPNs)*), and other health care professionals (social workers, physical therapists, and so forth), as appropriate. Services may also include homemaking and personal care services.

Home health care is a growing alternative to skilled nursing facilities and units (SNFs and SNUs) and to intermediate care facilities (ICFs) and units. Also called "in-home care" and "home care." See also *home life care.*

Often home health care is divided into three categories, depending on the intensity:

intensive home health care: Home care for persons who are seriously ill and require intensive medical and nursing attention.

intermediate home health care: Home care for persons with active but reasonably stable disease, that is, whose condition is not expected to change rapidly, and for whom less medical and nursing care is required than in the case of intensive home health care.

maintenance home health care: Home care for persons needing mostly personal care and support.

home health care program: An organization that provides medical and other health *services (1)* in the patient's home. Synonym(s): home care program.

home health services: See *home health care.*

home life care: Supportive services provided by an agency in order to permit an individual who is able to carry out the *activities of daily living (ADL)* to remain at home rather than being placed in an institution. The services are given by homemakers and home aids rather than by nurses. One benefit of having such trained assistance in the home is that the worker going into the home is in a position to detect the need for and to obtain nursing services as required. Home life care is distinguished from home health care in that home health care includes nursing services under the direction of a physician rather than simply homemaking care. See also *home health care.*

H

homemaker: See *home health aide.*

homeopathy: See *medicine (4).*

homogeneous: Composed of things which are the same, in contrast to "heterogeneous," which refers to a mixture. For example, in a homogeneous or "single-diagnosis" *Diagnosis Related Group (DRG)*, all the patients have the same diagnosis; on the other hand, a heterogeneous DRG is composed of patients with a variety of diagnoses.

homograft: See *allograft.*

hormone: A chemical substance, produced in the body and secreted internally, usually into the blood, which has effects on *organs* other than those in which it is produced. Most hormones are produced by endocrine organs.

hospice program: A program that assists with the physical, emotional, spiritual, psychological, social, financial, and legal needs of the dying patient and her family. The service may be provided in the patient's home or in an institution (or division of an institution) set up for the purpose. Volunteers are integral parts of the staff. *Bereavement care* for the family is also included.

hospital: A health care institution which has an *organized professional staff* and *medical staff* and *inpatient* facilities, and which provides medical, nursing, and related services. States have specific definitions for what may be called a "hospital," including, for example, a minimum number of beds, and the services which must be available. A given hospital may fit one or more of the following definitions:

accredited hospital: A hospital meeting the *standards* of the *Joint Commission on Accreditation of Healthcare Organizations (JCAHO)* and so certified by JCAHO (or, in Canada, by the *Canadian Council on Health Facilities Accreditation (CCHFA)).*

acute care hospital: A hospital which cares primarily for patients with *acute* diseases and injuries (that is, those with an *average length of stay (ALOS)* of 30 days or less), or in which more than half the patients are admitted to units with an ALOS of 30 days or less. Also called an acute hospital and short-term hospital.

affiliated hospital: A hospital that has some connection with another hospital, a training program, a multihospital system, a medical center, or some other organization.

certified hospital: A hospital recognized by the *Department of Health and Human Services (DHHS)* as meeting the standards necessary to be a *provider* for Medicare.

chronic disease hospital: See *long-term hospital*.

city hospital: A hospital controlled by a city government. While a hospital operated by a city is often referred to as a "municipal hospital" (and properly can be called that), the term *municipal hospital* refers to a hospital operated by any *municipal* government.

closed-staff hospital: A hospital which has a formal plan describing *medical staff* size and specialty needs. Such a hospital only accepts new applications to bring its medical staff up to size and to complete its specialty requirements. Except when vacancies exist in these respects, the medical staff is "closed."

community hospital: A hospital established primarily to provide services to the residents of the community in which it is located. Most community hospitals are nonprofit, non-federal, and for short term patients.

community-owned hospital: See *nonprofit hospital*.

county hospital: A hospital controlled by county government.

day care hospital: A hospital which treats, during the day, patients who are able to return to their homes at night.

deemed status hospital: A term used in the Medicare, Medicaid, and *Maternal and Child Health Programs* to indicate that the hospital had been deemed by the former *Professional Standards Review Organization (PSRO)* to meet the requirements of those programs with respect to *admissions review, continued stay review,* and *medical care evaluation.* The determinations of "deemed hospitals" in these matters had to be regarded as final, and the hospitals' demands for payment had to be honored.

delegated hospital: A hospital to which the former local *Professional Standards Review Organization (PSRO)* delegated authority to carry out review functions—*admissions review, continued-stay review,* and *medical care evaluation*—for Medicare, Medicaid, and *Maternal and Child Health* patients. The delegated hospital's own determinations on these matters had to be accepted by the paying agency.

disproportionate share hospital: A Medicare term for a hospital serving a higher than average proportion of low-income patients.

district hospital: A hospital controlled by a special political subdivision (a *hospital district*) created solely to operate the hospital and other health care institutions.

federal government hospital: A hospital controlled and operated by the federal government.

for-profit hospital: A hospital operated by a *for-profit corporation,* in which the profits are paid in the form of dividends to shareholders who own the corporation. A for-profit hospital is the same as an investor-owned hospital and a proprietary hospital; see also *publicly-owned hospital.*

general hospital: A hospital offering care for a variety of conditions and age groups. It is contrasted with a specialty hospital (for example, a children's hospital, or an "eye and ear" or psychiatric hospital).

government hospital: A hospital which is operated by a unit of government, usually the federal government. Hospitals operated by states are usually called *state hospitals,* and those operated by cities are usually called *municipal hospitals.*

investor-owned hospital: See *for-profit hospital.*

licensed hospital: A hospital *licensed* by the state licensing agency.

long-term hospital: A hospital providing long term care for patients not in an *acute* phase of an illness but who require more skilled services than those available in a *nursing home.* Synonym(s): chronic disease hospital.

municipal hospital: A hospital operated by a *municipal* government, usually a city.

night hospital: A hospital that treats, only at night, patients who are able to be out during the day.

nondelegated hospital: A hospital not qualified under its *Professional Standards Review Organization (PSRO)* to perform review functions (see *delegated hospital*).

nonprofit hospital: A hospital owned and operated by a corporation whose "profits" (excess of income over expense) are used for hospital purposes rather than returned to shareholders or investors as dividends.   "Nonprofit" does not necessary mean "tax-exempt."   To be tax exempt, an organization must not only be nonprofit, but also qualify under paragraph 501(c)(3) of the Internal Revenue Code as "scientific, religious, educational, or charitable" and have a determination to this effect from the IRS. The organization must also meet state requirements to be exempt from state taxes. Synonym(s): community-owned hospital, not-for-profit hospital.

not-for-profit hospital: See *nonprofit hospital*.

open-staff hospital: A hospital which has no formal plan as to *medical staff* size and *specialty* needs.   Such a hospital accepts new applications for appointment to the medical staff and for *clinical privileges*—it is "open" to such requests.   Such a hospital may have *exclusive contracts* with physicians or physician groups for certain administrative and clinical services, and these contracts would preclude other physicians from these activities for the lives of the contracts.   The existence of exclusive contracts does not make the staff closed.

private hospital: A hospital not operated by a government agency.   A private hospital may be either *for-profit* or *nonprofit*.

proprietary hospital: See *for-profit hospital*.

psychiatric hospital: A hospital specializing in the care of patients with mental illness.

publicly-owned hospital: A hospital operated by a corporation which offers ownership of shares to the general public.   The term is currently being applied to for-profit, investor-owned (proprietary) hospitals.

registered hospital: Short for "AHA-registered."   A hospital recognized by the *American Hospital Association (AHA)* as meeting its definition of a hospital and approved by its Board of Trustees for registration.

rehabilitation hospital: A hospital specializing in *rehabilitation* care.

satellite hospital: A hospital operated by another, "parent," hospital, at a location different than that of the parent hospital.

self-insured hospital: A hospital assuming the *risk (2)* of loss without an *insurance* policy. Commonly, a hospital would set aside its own funds to protect itself against financial loss, instead of purchasing an insurance policy from an insurance company. In many cases, however, even a so-called "self-insured" hospital will purchase a policy ("*excess coverage*") to protect against very large losses. For example, a hospital might self-insure for losses up to three million dollars, then have a policy to cover the next ten million dollars of loss.

short-term hospital: See *acute care hospital*.

specialty hospital: A hospital which cares for only a limited category of patients, such as psychiatric, orthopedic, or pediatric patients.

state hospital: A hospital operated by a state. Such hospitals are usually specialized, particularly for the care of contagious disease and psychiatric patients.

teaching hospital: A hospital with one or more *accredited* education programs in medicine, nursing, or the allied health professions.

university hospital: A hospital which is owned by or affiliated with a medical school and which is used in the education of physicians.

voluntary hospital: A hospital which is *private* (nongovernmental), *autonomous*, and self-supported.

hospital auxiliary: A organization, whose membership is from the community, whose purpose is to assist the hospital. Synonym(s): auxiliary.

hospital board: See *governing body*.

hospital chain: See *multihospital system*.

hospital consultant: See *health care consultant.*

hospital discharge abstract system: A system in which a number of hospitals submit coded, computer-ready, summaries (*discharge abstracts*) of clinical records to a central shared computer service. The summaries may be submitted on paper or via computer media. In return, the hospitals receive reports and analyses of their own data, which they need for their internal operations. In addition, by using standardized information, hospitals may obtain inter-hospital comparisons, and may establish a *data base (2)* which may be used, under the confidentiality rules of the system, for research. The prototype of such systems is the *Professional Activity Study (PAS)* of the *Commission on Professional and Hospital Activities (CPHA).*

hospital district: A special political subdivision created solely to operate the hospital and other health care institutions.

hospital engineer: A term sometimes used to designate the person responsible for the operation and maintenance of the equipment and the physical plant.

hospital information system (HIS): See *management information system (MIS).*

Hospital Insurance Program (HI): See *Medicare, Part A.*

hospital medical care hotel: A hotel operated by a hospital for patients who need certain services the hospital provides, but who can live in hotel surroundings, that is, without round-the-clock nursing. This is not a hotel for the families of patients.

hospital nursing care: Round-the-clock nursing care supervised at all times by a *registered nurse (RN)*, with the bedside care provided by both licensed nurses (registered nurses and licensed practical nurses (LPNs)) and auxiliary nursing personnel as appropriate for the patient.

Hospital Satellite Network (HSN): A hospital television network, to which several hundred hospitals subscribe. Some of its broad-

H

casts are "in the clear," that is, without charge, while others require a registration or fee.

Hospital-Sponsored Ambulatory Care Services (HO):   The chapter giving the *standards* for this component of the hospital in the 1990 *Accreditation Manual for Hospitals (AMH)* of the *Joint Commission on the Accreditation of Healthcare Organizations (JCAHO)*.

Hospital Statistics: The annual publication of the *American Hospital Association (AHA)* covering hospitals in the United States, and giving descriptions of each as well as tabulated data on hospitals.

hospitalization: A period of stay in the hospital.   Also, the placing of a patient in the hospital.

hospitalize: To admit a patient to a hospital in which that patient will be lodged.   The patient, once admitted, becomes an *inpatient*. See *admission*.

Hospitals: The official monthly publication of the *American Hospital Association (AHA)*.

hotel-hospital: A hotel facility operated by a hospital, at hotel rates, for use by patients and their families before and after hospitalization.   Such facilities are sometimes used for temporary care for elderly patients in order to give their family *caregivers* a rest.   If separated from the hospital, the hotel-hospital often provides shuttle bus service. Synonym(s): guest bed program.

house staff: The body of house officers, physicians and dentists in *residency* training in an *accredited graduate medical education* program in a *teaching hospital*. The house officers may or may not need to be *licensed*.

HPA: See *Health Policy Agenda for the American People*.

HRA: See *health record analyst*.

HSA: See *health systems agency*.

HSN: See *Hospital Satellite Network.*

HT: See *histologic technician/technologist.*

HTLV-III: Human T-lymphocyte virus type III. See *human immunodeficiency virus (HIV).*

human immunodeficiency virus (HIV): The virus which causes acquired immunodeficiency syndrome (AIDS). Synonym(s): human T-lymphocyte virus type III (HTLV-III), lymphadenopathy-associated virus (LAV), AIDS-related virus (ARV).

human T-lymphocyte virus type III (HTLV-III): See *human immunodeficiency virus (HIV).*

hyaline membrane disease (HMD): A disease of the lungs occurring in the newborn in which there is difficulty in breathing, sometimes fatal. It is sometimes referred to as *respiratory distress syndrome (RDS)*, although other conditions can cause RDS.

I

IA: See *intra-arterial*.

IADL: See *Instrumental Activities of Daily Living scale*.

iatrogenic illness: An illness or injury resulting from a diagnostic procedure, therapy, or other element of health care. An iatrogenic illness is often confused with a "nosocomial" illness, which simply · means an illness "occurring in a hospital."

IC: See *Infection Control*.

ICCS: See *International Classification of Clinical Services*.

ICD: See *International Classification of Diseases*.

ICD-9-CM: See *International Classification of Diseases, Ninth Revision, Clinical Modification*.

ICD-10: See *International Statistical Classification of Diseases and Related Health Problems*.

ICF: See *intermediate care facility*.

ICF/MR: See *intermediate care facility for the mentally retarded*.

ICP: Interdisciplinary care plan. See *interdisciplinary patient care plan (IPCP)*.

ICRC: Infant care review committee.

ICU: See *intensive care unit*.

IEEE: See *Institute of Electrical and Electronics Engineers*.

IG: See *inspector general*.

IHCA: See *individual health care account*.

IM (1): See *intramuscular*.

IM (2): Implementation monitoring. See *monitoring*.

IM (3): See *internal medicine*.

image: A picture or view.

imaging: A term which covers the variety of technologies which result in pictures (images) of body structures or functioning. The first imaging technology was, perhaps, medical illustration. Then came conventional *radiology (X-ray)*. The next technology to gain prominence was *computed (axial) tomography (CT or CAT)* scanning. To these have been added *magnetic resonance imaging (MRI)*, diagnostic *ultrasound, single photon emission tomography (SPET)*, and *positron emission tomography (PET)*. Many former Departments of Radiology in hospitals are now called Departments of Imaging.

IMC: See *indigent medical care*.

IMD: See *institution for mental diseases*.

immunity: The condition of being immune or insusceptible to an *agent (1)*. The term is most often used in regard to resistance to infectious disease—immunity to smallpox, diphtheria, colds, acquired immunodeficiency syndrome (AIDS), and the like. However, one may also speak, for example, of "stress immunity," the ability to resist stress, or "cold immunity," the ability to withstand cold. Immunity is relative, in that almost any immunity may be overwhelmed by either (1) a massive attack (such as contamination of a wound by barnyard dirt loaded with tetanus) or (2) general lack of resistance (an emaciated, starving person is unlikely to resist pneumonia); the combination of a massive attack and lack of resistance makes infection even more likely. Many modifiers are used with the term "immunity," but only a few are defined here:

acquired immunity: Immunity to infection which is the result of (1) *infection*, or (2) the administration of an *agent (1)*, such as a vaccine, either of which may stimulate the body to develop *active immunity*.

active immunity: A type of *acquired immunity* in which the body is stimulated to produce its own antibodies. This occurs either: (1) in response to an infection (which may or may not produce symptoms); or (2) in response to the inoculation of a vaccine, either a strain of killed bacteria or other infectious agent, or an attenuated (weakened) strain of the infectious agent (a strain which is able to stimulate the body to produce antibodies but not symptoms).

herd immunity: The relative immunity of a group of persons or animals as a result of the immunity of an adequate number (proportion) of the individuals in the group. The immunity may be *active immunity* or *passive immunity*. Herd immunity is actually an immunity against an epidemic, rather than the immunity of individuals against infection. For an epidemic to succeed, it must be possible for the disease to travel from one individual to another. When enough individuals are immune (perhaps 70 to 80 percent), the epidemic simply dies out. Herd immunity is fortunate for the public health control of contagious diseases, since the chance of being able to get everyone immunized is practically zero.

passive immunity: A type of *acquired immunity* that is conferred by giving to the person (or animal) immune substances developed in another animal or human. One example is tetanus antitoxin, an immune substance developed in a laboratory animal and transferred to the human patient by inoculation (injection). Such an antibody is prefabricated and immediately ready to repel the invasion of the infection (in this case, tetanus). Its protection is temporary, because the body eliminates the antitoxin as fast as it can (it is also a foreign substance) and thereafter the body is susceptible to tetanus again.

impaired: A descriptive term which, when applied to a professional such as a physician, usually encompasses physical handicaps, alcoholism, drug dependence, senility, mental illness, or, sometimes, behavior problems.

implant: To place a substitute organ, tissue, or device in a living body. The difference between implanting and transplanting is that implanting may involve a device (for example, a cardiac pacemaker, or an artificial hip joint, or a capsule of radioactive material) or an organ or tissue, while transplanting involves only organs or tissues. The term implant may also be used as a noun to indicate the organ or tissue implanted.

implementation monitoring: See *monitoring*.

implicit: "Naturally" a part of, although not specifically stated. For example, having to choose (or establish priorities) is implicit when one is on a fixed income or when the amount available for medical and hospital care is fixed. The necessity for choice (prioritizing) is implicit, once it is known that the income is fixed. If Medicare is the only source of funds for medical care, and there is not enough to purchase everything for everyone, choices will have to be made (rationing must occur). The necessity for choices (or rationing) is implicit (goes without saying), given that funds are limited. "Explicit," the term with which there is confusion, means specifically stated. In view of the limits on funds for Medicaid, the rationing proposed in 1990 by Oregon is explicit rationing. See *explicit*.

in-home care: See *home health care*.

in-house: Carried out within the organization, rather than brought in or done outside.

in vitro: In an artificial environment, as in a test tube. The similar term, "in vivo," means within a living body.

in vitro fertilization (IVF): The removal of one or more ova (eggs) from the mother, the *fertilization* of these ova outside the body (in a glass dish) by mixing them with sperm, and the transfer of the embryo thus established into the woman's uterus. IVF is a technique used in *noncoital reproduction*.

I

in vivo: In a living body. The similar term, "in vitro," means in an artificial environment, as in a test tube.

incentive: A reward for desired behavior. In health care, this term is used in regard to rewards to institutions and individuals for decreasing hospital and physician costs, and for encouraging patients to be frugal in demands for health care. Sometimes incentives are negative, for example, when a patient is required to pay the first dollars for a *service (1)* (this payment is called a deductible). The deductible is a "disincentive" to seek the care, and thus an incentive to be frugal.

incidence: The number of specified new events taking place in a defined period of time in a given area or population. It usually refers to cases of disease or injury, and is the numerator in the calculation of an incidence rate for the event in question. The denominator is the population at *risk (3)* within the given time period. Incidence is often confused with "prevalence," which applies to the number of events or cases of disease present in a given population at a given time.

incident: An event in the hospital which does not comport with the standards of the hospital, or which is unexpected and undesirable. For example, a patient leaving against medical advice (*AMA*) or a patient's adverse reaction to administration of a drug might be classified by a hospital as "incidents." Sometimes "incident" is used more narrowly to mean an accident (such as a fall) in which a patient is injured (or might have been injured) and for which the hospital may be liable. An incident report is completed for each incident, to assist in *quality management* and *risk management*. See also *adverse patient occurrence (APO)*.

income: Money earned during an *accounting period*, in contrast with *revenue*, which is the increase in *assets* or the decrease in *liabilities* during the accounting period.

income and expense statement: A standard part of a financial statement in which are shown the *revenues, costs,* and *expenses* of the organization for the *accounting period*. The other part of the financial statement is the *balance sheet*. Synonym(s): profit and loss statement (P & L), operating statement, income statement.

income statement: See *income and expense statement.*

incompetent (1): Lacking the ability to make decisions. Competency is relative, and standards of legal competency will vary according to the type of decision to be made. For example, competency to make decisions about one's own health care treatment requires the ability to understand one's condition, the options available, and the potential consequences of the various alternatives.

A person who is involuntarily committed to a psychiatric institution is not, just because of the commitment, legally incompetent. For example, that person would ordinarily still be able to make his own treatment decisions, and could legally enter into a contract. On the other hand, a comatose person is clearly incompetent to make decisions. Some classes of persons, for example minors (children), may be incompetent by law. See *minor.*

If a person is declared incompetent by a court, a legal guardian is appointed for that person. The person may be judged only unable to handle his financial affairs, and so the guardian will only make decisions about money and property management, and the incompetent person may still make personal decisions, such as those regarding health care. In other cases, the guardian may make personal decisions. Some guardians have the power to make both personal and property-related decisions. In any case, the court document appointing the guardian will state the authority of the guardian.

A legally incompetent person may still be sufficiently competent to make a valid will, since the requirements for competency in this area are less stringent. The testator (the person making a will) need only understand what property he owns, and be able to recognize the "natural objects of his bounty" (for example, his wife and children).

incompetent (2): A term applied to an individual who is considered unable to perform a task in an acceptable manner.

incubator: A special bed for an infant who needs control of its environment: temperature, humidity, and breathing (such as supplementary oxygen). An incubator also provides *isolation* for the infant. Incubators are used for *premature* infants and other infants with special problems, whether born in the hospital or elsewhere.

I

IND: Investigational new drug. See *drug*.

independent contractor: A person who works for himself and is not controlled by another, as distinguished from an employee. See *employee* for further discussion.

Independent Physician Association (IPA): A type of health care provider organization composed of physicians, in which the physicians maintain their own practices but agree to furnish services to patients who have signed up for a *prepayment plan* in which the physician services are supplied by the IPA. An IPA is not a *health maintenance organization (HMO)*, a *health care organization (HCO)*, or a *preferred provider organization (PPO)*.

independent practitioner: An individual, usually a person who gives patient care, who practices without supervision. In a hospital, an independent practitioner must ordinarily be *licensed* and also must be granted specific *clinical privileges* by the hospital.

index (1): A number expressing the relative size of a given statistic (number calculated from data) when compared with a reference value for that statistic. It is the result of dividing the given value of the statistic by the reference value. An example is the *consumer price index*.

index (2): A list, alphabetical or numerical, of items, created for the purpose of helping one find the items. Indexes are common in books. In the hospital, medical record indexes are maintained to assist in finding the records of individual patients, those cared for by each physician, those with certain diagnoses, and the like.

indicated: A term used by physicians meaning that, taking into account the patient's problems and condition, carrying out a given diagnostic procedure or treatment would be the wise course of action. For example, appendectomy (surgical removal of the appendix) is indicated in suspected acute appendicitis, unless there are factors in the patient's condition which outweigh the medical necessity for the operation. Such a factor might be, for instance, a concomitant illness which would add an intolerable risk to that of the surgery or anesthesia.

indication: A *finding* or piece of information which suggests or points to the proper next step in diagnosis or treatment of the patient. A certain set of symptoms and physical findings, for example, is an "indication" for diagnostic X-rays in a suspected fracture.

indicator: An "activity," "event," "occurrence," or *outcome* which is to be *monitored* and evaluated, under a *Joint Commission on Accreditation of Healthcare Organizations (JCAHO) standard*, in order to determine if those aspects conform to the standards. For each indicator, the hospital is expected to have developed *criteria* for use in evaluation.

indigent: A condition defined by the federal, state, or local government. Any individual whose income and other resources fall below the level defined is declared to be indigent. Note that *"medically indigent"* and "indigent" usually have different definitions.

indigent medical care (IMC): Care for patients whose income falls below a level usually set by statute or regulation as defining indigency. Such care is provided without charge or for reduced charges, but the institution must find the resources by "overcharges" to other patients (or their payers), supplementary appropriations, public subscription, or elsewhere.

individual health care account (IHCA): A proposed method of financing health care costs by giving tax advantages to individuals who establish and maintain personal "individual health care accounts (ICHAs)" similar in concept to individual retirement accounts (IRAs). Money placed in such accounts would be excluded from the individual's taxable income and would be invested, with principal and income to be used only for specified health care. ICHAs could be a replacement for financing by Medicare for the elderly, a supplement to Medicare, or both. Synonym(s): health IRA.

industrial engineering: The designing, installation, maintenance, and improvement of systems which integrate people, equipment, materials, and energy.

I

infant death: The death of an infant, defined as a death within the first year of life (after birth).

infection: An illness produced by an *infectious agent*. Several types of infection are discussed in the health care field:

community-acquired infection: An infection which the patient acquired before hospitalization (although it may manifest itself after admission to the hospital).

cross infection: See *nosocomial infection*.

hospital-acquired infection: See *nosocomial infection*.

nosocomial infection: An infection acquired in the hospital. Such an infection may not become evident until after discharge. Synonym(s): hospital-acquired infection, cross infection.

postoperative infection: A *nosocomial infection* (one acquired in the hospital) which was acquired during surgery and appeared later.

infection control: The policies and procedures used to prevent the transmission of *infection* from one infected individual to another. The term is used in connection with the protection of the professionals and other employees who may have contact with the infectious patient, and the protection of other patients. Infection-control measures include the use of protective clothing, hand-washing, precautions against needle-sticks, decontamination (of the patient's environment, and linens), disposal of wastes, and proper handling of laboratory specimens. The appearance of acquired immunodeficiency syndrome (AIDS) and hepatitis B in particular have stimulated increased emphasis on infection-control policies and procedures for all patients.

Infection Control (IC): The chapter giving the *standards* for this component of the hospital in the 1990 *Accreditation Manual for Hospitals (AMH)* of the *Joint Commission on the Accreditation of Healthcare Organizations (JCAHO)*.

infectious agent: See *agent*.

infectious diseases: A branch of *internal medicine*. One of the medical specialties for which *residency* programs have been approved by the Accreditation Council for Graduate Medical Education (ACGME). See *specialty*.

infectious waste: See *hazardous waste*.

infertile: Having reduced or absent capacity to reproduce; a condition which may or not be reversible. Infertility is not the same as having undergone *sterilization (2)*, a process intended to remove the capacity to reproduce.

informatics: An emerging term (seeking a standard definition) which is used to cover information along with its management, particularly by computer. Usually the field involved is used along with "informatics," e.g., "medical informatics."

> **medical informatics:** A term being applied to a field, being described as a new discipline, which covers medical (and related) information, both in traditional and electronic form, along with its management, particularly by computer methods. Included are the storage, retrieval, and use of the information (including, according to some authors, statistics).

information: A term generally used to mean *data* which have somehow been "digested" (manipulated, summarized, organized, or interpreted) so that inferences may more readily be drawn and decisions made than from "raw" data.

This book has defined "data" as material, facts, or figures on which discussion is held or from which inferences are drawn or decisions made (see the definition of *data*). No rigid standardization in terminology has appeared in this regard, although generally the term "information" is rarely applied to material which is "raw."

information system: A poorly defined term used to refer to anything from a pencil and paper to a full-blown computer system. Usually the term "information system" is modified by words specifying its purpose, such as *"management information system (MIS)."*

I

informed consent: See *consent.*

injunction: A court order prohibiting someone from doing something or, less commonly, ordering someone to do something. An injunction may be temporary (to preserve the status quo until a lawsuit is finally decided) or permanent (issued as part of the final decision of a lawsuit).

injury: The damage caused by an external force, as contrasted with an "illness," which simply indicates that the body is not in a healthy condition.

inpatient: A patient who receives care while being lodged in an institution.

inpatient care: Care rendered to patients who are lodged within a health care facility.

inpatient care institution: See *inpatient facility.*

inpatient day equivalents: A term used in compiling hospital statistics. The total number of *inpatient service days,* plus the volume of outpatient services expressed as (converted to) an estimate of inpatient service days. This computation has to use some sort of *relative value unit (RVU)* approach to convert outpatient services into inpatient service days. Synonym(s): adjusted inpatient service days.

inpatient facility: A health care institution which provides lodging and also nursing and continuous medical care for patients within a permanent facility with an *organized professional staff.* Synonym(s): inpatient care institution.

inpatient service day: See *day.*

inservice: Activities, ordinarily education or training, which are carried out without serious interruption of the employees' regular duties.

inservice director: The individual responsible for coordinating educational programs for all employees, including training of nursing aides and orderlies, in long-term care facilities.

inservice education coordinator: See *director of education*.

inservice training: Training carried out, usually within the institution, while employees carry out their regular duties. Inservice training may take the form of "courses" integrated into the work schedule, or "coaching." Also called staff development.

inspector general (IG): A federal official who reports to Congress and to certain heads of *agencies (1)* on the activities of the agencies. The post was created by statute. Agencies also have their own IGs who carry out similar functions with respect to the internal functions of the agency and outside programs which the agency funds.

Institute of Electrical and Electronics Engineers (IEEE): A national organization which has a group working on computer standards, some of which apply to medical systems.

institution for mental diseases (IMD): As defined by the *Department of Health and Human Services (DHHS)* for Medicaid, "an institution that is primarily engaged in providing diagnosis, treatment or care of persons with mental diseases." A hospital, skilled nursing facility (SNF), or intermediate care facility (ICF), for example, can also be an IMD for Medicaid purposes; the "overall character" of the institution governs.

institutional review board (IRB): A committee in an *investigator*'s institution set up to provide *peer review* for research programs supported by grants and contracts financed by the *Department of Health and Human Services (DHHS)*. Similar review is also required by the *Food and Drug Administration (FDA)* for investigational new drugs. The committee may not have as members any persons who have professional responsibility in the conduct of the research. The research proposal is reviewed in terms of institutional commitments and regulations, applicable law, standards of professional conduct and practice, and community attitudes. The committee also is to ensure that *informed consent* of subjects is obtained by adequate and appropriate methods, whether or not the research involves risk to the subjects.

Instrumental Activities of Daily Living (IADL) scale: A "standard scale of function" sometimes used to measure *severity of illness*. It is a portion of the Older American Resources and Services Questionnaire (OARS). The IADL scale involves ability to perform six *activities of daily living (ADL)*: dressing and undressing; walking; taking a bath or shower; going shopping for groceries or clothes; preparing meals; and doing housework. For each activity, a person can perform without help, with help, or not at all.

insurance: A method of providing for money to pay for specific types of losses which may occur. Insurance is a contract (the insurance policy) between one party (the insured) and another (the insurer). The policy states what types of losses (*risks (2)*) are covered, what amounts will be paid for each loss and for all losses, and under what conditions.

Two types of insurance commonly spoken of in health care are: (1) insurance covering the patient for health care *services (1)* (health insurance, also called a "third-party-payer"); and (2) insurance covering the health care provider for risks associated with the delivery of health care (liability to a patient for malpractice, for example).

captive insurance company: An insurance company formed to underwrite (insure) the risks of its owner(s). Increasingly, hospitals and other health care providers are forming or buying their own insurance companies, either alone or with other providers.

catastrophic insurance: Insurance intended to protect against the cost of a *catastrophic illness*, with "catastrophic" defined as exceeding a predetermined cost. Catastrophic insurance comes into play above that cost, in supplement of other insurance, and pays all or a percentage of the cost above the specified amount. Synonym(s): major medical insurance.

coinsurance: A type of insurance which requires that part of the charges be paid by the *beneficiary*, the primary purpose being to discourage small claims and "over-use" of services.

commercial insurance: In health care, usually any insurance for hospital or medical care other than that written by *Blue Cross and*

Blue Shield (BC/BS) (which, being nonprofit organizations, are thus "non-commercial").

general liability insurance: Insurance which covers the *risk (2)* of loss for most accidents and injuries to third parties (the insured and its employees are not covered) which arise from the actions or negligence of the insured, and for which the insured may have legal *liability*, except those injuries directly related to the provision of professional health care *services (1)* (the latter risks are covered by *professional liability insurance*). General liability insurance will pay for slips and falls of visitors on hospital premises, for example.

health insurance: Insurance which covers the patient for health care, including physician and hospital *services (1)*.

major medical insurance: See *catastrophic insurance*.

out-of-area insurance: Insurance carried by a *health care plan*, purchased from an insurance company, to pay for care for subscribers (*beneficiaries*) when they are away from home (out-of-area), away from the physicians and hospitals which would themselves provide the care if the patient were at home.

professional liability insurance: Insurance which covers the *risk (2)* of loss from patient injury or illness which results from *professional negligence* or other *professional liability*. Professional liability insurance pays *malpractice* claims. Often, a hospital's professional liability policy will not cover the actions of physicians on the medical staff, in which case those physicians need to obtain their own individual policies.

property insurance: Insurance which pays for damage to the insured's own property, for example, loss by fire.

self-insurance: Assumption of *risk (2)* of loss without an insurance policy. For example, a hospital deciding to "self-insure" would set aside its own funds to protect itself against financial loss, instead of purchasing an insurance policy from an insurance company. In many cases, however, even a so-called "self-insured" hospital will purchase a policy (*"excess coverage"*) to protect against very large losses. For example, a hospital might self-insure for losses up to three million dollars, then have a policy to cover the next ten million dollars of loss.

stop-loss insurance: Insurance carried by a *health care plan*, purchased from an insurance carrier, to reimburse the health care plan for costs of care for individual patients over a ceiling (for example, $10,000).

insurance clerk: See *reimbursement specialist (1)*.

insurance coverage: Generally refers to the amount of protection available and the kind of loss which would be paid for under an *insurance* contract with an insurer.

claims-made coverage: Insurance that will pay for *claims (1)* which are made during the period of time that the policy is in effect, for events which occur *after* the insurance policy's "retroactive date." For example, if a hospital has a claims-made insurance policy in effect for calendar year 1990, with a retroactive date of January 1, 1987, and a patient suffers an injury during a 1988 surgical procedure but does not notify (or sue) the hospital until 1990, the claim will be covered under the 1990 policy. If the surgery was in 1986, it will not be covered. See also *occurrence-based coverage*.

excess coverage: Extra high limits of insurance coverage, which will pay amounts over and above the original limits of a specified policy.

first-dollar coverage: Insurance which has no *copayment* or *deductible* provision; the insured does not have to pay the first dollar—the insurer pays it.

occurrence-based coverage: Insurance which will pay for claims only when the event which gives rise to the claim happens during the period of time that the policy is in effect, regardless of when the claim is made. For example, if a hospital has an occurrence-based insurance policy in effect only for calendar year 1990, and a patient suffers an injury during a 1988 surgical procedure, the claim will not be covered under the 1990 policy because the injury did not occur in 1990. See also *claims-made coverage*.

tail coverage: Insurance purchased to protect the insured after the end of a *claims-made* policy, to cover events which occurred during the period of the claims-made policy, but for which no claim was made during that period. This protects the insured in case a claim is made at a future date, after the original policy has lapsed.

umbrella coverage: A broad high limit liability policy, usually requiring underlying insurance. For example, a hospital may be insured for one million dollars for general liability and three million dollars for professional liability, with an umbrella of ten million dollars. The umbrella will pick up any excess liability over either policy, up to the ten million dollar additional limit.

integration: Integration is spoken of in health care today in terms of the linking together of components of the health care system:

horizontal integration: A linkage of hospitals (or other institutions and organizations) which are more or less alike, such as acute general hospitals, to form a *multihospital system*. The purpose of horizontal integration is to achieve economies of scale in operation, such as greater purchasing power and avoidance of duplication of facilities.

vertical integration: A linkage of hospitals (and other institutions and organizations) to form a system providing a range or continuum of care such as preventive, outpatient, acute hospital, long term, home, and hospice care. The purpose of vertical integration is to keep the patient population within the one system for as many of its health care needs as possible.

intensive care: Care provided to patients with life-threatening conditions who require intensive treatment and continuous monitoring.

intensive care unit (ICU): A hospital patient care unit for patients with life-threatening conditions who require intensive treatment and continuous monitoring. Such units are often set up separately for different kinds of patients, and a hospital may have several ICUs: medical, surgical, pediatric, neonatal, and others. Synonym(s): critical care unit.

neonatal intensive care unit (NICU): An intensive care unit for infants in the *neonatal* period. Sometimes shortened to "neonatal ICU."

intentional infliction of emotional distress: A *tort* where the wrongdoing consists of outrageous conduct which causes extreme mental suffering. This tort is also called outrage.

I

intentional tort: Wrongdoing (*tort*) which results in civil *liability (1)*, and which is done intentionally, maliciously, or recklessly (this is in contrast to *negligence*, which usually is done accidentally and without any intent to do harm).

interdisciplinary care plan (ICP): See *interdisciplinary patient care plan (IPCP)*.

interdisciplinary patient care plan (IPCP): A plan required by federal regulations for each patient in a *long term care facility (LTCF)*. The plan must define the patient's problems and needs, and must also set forth measurable goals, approaches to the care, and the profession (department or service) responsible for the care of the patient. An IPCP is sometimes referred to by the less correct terms: "interdisciplinary care plan (ICP)" or "patient care plan."

intermediary: See *fiscal intermediary*.

intermediate care: The second highest level of nursing care provided outside the acute hospital setting (the highest level is "skilled nursing care"), sometimes called "basic nursing care": nursing care for a patient whose professional nursing needs are less demanding than for skilled nursing care, but are of a nature to require overall supervision by a *registered nurse (RN)*. This supervision requirement is ordinarily met by having an RN in charge for one shift each day. Intermediate care patients typically can participate to some extent in the *activities of daily living (ADL)*.

The payer (a government program such as Medicare and Medicaid, insurance or other prepayment program) typically has its own definition of the term, under which specific procedures and services are included as intermediate care, while others are excluded. It is wise to consult the regulations governing the program, such as Medicare, or the terms of the insurance contract, for specific inclusions and exclusions. See also *skilled nursing care*.

intermediate care facility (ICF): A *free-standing facility (2)* which provides "intermediate care" (the second highest level of nursing care, sometimes called "basic nursing care"). Such a facility would typically have a *registered nurse (RN)* on site during at least one nursing shift, rather than for two nursing shifts as in a "skilled nursing facility" (SNF). See *intermediate care*.

intermediate care facility for the mentally retarded (ICF/MR): A *free-standing facility (2)* which provides *intermediate care* for mentally retarded patients. See *intermediate care facility (ICF)*. Synonym(s): community residential facility.

intermediate care unit: A portion of a *skilled nursing facility (SNF)* which is organized so as to provide "intermediate care" (the other portion of the SNF, that portion giving "skilled nursing care," would be the facility's "skilled nursing unit" (SNU)). Rarely is an intermediate care unit a portion of an acute hospital. The acronym ICU for an intermediate care unit should be avoided since ICU is much more likely to be interpreted "intensive care unit." See *intermediate care* and *skilled nursing care*.

intermediate life support: A term used in emergency services with particular reference to the prevention and treatment of *shock (1)*. This term may have a specific definition in a state's statutes or regulations concerning emergency medical care.

intermittent care: A variety of *home health care* which includes daily care for a two- to three-week period and thereafter under "exceptional circumstances."

intern: A person who has already had formal training in a profession who is now obtaining supervised practical training. The term is no longer restricted to physicians; in fact, the physician intern of the past is now called a *first year resident physician*.

internal disaster plan: See *disaster preparedness plan*.

internal medicine (IM): That branch of medicine which deals especially with diagnosis and medical (non-surgical) therapy of disorders and diseases of the internal structures of the body. One of the medical specialties for which *residency* programs have been approved by the Accreditation Council for Graduate Medical Education (ACGME). See *specialty*.

The physician who specializes in internal medicine is an *internist* (not to be confused with *intern* (a professional undergoing practical training)). See also *internist*.

I

International Classification of Clinical Services (ICCS): A *classification (1)* and *coding* system developed by the *Commission on Professional and Hospital Activities (CPHA)* for certain hospital-provided services in order to standardize patient care data and to facilitate computer handling of those data. Schemas are available for laboratory services, diagnostic imaging, and drugs. Similar schemas are under development for supplies, anesthesia, cardiology, respiratory therapy, physical medicine, nursing, and other categories.

International Classification of Diseases (ICD): A publication of the World Health Organization (WHO), revised periodically, and now in its 9th Revision, dated 1975. The full title is *The International Classification of Diseases, Injuries, and Causes of Death.* This classification, which originated for use in *classifying (2)* deaths, is used world-wide for that purpose. In addition, it has been used widely in the United States for hospital *diagnosis* classification since about 1955 through adaptations and modifications made in the United States of the 7th, 8th, and 9th Revisions. Modification was required for hospital use since, as discussed under *classification (1)*, the purpose of the classification determines the pigeonholes; for example, "death pigeonholes" are quite different, in many instances, from those for illnesses and injuries. The modification in current use, the *International Classification of Diseases, Ninth Revision, Clinical Modification (ICD-9-CM)*, published in 1978, has been in official use in the United States since 1979.

The 10th Revision, due in 1992, will contain additional reasons why people seek help from, and how they are affected by, both the public health programs and the health care systems of the world. Its title will be *The International Statistical Classification of Diseases and Related Health Problems.*

International Classification of Diseases, Ninth Revision, Clinical Modification (ICD-9-CM): The *classification (1)* in current use for *coding* of diagnoses and operations for indexing *medical records* by *diagnoses* and *operations*, for compiling hospital statistics, and for submitting bills in the *prospective payment system (PPS).* ICD-9-CM is published by the *Commission on Professional and Hospital Activities (CPHA)* and by the federal government. "*Annotated ICD-9-CM,*" published by CPHA, is a version color-coded to alert users to reimbursement-related issues.

International Statistical Classification of Diseases and Related Health Problems (ICD-10): The 10th Revision of *The International Classification of Diseases*, due to be published by the World Health Organization (WHO) in 1992. The original volume, published in 1900, was called *The International List of Causes of Death*. Subsequent revisions, about every ten years, have broadened the scope of the volume to include causes of injury and illness, their external causes, and "other factors influencing health status and contact with health services." The name was changed with the 7th Revision (1955) to *The International Classification of Diseases, Injuries, and Causes of Death*. This title was used for the 8th and 9th Revisions as well. With the 10th Revision, the title shown above has been adopted. In view of the widespread use of *ICD-9* in the United States, it is likely that the 10th Revision will be referred to as "*ICD-10*," despite the fact that this short title no longer reflects the actual title of the classification.

Major changes from the 9th Revision include the adoption of alphanumeric codes (previously most of the codes were numeric), the provision of categories for additional "other factors" (see *problem*), changes in the details of categories throughout the classification, changes in the chapters and chapter headings, and the inclusion of the previous "supplementary classifications" as chapters within the classification itself. A comparison between *ICD-9* and *ICD-10* is shown in the table on pages 234 -235.

internist: A physician who practices *internal medicine*, that branch of medicine dealing especially with the diagnosis and medical (non-surgical) treatment of disorders and diseases of the internal structures of the body. The "internist" is not to be confused with an "intern," a physician (or other professional) in training.

A physician who covers the entire field of internal medicine is a "general internist"; one who specializes usually carries the "-ist" designation for the specialty. Within internal medicine there are a number of specialties; one specialty, for example, is cardiology (diseases of the heart), and the internist specializing in cardiology is a "cardiologist." (For a complete listing of *specialties*, see that term.) A general internist is a *primary care physician* because he provides one path of entry to medical care—first evaluating the whole patient and her needs, and then obtaining "secondary" (*specialist*) *consultation* and care as appropriate. The specialized internist, for example, the cardiologist, may at times provide primary care but is, generally speaking, a *secondary care physician*.

I

general internist: An *internist* who does not specialize within the field of *internal medicine*; such an internist is a *primary care physician*.

interrogatories: Written questions sent by one party in a lawsuit to the adverse (opposing) party, in preparation for the trial of the suit. Interrogatories are part of the process of *discovery*, and must be answered by the adverse party within a certain amount of time.

Interstudy: A nonprofit health care research body, a "think tank," located in Minneapolis, Minnesota.

intervening cause: Something which happens after an act of *negligence* and which causes the resulting injury. If the intervening cause is significant, it may relieve the person who was originally negligent of legal *liability (1)*; in this case, it is usually called a "superceding" cause. May also be called intervening force or intervening act. See also *proximate cause*.

intervention: A term which, in clinical use, means an action which is intended to interrupt the course of events which are in progress. For example, a surgeon intervenes in appendicitis by operating and removing the appendix (performing an appendectomy); the operation is a surgical intervention. See also *nursing intervention*.

intra-arterial (IA): Given into a patient's artery (for example, via a needle). For some purposes, the injection is given into a vein rather than an artery, and is then "intravenous (IV)." The injection may be made for the administration of medication or as a part of a diagnostic procedure.

intramuscular (IM): A method of administration of medication or nourishment, in which an injection is given into a patient's muscle.

intrapreneur: A person *within* an organization who creates a new venture or "product" for the organization, as contrasted with an "entrepreneur," a person who organizes a new venture and assumes the risk.

intrauterine device (IUD): A *contraceptive* device which is inserted into the uterus and left there for an extended period of time.

intravenous (IV): An injection given into a patient's vein (for example, via a needle). For some purposes, the injection is given into an artery rather than a vein, and is then "intra-arterial (IA)." The injection may be made for the administration of medication or nourishment or as a part of a diagnostic procedure.

inurement: Private gain from corporate activities. A *nonprofit corporation* cannot keep its tax exempt status if there is "inurement" to individuals or proprietary (for-profit) interests. One common area in which inurement issues are raised today is physician recruitment. Hospitals often provide incentives to attract physicians in needed specialties. If the hospital contracts to pay the physician a salary in excess of reasonable compensation for services, or provides an interest-free loan to the physician, these incentives may be considered by the Internal Revenue Service (IRS) to be inurement and thus jeopardize the hospital's tax exempt status. The hospital must show that it (and the community) receive measurable value for the incentives provided. Inurement issues are also sometimes raised by hospital *joint ventures*.

invasion of privacy: A *tort* in which the wrongdoing is the subjecting of a person to unreasonable, unwanted publicity. For example, a physician was successfully sued by a patient for publishing "before" and "after" pictures of the patient's cosmetic surgery without her permission.

invasive: A term describing a diagnostic or therapeutic procedure or technique which requires penetration of the skin or mucous membrane, either by incision (cutting) or insertion of a needle or other device. A biopsy (removing a portion of tissue for examination and analysis) is invasive, as is the removal of a specimen of blood; an X-ray is *noninvasive*, as is *extracorporeal shock wave lithotripsy (ESWL)*, in which the patient is immersed in a special bath through which the shock wave is administered.

investigator: A term used for anyone doing investigation. In health care, "investigator" means an individual who is carrying out research under federal regulation; he must meet certain standards of *informed consent* of subjects, *peer review*, reporting, and accounting.

I

CH.	*ICD-9*	*ICD-10*	*ICD-9 Chapter Title*	*ICD-10 Chapter Title*
I	001–139	A00–B99	Infectious and Parasitic Diseases	Certain Infectious and Parasitic Diseases
II	140–239	C00–D49	Neoplasms	Neoplasms
III	240–279		Endocrine, Nutritional and Metabolic Diseases and Immunity Disorders	
III		D50–D99		Diseases of Blood and Blood-forming Organs and Certain Disorders Involving the Immune Mechanism
IV	280–289		Diseases of Blood and Blood-forming Organs	
IV		E00–E99		Endocrine, Nutritional and Metabolic Diseases
V	290–319	F00–F99	Mental Disorders	Mental and Behavioral Disorders
VI	320–389	G00–G99	Diseases of the Nervous System and Sense Organs	Diseases of the Nervous System
VII	390–459		Diseases of the Circulatory System	
VII		H00–H59		Diseases of the Eye and Adnexa
VIII	460–519		Diseases of the Respiratory System	
VIII		H60–H99		Diseases of the Ear and Mastoid Process
IX	520–579		Diseases of the Digestive System	
IX		I00–I99		Diseases of the Circulatory System
X	580–629		Diseases of the Genitourinary System	
X		J00–J99		Diseases of the Respiratory System
XI	630–676		Complications of Pregnancy, Childbirth, and the Puerperium	
XI		K00–K99		Diseases of the Digestive System

The title row of the table reads: *ICD-9 vs ICD-10:* Comparison of Chapters, Codes, and Titles

CH.	ICD-9	ICD-10	ICD-9 Chapter Title	ICD-10 Chapter Title
XII	680-709	L00-L99	Diseases of the Skin and Subcutaneous Tissue	Diseases of the Skin and Subcutaneous Tissue
XIII	710-739	M00-M99	Diseases of the Musculoskeletal System and Connective Tissue	Diseases of the Musculoskeletal System and Connective Tissue
XIV	740-759		Congenital Anomalies	
		N00-N99		Diseases of the Genitourinary System
XV	760-779		Certain Conditions Originating in the Perinatal Period	
		O00-O99		Pregnancy, Childbirth and Puerperium
XVI	780-799		Symptoms, Signs and Ill-Defined Conditions	
		P00-P99		Certain Conditions Originating in the Perinatal Period
XVII	800-999		Injury and Poisoning	
		Q00-Q99		Congenital Malformations, Deformations, and Chromosomal Abnormalities
XVIII		R00-R99		Symptoms, Signs, and Abnormal Clinical and Laboratory Findings Not Elsewhere Classified
XIX		S00-T99		Injury, Poisoning and Certain Other Consequences of External Causes
XX		V01-Y99		External Causes of Morbidity and Mortality
XXI		Z00-Z99		Factors Influencing Health Status and Contact with Health Services
	E800-E999		Supplementary Classification of External Causes of Injury and Poisoning	
	V01-V82		Supplementary Classification of Factors Influencing Health Status and Contact with Health Services	

I

involuntary commitment: The admission of a person to a mental health care facility against that person's will. Involuntary commitment is the result of a court proceeding. In most jurisdictions, mental illness alone is insufficient for an involuntary commitment. Usually, at least one of the following factors must also be present: (1) the person is incapable of taking care of himself; (2) he is likely to injure himself (intentionally or unintentionally); or (3) he is likely to injure another (intentionally or unintentionally).

involuntary smoking: Inhaling air containing tobacco smoke produced by other persons who are smoking. It is also called passive smoking. Synonym(s): passive smoking.

IPA: See *Independent Physician Association.*

IPCP: See *interdisciplinary patient care plan.*

IRB: See *institutional review board.*

irrigation: Flushing by use of a liquid.

IRS: Internal Revenue Service.

isobar: See *nuclide.*

isolation: Arrangements made so that (as completely as possible) an individual is neither able to *contaminate* (transfer bacteria, or other infectious agents or harmful substances to) others nor able to be contaminated by them. Isolation may be applied to an individual patient or person or to a group. A patient highly susceptible to infection, such as a premature infant, may be isolated from other patients and from hospital and medical personnel for his own protection (in some instances such isolation systems result in entire *"clean rooms"* being set up). A person with a contagious disease may be isolated from those who are not ill for the protection of others. A physician or hospital employee may also use isolation techniques when he has a cold, for example, in order to protect patients and other hospital personnel. Depending on the situation, the isolation may attempt to prevent direct physical contact, transfer of infectious material by air (air currents, sneezing, and so on), contamination of water supply or sewage, or contamination of objects, such as linens and dishes.

isomer: See *nuclide*.

isotope: See *nuclide*.

IUD: See *intrauterine device*.

IV: See *intravenous*.

IVF: See *in vitro fertilization*.

J

JAMA: See *Journal of the American Medical Association.*

Jarvik heart: A type of artificial (man-made) heart developed by Robert Jarvik, MD. In its present state of development, the Jarvik heart is used as a "bridge" before a heart transplant. The heart is powered from outside the body.

JCAH: See *Joint Commission on Accreditation of Hospitals.*

JCAHO: See *Joint Commission on Accreditation of Healthcare Organizations.*

JCAHO standard: See *standard.*

Joint Commission on Accreditation of Healthcare Organizations (JCAHO): An independent, nonprofit, voluntary organization sponsored by the American College of Physicians (ACP), the American College of Surgeons (ACS), the American Hospital Association (AHA), the American Medical Association (AMA), and other medical, dental, and health care organizations. JCAHO is the successor to the *Hospital Standardization Program (HSP)* of the ACS. It is based in Chicago, Illinois. Governance is by a Board of Commissioners designated by the sponsoring organizations.

JCAHO develops *standards* and provides *accreditation* surveys and *certification* to hospitals and to other health care organizations, such as psychiatric facilities, long term care facilities, ambulatory care, and hospital care. It also offers education programs, consultation, and publications. It should be noted that the JCAHO *Accreditation Manual for Hospitals (AMH)*, published annually, has a glossary defining terms as used by JCAHO. The JCAHO is often referred to simply as the Joint Commission. It was formerly (until 1987) called the Joint Commission on the Accreditation of Hospitals (JCAH).

Joint Commission on Accreditation of Hospitals (JCAH): The former name of the *Joint Commission on the Accreditation of Healthcare Organizations (JCAHO)*.

joint conference committee: A hospital committee with members from the *governing body*, the *medical staff*, and the hospital management (administration). Its purpose is to facilitate understanding and communication, not to introduce a channel of management which competes with the *line* channels of the hospital administration and the *medical staff organization (MSO)*.

joint planning: Planning carried out jointly by two or more institutions, which may or may not envision sharing of services and facilities. See *shared services*.

joint venture: A business arrangement between two or more parties to share profits, losses, and control. In health care, the term usually indicates a formalized cooperative effort between the hospital and its *medical staff* (or physicians from its medical staff), as opposed to a relationship in which the two, hospital and physicians, are in competition with one another. For example, a joint venture may be established in order to set up a diagnostic facility.

The legal form of the joint venture may be a *partnership* (general or limited), lease arrangement, *corporation*, or other form suited to the requirements of the venture. Sometimes the term "joint venture" is used synonomously with "partnership"; however, while a partnership may be a joint venture, not all joint ventures are partnerships. "Joint venture" may also have a specific legal meaning under state law.

Joint ventures may raise legal concerns for hospitals; see *antitrust, fraud and abuse, inurement, safe harbor regulations, Stark bill*.

Journal of the American Medical Association (JAMA): The weekly clinical publication of the *American Medical Association (AMA)*.

judicial law: See *common law*.

K

KCF: See *key clinical findings*.

key clinical findings (KCF): A term used in the *Medisgroups II* method of measuring the *severity* of a patient's illness or injury. KCFs are found in a "standardized medical glossary," a list of "...objective clinical findings (e.g. lab test results)..." Severity is defined in the KCF system as likelihood of organ failure.

kininase: See *angiotensin-converting enzyme (ACE)*.

KIPS: Key Indicators, Probes, and a Scoring method. "KIPS" is an initialism used by the *Joint Commission on the Accreditation of Healthcare Organizations (JCAHO)* for evaluating compliance with certain JCAHO requirements for *accreditation*. JCAHO publishes a *KIPS Survey Guide*.

KIPS Survey Guide: A publication of the *Joint Commission on the Accreditation of Healthcare Organizations (JCAHO)*. It contains Key Indicators, Probes, and a Scoring method for evaluating compliance with certain JCAHO *standards*.

Kirklin system: A method of *staging tumors*.

L

labor: The process the mother goes through in giving birth.

labor-delivery-recovery-postpartum suites (LDRPS): Hospital suites in which a maternity patient can remain in the same suite from admission to the hospital, through *labor*, *delivery*, and recovery in the *postpartum* period until the time of *discharge*. Procedures such as caesarean sections are not performed in such suites, however. In some hospitals LDRPSs are replacing *labor-delivery-recovery suites (LDRSs)* in which the postpartum period requires the patient's transfer to another room.

labor-delivery-recovery suites (LDRS): Hospital suites in which a maternity patient stays from the time of *admission*, through *labor* and recovery from *delivery*. The *postpartum* portion of the hospital stay is provided in other quarters. In some hospitals LDRSs are being replaced by labor-delivery-recovery-postpartum suites (LDRPSs) in which the entire stay (except for such procedures as caesarean sections) is in the one suite.

labor room: A room for maternity patients who are in *labor*. A labor room is not to be confused with the *delivery room*, where actual birth takes place.

laboratory: A facility where testing, research, experimentation, and sometimes preparation of scientific equipment and substances is carried out. In a hospital, when the word "laboratory" is used alone, it refers to the *clinical laboratory*. See also *pathology laboratory*.

clinical laboratory: A laboratory for examining materials from the human body. The examinations typically fall under headings such as *hematology, cytology, bacteriology, histology, biochemistry, toxicology,* and *serology.*

LAN: See *local area network.*

laparascopic surgery: Abdominal surgery carried out by inserting instruments for seeing inside the abdomen and instruments for manipulation (such as cutting, application of lasers, sewing) through small incisions, often under local anesthesia. When surgery by this method is appropriate for a given patient, it is usually preferable, because the procedure usually becomes one for "same-day" (ambulatory) surgery. The technique is being used for gallbladder removal (laparascopic cholecystectomy), for example.

laptop computer: See *computer.*

LAV: Lymphadenopathy-associated virus. See *human immunodeficiency virus (HIV).*

LDRPS: See *labor-delivery-recovery-postpartum suites.*

LDRS: See *labor-delivery-recovery suites.*

leave of absence (LOA): A predetermined period of time during a hospital stay when the patient is permitted to be away from the hospital, with the understanding that the patient will return at the end of the period. An LOA may be for a few hours, a day, or several days. A leave is granted by the *attending physician,* who has satisfied herself that the patient's condition warrants the absence. The patient's departure is not a *discharge,* and the return is not an *admission.* There is debate as to whether the absent days are a part of the patient's *length of stay (LOS).* Questions also arise as to responsibility for the patient on LOA, that is, whether the hospital or patient is liable if the patient's condition worsens or there is an accident.

length of stay (LOS): The number of days between a patient's *admission* and *discharge.* The day of admission is counted as a day, while the day of discharge is not. This abbreviation is often misused when the intent is to refer to *average length of stay (ALOS)*.

average length of stay (ALOS): A standard hospital statistic. For a given group of patients, their total *lengths of stay (LOSs)* are added together, and that total is divided by the total number of patients in the group. For a "hospital ALOS," the formula adds together the LOSs of all patients discharged from the hospital (for their entire stays) in a given time period, and divides that sum by the number of patients discharged in that same time period. ALOS is often incorrectly referred to as "LOS"; however, LOS means "length of stay" and pertains to an individual patient.

The ALOS may be calculated not only for the entire hospital, but also for specific age groups or *Diagnosis Related Groups (DRGs)*, for example. It may also be calculated in a more refined ("normalized") manner by making an *adjustment* for the *case mix* of the hospital. An ALOS which adjusts for the age distribution of the patients, for example, makes for fairer comparisons between hospitals than one without such an adjustment; adjusting for additional factors, such as the distribution of patients among DRGs, further improves the statistic for interhospital comparison purposes.

level of care: The amount (intensity) and kind of professional nursing care required for a patient in order to achieve the desired medical and nursing care objectives for the patient, that is, to carry out the orders of the attending physician and to meet the patient's nursing care needs. The term "levels of care" is primarily used outside the acute hospital, where three levels of care are recognized: *skilled nursing care* (the highest level), *intermediate care*, and *rest home care* (custodial care, the lowest level).

Levels of care (and facilities to provide them) have specific definitions in Medicare, Medicaid, and other payment programs, and also under statutes and regulations of the various states. The determination of the level of care to be provided to a given patient is a serious matter; on the one hand, the patient should be placed at the lowest level of care commensurate with his needs as a matter both of appropriate care and of economy, while, on the other hand, payment is greater for each succeedingly higher level of care. See also *care*.

L

leverage: A financial term, meaning financing by borrowing, that is rarely used in health care except with modifiers:

financial leverage: The ratio of total *debt* to total *assets* (in a stock corporation, the ratio of *long-term debt* to *shareholders' equity*). Financial leverage is also called "capital leverage." An institution uses financial leverage (it "trades on its equity") when it believes it has "positive leverage," that is, that it can use the money obtained by *debt financing* (using borrowed money) to earn more money than it costs to borrow the money (interest and taxes). Should the cost of borrowing exceed the added revenue, the situation is one of "negative leverage."

operating leverage: The ratio of *fixed costs* to *variable costs*. When it takes very little added labor or materials to provide added units of service or products, the operating leverage is high (and the *marginal cost* of added units is low); a greater volume brings accelerated profits, once the *break-even point* is reached. The higher the proportion of the costs that are variable (that is, the lower the operating leverage) the greater an increase in units of service or products will be required to increase profits.

leveraged: Financed largely by borrowed funds.

LHEG: See *local healthcare executive group*.

liability (1): Responsibility to do something, pay something, or refrain from doing something. Liability is used to refer to a legal obligation, often one which must be enforced by a lawsuit.

corporate liability: Legal responsibility of a corporation, rather than of an individual. In the health care context, the term is often used to denote a specific type of responsibility: that of the hospital as an institution (corporation) to exercise reasonable care in selecting, retaining, and granting *privileges* to members of its *medical staff*. A hospital may be liable to a patient injured by a physician (or other health professional) if the hospital knew or should have known that the physician was not competent to perform the procedure involved (or to otherwise treat the patient), and did not reasonably act to protect the patient (for example, by restricting that physician's privileges or by requiring supervision). "Knew" means that the hospital may not "look the other way" if it learns of problems with a physician which could endanger patients;

L

"should have known" means that the hospital must diligently investigate a physician's credentials prior to granting staff privileges, *and* that the hospital must systematically monitor the care provided by that physician, once on the staff. See also *privileges* and *credentialing*.

joint and several liability: The responsibility of more than one *defendant* to share in legal liability to a *plaintiff*. If the defendants (for example, the hospital and a physician) are jointly and severally liable, each is responsible to pay the entire judgment to the plaintiff (although the plaintiff cannot collect more than the amount of the judgment).

product liability: An area of law which imposes legal responsibility on manufacturers (and in some cases distributors and retailers) of goods which leave the factory in an unreasonably dangerous condition, and which in fact cause harm to someone because of that condition. Product liability does not require proof that the manufacturer was *negligent* (careless) in designing or producing the item.

professional liability: A legal obligation which is the result of performing (or failing to perform) something which one does (or should have done) as a professional. A physician who drives carelessly and injures another will be simply "liable" for that person's injuries; the fact that she is a physician is not relevant to the fact that she injured the other person. If that same physician carelessly misses a diagnosis and again injures another, the legal responsibility is called "professional liability," since her actions as a physician caused the injury. Sometimes the phrase "professional liability" is used interchangeably with "professional *negligence*," but that usage is inaccurate because a professional can become liable for reasons other than negligence (for example, by improperly disclosing a patient's confidences, operating without *informed consent*, or abandoning a patient).

strict liability: Legal responsibility for injury which is imposed regardless of any fault, or lack of fault. A plaintiff suing under strict liability does not need to show that the defendant was negligent, reckless, or malicious. The plaintiff does, however, still need to prove the existence of a defect (such as in a product) or an action (such as selling liquor to an intoxicated person) and that the defect or action caused the plaintiff's injuries.

L

liability (2): In finance, an obligation to pay. Liabilities are shown on an institution's *balance sheet* under such headings as "accounts payable" (money owed to vendors and others), "accrued salaries" (when a statement is drawn before checks have been issued for a given pay period), and the like.

current liability: A liability due within one year.

Libby Zion case: A 1986 legal case involving the death in 1984 of an 18-year old woman, Libby Zion, in New York. The woman died a few hours after admission to a hospital from its emergency department. Ms. Zion's father claimed that her care had been inadequate, and a grand jury investigation later followed. While the grand jury did not return a criminal indictment, it did make a number of recommendations regarding emergency room staffing, supervision of physicians in training, regulation of work hours for *interns* and junior *resident physicians*, restraint of patients (and the care of patients under restraint), and protection of patients from *contraindicated* combinations of drugs. Each recommendation— particularly that of limiting the number of hours a physician in training may work consecutively—has attracted a good deal of attention in New York and nationally.

libel: Written words which injure the reputation of another; written *defamation*. Oral defamation is called "slander." See *defamation*.

licensed: Having a legal right, granted by a government *agency (1)*, in compliance with a statute governing a profession (such as medicine or nursing), occupation, or the operation of an activity (such as a hospital).

licensed beds: The number of beds which the state licensing agency authorizes the hospital to operate on a regular basis. See *bed capacity*.

life care: A *long-term care* arrangement ("*alternative*") in which all care required for the lifetime of the participant is provided. A retirement home which agrees to provide not only facilities for independent living, but also nursing care and hospitalization to residents as needed, is a "life care community."

Life Safety Code: A code of construction and operation for buildings, intended to maximize fire safety, issued and periodically revised by the *National Fire Protection Association (NFPA)* of Quincy, Massachusetts. Compliance with this code (also known as NFPA 101) is required of hospitals seeking *accreditation* by the *Joint Commission on the Accreditation of Healthcare Organizations (JCAHO)*.

life signs: See *vital signs*.

life support system: Equipment and services, including administration of nutrition and fluids, which support one or more of the life-sustaining functions of circulation (heart), respiration (breathing), nutrition, and kidney function. When a patient is completely dependent on artificial (mechanical) means for maintenance of one or more of these functions, stopping or removing the equipment will cause death, and the stopping or removal is referred to as "termination of life support systems."

lifetime reserve: A Medicare term referring to the pool of 60 days of hospital care upon which a patient may draw after she has used up the maximum Medicare benefit for a single *spell of illness*.

line: A term used in the context of "line and staff," which refers to authority in an organization. Line authority is *hierarchical*: a floor nurse reports to a head nurse, who in turn reports to the chief of nursing, who in turn reports to the chief executive officer of the hospital who, finally, reports to the governing body. Only a person higher in this series is authorized to "give orders" to a person lower in the series.

The contrast is with "staff," which refers to persons who assist in the operation of the organization by furnishing services to line personnel. Staff personnel do not have authority to "give orders" (except within the narrow limits of the staff group itself). The chief of nursing is a line person. The controller is a staff person, although the controller may also have line authority for the business office, for example.

line and staff: A phrase used in organizations describing the two kinds of roles played by personnel. "Line" pertains to positions in the "chain of command" in which superiors direct subordinates at a series of levels, and "staff" refers to positions in which in-

L

dividuals (or components of the organization) are not in the "chain of command" but are employed to provide assistance to those in line positions.

linear regression: See *regression*.

liquidity: The ability to turn *assets* into cash.

lithotripsy: Fragmentation (shattering) of stones (kidney, urinary tract, and bladder stones, as well as gallstones). Several methods are in use or under development: *electrohydraulic lithotripsy (EHL)*, which produces shock waves at or near the stone through the use of a probe; *ultrasonic lithotripsy (UL)*, which produces a drilling effect; and *extracorporeal shock wave lithotripsy (ESWL)*, in which shock waves are generated in a bath in which the patient is placed. The latter method is the most widespread in current use. Lithotripsy is *noninvasive*; the patient is spared surgery requiring invasion of her body.

lithotriptor: A device for fragmenting stones in the urinary tract without *invasive* surgery. See *lithotripsy*.

living-in unit: A hospital room where a mother can assume care of her newborn infant under the supervision of the hospital's nursing personnel. This term may also apply to relatives or others assisting in the care of a chronically ill or other type of patient.

living will: A will concerning the life of the individual executing the will, in contrast with the usual "last will and testament" in which the subject matter is the disposition of property (this could be thought of as a "property will") and custody of minor children. In many states, individuals may execute "living wills" concerning the circumstances under which they wish to refuse, or discontinue the use of, life-support measures administered to themselves should they become *incompetent (1)*. Living will statutes (also known as *right to die* laws or *natural death acts*) govern the execution and enforcement procedures for living wills. At least one state (New Hampshire) calls the living will a "terminal care document."

The "life-sustaining procedures act," proposed by the National Conference of Commissioners on Uniform State Laws, suggests the following language for a living will: "If I should have an incurable or irreversible condition that will cause my death within a relatively short time, and if I am unable to make decisions regarding my medical treatment, I direct my attending physician to withhold or withdraw procedures that merely prolong the dying process and are not necessary to my comfort or to alleviate pain."

LOA: See *leave of absence.*

local area network (LAN): The hardware and software allowing two or more *computers* to be connected together over a small geographic area (typically an office, or one building). It is distinguished from a "wide area network" (WAN) which connects computers, other networks, or both over large geographical distances.

LANs are becoming increasingly important in allowing *microcomputers* (PCs) to be connected to each other; they allow PC users to share data and facilities which once required the use of *mini* or *mainframe* computers. However, a major stumbling block to even greater acceptance of LAN technology is the lack of standards in network "protocols."

local healthcare executive group (LHEG): Any association of health care executives in a local area, either formal or informal, designed to provide *networking* opportunities. A variety of such groups exist under many names, the earliest perhaps being "young administrators' groups."

locality rule: A legal doctrine which states that the *standard of care (2)* in a *malpractice* lawsuit will be measured by the degree of care exercised by similar professionals within the same geographic area (locality), rather than within the world, nation, state, or profession at large. Some states use this rule; others do not.

long-term care (LTC): Care for patients, regardless of age, who have chronic diseases or disabilities, and who require preventive, diagnostic, therapeutic, and supportive services over long periods of time. LTC may call on a variety of health care professionals (such as physicians, nurses, physical therapists, and social workers) as well as non-professionals (family, others) and may be delivered in a health care or other institution or in the home.

Long-term care customarily refers to those for whom the care is thought to be necessary for the rest of their lives, i.e., for whom

L

the disability is thought not to be reversible. When the prediction is that the person can be returned to a more independent mode of living, the person is placed under *skilled nursing* or *intermediate care* (under "extended care" rather than "long-term care"). Rehabilitation efforts are, however, made for persons in long-term care, and some of them do recover sufficiently to become less dependent.

long-term care alternatives (LTC alternatives): *Alternatives* to the traditional *nursing home.*

long-term care facility (LTCF): A *facility (2)* which provides lodging and health care services to patients with *chronic* health care needs.

LOS: See *length of stay.*

loss: Excess of expense over income. Actually means a decrease in *assets.* The defining phrase "negative fund balance" is often used in *nonprofit corporations* as a substitute for the word "loss."

low birth weight: A weight of 2500 grams or less (5 pounds, 8.2 ounces) at birth.

very low birth weight: A weight of 1500 grams (3 pounds, 4.5 ounces) or less at birth.

LPN: Licensed practical nurse. See *nurse.*

LTC: See *long-term care.*

LTC alternatives: See *long-term care alternatives.*

LTCF: See *long-term care facility.*

LVN: Licensed vocational nurse. See *licensed practical nurse (LPN)* under *nurse.*

lymphadenopathy-associated virus (LAV): See *human immunodeficiency virus (HIV).*

M

M & E: Monitoring and evaluation. An abbreviation used by the *Joint Commission on the Accreditation of Healthcare Organizations (JCAHO)*.

MA (1): Medical audit. See *patient care audit*.

MA (2): See *market administration*.

MA (3): See *medical assistant*.

MA (4): See *Management and Administrative Services*.

MAAC: See *maximum allowable actual charges*.

magnetic resonance imaging (MRI): See *nuclear magnetic resonance imaging (NMRI)*.

mainframe computer: See *computer*.

mainstreaming: A policy of providing services to special classes of individuals within the organizational structure which serves the general population. For example, handicapped children, often educated in special classrooms, are "mainstreamed" when they are educated in the regular classroom. The term is now being applied in health care in some instances.

Major Diagnostic Category (MDC): A term used in the *prospective payment system (PPS)*. All patients are ultimately classified into

M

one of the 468 *Diagnosis Related Groups (DRGs)* (*categories*). On the way to that classification, each patient first falls into one of 23 MDCs on the basis of his *principal diagnosis*; the patient is then further classified according to age, complications, whether an operating room procedure was performed, and so forth.

malice: A legal term which describes the state of mind of someone doing a wrongful act intentionally, with the purpose of doing injury or with reckless disregard as to whether the act will result in injury.

malicious prosecution: Legal grounds upon which a *defendant* may countersue a *plaintiff* if the plaintiff's lawsuit was totally frivolous and without any merit, and was brought simply to harass the defendant. To prove a case of malicious prosecution, the plaintiff's case must have been decided in favor of the defendant, and the defendant must show that there was no probable cause to believe that the defendant was liable and that the plaintiff (or plaintiff's attorney) acted with *malice* in bringing the suit. Given those restrictions, physicians have had very limited success in suing malpractice plaintiffs for malicious prosecution.

malignant: As applied to a tumor, one which is subject to unlimited growth and extension or dispersal within the body, often leading to death.

malpractice: A failure of care or skill by a *professional*, which causes loss or injury and results in legal *liability (1)*. This narrow definition means the same as *professional negligence*. Some individuals use the term "malpractice" more broadly to describe all acts by a health care professional in the course of providing health care—including *breach of contract*—which may result in legal liability.

mammogram: A *diagnostic X-ray* of the breast, usually for the purpose of detecting a *tumor*. *Nuclear magnetic resonance images (NMRIs)* are being tried as a supplement or substitute for the mammogram.

mammography: The making of *X-ray images* of the breast (*mammograms*).

managed care: Any arrangement for health care in which someone is interposed between the patient and physician and has authority to place restraints on how and from whom the patient may obtain medical and health services, and what *services (1)* are to be provided in a given situation. Under the terms of a *prepaid health plan*, for example, the payer may require: that except in an emergency, a designated person (a *gatekeeper*) be the patient's first contact with the health care services; that all care be authorized and coordinated by the gatekeeper rather than permitting the patient to go directly to *specialists*; that only certain physicians and facilities be used (if the prepayment plan is to pay for the services); that *preadmission certification* precede hospitalization; that *second opinions* be obtained for *elective surgery*; and that certain care be delivered in the *outpatient* setting. Although the primary stimulus for introducing managed care was to attempt to keep costs down, there is increasing interest in trying to see that each patient gets the care indicated and is spared unnecessary or ill-advised care.

managed care firm: A term applied to a variety of organizations which contract to provide management services for the reduction and control of health care costs to corporations, insurers, and third-party administrators. Managed care firms employ such methods as making decisions as to what care is to be given individual patients and where it will be provided, negotiating contracts with providers as to quantities of and prices for services (often discounts), and auditing and approving the bills for the services the patients receive. Sometimes the managed care firm offers a stipulated care package for a prearranged capitation fee. Typically such firms do not themselves provide care and do not operate hospitals or other health care facilities. Managed care firms often contend that they can reduce the costs of health care for a client by 25 percent or more.

managed care plan: An organization providing *managed care*, a method of arranging for health care to achieve certain goals: (1) to benefit the individuals served by the plan, and, at the same time, (2) to benefit the population being served, and (3) to provide *services (1)* in the most efficient, effective, and economic manner in view of the finite resources available. A managed care plan has a defined group of providers and an identified group of enrollees to be served. Forward-looking plans develop explicit standards of care to be required of its providers, and are concerned not only with treatment and amelioration of disease, but also with prevention. The plan may or may not operate its own hospitals or other health care facilities. The financing is typically prearranged by *capitation*.

management (1): The plan and course of action for the care of the patient.

management (2): In an organization, the task of getting things done systematically by, through, or with people with the necessary tools and facilities.

service management: A philosophy of management which emphasizes *"service (5)"* to mean satisfaction of the demands and wishes of the "customer" and attention to his perceptions, rather than paying primary attention to the "products" provided or satisfying the provider (the hospital or physician, for example).

Management and Administrative Services (MA): The chapter giving the *standards* for this component of the hospital in the 1990 *Accreditation Manual for Hospitals (AMH)* of the *Joint Commission on the Accreditation of Healthcare Organizations (JCAHO)*.

management information system (MIS): An essentially undefined term, applied to any system set up to provide information to or for management. There is no agreement on the kinds of information to be carried or the technology used. The term "MIS" often implies that a computer is involved—sometimes the hospital's computer system, sometimes *shared services* with outside computers, and sometimes a *hospital discharge abstract system*. The *information* may include data on, for example, patients, finance, personnel, production, or the health care industry.

case-mix management information system (case-mix MIS): An information system which combines and correlates, on an individual patient basis, medical data abstracted from the hospital medical record of the patient (*discharge abstract*) and from the patient's bill. Data analyses and displays relate *charges*, by *Diagnosis Related Groups (DRGs)*, to receipts or allowances for those DRGs for the hospital and for individual physicians. A case-mix MIS may be provided *in-house*, off-site, or through *shared services*. See also *case-mix*.

hospital information system (HIS): A term applied to any system in a hospital dealing with information, usually with a computer involved. The kinds of data carried in the system will vary from hospital to hospital; there is no agreement yet on criteria which a system must meet to carry this title. An HIS is one kind of management information system (MIS).

manager: Any individual who is responsible for directing the activities of an organization or one of its components. In the hospital field, however, the title of "manager" is rarely given to high ranking persons, particularly in the professions; the chief executive officer (CEO) and the chief of nursing are not called "managers." The title is more likely to be used in such areas of the hospital as housekeeping, maintenance, and the like.

MAP: See *Medical Audit Program.*

marginal worker: See *contingent worker.*

market administration (MA): A type of administration of an organization in which the focus is on the institution's markets. In a hospital, MA focuses on the hospital's markets, such as women, the elderly, or specific payers. Other types of administration are the traditional *functional administration (FA),* in which the focus is on the functional components (in a hospital, nursing and pathology, for example) and *product administration (PA),* in which the structure revolves around "products" (in a hospital, surgery and internal medicine, for example).

market-driven system: An economic system which responds to the demands of the market, that is, those of the purchaser. The term is currently being applied in health care with the emergence of competitive health care delivery plans which seek to attract "customers" by offering (1) more of what the customers want (amenities as well as services) or (2) attractive prices (that is, price competition). Note that the "customer" is the person paying for the service, and is not necessarily the "consumer" (the patient).

In health care, a "market-driven system" is contrasted with the traditional health care system, which could be labelled "provider-driven" to indicate that the providers (physicians, other professionals, and institutions) "prescribed" and furnished those *services*

M

(1) which they considered to be best for the patients. Such a system sought to meet the provider-determined needs of the patients rather than the demands of the purchasers. Even in a market-driven system, however, the purchaser seeks professional advice in determining what he should demand.

marketing: Activity to publicize a hospital or service, and to increase its use. See also *demarketing*.

MAS: See *medical audit study*.

mass number: See *nuclide*.

materiel: The materials and tools necessary to do any given work, as contrasted with the personnel needed to do the work.

maternal and child health program (MCH program): A program providing preventive and treatment services for pregnant women, mothers, and children. The services may include health education (often with particular attention to nutrition) and family planning. Funding may be from federal, state, or local sources. One source of funds has been the United States Maternal and Child Health Program under the Social Security Act.

maternal death: In public health (vital) statistical usage, a death of a pregnant woman or of a woman within a specified time period after delivery (the time period ranges from 42 days, as defined by the World Health Organization, to one year in some jurisdictions). Maternal deaths are sometimes classified as direct (due to some element of the pregnancy, labor, or immediate recovery period), indirect (due to some disease not related to obstetric causes but aggravated by the pregnancy), and as nonmaternal (for example, from unrelated accidents). See also *maternal death rate* under *death rate*.

maternity: The condition of being a mother.

maternity patient: A patient who is under medical or hospital care because she is pregnant. Synonym(s): obstetric patient.

maximum allowable actual charges (MAAC): Limits for physician charge increases which were set by federal statute enacted in 1986. The statute applies only to physicians who are "non-participating" (that is, who have not agreed to accept the Medicare payment allowance as full payment). The limits apply to average charges, rather than charges for specific *services (1)*; thus, compliance must be evaluated retrospectively, and enforcement is complicated.

MCAT: See *Medical College Admission Test*.

MCES: Medical care evaluation study. See *patient care audit*.

MCH program: See *maternal and child health program*.

MD: See *Doctor of Medicine*.

MDC: See *Major Diagnostic Category*.

mean: By itself, this term usually means *arithmetic mean*, which is the ordinary *average*—namely the sum of a set of quantities divided by the number of quantities in the set.

geometric mean: The nth root of the product of n items. For example, the geometric mean of 2 and 8 is 4, since 4 is the 2nd root (square root) of 2 x 8, or 16. Geometric means of hospital *lengths of stay (LOSs)*, compiled from reference data, are sometimes used as standards in LOS comparisons.

med: Short for *medication*.

Medi-Cal: *Medicaid* in California. Since each state administers Medicaid, the program in California is unique (as are the programs in the other states).

median: A statistical term. The middle point in a series of things arranged in order of size. The median for the series 7, 8, 9, 10, and 51 is 9, the third of the five items. For the same series, the *mean* (arithmetic average) for that series would be 17 (the sum, 85, divided by the number of quantities, 5). When the series has an even number of items, the median is customarily calculated as the average of the two middle items.

M

mediation: A method of settling disputes by bringing the parties together to agree on a solution, rather than having a third party (such as an *arbitrator*, judge, or jury) make the decision for them. Mediation, usually done with the assistance of a mediator (someone trained in dispute resolution), may be private or may be connected to the court system. Some states have laws requiring or encouraging mediation as an alternative or supplement to costly, time-consuming lawsuits or trials.

Medicaid: The federal program which provides health care to *indigent* and *medically indigent* persons. While partially federally funded, the Medicaid program is administered by the states, in contrast with Medicare, which is federally funded and administered at the federal level. The Medicaid program was established in 1965 by amendment to the Social Security Act, under a provision entitled "Title XIX—Medical Assistance."

medical: When applied as an adjective (as in "medical treatment"), this term means "nonsurgical," that is, the avoidance of the surgical methods of operation and manipulation. Synonym(s): nonsurgical.

Medical Assistance: See *Medicaid*.

medical assistant (MA): One of the 26 *allied health professionals* for whom the American Medical Association's *Committee on Allied Health Education and Accreditation (CAHEA)* has accredited education programs.

medical association: See *medical society*.

medical audit (MA): See *patient care audit*.

Medical Audit Program (MAP): A specific program of data display formerly offered by the *Commission on Professional and Hospital Activities (CPHA)* as part of the *Professional Activity Study (PAS)* system. Clinical data on patient condition and diagnostic procedures, along with diagnoses and therapy, were used to show patterns of care useful in the evaluation of care. See *patient care audit*.

medical audit study (MAS): The operational unit of a "medical audit." See *patient care audit*.

medical care: Traditionally, care which was under the direction of a physician. More recently, "medical care" has also come to refer only to those portions of the care provided directly or personally by a physician, with the care given by other professionals (such as nursing care, rehabilitation, and the like) excluded, or at least semi-independent, from the definition. For example, "evaluation of medical care" has been replaced in most usage by "evaluation of patient care"; the latter term not only focuses on the patient, but also ensures that all components of the care—not just what the physician does—are included.

medical care evaluation: The evaluation of the quality of medical care. Usually refers to the patient care audit (medical audit), which is a retrospective review of the quality of care of a group of patients, ordinarily a group with the same diagnosis or therapy. See *patient care audit*.

medical care evaluation study (MCES): See *patient care audit*.

medical center: An essentially undefined term which may refer to a single institution, but is usually taken to mean that there is more to the institution than merely a single hospital—perhaps several hospitals in a complex, or perhaps a wider range of facilities and services than an ordinary hospital is likely to offer. The term does not automatically imply that the institution is an academic center, nor is there any licensure requirement before the term may be used.

academic medical center: A medical center which ordinarily consists of a *university hospital* and medical school, often along with other *teaching hospitals*, research organizations and their laboratories, outpatient clinics, libraries, and related facilities.

Medical College Admission Test (MCAT): A national examination, similar to the Scholastic Aptitude Test (SAT), which most medical schools require of individuals seeking admission to medical school. The test was developed by the Association of American Medical Colleges (AAMC).

M

medical director (1): A physician, usually employed by the hospital, who serves as the administrative head of the *medical staff organization (MSO)*. "Medical director" tends to be the title for the *chief of staff* when that person is a paid hospital employee. The title may also be "vice president for medical affairs" or something similar. This term is discussed further under *chief of staff*.

medical director (2): A physician, in a *long term care facility (LTCF)*, retained to coordinate the medical care in the facility, to ensure adequacy and appropriateness of the medical *services (1)* provided to each patient, and to maintain surveillance of the health status of employees. An LTCF is required to have a medical director.

medical education: Medical education is carried out at several levels:

> **continuing medical education (CME):** The education of practicing physicians through refresher courses, medical journals and texts, attendance at regularly scheduled teaching programs, approved self-study courses (both traditional and computer-assisted), and so forth. CME programs are provided by medical schools, professional organizations, publishing companies, educational organizations, and hospitals. The necessity for continuing education is well accepted by the medical profession. In some states, CME is required for continued licensure.

> **graduate medical education (GME):** Formal education in *residency* programs. Graduate medical education is only available to those holding Doctor of Medicine (MD) or Doctor of Osteopathy (DO) degrees.

> **undergraduate medical education (UGME):** Education in medicine prior to the granting of the *Doctor of Medicine (MD)* or *Doctor of Osteopathy (OD)* degree.

Medical Group Management Association (MGMA): The national association of business managers of medical groups (*group practices*).

medical history: The portion of the patient's *medical record* containing the essential medical (and social) information about the patient and his family (ancestors, blood relatives, and siblings), spouse and household, past personal injuries and illnesses, and development of the present problems. The history may be recorded using the traditional method of "systems review," under headings such as "respiratory," "past illnesses," "cardiac," and the like; or, it may be recorded in the newer method, the *problem oriented medical record (POMR)*, in which each of the patient's *problems* is traced separately. A medical history is often referred to simply as a "history."

Medical Illness Severity Grouping System (MedisGroups): A proprietary system for *classifying (2)* hospital patients by *severity of illness* using *objective* data specially *abstracted* from the patients' *medical records*. This *classification (1)* is a contender for use in supplementing the *Diagnosis Related Group (DRG)* classification to allow for severity. It was developed by MediQual Systems, Inc.

medical illustrator (MI): One of the 26 *allied health professionals* for whom the American Medical Association's *Committee on Allied Health Education and Accreditation (CAHEA)* has accredited education programs.

medical indigence: As defined in a statute or administrative rule, the state of having insufficient income to obtain health care services without depriving oneself or one's dependents of the necessities of living.

medical informatics: See *informatics*.

medical laboratory technician—associate degree (MLT-AD): A medical laboratory technician trained in an *associate degree (AD)* program. One of the 26 *allied health professionals* for whom the American Medical Association's *Committee on Allied Health Education and Accreditation (CAHEA)* has accredited education programs.

medical laboratory technician—certificate (MLT-C): A medical laboratory technician trained in a hospital training program. One of the 26 *allied health professionals* for whom the American Medical Association's *Committee on Allied Health Education and Accreditation (CAHEA)* has accredited education programs.

Medical Literature Analysis and Retrieval System (MEDLARS): A computerized *data base access system* of the United States National Library of Medicine (a federal governmental agency).

M

Medical Management Analysis (System) (MMA): A proprietary system for carrying out *occurrence screening*; a method for detecting cases in which there was a possible quality problem. Its author is Joyce W. Craddick, MD, president of Medical Management Analysis Consulting and Education Services, Inc., of Auburn, California.

medical neglect: Withholding medically indicated treatment from a child, a form of child abuse and neglect. See *Child Abuse Amendments*.

medical oncology: A branch of *internal medicine* which deals with *tumors*. One of the medical specialties for which *residency* programs have been approved by the Accreditation Council for Graduate Medical Education (ACGME). See *specialty*.

medical practice act: A state statute governing the practice of medicine within the state.

medical practice plan: In a medical school setting, an official document setting forth the policies under which patient services are rendered by medical school faculty physicians, the method of obtaining reimbursement, and the disposition of the funds obtained for such services. The detail of procedures is usually covered in the document. Synonym(s): clinical practice plan, faculty practice plan.

medical record: A file kept for each patient, maintained by the hospital (the physician also maintains a medical record in his own practice), which documents the patient's problems, diagnostic procedures, treatment, and outcome. Related documents, such as written *consent* for surgery and other procedures, are also included in the record. The Joint Commission on Accreditation of Healthcare Organizations (JCAHO) places great importance on the medical record in the accreditation process, and its *Accreditation Manual for Hospitals (AMH)* contains an extensive description of the desired and required contents of the medical record.

Ordinarily the record is kept on paper, but it may also be in computer (electronic) media. Occasionally a hospital keeps a separate medical record for each hospitalization (hospital *admission*); the better practice is to use the "unit record system," that is, keep a "unit record" for each patient, with all records of the patient's successive hospitalizations in the patient's unit file.

The record itself is usually organized in either the "traditional" or "problem-oriented" method (see below). The medical record is also called the clinical record, the patient's chart, or simply the chart. See also *medical record entry* and *nursing record*.

online medical record (OMR): A medical record kept in a computer, with constant instantaneous access via a *computer terminal* and sometimes with other forms of data entry, such as *point of sale (POS)* terminals for laboratory and other data.

problem-oriented medical record (POMR): A medical record organized around the problems presented by the patient. (See the definition of *problem*.) A common form of organization of the POMR is "SOAP": Subjective (complaints), Objective (observations, test results), Assessment, and Plan for each problem. The same principle is increasingly used for nursing information and that of other professionals in the medical record; that is, nursing and other information is recorded in connection with the problem(s) to which it pertains. Sometimes shortened to "problem-oriented record."

problem-oriented record (POR): See *problem-oriented medical record*.

traditional medical record: A medical record organized according to "presenting complaint," "*history*," "review of systems" (such as cardiovascular and respiratory), "physical examination," and the like. The nursing record is traditionally organized chronologically.

medical record abstracter: A person who extracts a specific predetermined array of information from a *medical record*, usually on a precoded form to be used as input into a *hospital discharge abstract system*.

medical record administrator (MRA): A person, formerly called a "medical record librarian," who has met the requirements of the *American Medical Record Association (AMRA)* as to training in *medical record science*, including a course in the management of the medical record department of a health care institution. Educational requirements are higher than for the title of *medical record technician*. One of the 26 *allied health professionals* for whom the

M

American Medical Association's *Committee on Allied Health Education and Accreditation (CAHEA)* has accredited education programs.

medical record analyst (MRA): See *health record analyst*.

medical record designee: The individual in a *long term care facility (LTCF)* assigned the responsibility of maintaining *medical records* on all patients. Note that this term applies to the duty, not to the qualifications, of the individual.

medical record entry: Something written in the *medical record*. Certain members of the health care team, such as physicians, nurses, respiratory therapists, physical therapists, etc., are permitted by the hospital to write in the medical record. Each person doing so follows a certain protocol, which includes dating the written information and *authenticating* (signing) it. Customarily, a notation made by one person at one time is called an entry. "Written" may include computer and audio entries; any type of recording approved for that hospital's medical record system.

medical record index: A system of indexing *medical records* so that they can be located according to several factors, such as by patient name, diagnoses, procedures, physicians, and surgeons.

medical record librarian (MRL): An obsolete term for *medical record administrator (MRA)*.

medical record professional: A general term covering *medical record administrators (MRAs), medical record technicians (MRTs), registered record administrators (RRAs), accredited record technicians (ARTs)*, and the like.

medical record science: The allied health profession dealing with *medical records*. Medical record science concerns record content, medical terminology, medical *classification*, medical record administration, medicolegal aspects, information retrieval, and the like.

Medical Record Services (MR): The chapter giving the *standards* for this component of the hospital in the 1990 *Accreditation Manual for*

M

Hospitals (AMH) of the *Joint Commission on the Accreditation of Healthcare Organizations (JCAHO).*

medical record technician (MRT):   A person who carries out certain technical duties with respect to *medical records*. The MRT's formal training is somewhat less than for the *medical record administrator (MRA)*. One of the 26 *allied health professionals* for whom the American Medical Association's *Committee on Allied Health Education and Accreditation (CAHEA)* has accredited education programs.

The *American Medical Record Association (AMRA)* provides a *credential examination* service for qualified persons. Passing the examination permits the use of the title "Accredited Record Technician (ART)."

medical review agency: An *agency (1)* established under the *prospective payment system (PPS)* to carry out certain surveillance functions with respect to hospital and physician performance and detection of fraud.

medical society: A term generally used with reference to a geographically defined association of physicians, for example, a city, county, state, or national medical society. Associations whose membership is made up of *specialists* (for example, surgeons) are usually called "specialty societies." The *medical staff organization (MSO)* of a hospital is not a medical society. Synonym(s): medical association.

medical staff: The physicians, dentists, and other professionals who are members of the "medical staff," that is, they are members of the *medical staff organization* of the hospital. Each individual must have been formally appointed to the medical staff by the *governing body*, and been authorized by that body to treat patients, independently, in the hospital. Appointment to the medical staff must be based on the individual's having full licensure, and having met the hospital's own requirements.

Each medical staff member is granted specific clinical *privileges* by the governing body and is subject to the medical staff bylaws and rules and regulations and to review under the hospital's quality management program. In addition, all members must be reappointed periodically (JCAHO requires that appointments may not be for more than two years) and their privileges reaffirmed.

M

For a discussion of the procedures for admitting physicians and other professionals to the medical staff, see *credentialing*; for more detail regarding clinical privileges, see *privileges*.

Physician practitioners on the medical staff are authorized to admit patients. Nonphysician practitioners usually do not have admitting privileges.

Members of the medical staff are often erroneously referred to as "hospital staff" or merely "staff"; in better usage, "hospital staff" refers to hospital employees, while "staff" alone is ambiguous unless taken in context.

One classification of medical staffs as bodies is that they are "closed" or "open"; see *closed staff* and *open staff*.

Medical staff members fall into a number of classifications:

active medical staff: Medical staff members with full clinical *privileges* (according to their abilities, as awarded by the *governing body*), and with full responsibilities with respect to *medical staff organization (MSO) activities*, such as committee membership.

associate medical staff: Persons eligible to apply for medical staff membership, who have applied for membership, who have been awarded limited clinical *privileges* on an interim basis, and whose participation in *medical staff organization (MSO) activities* is somewhat limited. New medical staff members may be appointed to the associate medical staff for the first year, for example. Sometimes called the "provisional medical staff."

courtesy medical staff: Medical staff members who admit patients only occasionally, or who only consult, and so are granted limited *privileges* (less than those of active staff members) and are not required to participate in *medical staff organization (MSO) activities*.

honorary medical staff: Persons whose professional qualifications make them eligible for medical staff membership, but who do not have the *privileges* of admitting patients and who do not participate in *medical staff organization (MSO) activities*. Typically, honorary medical staff are retired members of the medical staff.

provisional medical staff: See *associate medical staff*.

Medical Staff (MS): The chapter giving the *standards* for this component of the hospital in the 1990 *Accreditation Manual for Hospitals*

M

(AMH) of the *Joint Commission on the Accreditation of Healthcare Organizations (JCAHO)*.

medical staff bylaws: The portion of the *bylaws* of the hospital pertaining to the rights and obligations of physicians and others as members of the *medical staff organization (MSO)* of the hospital. Typically the bylaws are drafted and proposed by the medical staff organization, but they are approved and adopted by the *governing body*, and their force stems from this governing body action. Serious consideration is being given to separating the traditional medical staff bylaws to retain organizational matters within the medical staff bylaws, but to create a separate policy on credentials matters (appointment, reappointment, and clinical privileges) so that the separate documents may be more easily amended, if necessary, and to minimize potential legal problems (such as antitrust allegations, which may charge that the medical staff has too much control over credentials decisions if the process is entirely within the medical staff bylaws).

medical staff corporation: Sometimes a *medical staff organization (MSO)* incorporates itself, and the matters which are ordinarily the subject of the medical staff *bylaws* are then handled by contract between the medical staff corporation and the hospital corporation, much as an emergency services corporation could be contracted with to provide emergency department services.

medical staff organization (MSO): An organization of the *medical staff* members formed to carry out two functions: (1) to provide the management structure through which the hospital policies which pertain to the medical staff members are carried out, with particular attention to the quality of care; and (2) to serve as the spokesperson for the physicians to the *governing body*. This organization is variously referred to as the "medical staff," the "organized medical staff," the "medical staff organization," or simply the "MSO."

medical staff organization activities (MSO activities): A term used to include both the rights and duties of *medical staff organization (MSO)* membership. The rights include, primarily, the right to vote in MSO meetings as full members of the MSO. The duties include carrying out the functions which devolve on full members under the *medical staff bylaws,* including committee membership and participation, and accepting the supervision and sanctions laid out in the bylaws. All MSO members are governed by the medical staff bylaws, which contain some provisions which affect all classes of members, such as those dealing with professional and personal conduct and completion of medical records.

Medical Subject Headings (MeSH): The annual authority list for the subject analysis of the biomedical literature in the National Library of Medicine (NLM). The list is divided into two sections, an alphabetical list of the subjects along with their reference code numbers (MeSH numbers), and a "tabular list," called a "tree structure," in which the subjects are categorized and subdivided, often to several levels, according to the hierarchical arrangement of the classification. Any document in the literature will be classified under as many subjects as are logically necessary. The volume is published by NLM but may only be obtained from the National Technical Information Service of the United States Department of Commerce. See also *tree structure.*

medical technologist (MT): A person who performs chemical, microscope, and bacteriological examinations on human tissues, blood, and other specimens of or from the body. The medical technologist works under the supervision of a physician or other scientist, and typically has been trained in a medical technology training program (*accreditation* is available for such programs, but a person may be called an MT without having gone through an accredited program). One of the 26 *allied health professionals* for whom the American Medical Association's *Committee on Allied Health Education and Accreditation (CAHEA)* has accredited education programs.

medically indigent: The condition, as defined by the federal, state, or local government, of lacking the financial ability to pay for one's medical care. Any individual whose income and other resources falls below the defined level is declared to be medically indigent and may qualify for public assistance. Note that "medically indigent" and *"indigent"* are usually defined differently.

Medicare: The federal program which provides health care to persons 65 years of age and older and to others entitled to Social

Security benefits. Medicare is administered at the federal level, as contrasted with *Medicaid*, which is administered by the states. Medicare was established in 1965 by amendment to the Social Security Act, the pertinent section of the amendment being "Title XVIII—Health Insurance for the Aged." There are two parts to Medicare:

Medicare, Part A: The hospital care portion (Hospital Insurance Program (HI)) of Medicare. Individuals who (1) are age 65 and over and who qualify for the Social Security "Old Age, Survivors, Disability and Health Insurance Program" or who are entitled to railroad retirement benefits; (2) are under age 65 but have been eligible for disability for more than two years; or (3) qualify for the *end stage renal disease (ESRD)* program are automatically enrolled in Part A of Medicare. Synonym(s): Hospital Insurance Program (HI).

Medicare, Part B: The part of Medicare through which persons entitled to *Medicare, Part A*, the Hospital Insurance Program, may obtain assistance with payment for physicians' services. Individuals participate voluntarily through enrollment and the payment of a monthly fee.

Medicare Insured Group (MIG): An organizational concept allowing businesses or labor unions to distribute Medicare funds to retired employees. By targeting a specific group of retirees, it is hoped that costs can be lowered through the use of managed care.

medication: A term used in health care to cover both *prescription drugs* and *nonprescription drugs* (over-the-counter drugs). Often shortened to "med" or "meds."

medication administration: The giving of a single dose of a *medication* (drug) to a patient.

medication error: A failure of some kind in the process of medication administration. The process begins when the physician writes a medication order. It is often transcribed (perhaps by a clerk or secretary), then communicated to the hospital pharmacy, where the prescription is filled and the medication sent back to the patient care unit. A nurse (or other qualified professional) gives the medication to the patient, observing the "5 R's" of medication administration: (1) right medication, (2) right dosage, (3) right patient, (4) right time, and (5) right route of administration (for example, oral, intravenous, or intramuscular).

Mistakes can happen at any one or more points along way. For example, the pharmacy may dispense the wrong drug, or the nurse may give it to the wrong patient. Any of these is a medication error, although the term is often used more narrowly to refer to a nursing error. A medication error may be harmless or have serious consequences, and there may be disagreement as to what in fact constitutes an "error" (for example, a ten-minute delay might constitute serious error in one instance, but be totally insignificant in another, depending upon the drug and the patient's condition). A written medication error report is usually completed for each error as part of the hospital's *quality management* process. Only through careful analysis of medication errors can it be determined whether errors are due to lack of skill, lack of education, or problems with the process itself.

The term "medication error" does not refer to inappropriate usage of drugs; drug usage is reviewed by the *medical staff.* See *drug utilization, peer review,* and *pharmacy and therapeutics committee.*

medication order: A written order by a physician, dentist, or other authorized individual for a *medication* (either a *prescription drug* or a *nonprescription drug*) to be given to a specific inpatient. A similar order written for a prescription drug for an outpatient or outside the hospital is a "drug prescription." For a nonprescription drug (an over-the-counter drug), no similar paperwork is required outside the hospital.

medicine (1): A substance administered to treat disease.

medicine (2): The science and art of the diagnosis and treatment of disease and the maintenance of health.

medicine (3): A general method of treatment of disease by means other than surgical; that is to say, "medical treatment" is treatment without surgery (without operation or manipulation).

medicine (4): A system of *diagnosis,* and particularly *treatment,* based upon a specific theory of disease and healing:

allopathy: A system of medicine based on the theory that successful therapy depends on creating a condition antagonistic to or incompatible with the condition to be treated. Thus drugs such as antibiotics are given to combat diseases caused by the organisms to which they are antagonistic. Allopathy is the predominant system in the United States, and its practitioners are Doctors of Medicine (MDs).

chiropractic: A system of medicine based on the theory that disease is caused by malfunction of the nerve system, and that normal function of the nerve system can be achieved by manipulation and other treatment of the structures of the body, primarily the spinal column. A practitioner is a chiropractor, Doctor of Chiropractic (DC).

homeopathy: A system of medicine based on the theory that diseases should be combatted (1) by giving drugs which, in healthy persons, can produce the same symptoms from which the patient is suffering, and (2) by giving these drugs in minute doses.

osteopathy: A system of medicine which emphasizes the theory that the body can make its own remedies, given normal structural relationships, environmental conditions, and nutrition. It differs from *allopathy* primarily in its greater attention to body mechanics and manipulative methods in diagnosis and therapy. Osteopathy is second to allopathy in number of practitioners in the United States. Osteopathic physicians are granted the Doctor of Osteopathy (DO) degree (note that an "OD" is not an "osteopathic doctor," but an *optometrist*, an "optometric doctor").

MedisGroups: See *Medical Illness Severity Grouping System.*

MEDLARS: See *Medical Literature Analysis and Retrieval System.*

MEDLARS-on-line (MEDLINE): A telephone linkage system between a number of United States medical libraries and the *Medical Literature Analysis and Retrieval System (MEDLARS)* of the *National Library of Medicine.*

MEDLINE: See *MEDLARS-on-line.*

meds: Short for *medications.*

M

mental distress: See *emotional distress*.

mental health: The state of being of the individual with respect to emotional, social, and behavioral maturity. Although the term is often used to mean "good mental health," mental health is a relative state, varying from time to time in the individual, with some people more mentally healthy than others.

Merck Manual: A widely-used reference on diagnosis and treatment of disease, published by Merck, Sharpe, and Dohme.

Merck Manual of Geriatrics: A companion volume to the *Merck Manual*, concerning the diagnosis and treatment of disease in aging patients, published by Merck, Sharpe, and Dohme.

merger: The formal union of two or more corporations (such as hospitals) into a single corporation. In a merger, one of the original corporations retains its identity and continues to exist, while the other corporations are merged into it and lose their former identities. A *consolidation* is similar to a merger, except that all of the corporations which unite cease to exist, and a new corporation is formed with its own new identity. In either case, the surviving or consolidated corporation acquires the assets and assumes the liabilities of the former corporations.

MeSH: See *Medical Subject Headings*.

meta-analysis: A research method which entails taking several studies on a given topic and analyzing those studies together, thus making a large study out of them. The method is of relatively recent development, and much attention is being given to improving the methodology itself. The study resulting using meta-analysis is also called a "meta-analysis."

method effectiveness: When a treatment fails to achieve its intended results, the failure may be due to the method employed or its use. For example, a contraceptive failure may occur because the method was inadequate or because it really was not employed or was employed improperly. Thus the "method effectiveness" or the "use effectiveness" of the contraceptive may have been at fault, and the failure may have been a "method failure" or a "use failure."

method failure: When a treatment fails to achieve its intended results, the failure may be due to the method employed or its use. For example, a contraceptive failure may occur because the method was inadequate or because it really was not employed or was employed improperly. Thus the "method effectiveness" or the "use effectiveness" of the contraceptive may have been at fault, and the failure may have been a "method failure" or a "use failure."

metric system: See *Systeme International (SI) units*.

MGMA: See *Medical Group Management Association*.

MI (1): See *myocardial infarction*.

MI (2): See *medical illustrator*.

microbiology: The science dealing with microbes (microscopic—and smaller—organisms).

  medical microbiology: Microbiology as it pertains to medicine, a branch of *pathology*. One of the medical specialties for which *residency* programs have been approved by the Accreditation Council for Graduate Medical Education (ACGME). See *specialty*.

microcomputer: See *computer*.

microscopic anatomy: See *histology*.

MIG: See *Medicare Insured Group*.

minicomputer: See *computer*.

minimal differential risk: A concept applied to evaluate the difference in risk between two treatments or procedures, particularly in research, when there is very little difference in risk of an undesirable outcome between standard, commonly accepted therapy used for the condition and the experimental therapy under study.

minor: A person who has not yet reached the age required by law for a particular purpose. The age may vary from state to state;

however, in most states, for most purposes (such as voting or making contracts) the age of majority is 18 years.

A minor is usually legally *incompetent* to give consent for treatment. However, in many states a minor may give valid consent if he is married, emancipated (living away from home and supporting himself), or sufficiently mature (emotionally and intellectually capable of understanding his disease, need for treatment, and so forth). In addition, many states have specific ages at which even an (otherwise incompetent) minor can consent; for example, to testing and treatment for venereal disease or for drug or alcohol abuse, or to make a decision whether to remain in a psychiatric hospital.

minutes: The written record of the proceedings of a body or group. In health care, such bodies include the governing body, the medical staff, and committees of the hospital and medical staff. Minutes should include the date of the meeting, who was present, and who wrote the minutes. Topics should be listed separately for ease of reading and retrieval of information, and all significant actions taken by the body should be noted. Minutes need not (and should not) include "minute" detail of discussions (usually, the fact that a topic was discussed, and whether action was taken, is sufficient), who said what, who made or seconded a motion, or who voted for what (unless a request is made to note names of voters). Excessive detail can inhibit the free speech necessary for intelligent decision-making. Minutes may in some instances become evidence in a lawsuit or other legal proceeding, so their accuracy and conciseness is important.

MIS (1):   See *management information system.*

MIS (2):   Manager of information systems.

miscarriage: The spontaneous (without outside efforts) termination of a pregnancy before the middle of the pregnancy, the middle of the second trimester.

MLT-AD: See *medical laboratory technician—associate degree.*

MLT-C: See *medical laboratory technician—certificate.*

M

MMA: See *Medical Management Analysis (System)*.

MND: See *motoneuron disease.*

modality: A therapeutic (treatment) method employing electrical or physical (as contrasted with chemical or other) means. "Modality" is often used incorrectly as a synonym for "method."

modem: A device used to transfer *digital* information over telephone lines, which are basically *analog*. Its most common application is to connect *computer terminals* or computers to other computers a great distance away. "Modem" is a word formed from "MOdulate/DEModulate." Modems are characterized by their speed capability (baud rate), type (synchronous versus asynchronous), and compatibility with various hardware and software.

modified diet: A diet other than the regular (or "house") diet; one which is tailored to the individual's nutritional needs in terms of calories, food elements, or other factors. Synonym(s): special diet.

monitor parameter: See *parameter.*

monitoring: Keeping track of events in a systematic fashion. The term is applied to monitoring the *quality* of *medical care*, monitoring the *performance* of physicians, and monitoring *patient condition* and response to care. The events, activities, and other measurements monitored are called monitor *parameters.*

implementation monitoring (IM): An approach used by the *Joint Commission on the Accreditation of Healthcare Organizations (JCAHO)* with respect to evaluating an institution's progress toward compliance with certain new or revised JCAHO *standards.* Effective in 1985, JCAH adopted a policy of designating certain standards for implementation monitoring. These are standards for which it believes that an institution will require more than the usual time to achieve compliance, and for which the institution will be required to submit reports of progress toward compliance. This approach is not a substitute for *Type I recommendations* (contingencies), under which *accreditation* is granted subject to correction of deficiencies within a specified time period. Lack of compliance with "implementation monitoring recommendations" does not affect the accreditation status of the hospital.

monogamous: A relationship between a doctor and a hospital in which a doctor does all his hospital work in a single hospital.

monopoly suicide: An economic phenomenon referring to the observation that any monopoly enterprise which succeeds in raising its prices to the point where "windfall" profits occur will attract such competition into the field that the monopoly will be destroyed.

morbidity: Illness, injury, or other than normal health. This term is often used in describing a *rate (2)* (a statistical term). One type of hospital morbidity rate, for example, is the postoperative infection rate; it is the number of patients with infections following surgery, expressed as a *proportion* of those undergoing surgery, within a given period of time.

comorbidity: As used in the *prospective payment system (PPS)*, a diagnosis present *before* hospitalization which is thought to extend the hospital stay at least one day for roughly 75 percent or more of the patients with a given principal diagnosis. The presence of a comorbidity is reported in the PPS by placing, as a secondary ICD-9-CM diagnosis code in the patient's bill, a condition defined by PPS as a comorbidity. See also *complication*.

compression of morbidity: The situation which results if persons are healthy until later in life than at present, that is, if disability is postponed more than death, so that an individual's period of disability preceding death is shorter, and the older population is both "older and healthier." The converse could be called "expansion of *morbidity*," so that the population becomes "older and sicker." Which will occur is not known; guesses about this aspect of the aging of the population are critical in planning for *long-term care*.

mortality: A term that applies to death. This term is usually used in the phrase "mortality rate," which means the number of patients who died expressed as a *proportion* of those at risk. See *death rate*.

motoneuron disease (MND): A class of degenerative muscle disorders, which includes amyotrophic lateral sclerosis (Lou Gehrig's disease) and multiple sclerosis. The diseases in the class all result in increasing muscular weakness and lack of muscle control. The causes of MND are not known.

mouse: A computer input device (like the keyboard) which fits into one hand, rolls around on the desktop, and is attached to the computer by a thin cable (the mouse's "tail"). The mouse is used as a "pointing" device to move the cursor on the *cathode ray tube (CRT)* screen. It has two or three buttons which can be "clicked" to make selections presented on the screen. Mouse travel is measured in units called "mickeys." Software which makes extensive use of mouse input is often referred to as having a "point and shoot" interface.

MR: See *Medical Record Services*.

MRA (1): See *medical record administrator*.

MRA (2): Medical record analyst. See *health record analyst*.

MRDD: Mentally retarded/developmentally disabled individuals.

MRI: Magnetic resonance imaging. See *nuclear magnetic resonance imaging (NMRI)*.

MRI scanner: See *nuclear magnetic resonance imaging scanner (NMRI scanner)*.

MRL: See *medical record librarian*.

MRT: See *medical record technician*.

MS (1): See *multiple sclerosis*.

MS (2): See *Medical Staff*.

MSN: Master of Science in Nursing.

M

MSO: See *medical staff organization*.

MSO activities: See *medical staff organization activities*.

MT: See *medical technologist*.

multidisciplinary: Made up of individuals from different fields. In the hospital, a committee on patient care which has members who are physicians, nurses, and managers, for example, is a multidisciplinary committee.

multihospital system: A term which technically pertains to two or more hospitals under a single *governing body*. In current usage, "multihospital system" also applies to a number of formal and informal arrangements among hospitals, varying from sharing of one or two services, through a variety of leasing, sponsoring, and contract-managing schemes, to full-blown single ownership of two or more facilities. Synonym(s): chain organization, hospital chain.

multihospital system code: A number which identifies the specific *multihospital system* to which a given hospital belongs. This code is used by the *American Hospital Association (AHA)* in its listing of hospitals in its annual *Guide to the Health Care Field*.

multiple sclerosis (MS): A nervous system disease.

municipal: Pertaining to a governmental unit. While "municipal" is commonly used to refer to a local governmental unit, such as a city or town, it can also be used in a broad sense to refer to the internal affairs of a state, nation, or people.

musculoskeletal: Pertaining to the muscles and the skeleton.

musculoskeletal oncology: One of the medical specialties for which *residency* programs have been approved by the Accreditation Council for Graduate Medical Education (ACGME). See *specialty*.

myocardial infarction (MI): The medical diagnosis for the most frequent form of "heart attack" (other conditions are also often called "heart attacks" by laypersons). An "infarction" is an area of destruction of tissue, here heart muscle ("myocardial") tissue, caused by interference with the blood supply to the area. In an MI, the infarction is the result of the blockage of one of the arteries supplying blood to the heart muscle. The surgical procedures used to improve circulation to the heart, coronary artery bypass grafts (CABG) and balloon angioplasties, are done to prevent MIs and also the symptoms, such as poor cardiac function and angina, resulting from insufficient oxygen supply to the heart muscle.

N

NACHRI: National Association of Children's Hospitals and Related Institutions, Inc.

NAQAP: See *National Association of Quality Assurance Professionals*.

NARL: See *no adverse response level*.

National Association of Quality Assurance Professionals (NAQAP): A national organization of individuals whose duties include *quality assurance (QA)* activities. See *quality assurance professional (QAP (1))* for a list of some of the individuals eligible for membership.

National Board of Medical Examiners (NBME): An independent nonprofit organization that tests and *certifies* students and graduates of United States and Canadian medical schools.

National Fire Protection Association (NFPA): The organization which issues the *Life Safety Code* with which the *Joint Commission on Accreditation of Healthcare Organizations (JCAHO)* expects health care institutions to comply.

National Formulary (NF): A publication of the *United States Pharmacopeia Convention (USPC)* containing recipes for the standard preparation (compounding) of medicinal drugs.

National Health Corps: A federal program for providing medical, dental, and nursing services to rural areas of the United States.

National Hospital Panel Survey: A monthly statistical survey of 30 percent of the *community hospitals* of the United States, conducted by the *American Hospital Association (AHA)*, concerning finances, utilization, staffing, and other key indicators of hospital performance, with data available within 90 days of the reporting period. Synonym(s): AHA/National Hospital Panel Survey.

National Institutes of Health (NIH): A federal agency (of the Department of Health and Human Services (DHHS)) based in Bethesda, Maryland, which carries out research and programs related to certain specific types of diseases, such as mental and neurological disease, arthritis, cancer, and heart disease. There is an "institute" for each of the categories of disease for which NIH has programs.

National League for Nursing (NLN): The national organization concerned with all of nursing. It is a membership organization of individuals and of agencies, and includes nurses, related professionals, and consumers. It is the official *accrediting* agency for schools of nursing (professional and vocational). Continuing education programs are conducted nationally on a variety of nursing and nursing education topics. Consultation on programs and management is available to educational institutions and providers. (The *American Nurses Association (ANA)*, although also national, is primarily an association of constituent state associations of individual nurses, and is concerned with their welfare and professional performance.)

National Library of Medicine (NLM): The United States National Library of Medicine in Washington, DC.

National Practitioner Data Bank: A clearinghouse for information on disciplinary and *malpractice* actions against physicians created by the *Health Care Quality Improvement Act (HCQIA)* of 1986, which went into operation in 1990. The Act requires that (1) an insurance company (or other entity) which makes a payment on a malpractice claim (whether in settlement or pursuant to a court decision), (2) a state board of medical examiners which imposes a sanction on a physician, and (3) a health care entity (such as a hospital) which takes a professional review action adversely affecting a physician's privileges for more than 30 days, must report these actions to the Data Bank. Eligible parties may then inquire of the Data Bank for information about a particular physician; for example, a hospital may inquire prior to granting *privileges*. If a hospital fails to comply with the reporting requirements, it loses for three years the protection it would otherwise have under the Act. See *Health Care Quality Improvement Act (HCQIA)*.

National Society of Patient Representatives: An association of patient representatives (*patient advocates*) which is an affiliate of the *American Hospital Association (AHA)*.

natural death act: Legislation governing procedures by which a *competent* person can execute a document, such as a *living will*, *durable power of attorney*, or *health care proxy*, concerning the withholding or withdrawal of life-sustaining treatment, should she become *incompetent (1)*. A living will expresses the person's own wishes regarding *extraordinary treatment*, while the durable power of attorney or health care proxy authorizes someone else to make treatment decisions for the person who becomes incompetent to make them herself. See also *right to die*.

natural history: The ordinary course of a disease. For example, the common cold has an incubation period before symptoms and signs appear, a period when the patient is noticeably ill, and then a recovery phase; this is the natural history of the common cold. Treatment is intended to modify the natural history of the disease.

NBME: See *National Board of Medical Examiners*.

necropsy: See *autopsy*.

NEDEL: See *no epidemiologically detectable exposure level*.

negative incentive: See *disincentive*.

negligence: The failure to exercise reasonable care. In addition to its ordinary meaning, negligence has a specific legal meaning; it is one kind of *tort* which results in legal *liability (1)*. The tort of negligence requires a duty to exercise reasonable care; a failure to exercise such care; and an injury which was *proximately caused* by that failure. One may commit a careless act, but if no one is injured as a result, there is no "negligence" as far as legal liability is concerned.

professional negligence: In the context of health care, professional negligence is the failure of a *professional* to exercise that degree of care and skill practiced by other professionals of similar skill and training (and, in some states, in the same geographic locality) under similar circumstances (see *standard of care (2)*). Such lack of care alone, however, will not result in legal liability; there must be an injury to the patient, and the injury must have been caused by the negligent act.

negligence per se: Legal *liability (1)*, based on negligence, which is established in a lawsuit by showing that a law (*statute*) was violated. Violation of a law, by itself, does not prove negligence. For example, driving without the current automobile registration required by state law will not make a driver liable for hitting a pedestrian, in the absence of any carelessness or fault of the driver. To establish negligence per se, a plaintiff must prove that: (1) the law was violated by the *defendant*; (2) the plaintiff was injured as a result of the violation; (3) the plaintiff was a person whom the law was intended to protect; and (4) the harm which resulted was the type of harm to be avoided by the law.

An example of negligence per se in health care would be the failure of a physician to report a case of suspected child abuse to the child protection authorities (a requirement commonly imposed by state law), where the child is further injured because no one intervened to protect her.

negotiated underwriting: A private sale of *bonds* by their issuer as contrasted with advertisement for public bids. Most hospital bond underwritings are negotiated because of special marketing considerations.

neighborhood health center: A *facility (2)*, located where it will be easy for patients to go, which provides various services short of *inpatient* care.

NEJM: See *New England Journal of Medicine*.

neo-no-fault compensation: See *patients' compensation*.

N

neonatal: A term pertaining to the infant's first four weeks (28 days) after birth.

neonatal-perinatal medicine: The branch of *pediatrics* dealing with the newborn infant at and around the time of birth. One of the medical specialties for which *residency* programs have been approved by the Accreditation Council for Graduate Medical Education (ACGME). See *specialty*.

neonatology: The science and art of diagnosis and treatment of disorders of the infant in the neonatal period—the first four weeks (28 days) after birth.

nephrology: A branch of *internal medicine* which deals with diseases and disorders of the urinary system and with kidney function. One of the medical specialties for which *residency* programs have been approved by the Accreditation Council for Graduate Medical Education (ACGME). See *specialty*.

net worth: *Assets* minus *liabilities*; also called "equity."

networking: An informal relationship among individuals for exchange of information, counsel, and planning; a *support group*.

neural network machine: See *neurocomputer*.

neural tube defect (NTD): A specific kind of *birth defect* involving the brain and spinal cord.

neurocomputer: See *computer*.

neurological surgery: One of the medical specialties for which *residency* programs have been approved by the Accreditation Council for Graduate Medical Education (ACGME). See *specialty*.

neurology: The branch of medicine which deals with the nervous system, its functions and its diseases and disorders. One of the medical specialties for which *residency* programs have been approved by the Accreditation Council for Graduate Medical Education (ACGME). See *specialty*.

neuropathology: The branch of *pathology* which deals with the nervous system. One of the medical specialties for which *residency* programs have been approved by the Accreditation Council for Graduate Medical Education (ACGME). See *specialty*.

newborn: A baby from the time of birth through the first 28 days of life. Used as an adjective, "newborn" pertains to this period of life.

New England Journal of Medicine (NEJM): The weekly clinical journal of the Massachusetts Medical Society.

NF: See *National Formulary*.

NFPA: See *National Fire Protection Association*.

NFPA 101: See *Life Safety Code*.

NGT: See *Nominal Group Technique*.

NGT process: See *Nominal Group Technique*.

NHLA: National Health Lawyers Association.

NICU: See *neonatal intensive care unit*.

NIH: See *National Institutes of Health*.

NLM: See *National Library of Medicine*.

NLN: See *National League for Nursing*.

NM: See *Nuclear Medicine Services*.

NMR: See *nuclear magnetic resonance*.

NMR scanning: Nuclear magnetic resonance scanning. See *nuclear magnetic resonance imaging*.

N

NMRI: See *nuclear magnetic resonance imaging.*

NMRI scanner: See *nuclear magnetic resonance imaging scanner.*

NMT: See *nuclear medicine technologist.*

no adverse response level (NARL): A measure, derived from animal studies, of the level of contamination in a soil below which there is hazard to humans.

no-code order: See *do not resuscitate order (DNR).*

no epidemiologically detectable exposure level (NEDEL): One of several measures used to advise on the hazards of environmental exposure to toxic substances in the soil. The NEDEL is calculated by making studies of appropriate populations of humans exposed to the toxic *agent (1)* in the soil, and determining whether the persons show significantly elevated levels of the toxic agent, symptoms of toxicity, or both. The measure was developed by the *Centers for Disease Control (CDC)* and the Montana Department of Health and Environmental Sciences.

Other measures have been developed from studies of laboratory animals: the *no observable defect level (NOEL)*; the *no adverse response level (NARL)*; and the *acceptable daily intake (ADI).*

no-fault: A system of compensation for persons who have been injured or adversely affected, without the need to prove fault or wrongdoing. No-fault systems are presently in use to compensate auto and industrial accident victims (see *workers' compensation*). Several no-fault (or no-fault-like) plans have been suggested for the health care area; see, for example, *patients' compensation.*

no observable effect level (NOEL): A measure, derived from animal studies, of the level of contamination in a soil below which there is hazard to humans.

NOEL: See *no observable effect level.*

nomenclature: A system of terms used in a particular science.

nominal group: A group "in name only." A type of group described by Delbecq, Van de Ven, and Gustafson in which individuals are together in the process known as the *Nominal Group Technique (NGT)*.

Nominal Group Technique (NGT):   A process developed by Delbecq, Van de Ven, and Gustafson for "increasing the creative productivity of group action, facilitating group decisions...and saving human effort and energy..." A nominal group is a group "in name only," a type of group in which individuals are together but do not talk or interact until late in the NGT process.

noncoital reproduction: Reproduction by any one of a number of techniques other than sexual intercourse (coitus). A variety of techniques may be employed, including *artificial insemination by a donor (AID), artificial insemination by the husband (AIH), surrogate mother (SM), in vitro fertilization (IVF), surrogate embryo transfer (SET),* and *frozen embryo (FE)*.

nonexempt distinct part unit: A term used in Medicare, apparently to mean a part of the hospital considered by Medicare to qualify for a different pay rate than another part. For *transfer in* or *transfer out* purposes, Medicare considers a nonexempt distinct part equivalent to another hospital (see *transfer in*).

nonfederal: Not owned or operated by the federal government.

nonhospital ambulatory care organization: A type of organization for which the *Joint Commission on Accreditation of Healthcare Organizations (JCAHO)* uses a separate manual for *accreditation* surveys.

noninvasive: A diagnostic or therapeutic procedure or technique which does not require penetration of the skin or mucous membrane by a needle or surgical instrument. The various *imaging* scanners, for instance, are noninvasive. See *invasive*.

nonphysician practitioners: A term used primarily in connection with *medical staff* membership under the *Joint Commission on Accreditation of Healthcare Organizations (JCAHO)* medical staff *standards*. JCAHO standards, which became effective in 1985, allow

N

nonphysician practitioners on the medical staff. Nonphysician practitioners include dentists, podiatrists, clinical psychologists, nurse midwives, and chiropractors. Of these, only podiatrists and qualified oral surgeons are likely to be granted *privileges* to admit patients under their own authority.

nonprofit: See *nonprofit corporation* under *corporation* and *nonprofit hospital* under *hospital*.

nonsurgical: See *medical*.

nonviable (1): Not capable of living, as a baby born below a certain birth weight.

nonviable (2): Not capable of being carried out or of succeeding, for example, "nonviable plans."

nosocomial: Originating in a hospital. The term is sometimes confused with "iatrogenic," which refers to a disease or injury resulting from a diagnostic procedure, therapy, or other element of health care.

nosology: The branch of medical science that deals with the *classification (1)* of diseases.

not to be coded: See *do not resuscitate order (DNR)*.

notebook computer: See *computer*.

NR: See *Nursing Services*.

NTD: See *neural tube defect*.

nuclear isomer: See *nuclide*.

nuclear isotope: See *nuclide*.

nuclear magnetic resonance (NMR): A *physical* phenomenon brought about in the body by subjecting the body to radio frequency fields in a strong magnetic field. It does not use *radioactive* materials or *X-rays*. NMR is used in *nuclear magnetic resonance imaging (NMRI)* and the study of certain *biochemical* activity.

nuclear magnetic resonance imaging (NMRI): A diagnostic technique for creating *cross-section*al *images* of the body by the use of *nuclear magnetic resonance (NMR)*. NMRI can also provide information on tissue *biochemical* activity. The procedure is *noninvasive*. The device used is called an NMRI (or MRI) scanner. Synonym(s): magnetic resonance imaging (MRI), zeumatography, spin density.

nuclear magnetic resonance imaging scanner (NMRI scanner): The diagnostic machine used to carry out *nuclear magnetic resonance imaging (NMRI)*. Synonym(s): MRI scanner.

nuclear magnetic resonance scanning (NMR scanning): See *nuclear magnetic resonance imaging.*

nuclear medicine: The use of radioisotopes (*radioactive* forms of chemical elements) to diagnose and treat patients and for investigation. Some applications provide *imaging* ("pictures" of body structures and functions), while others provide diagnostic tests and treatment for diseases. One of the medical specialties for which *residency* programs have been approved by the Accreditation Council for Graduate Medical Education (ACGME). See *specialty.*

Nuclear Medicine Services (NM): The chapter giving the *standards* for this component of the hospital in the 1990 *Accreditation Manual for Hospitals (AMH)* of the *Joint Commission on the Accreditation of Healthcare Organizations (JCAHO).*

nuclear medicine technologist (NMT): One of the 26 *allied health professionals* for whom the American Medical Association's *Committee on Allied Health Education and Accreditation (CAHEA)* has accredited education programs.

nuclide: A term used in atomic physics, meaning a species of atoms having a specific mass number *and* a specific atomic number. It has become the custom to refer to "radioactive nuclides" rather

N

than "radioactive isotopes" in nuclear medicine, hence the brief discussion of the terms here (see also *atom*):

atomic number: Each atom (the smallest particle of matter which exhibits unique *chemical* properties) has a nucleus surrounded by electrons. The chemical properties of the atom are determined by the number of "protons" in its nucleus. The number of protons in the nucleus also determines the atomic number of the element (the term element is applied to a collection of atoms of one chemical type). The element carbon, which has 6 protons, thus has the atomic number "6."

mass number: The nucleus of an atom also contains one or more "neutrons." Adding together the numbers of protons and neutrons in an atom's nucleus gives its atomic mass, known as its mass number. A given element, while retaining its chemical properties, can have atoms of different masses, depending on the numbers of neutrons in their nuclei. As a matter of fact, most elements occur in nature as mixtures of atoms with the same atomic number but different mass numbers. The most common form of carbon (over 98 percent of it in nature), for example, has 6 protons and 6 neutrons, therefore its atomic mass = 12; a rare form of carbon, which has the same chemical properties (but is radioactive), has 6 protons and 8 neutrons; its atomic mass = 14.

notation: When one describes an atom, one must give both its atomic mass and its name or atomic number (sometimes both name *and* atomic number). This is done in one (or both) of two ways: (1) give the full chemical name and the atomic mass (the two separated by a hyphen), or (2) give first the mass (number of protons + number of neutrons) as a superscript followed by the abbreviation for the element's chemical name. Carbon (atomic number 6) with the most common atomic mass, 12 (6 protons plus 6 neutrons) would be given as"carbon-12" or ^{12}C. Sometimes for safety, the expression would be ^{12}C (carbon-12). Radioactive carbon, with 6 protons and 8 neutrons, would be given as "carbon-14" or ^{14}C. An alternative notation would give the atomic mass as a leading superscript, and the atomic number as a leading subscript, thus carbon-14 could be given as $^{14}_{6}C$.

isotopes: When two or more atoms have the same atomic number but different atomic mass, they are different nuclides, but they are called isotopes (of the element in question). In the case of carbon, for example, seven different masses have been found: atoms all with the 6 protons making the element carbon, but with 4, 5, 6, 7, 8, 9, or 10 neutrons, producing the seven carbon isotopes: carbon-10, carbon-11, carbon-12, carbon-13, carbon-14, carbon-15, and carbon-16.

isobars: When the mass number of two or more different nuclides is the same, but the atomic number is different, the nuclides are called isobars. For example, some atoms of titanium, vanadium, and chromium all have a mass number of 50: ^{50}Ti (titanium-50), ^{50}V (vanadium-50), and ^{50}Cr (chromium-50). These three elements are called isobars (not isotopes).

radioactivity: In general, the greater the difference between the numbers of protons and neutrons in a given nuclide, the more "unstable" the nuclide, and the more likely it is to be radioactive, that is, for its nucleus to disintegrate spontaneously, and for it to give off ionizing radiation in the process. Two of the nuclides (isotopes) of carbon, carbon-12 and carbon-13, are stable; the other four, including carbon-14, are radioactive.

nuclear isomers: Not all radioactive nuclides have the same "half-life" or "degree" of radioactivity. Bromine, atomic number 35, for example, has a nuclide with mass number 80 which is found to exist as a mixture of nuclides with different half-lives, known as different metastable states. These are expressed as "bromine-80" and "bromine-80m," or "^{80}Br" and "^{80}mBr." When, as in this example, two or more of the same nuclides differ in some physical respect, they are called isomers.

nurse: A person qualified by accredited formal training at an academic or diploma school of nursing to provide nursing services (usually these services are defined by state statutes). Modifying words or phrases which accompany the word "nurse" may describe either the nurse's duties or qualifications:

N

associate nurse: Usually, a nurse who is responsible for carrying out a primary nurse's care plans, although in some states the term is used for a *diploma nurse* or a nurse with an *associate degree (AD)*.

cardiac care nurse: A nurse specially qualified by educational preparation to care for cardiac (heart) patients.

certified critical care nurse (CCRN): A *credential* granted by the American Association of Critical-Care Nurses (AACN) which validates competence in critical care nursing. The CCRN credential is awarded on the basis of a test administered by the Center for Occupational and Professional Assessment (COPA) of the Educational Testing Service (ETS). In 1988 about 24,000 critical care nurses held this credential. Certification is valid for three years, and may be continued by recertification.

certified nurse: A *registered nurse (RN)* who has obtained a *credential* of *certification* in a specialty. About 40 percent of the certified nurses in the United States have their credentials from the *American Nurses' Association (ANA)* which examines and certifies in 17 clinical and two administrative areas of nursing (1989):

> Adult Nurse Practitioner
> Clinical Specialist in Adult Psychiatric
>   and Mental Health Nursing
> Clinical Specialist in Child and Adolescent
>   Psychiatric and Mental Health
> Clinical Specialist in Gerontological Nursing
> Clinical Specialist in Medical-Surgical Nursing
> Community Health Nurse
> Family Nurse Practitioner
> General Nursing Practice
> Gerontological Nurse
> Gerontological Nurse Practitioner
> Medical-Surgical Nurse
> Nursing
> Nursing Administration
> Nursing Administration Advanced
> Pediatric Nurse
> Pediatric Nurse Practitioner
> Perinatal Nurse
> Psychiatric Nurse
> School Nurse
> School Nurse Practitioner

certified school nurse: A *school nurse* who has met certain criteria determined by the State Board of Education and who has been *certified*.

charge nurse: A *registered nurse (RN)* "in charge of" nursing in a *patient care unit* during a given work period.

circulating nurse: A *registered nurse (RN)* whose duties are to "circulate" in the operating room and be responsible chiefly for the patient's environment, and to wait on members of the surgical team who are in sterile attire, but not actually assist in surgical operations. See also *scrub nurse*.

clinical nurse specialist: A *registered nurse (RN)* with a Masters of Science (MSN) degree in nursing who has acquired advanced knowledge and clinical skills in a specific area of nursing and health care.

community health nurse: Any nurse working in the community. The term denotes the setting for the practice. Thus, a community health nurse may be a nurse providing care in the home, a *school nurse*, an *occupational health nurse*, or a *public health nurse*—in fact, any nurse not practicing specifically in a health-related facility setting.

A "community health nurse specialist" is a nurse with at least a master's degree who is practicing in the community. The degree may be in any area of nursing. The term "community health nurse" is sometimes confused with *public health nurse (PHN)*, which is a recognized *specialty* in nursing, and with *public health nursing*, which has a specific focus.

critical care nurse: A *registered nurse (RN)* specially qualified to care for critically ill patients, usually in an *intensive care unit (ICU)*. Synonym(s): intensive care nurse.

degree nurse: A nurse whose nursing education was obtained in an educational institution which granted an academic degree. The degree referred to is usually Bachelor of Science in Nursing (BSN).

diploma nurse: A nurse whose nursing education was obtained in a hospital school of nursing which granted a *diploma* rather than an academic *degree*.

float nurse: A nurse assigned to various *patient care units* of the hospital depending on their staffing needs, rather than regularly assigned to the same unit; thus, such a nurse "floats." Synonym(s): prn nurse.

floor nurse: A nurse working on, but not in charge of, a *patient care unit*.

general duty nurse: A *registered nurse (RN)* whose duties do not require specialty preparation. The term is ordinarily used with hospital nursing.

graduate nurse: Ordinarily, a nurse who has graduated from a professional nursing education program but who does not hold a valid state license. Although a registered nurse (RN) logically could be called a "graduate nurse," since he has "graduated" from a nursing program, that term instead refers to the lack of a license.

head nurse: A *registered nurse (RN)* whose duty is to be in charge of a *patient care unit* on an ongoing basis. This nurse is the *charge nurse*'s superior, since the head nurse's responsibility continues through all work shifts, while the charge nurse's responsibility is only for the shift when the charge nurse is present. The title and the management system vary from hospital to hospital.

intensive care nurse: See *critical care nurse*.

licensed practical nurse (LPN):   A person *licensed* by the state to carry out specified nursing duties under the direction of a *registered nurse (RN)*. Must have had formal training in a practical or vocational nursing education program. Same as licensed vocational nurse (LVN).

licensed vocational nurse (LVN):   See *licensed practical nurse (LPN)*.

occupational health nurse: A *registered nurse (RN)* who works in the field of *occupational health*. Although not required, many have advanced preparation in occupational health or *public health*.

operating room nurse (OR nurse):   A *registered nurse (RN)* with special qualifications for working in the operating room. An OR nurse may be a *circulating nurse* or a *scrub nurse*, or may act in a supervisory capacity.

pool nurse: A *registered nurse (RN)* or *licensed practical nurse (LPN)* (also known as a licensed vocational nurse (LVN)) who is not a member of the *nursing staff* of an institution but who is hired through an agency to provide patient care on a temporary basis (for example, one shift) when sufficient regular nursing staff are not available to provide such care.

practical nurse: A person who has had formal training in a practical or vocational nursing education program. When a practical nurse has been *licensed* by the state to carry out specified nursing duties under the direction of a *head nurse* or *nursing team* leader, that person may assume the title of *licensed practical nurse (LPN)*. A practical nurse is also called a vocational nurse.

primary nurse: A *professional nurse* who is responsible around the clock for planning, supervising, and, when present, giving nursing care to an assigned group of patients. This approach to nursing care is replacing *team nursing*, in which a "committee" rather than an individual carries out these functions.

private-duty nurse: A *registered nurse (RN)* who is employed by the patient.

prn nurse: See *float nurse*.

professional level nurse: A term proposed to designate a nurse whose training was in a four-year approved *baccalaureate program* in nursing. If the term is adopted, nurses trained in a *diploma program* or an *associate degree (AD) program* in a degree-granting institution would then be called *technical level nurses*.

professional nurse: Usually, a nurse educated in an approved *baccalaureate program* in nursing. There is a movement toward using the term *"professional level nurse"* for those educated in four-year college and university programs, and calling those with *associate degrees (ADs)* and *nursing diplomas* "technical level nurses." However, both professional level nurses and technical level nurses, when they are *registered nurses (RNs)*, are considered "professional nurses," in contrast with *licensed practical nurses (LPNs)* (licensed vocational nurses (LVNs)).

public health nurse (PHN): A nurse who has received specific educational preparation and supervised clinical practice in *public health nursing*. At the basic level, a PHN is one who holds a *baccalaureate degree* in nursing that includes this preparation; this nurse may or may not practice in a governmental health agency but has the initial qualifications to do so. A *public health nurse specialist* is prepared at the graduate level (master's or doctoral degree) with a focus on the public health sciences.

N

registered nurse (RN): A nurse who has been granted a "registered nurse" license by the state. (States also grant *practical nurses* licenses, which are not the same as "RN" licenses.) Nurses educated in state approved *baccalaureate programs* in nursing or in *associate degree programs* in nursing (in degree-granting institutions), and those trained in hospital schools of nursing, are eligible to sit for *registration* licensing examinations given by state boards of nursing. The registration license is intended to ensure minimum levels of competence and thus protect the public, not to indicate the educational background of the nurse. Registration typically requires periodic renewal.

school nurse: A nurse employed by a school. School nursing is a specialty in nursing, and *school nurse practitioners (SNPs)* have begun to appear. In some states, school nurses must meet certain criteria determined by the State Board of Education and be *certified*.

scrub nurse: An *operating room nurse (OR nurse)* who assists the surgeon in surgical operations, who "scrubs up" for surgery and is in sterile attire. A scrub nurse must be a registered nurse. See also *circulating nurse*.

team nurse: A nurse who is a member of a nursing team. A nursing team is a group of *registered nurses (RNs)* and ancillary personnel who provide nursing services, under a team leader, for a designated group of inpatients during a single nursing shift. See also *primary nurse*.

technical level nurse: A proposed term for a nurse whose education was in an *associate degree (AD) program* in nursing (in a degree-granting institution) or in a *diploma program in nursing*.

vocational nurse: See *practical nurse*.

nurse anesthetist: A nurse who administers *anesthesia* under the supervision of a physician or dentist, and who can assist in the care of patients who are in *critical* condition. A nurse anesthetist has special training in *anesthesiology*. A nurse anesthetist meeting the *certification* requirements of the *Council on Certification/Council on Recertification of Nurse Anesthetists* may use the *credential* "certified registered nurse anesthetist."

nurse clinical instructor: A *registered nurse (RN)* who carries out *clinical* teaching, with patients, for nursing students.

nurse clinician: A *registered nurse (RN)* who has had advanced study in a specific area of nursing practice, who may identify and diagnose problems of clients, and who may function independently under standing orders. Synonym(s): clinical nurse specialist.

nurse midwife: A *registered nurse (RN)* with special qualifications in *obstetric* and *neonatal* (newborn) care, certified by the *American College of Nurse Midwives (ACNM)* (a voluntary body) to manage maternal and *perinatal* care in normal pregnancy, labor, and childbirth.

nurse practice act: A state statute (law) governing the practice of nursing within the state.

nurse practitioner: A *registered nurse (RN)* who had completed a nurse practitioner program at the *master's* or *certificate* level beyond basic nursing education. Nurse practitioners have qualifications which permit them to carry out expanded health care evaluation and decision-making regarding patient care. Nurse practitioners are, in turn, specialized into "family nurse practitioners," "gerontological nurse practitioners," "school nurse practitioners," and the like. The term "practitioner" implies a certain degree of independence from the supervision of a physician in making decisions and carrying out acts, with the boundaries of this independence stipulated by state law. Nurse practitioners are ordinarily regulated by state nurse practice acts.

pediatric nurse practitioner (PNP): A *registered nurse (RN)* who has completed a program of advanced study of nursing care and health care maintenance of children from birth through adolescence.

nursing aide: A person who, under the supervision of an authorized member of the *nursing staff,* carries out non-specialized duties and personal care activities. Synonym(s): nursing assistant.

nursing assistant: See *nursing aide.*

nursing care objectives: One item of content of a *nursing care plan* giving the specific aims of the nurse with respect to reducing the

N

patient's stress and improving the patient's ability to adapt to the situation.

nursing care plan: A formal written plan of care and activities for a patient. Typically, the physician's activities are not part of the plan; the plan pertains to nursing and to other *services (1)*, and is part of the *nursing record*. Synonym(s): care plan.

nursing department: See *nursing service*.

nursing diagnosis: The description of the individual's actual or potential health needs which are amenable to *nursing intervention*. The focus of the nursing diagnosis is on the individual's response to illness or other factors that may adversely affect the attainment or maintenance of wellness. These diagnostic acts are distinct from those of medical and dental diagnosis. To illustrate, the physician's diagnosis may be "hypertension" (high blood pressure). Certain nursing diagnoses commonly are found for patients with hypertension; for example, "nutrition, alteration in, more than body requirements," because obesity may aggravate hypertension. The nursing intervention would therefore include patient education to reduce intake of salt, fats, and sugar.

nursing differential: An allowance originally added to payments for Medicare patients in recognition of the greater cost of providing nursing services to elderly patients.

nursing diploma: A credential given an individual on successful completion of the course of instruction in nursing given by a hospital school of nursing. An individual completing the nursing course in an academic program, that is, one offered by an educational institution, receives a nursing degree rather than a nursing diploma. Both degree and diploma holders are eligible to be *licensed* as a *registered nurse (RN)*.

nursing director: See *nursing service administrator*.

nursing home: An institution which provides continuous nursing and other *services (1)* to patients who are not acutely ill, but who need nursing and personal services as *inpatients*. A nursing home has permanent facilities and an *organized professional staff*.

academic nursing home: A nursing home affiliated with or operated by an institution providing *medical residency* training, with goals of research and the education of health care professionals in addition to the provision of patient care. The education programs may include medicine, nursing, social work, psychology, speech pathology, audiology, pharmacy, gerodentistry, occupational therapy, and other disciplines.

nursing intervention: An action performed by a nurse to prevent illness or its complications and to promote, maintain, or restore health.

nursing order: A statement written by the nurse that specifies the *nursing interventions* that all nurses caring for the patient should follow.

nursing process: A systematic manner for determining the client's problems, making plans to solve them, initiating the plan or assigning others to implement it, and evaluating the extent to which the plan was effective in resolving the problems identified. The five steps in the process are assessment, diagnosis, planning, implementation, and evaluation.

nursing record: That portion of the *medical record* which is the responsibility of the nurse. It contains the *nursing care plan*, *nursing orders*, and "nurse's notes" regarding the patient's response. It provides a sequential record of all nursing activities on behalf of the patient as well as accountability and validation of orders (physician and nurse) being carried out. When the nurse maintains a similar record for a person who is not ill, the person is referred to as a "client."

nursing service: The department of the hospital which provides *nursing services*. Synonym(s): nursing department.

nursing service administrator: A *registered nurse (RN)* responsible for the overall administration and management of *nursing services* in a hospital. It is the highest nursing position in the hospital. The nursing service administrator may have the title "vice-president for nursing" or some similar title. The former title was "nursing

N

director." Synonym(s): nursing director, nursing service director, chief of nursing.

nursing service director: See *nursing service administrator.*

nursing services: Those services normally provided by nurses, including personal care, administration of drugs and other medications and treatments, assessment of patients' needs and care requirements, and preparation of care plans for individual patients. Nurse practice acts (laws) in the various states place limitations on the tasks (for example, administration of intravenous medication) which can be performed by *registered nurses (RNs)*, *licensed practical nurses (LPNs)*, and allied personnel, with and without supervision.

Nursing Services (NR): The chapter giving the *standards* for this component of the hospital in the 1990 *Accreditation Manual for Hospitals (AMH)* of the *Joint Commission on the Accreditation of Healthcare Organizations (JCAHO).*

nursing staff: Those persons employed by a nursing service (nursing department). The nursing staff may include not only *registered nurses (RNs)*, *practical nurses*, and *nurses aides*, but also clerical and other support persons.

nursing team: A group of *registered nurses (RNs)* and auxiliary nursing personnel who provide *nursing services*, under a nursing team leader, for a designated group of patients.

nursing team leader: A *registered nurse (RN)* in charge of a *nursing team.*

nursing unit: See *patient care unit (PCU).*

nurturing: The provision of nourishment. In health care, the nourishment under consideration is that required for the mental, spiritual, emotional, and social well-being of the patient and family as well as their physical well-being. The topic is getting increasing attention as hospital stays are becoming shorter and hospitalization is often being avoided altogether; the nurturing formerly provided by the hospital is proportionately reduced. The situation is compounded in today's society by many factors, including family members' diminished acceptance of responsibility for nurturing one another. Health care organizations, community and church support groups, and others are increasing their efforts to assist with nurturing in the home and other settings.

nutrition: A field of science dealing with the relationships of food products and eating patterns to the development, growth, maintenance, and repair of living organisms.

nutrition assessment: Determining the nutritional status of an individual or a group through physical, biochemical, or dietary intake indicators.

anthropometric assessment: Measurement of an individual's height, weight, skin fat folds, arm circumference, elbow breadth, or other body measures for the purpose of assessing nutritional status, growth, and development. Synonym(s): anthropometry.

anthropometry: See *anthropometric assessment*.

biochemical assessment: The use of laboratory tests on urine, blood, blood fractions, and other tissue, to describe an individual's nutritional status. For example, sodium excretion (in urine) can be used to measure compliance with a low sodium diet in hypertensive patients.

dietary assessment: Analysis of the nutrient constituents of foods as recorded in a food history. The histories are compiled by trained interviewers doing dietary recalls, by individuals keeping food diaries, or through checking off the frequency of foods consumed, to arrive a food frequency pattern. Analyses of nutrient constituents can be done using a number of specially developed computer programs or by using printed reference materials such as the United States Department of Agriculture (USDA) *Handbook 8* series.

The assumption is made that consuming amounts of nutrients meeting a standard such as the United States National Academy of Sciences' "Recommended Dietary Allowances" (RDAs) ensures better health through a good nutritional status.

N

nutritionist (1): A person who works in the area of *nutrition* for either animals or humans. A nutritionist in the field of human nutrition has usually had training that includes chemistry, biochemistry, human physiology and psychology, as well as food science and nutrition. However, there is no consensus among national groups about minimum qualifications needed to call oneself a nutritionist. Currently, anyone who wishes to do so may call herself a nutritionist.

nutritionist (2): A generic term for a health professional specializing in health and nutrition relationships; the American Hospital Association uses the term as a job classification for registered dietitians.

public health nutritionist: A health professional specializing in assessment of community nutrition needs and in planning, organizing, implementing, and evaluating appropriate nutrition related services. Public health nutritionists are often members of a publicly funded health agency such as city, county and state health departments. They usually serve selected groups having special nutritional needs such as mothers and children, pregnant teenagers, and the poor.

nutritionist (3): A *dietitian* licensed by the state. Not all states require dietitians to be licensed.

O

objective: A term used to describe "reality" as it can be determined by observations made by individuals who are not experiencing the event. A broken arm is objective in that it can be observed by others. "Objective" is used in contrast with "subjective," which refers to reality as perceived by an individual. Pain is subjective in that only the person experiencing it can describe it.

obstetric patient: See *maternity patient*.

obstetrics: The branch of medicine dealing with pregnancy and the delivery of babies.

obstetrics-gynecology: The specialty of medicine dealing with disorders of the female reproductive system, pregnancy, and the delivery of babies. One of the medical specialties for which *residency* programs have been approved by the Accreditation Council for Graduate Medical Education (ACGME). See *specialty*.

occasion of service: A specific act of *service (1)* provided a patient, such as a test or procedure.

occupancy rate: The *ratio* between *occupied* and *available beds*, expressed as a percentage. The rate is calculated by dividing the average number of beds occupied for a given time period by the average number of beds available for that same time period (and multiplying by 100 to create the percentage). Sometimes the term "occupancy" alone is used.

O

occupational health: An area of specialization in health care which concerns the factors (such as working conditions and exposure to hazardous materials) in an occupation that influence the health of workers in that occupation, and which is concerned generally with the prevention of disease and injury and the maintenance of fitness (because these factors are important in maintaining a stable work force).

occupational health nursing: Nursing which involves care to individuals in the work setting. Its purpose is to promote health, and improve *productivity* and social adjustment.

occupational medicine: The branch of *preventive medicine* which deals with *occupational health*. One of the medical specialties for which *residency* programs have been approved by the Accreditation Council for Graduate Medical Education (ACGME). See *specialty*.

Occupational Safety and Health Administration (OSHA): A federal *agency (1)* responsible for developing and enforcing regulations regarding safety and health among workers in the United States.

occupational therapist (OT): One of the 26 *allied health professionals* for whom the American Medical Association's *Committee on Allied Health Education and Accreditation (CAHEA)* has accredited education programs.

occupational therapy (OT): Treatment by means of "occupational" activities, that is, tasks which are constructive and often will permit gainful employment. Occupational therapy is used primarily with disabled individuals, but is also used in retraining individuals after illnesses and accidents.

occurrence reporting: A system of reporting cases which have been detected in *occurrence screening* and then, in the judgment of reviewers, merit further study within the hospital. This is a step in the *Medical Management Analysis (MMA)* system employed by some hospitals in quality management.

occurrence screening: See *screening*.

occurrence-based coverage: See *insurance coverage.*

office audit system: A technique reported from Canada in which a review team goes into the offices of physicians whose practice is outside the hospital, and examines patient records (*medical records*) for the purpose of determining the *quality of care.*

Office of Management and Budget (OMB): The agency in the federal executive branch which prepares and monitors the budget.

Office of Technology Assessment (OTA): A Congressional investigative body whose duties have to do with assessing the merits and applications of technology.

office visit: All *services (1)* provided a patient in the course of a single appearance for care at a physician's office.

officer: A person holding a position of authority, either by election or appointment, in an organization. In a corporation, the officers are appointed by the corporate directors to manage the day-to-day affairs of the corporation, and have specific authority and responsibilities given to them by the directors and by law.

OMB: See *Office of Management and Budget.*

ombudsperson: See *patient advocate.*

OMR: See *online medical record.*

OMT: See *ophthalmic medical technician/technologist.*

oncology: The branch of medicine which is concerned with the diagnosis and treatment of tumors.

online medical record (OMR): A *medical record* kept in a computer, with constant instantaneous access via a *computer terminal* and sometimes with other forms of data entry, such as *point of sale (POS)* terminals for laboratory and other data.

O

ONTR: Order not to resuscitate. See *do not resuscitate order (DNR)*.

OP: See *outpatient*.

OP service: See *outpatient service (1)* and *(2)*.

OPA: See *organ procurement agency*.

open account: An arrangement between a buyer and a seller under which payment is to be made at some future time for goods or services.

open medical staff: See *open staff*.

open staff: A *medical staff* in a hospital which has no formal plan describing its desired medical staff size and *specialty* needs, and which, therefore, accepts new applications for medical staff membership and clinical privileges at any time.

operating room (OR): A room specially equipped for the performance of surgical operations.

operating room procedure: A term which, on its face, describes a surgical treatment of a patient, performed in the hospital's *operating room*. However, the term has a special function under the *prospective payment system (PPS)*: if a patient has an "operating room procedure," that patient is placed in a different payment category than a patient in the same *Major Diagnostic Category (MDC)* who does not have an operating room procedure. For the purpose of making this allocation of patients, an arbitrary list of procedures (actually, a list of procedure codes) has been established by the Health Care Financing Administration (HCFA). If the patient's *data set* submitted for payment has a code shown on the HCFA's list as an operating room procedure, that patient is considered to have had an operating room procedure, no matter where the procedure was actually done.

operating statement: See *income and expense statement*.

operation: Sometimes an operation is defined as identical with a "surgical procedure." In general usage, however, the term "operation" is rarely used for a single procedure; the term suggests an event of sufficient magnitude that it requires special preparation of the patient, use of an operating room, assistance to the operator by nurses and often other surgeons, sometimes anesthesia, and postoperative care. The term "procedure," on the other hand, usually refers to something which is discrete, and for which a relatively short time is required for execution.

An operation often actually consists of a number of procedures, and the array of procedures which make up a given operation will vary from patient to patient. For example, cholecystectomy (gall bladder removal) for one patient may include "exploration of the common bile duct," while for another, this procedure may be omitted. For this reason, a proper description of an operation requires that its procedures be listed.

ophthalmic medical technician/technologist (OMT): One of the 26 *allied health professionals* for whom the American Medical Association's *Committee on Allied Health Education and Accreditation (CAHEA)* has accredited education programs.

ophthalmology: The branch of medicine dealing with the eye, its physiology, anatomy, diseases, and so on. One of the medical specialties for which *residency* programs have been approved by the Accreditation Council for Graduate Medical Education (ACGME). See *specialty*.

opticianry: The discipline of making, selecting, fitting, and adjusting eyeglasses, contact lenses, and other ophthalmic devices.

optometry: The branch of science which deals with measurement of vision and the effects of lenses and prisms on vision. Optometry is not a branch of *medicine (4)*.

OR: See *operating room*.

oral surgeon: A *dentist* who specializes in surgical treatment of disorders, diseases, and injuries of the jaws and adjacent structures.

O

order (1): Doctor's order. A directive from a physician to a nurse or other individual as to drugs, treatments, examinations, and other care to be given to a patient.

order (2): A command of a court (judge) that a certain action be taken or not taken. A court order may be made before or during a lawsuit; a final order is issued once the case has been formally decided.

order not to resuscitate (ONTR): See *do not resuscitate order (DNR)*.

orderly: A hospital attendant, without professional qualifications, who does heavy or routine work, such as transporting patients.

organ: A part of the body which carries out a specific activity or function, for example, digestion.

organ procurement: The obtaining of human organs from *donors* for *transplantation* into other humans who need them.

organ procurement agency (OPA): An agency set up to keep records of persons needing organ *transplants* and donor organs available, and to match the two with such speed that the surgery can be performed.

organized medical staff: See *medical staff organization*.

organized professional staff: An ill-defined term, applied primarily to hospitals, which refers to the formal organization of the health care *professionals* on its staff. Usually there must be one or more physicians on the staff, and the term may also imply delegation of certain responsibilities with respect to the *quality of care* of the organized professional staff. The term "organized medical staff" is, in contrast, well defined by the *Joint Commission on Accreditation of Healthcare Organizations (JCAHO)*; see *medical staff organization*. Synonym(s): organized staff.

organized staff: See *organized professional staff*.

orthodontics: The branch of dentistry which deals with prevention and treatment of misalignment of the teeth and the jaws.

orthognathic: Dealing with the face and teeth. Orthognathic surgery is aimed at correcting deformities in these structures.

orthopedic: Pertaining to the bones and joints and the musculoskeletal system (the spine, extremities, and related structures).

orthopedic sports medicine: One of the medical specialties for which *residency* programs have been approved by the Accreditation Council for Graduate Medical Education (ACGME). See *specialty*.

orthopedic surgery: Surgery dealing with the spine, extremities, and related structures. One of the medical specialties for which *residency* programs have been approved by the Accreditation Council for Graduate Medical Education (ACGME). See *specialty*.

OSHA: See *Occupational Safety and Health Administration*.

osteopath: A physician (Doctor of Osteopathy (DO)) who has been trained in and practices *osteopathy* (osteopathic medicine). By contrast, a Doctor of Medicine (MD) practices *allopathy* (allopathic medicine). See *medicine (4)*.

A few decades ago, the distinction in theory and procedures permitted the two (osteopathy and allopathy) under licensing acts was marked; today, the distinctions are in matters of detail, and licensure tends to give DOs and MDs equal permission for the practice of medicine.

osteopathy: See *medicine (4)*.

OT (1): See *occupational therapy*.

OT (2): See *occupational therapist*.

OTA: See *Office of Technology Assessment*.

OTC: Over-the-counter drug. See *nonprescription drug* under *drug*.

O

otolaryngology: The branch of medicine dealing with the ear and larynx and other elements of the upper respiratory system.   One of the medical specialties for which *residency* programs have been approved by the Accreditation Council for Graduate Medical Education (ACGME).   See *specialty*.

otorhinolaryngology (ENT):   The medical specialty dealing with the ears (-oto), nose (-rhino), and throat (-laryngo), hence the acronym "ENT."

outcome: A term used very loosely, particularly in evaluating patient care and the health care system and its components.   When used for populations or the health care system, it typically refers to changes in birth or death rates, or some similar global measure.   In contrast, it may refer to the "outcome" (finding) of a given diagnostic procedure.   It may also refer to cure of the patient, restoration of function, or extension of life, sometimes with an attempt to introduce into the calculation some quantification of the *quality of life*.

　　When used in *quality management,* it is difficult to find in what dimensions and at what time in the history of the patient's problem outcome is to be determined.   It is commonly stated that three things can be measured in relation to quality: structure, process, and outcome.   "Structure" refers to resources, and "process" refers to the things done for the patient.   There is a tendency on the part of some individuals to take an "either-or" position, to the effect that one need only be concerned with one of the three dimensions. This tendency is not logical; all three must be considered.   Clearly, certain structure is needed; and equally clearly, there is no way to change outcome except through changing process, since "outcome 'tells on' process."

outlier: A patient who requires an unusually long stay or whose stay generates unusually great cost. The term is used in the *prospective payment system (PPS)*.   About five or six percent of the budgets for regional and national rates have been set aside for payments for outliers.   Outliers provide an escape hatch for the hospital, because they allow the hospital to negotiate for a fee higher than the *Diagnosis Related Group (DRG)* price which would otherwise apply to the patient.   Outliers are of two kinds:

cost outlier: An unusually costly case.

stay outlier: An unusually long stay. Also called day outlier.

outpatient (OP): A person who receives care without taking up lodging in a care institution.

outpatient clinic: A facility for the diagnosis and treatment of *ambulatory* patients. The term is usually applied to a unit of a hospital.

outpatient service (1) (OP service): Service provided to patients who do not require lodging in a care institution.

outpatient service (2) (OP service): An activity of the hospital which consists of providing care to *outpatients* (patients who do not require lodging).

outpatient surgery: Surgery performed on an *outpatient*, with arrival and departure on the same day. If the patient has to be kept over night, he is admitted and then discharged the next day. Same as ambulatory surgery and same-day surgery.

outrage: See *intentional infliction of emotional distress*.

over-the-counter (OTC) drug: See *nonprescription drug* under *drug*.

P

P & L: Profit and loss statement. See *income and expense statement.*

P & T: See *pharmacy and therapeutics.*

PA (1): See *Pathology and Medical Laboratory Services.*

PA (2): Physician advisor.

PA (3): See *physician assistant.*

PA (4): See *physician's assistant.*

PA (5): See *product administration.*

PA (6): Professional association. See *professional corporation* under *corporation.*

PA (7): See *public accountant.*

PABV: See *percutaneous aortic balloon valvuloplasty.*

PAC (1): See *political action committee.*

PAC (2): See *preadmission certification.*

PAC (3): See *products of ambulatory care.*

pain and suffering: The noneconomic injury which accompanies the physical injury a *malpractice* victim suffers as a result of the professional negligence, for which the law allows an amount of money to be paid to the victim as compensation. Some states limit the amount which can be awarded for pain and suffering in malpractice lawsuits.

pain management program: A specialized medical program for the management of *chronic* (and sometimes *acute*) pain, employing a multidisciplinary approach with medical, nursing, and allied health professionals. The national cost of treating pain is said to rank as the third highest health care cost, led only by cancer and heart disease.

panel (1): A group of individuals, such as physicians. The term is used for groups such as the physicians who form a *preferred provider organization (PPO)*, and those who are convened to review a grant application.

panel (2): In law, a group of people given the duty to review information, receive evidence, and make a decision. In a court of law, a panel may be comprised of judges; in other contexts, it may be made up of experts or laypersons. Also, the group of potential jurors from which a jury will be selected is called a "panel."

pretrial screening panel: In *malpractice* cases, a group of physicians who review the case before trial and make a recommendation as to whether there was malpractice, and if so, the dollar amount of *damages* the *plaintiff* suffered as a result of it. The purpose is to encourage settlement; if one party turns down a settlement based on the recommendation, that party may be penalized if she loses at trial.

parachute: An arrangement with an *employee*, particularly an officer or executive of a corporation, which protects the employee financially in the event of loss of employment. The arrangement may be a stipulated severance payment, an employment contract with a substantial notice of severance requirement, insurance, or other protection. A handsome severance arrangement is a "golden parachute."

parallel associative network: See *neurocomputer* under *computer*.

P

parallel distributed processor: See *neurocomputer* under *computer.*

paramedical personnel: A term derived from "para-," meaning "beside." Paramedical personnel, who prefer to be called "allied health professionals," are not physicians, but work in the health field. The term does not apply to nurses and pharmacists. Paramedical personnel may be dietitians, emergency medical technicians, and so on. There are some 26 allied health professions for which educational standards have been developed. For a list of occupations for which programs have been accredited by the *Committee on Allied Health Education and Accreditation (CAHEA),* see that listing.

parameter: A term gaining the favor of physicians in referring to statements which delineate the ways in which it is acceptable for physicians to treat patients. Recent American Medical Association (AMA) statements indicate an interpretation of the term "standard" as referring to a rigid rule, any deviation from which is subject to censure, and "parameter" as referring to "an acceptable range of options." It would seem that any properly drawn standards should allow adaptation to the peculiar problem presented by the individual patient, the skills of the physician, and the resources available. The argument apparently is over the breadth of the standard rather than the concept that certain practice is acceptable, but other practice is not. Note that an earlier, and current, usage of the term "parameter" is to mean "the thing measured," as in *"monitor parameters."*

monitor parameter: Anything being kept track of systematically. The term originated in connnection with quality assessment, in which certain key data, such as death rates, infection rates, average length of stay, and the like, were identified as giving such useful information that running records should be kept, that is, that they should be monitored. The infection itself is the "thing," or parameter, the numbers of infections are its "value" and are the statistics monitored.

parens patriae: "Parent of his country." A legal term referring to the power of the state to protect its people—specifically, those unable to care for themselves, such as *minors* (children) and the mentally *incompetent.*

parent: A term applied to both the father and mother of a child. With the advent of *noncoital reproduction*, it has become necessary to distinguish among the genetic parents, the gestational mother, and the rearing parents:

genetic parent: The parent who furnished the sperm (the genetic father) or the ovum (the genetic mother).

gestational parent: The woman who bore the child (the father, who cannot bear a child, cannot be a gestational parent). The gestational mother may also be the *genetic mother*, the *rearing mother*, or neither.

rearing parent: The parent who actually rears the child. This term would apply to both father and mother, and is used in connection with both *noncoital reproduction* and adoption.

Pareto: An Italian economist after whose discoveries J.M. Juran, an authority on quality, named the *Pareto principle*.

Pareto analysis: See *Pareto principle*.

Pareto principle: A principle which states that in any series of steps in a process, such as the diagnosis of a patient's problem, there are a "vital few" steps and a "trivial many." The procedure for identifying the vital few and the trivial many is called a *Pareto analysis*. The Pareto analysis makes feasible productive efforts at quality improvement since, once the "vital few" steps where efforts pay off can be identified, appropriate action can be taken. The Pareto principle is also the key to optimizing the care possible under a condition of limited resources. The principle was developed by J.M. Juran, an authority on quality, and named after an Italian economist named Pareto.

partial hospitalization: Treatment which involves the use of hospital *day beds* or *night beds* or *adult day care* services on a regularly scheduled basis. The services provided may include medical, social, nutritional, psychological, and others.

partnership: Two or more people (or organizations) carrying on a business for profit (for the purpose of making money). The law recognizes such an enterprise as a legal partnership, whether or not the partners have a verbal or written partnership agreement.

P

In a general partnership, the partners share profits, losses, and management of the business, and are all equally liable should the partnership be sued. In a limited partnership, there is at least one general partner who manages the business, and one or more limited partners who put in money and share profits and losses, but who are liable only to the extent of their investments, and who do not have management control. To be recognized as a limited partnership, however, the business must comply with legal formalities.

parturition: See *delivery.*

PAS (1): See *preadmission screening.*

PAS (2): See *Professional Activity Study.*

passive smoking: See *involuntary smoking.*

PAT: See *preadmission testing.*

pathological: Abnormal. When the body structure or function is not normal, it may be called "pathological." When function or structure is normal, it is called "physiological."

pathology: The branch or *specialty* of medicine which is concerned with the structures of the body and their physiology (vital processes), and in particular the changes in both structure and physiological function which occur in disease. One of the medical specialties for which *residency* programs have been approved by the Accreditation Council for Graduate Medical Education (ACGME). See *specialty.*
See also *pathology laboratory.*

anatomic pathology: The study of *tissues* removed at surgery, of biopsy specimens (specimens of tissue removed purely for examination by the pathologist), and of *autopsy* material. Anatomic pathology may be either gross (the study of an entire tissue, typically as visible to the naked eye) or microscopic.

clinical pathology: The study of body tissues and fluids, with particular attention to changes in physiology (function) and biochemistry in disease. The site of the clinical pathology services in the hospital is the *clinical laboratory*, where biochemical and other examinations are made of materials obtained from the body and body fluids.

forensic pathology: The branch or specialty of pathology which deals with legal issues, particularly crime, and the cause of violent or mysterious death. Estimation of the time of death is also a forensic matter. A growing concern in forensic pathology is toxicology, the study of poisonous substances, their effects, and their detection in the body.

surgical pathology: The branch or specialty of pathology which deals with tissues removed in surgical operations. It includes the examination of tissue during operation (often by frozen section) in order to help the surgeon determine the appropriate procedure for the remainder of the operation; it also includes the examination of tissue after surgery. During the operation, a determination as to whether the tissue is cancerous (malignant) may greatly influence the extent and type of surgery.

Pathology and Medical Laboratory Services (PA): The chapter giving the *standards* for this component of the hospital in the 1990 *Accreditation Manual for Hospitals (AMH)* of the *Joint Commission on the Accreditation of Healthcare Organizations (JCAHO)*.

pathology laboratory: A *laboratory* used in *anatomic pathology*. Pathology, the study of the structures, organs, and tissues of the body in disease, is divided into several major specialties, including anatomic pathology, which deals with tissues removed in surgery and with *autopsy* material. It is in the pathology laboratory that organs removed in surgery are studied for the presence of disease and its nature (such as infections, cancer, and the like). This laboratory is also the place where autopsies are performed.

Other major divisions of pathology include *clinical pathology* and *forensic pathology*. Clinical pathology is concerned with analysis of materials obtained from the body, such as blood and urine. The laboratory for this service is called the clinical laboratory. Every hospital will have both a pathology laboratory for anatomic pathology and a clinical laboratory, or will make arrangements for laboratory services, both anatomic and clinical, which are acceptable to the accrediting and licensing agencies.

Forensic pathology, dealing with crime, typically has its

P

laboratory in a municipal hospital or with a law enforcement organization.

patient: A person who has established a contractual relationship with a health care provider for that provider to care for that person. A patient may or may not be ill or injured. A patient who is ill or injured, or who otherwise presents a health problem, is often referred to as a "case."

patient advocacy: An allied health field developed to help patients with their complaints and problems in relation to medical care and hospital and other health care services, and with the protection of their rights. The practitioner may be called a patient advocate, a patient representative, a health advocate, or an ombudsperson. See also *health advocacy*.

patient advocate: A person who helps patients with their complaints and problems with medical care and hospital and health care services and with the protection of their rights. The field is called "patient advocacy," one area of *health advocacy*. Synonym(s): ombudsperson, patient representative, health advocate.

patient assistance services: Things done by volunteers for patients, such as reading to them and providing library services and toiletries.

patient care audit (PCA): The preferred term for the process also called "medical audit" or "medical care evaluation study." A patient care audit is a retrospective review of the *quality of care* of a group of patients, ordinarily a group with the same diagnosis or therapy. The review is based on medical records, and matches the care against *standards of care (1)*. "Patient care audit" is the preferred term because it indicates that the focus of the study is the care received by the group of patients, rather than the performance of physicians, nurses, or other caregivers.

patient care committee: A hospital committee, typically composed of medical, nursing, and other disciplines involved in direct patient care, along with hospital administration. The purpose of the committee is to monitor patient care practices, evaluate them against standards, and improve care through better liaison among the departments involved.

patient care coordinator (1): An individual assigned the responsibility for coordinating all care given to a patient in a *long term care facility (LTCF)*.

patient care coordinator (2): A *registered nurse (RN)* who manages, coordinates, or directs a nursing service, such as obstetrics, among two or more *patient care units*.

patient care management: The determination of processes and procedures (such as diagnostic testing, administration of drugs, surgery, nursing, physical therapy, and others), their scheduling, and arranging for them in the care of the individual patient.

patient care manager (PCM): A term which has been suggested as the preferred term to designate the person who is responsible for determining the *services (1)* to be provided to a patient and coordinating the provision of the appropriate care. The purposes of the PCM's function are: (1) to improve the quality of care by considering the whole patient, that is, all the patient's problems and other relevant factors; (2) to ensure that all necessary care is obtained; and (3) to reduce unnecessary care (and cost). When, as is often the case, the PCM is a physician, she is a *primary care physician* and usually must, except in an emergency, give the first level of care to the patient before the patient is permitted to be seen by a *secondary care* physician (*specialist*). In fact, the PCM must refer the patient for the secondary care. It has been suggested that the term "PCM" replace the widely-used term "gatekeeper," but "gatekeeper" is likely to be retained as well.

patient care plan: See *interdisciplinary patient care plan (IPCP)*.

patient care policies: Written policies that a *long term care facility (LTCF)* is expected to maintain, which govern nursing care and related medical and other *services (1)* to be provided.

patient care quality: See *quality of care*.

P

patient care unit (PCU): An organizational part of the hospital where *inpatients* are lodged during their hospitalization. Synonym(s): nursing unit, unit.

patient condition: A brief statement of "how ill" the patient is. Patient condition is described to relatives, other professionals, and in public information releases. It may be described in terms of progression of the illness, for example, as "improving" or "stable." It may also be described in terms of likelihood of favorable outcome, for example, "good," "fair," "poor," "serious," or *"critical."* In general, this latter series progresses from high likelihood of recovery (good) to low (critical). While health care professionals often use these terms in communicating with each other about patients, terms describing patient condition may also reflect specific patient needs, and may use measurements which translate the condition into requirements for nursing service in order better to provide the necessary hours of skilled or other nursing care. See also *severity of illness* and *staging.*

patient days: The total number of *inpatient service days,* for all patients, during a specified period of time (for example, a month). Ordinarily this number will be expressed in three segments—adult days, pediatric days, and newborn days—since there almost certainly will be a desire to relate the usage in these three segments to the "adult inpatient bed count," the "newborn bed count," and the "pediatric inpatient bed count." Each bed count multiplied by the number of days in the period gives the "available bed days," the denominator in computing the *occupancy rate.* See also *bed, bed count,* and *day.*

patient dumping: See *dumping.*

patient management categories (PCMs): A method of quantifying *severity of illness* based on the perceived needs of the patient for diagnostic and therapeutic services. This method, as currently applied, gives only one assessment for the episode of care, and relies on the subjective judgment of professional reviewers of the patient's medical record rather than objective data. Thus it does not offer help in viewing the patient's response to treatment.

patient representative: See *patient advocate.*

P

patient's chart: See *medical record*.

patient's data set: A computer record of selected data items about an *episode of care*, including identity of the patient, identity of the physician, dates of care, diagnoses, procedures, reference to the original medical record, and other information.

Patient's Bill of Rights: A statement adopted by the *American Hospital Association (AHA)* in 1973 giving some 12 "rights" to which it felt that hospital patients were entitled. These include the right of the patient to be included in making treatment decisions, to be treated with dignity, to have privacy, and so forth. In several states, legislation has been passed codifying and augmenting these rights; some states extend these rights to nonhospitalized patients.

The *Joint Commission on Accreditation of Healthcare Organizations (JCAHO)* also requires hospitals to have policies concerning patient rights, and in an opening chapter of its *Accreditation Manual for Hospitals* (1990) entitled "Rights and Responsibilities of Patients," rights and responsibilities considered "reasonably applicable to all hospitals" are given. Rights are listed under the following headings: (1) Access to care, (2) Respect and Dignity, (3) Privacy and Confidentiality, (4) Personal Safety, (5) Identity, (6) Information, (7) Communication, (8) Consent, (9) Consultation, (10) Refusal of Treatment, (11) Transfer and Continuity of Care, (12) Hospital Charges, and (13) Hospital Rules and Regulations. Responsibilities are listed under: (1) Provision of Information, (2) Compliance Instructions, (3) Refusal of Treatment, (4) Hospital Charges, (5) Hospital Rules and Regulations, and (6) Respect and Consideration.

patients' compensation: A *no-fault* system for compensating patients who suffer harm as a result of some aspect of medical or hospital care, proposed as an alternative to *malpractice* litigation. Synonym(s): neo-no-fault compensation.

patients' rights: See *Patient's Bill of Rights*.

Patrick case: A United States Supreme Court case which ruled that physicians are not immune from liability for *antitrust* violations in connection with their activities on hospital *peer review* committees.
Dr. Patrick, a general surgeon, was a member of the *medical staff*

P

of the only hospital in a community of about 10,000 people. He was also an employee of a private group medical practice, of which a majority of the hospital medical staff were either partners or employees. Dr. Patrick was offered a partnership with the clinic but declined, and instead opened up his own private practice. After this, clinic physicians refused to deal professionally with Dr. Patrick, and eventually a hospital staff committee (largely comprised of clinic partners) recommended that his *privileges* be terminated.

Dr. Patrick brought a lawsuit against the partners for violation of federal antitrust law, alleging that the hospital peer review proceedings were initiated to reduce competition rather than to improve patient care. The trial court jury found in favor of Dr. Patrick and awarded him $650,000 in *damages*. Under federal antitrust law, this amount was trebled to nearly two million dollars (attorney's fees and costs raised the award to over $2,000,000). The defendants appealed and the Court of Appeals reversed, stating that the peer review activity was immune from suit because peer review committees were mandated by state law, and thus their activities were "state action." (However, in a footnote the Court of Appeals characterized the defendants' conduct as "shabby, unprincipled, and unprofessional.")

The United States Supreme Court ruled that state action immunity did not apply because the peer review was not actively supervised by the state. Although a doctor in that state presumably could appeal to a court for review of an adverse peer review decision, the reviewing court would not look at the substance of the decision, but only decide whether proper procedures had been followed by the hospital. Thus, the state did not protect physicians from abuses by peer reviewers. *Patrick v. Burget*, 486 U.S. 94, 108 S.Ct. 1658 (1988), *rev'g* 800 F.2d 1498 (9th Cir. 1986).

payback period: The period of time it will take a new item of equipment to produce revenues or result in savings equal to its cost.

payer: An organization or person who furnishes the money to pay for the provision of health care services. A payer may be the government (for example, Medicare), a nonprofit organization (such as *Blue Cross/Blue Shield (BC/BS)*), *commercial insurance*, or some other entity. In common usage, "payer" most often means *third party payer*.

PC (1): Personal computer. See *microcomputer* under *computer*.

PC (2): See *professional corporation* under *corporation*.

PC-stager: See *personal computer stager*.

PCA: See *patient care audit*.

PCC: See *primary care center*.

PCM: See *patient care manager*.

PCMs: See *patient management categories*.

PCU: See *patient care unit*.

PDR: See *Physicians' Desk Reference*.

PDR *for Nonprescription Drugs*: An annual publication of the Medical Economics Company which is a compendium of information on *over-the-counter drugs*. This publication is a companion volume to the *Physicians' Desk Reference (PDR)*, which deals with *prescription drugs* and *diagnostic products*.

pediatric: Pertaining to children.

pediatric cardiology: A branch of *pediatrics*. One of the medical specialties for which *residency* programs have been approved by the Accreditation Council for Graduate Medical Education (ACGME). See *specialty*.

pediatric endocrinology: The branch of *pediatrics* dealing with *endocrinology*. One of the medical specialties for which *residency* programs have been approved by the Accreditation Council for Graduate Medical Education (ACGME). See *specialty*.

pediatric hemato-oncology: The branch of *pediatrics* dealing with diseases of the blood and blood-forming organs and with tumors. One of the medical specialties for which *residency* programs have been approved by the Accreditation Council for Graduate Medical Education (ACGME). See *specialty*.

pediatric nephrology: The branch of *pediatrics* which deals with diseases of the urinary system or kidneys. One of the medical specialties for which *residency* programs have been approved by the Accreditation Council for Graduate Medical Education (ACGME). See *specialty*.

pediatric nurse practitioner (PNP): See *nurse practitioner*.

pediatric orthopedics: Orthopedic surgery applied to infants and children. One of the medical specialties for which *residency* programs have been approved by the Accreditation Council for Graduate Medical Education (ACGME). See *specialty*.

pediatric surgery: The branch of surgery dealing with children. One of the medical specialties for which *residency* programs have been approved by the Accreditation Council for Graduate Medical Education (ACGME). See *specialty*.

pediatrics: The branch of medicine dealing with children. The upper age limit for pediatrics varies with the region of the country and the hospital. One of the medical specialties for which *residency* programs have been approved by the Accreditation Council for Graduate Medical Education (ACGME). See *specialty*.

peer review: Review by individuals from the same discipline and with essentially equal qualifications (peers). "Peer review" usually means review of the performance of a physician, done by other physicians. It may also be used for reviews of other disciplines' performance (for example, the performance of nurses, with the review done by other nurses). Peer review sometimes leads to reduction or denial of clinical *privileges* of a physician (or other professional) whose performance is reviewed. It is therefore especially important that the process be done fairly and in *good faith* to avoid legal liability. See *antitrust, credentialing, defamation, due process, Health Care Quality Improvement Act, Patrick case*, and *tortious interference with business relationship*.

"Peer review" sometimes has a narrower meaning, which can be determined only after careful listening and asking: (1) some use the term only for review conducted by a group of physicians appointed by a *medical society*; (2) some use it as a synonym for a *patient care audit*; and (3) some use it only when the reviewers are physicians.

The term is also used in connection with review of research projects funded by the *National Institutes of Health (NIH)*.

peer review committee: A committee, usually set up by a *medical society*, to carry out the review of physicians' performance. The term is also applied to such a committee of a hospital department or the *medical staff*, whose function is to carry out *peer review*.

Peer Review Organization (PRO): An organization set up as a part of the *prospective payment system (PPS)* to carry out certain review functions under contract from the *Health Care Financing Administration (HCFA)*. PROs are external to the hospital; some were formerly *Professional Standards Review Organizations (PSROs)* and the functions of PROs are similar to those performed by PSROs.

The duties of the PRO include, for example: determining whether the medical records of Medicare patients support the diagnoses and procedures stated in the claims submitted; determining whether a changing pattern of care in a hospital, as reflected in its claims submitted, represents an actual change in the kinds of patients or their treatment, or is a fictitious result of the claims submission and reporting system; reviewing the medical necessity of DRG *outliers*; reviewing cardiac pacemaker implantations; and attempting to achieve certain changes in performance in hospitals within the jurisdiction of the PRO. A PRO is not the same as a hospital or medical society *peer review committee*.

People's Medical Society, The: A nonprofit patients' advocacy group, with membership (1987) stated to be about 85,000. Its headquarters are in Emmaus, Pennsylvania.

per diem rate: A *rate (1)* established by dividing total costs (plus a percentage for excess of income over expenses) by the total number of inpatient days of care for the same period. Thus the per diem rate is the same for each patient, regardless of the patient's illness, its severity, or the diagnostic or therapeutic measures required.

P

per se: "By itself." In *antitrust* law, the term refers to activities which, by themselves, are violations of the antitrust laws; no proof of intent, effect on competition, and so forth are required. Price-fixing (two or more competitors agreeing on prices) is a "per se" violation of the *Sherman Act*.

percentile: The size or magnitude of that element, in a series of elements that are arranged in order of magnitude, whose location in the series is at the designated percentage of the way from the small end of the series to the large end. For example, the 50th percentile is the magnitude of the element that is 50 percent of the way through the series—namely, the magnitude of the middle element, if the series has an odd number of elements. (Thus the 50th percentile is the same as the *median*).

Algorithms (sets of rules) for calculating percentiles vary, and so their results for a given series may also vary somewhat. This is because the concept of "percentile" is not precise. The following example gives some results of one commonly used algorithm:

Grading of students is a familiar use of the percentile. All the test scores (either percentages or raw scores) are placed in order from lowest to highest. If there are 80 students in the class, the 40th test score (from either end) is the 50th percentile (also known as the median). The 60th test score (from the low end) is the 75th percentile, the 72nd (again from the low end) is the 90th percentile (90 percent of 80 students (scores) is 72).

percutaneous: Through the skin.

percutaneous aortic balloon valvuloplasty (PABV): Correction of the narrowing of the aortic valve of the heart by expanding a balloon within the valve. The balloon is at the tip of a *catheter* (a thin tube) which is threaded through an artery to the heart after insertion through the skin ("percutaneous"). The process requires viewing the progress of the catheter by *X-ray* so that the catheter can be guided to the proper location.

percutaneous transluminal coronary angioplasty (PTCA): A technique for correcting a narrowing in the diameter of an artery in the heart muscle. A needle is inserted into the skin ("percutaneously") and then into an artery, usually in the groin. A thin tube (*catheter*) with a balloon at its tip is passed through the needle and threaded "upstream" inside the artery ("transluminally") into the heart artery where the narrowing has been detected by an earlier *X-ray* examination. The movement and placing of the catheter tip are guided visually by the physician who can see the catheter and its tip with the aid of a "live" X-ray. When the balloon is in the narrowed section of the artery, it is inflated, the artery is forced open, and the obstruction is thus cleared. The procedure is *invasive*, but far less traumatic than open heart surgery. PTCA can be repeated if the narrowing recurs. Synonym(s): balloon angioplasty.

PERF: See *perfusionist*.

performance: The actual carrying out of an activity. The term occurs especially in connection with physician's *privileges*, where the trend is to attempt to grant privileges, and to continue or terminate them, not only on the basis of the individual's *credentials*, but also on her performance, that is, the skill with which she carries out the activities under review. To be able to evaluate performance accurately requires considerable sophistication in the collection and analysis of data about the performance demonstrated.

perfusion: Pouring through, especially the circulating of blood or other liquid through an organ or tissue. In certain cardio-vascular surgery, this flow is assisted by mechanical pumping devices, such as a *heart-lung machine*.

perfusionist (PERF): One of the 26 *allied health professionals* for whom the American Medical Association's *Committee on Allied Health Education and Accreditation (CAHEA)* has accredited education programs.

perinatal: Pertaining to the infant in the period shortly before and after birth. It is often (but not always) defined as beginning with the completion of the 28th week of gestation (pregnancy) and ending one to four weeks after delivery.

periodic interim payment (PIP): A system of providing Medicare funds to *providers* on a regular basis. Periodic payments may be made monthly or semi-monthly to a hospital, home health agency, or skilled nursing facility in the Medicare program, based on the institution's estimated annual Medicare revenue. Adjustments are made later when actual revenue figures become available. Such a system of payment is also sometimes employed by other *payers*.

periodic payments: A payment arrangement which allows money due to be paid in installments, over time, instead of in a lump sum. The term is used in regard to settlements (or judgments) in *malpractice* cases, which allow the *defendant* to pay for the patient's health care and other needs as those expenses accrue, or to pay a fixed sum in even portions over a given number of years.

peripheral worker: See *contingent worker*.

peritoneal dialysis: A technique for removal of the waste materials which would have been removed by the kidneys in a normally functioning individual. The technique involves introducing a fluid into the person's abdomen (peritoneal cavity) where the waste materials pass from the body into the fluid, which is then removed. Peritoneal dialysis may be done either in an institution or on an ambulatory basis. See also *renal dialysis*.

personal care services: Those *services (1)* required to take care of the *activities of daily living (ADL)*.

personal computer stager (PC-stager): A method for quantifying the *severity of illness* using data specially abstracted from the *medical record*. See *microcomputer* for definition of "personal computer."

personal services: Usually, services which are provided simply because the recipient wants them, rather than because they are essential to her medical or other care. Examples include beauty parlor services, catered meals, and the like. Such services are not included in the *benefits* of a health care plan. See also *personal care services*.

PET: See *positron emission tomography*.

PH: See *Pharmaceutical Services*.

phacoemulsufication: The liquidizing of cataracts and their removal by suction, using *ultrasound*.

Pharmaceutical Services (PH): The chapter giving the *standards* for this component of the hospital in the 1990 *Accreditation Manual for Hospitals (AMH)* of the *Joint Commission on the Accreditation of Healthcare Organizations (JCAHO)*.

pharmacist: A person who is *licensed* to prepare, dispense, and control *prescription drugs*. A pharmacist need not be a *pharmacologist*.

pharmacologist: A person trained in the science of *drugs*—their properties and reactions, and their therapeutic effects and *(drug) interactions*. A pharmacologist need not be *licensed*, and is not necessarily a *pharmacist*.

pharmacology: The science dealing with drugs, their composition, preparation, chemical properties, actions, and uses.

pharmacopeia: A document containing recipes for the preparation (compounding) of medicinal *drugs* and also standards for their strengths and purities. Many nations adopt official pharmacopeias. In the United States, the United States Pharmacopeia Convention (USPC) issues the *Pharmacopeia of the United States of America (USP)*, which is a legal standard. By contrast, a *formulary* need not contain the information about strengths and purities.

pharmacy (1): The art and science of preparing and dispensing *medicine (1)* (substances administered to treat disease).

pharmacy (2): The internal "drugstore" of the hospital which serves the hospital *inpatients* and other units of the hospital, such as the emergency department, which administer drugs.

pharmacy (3): A public drugstore.

pharmacy and therapeutics (P & T): Usually, a committee of the *medical staff organization (MSO)*, or of the hospital, which concerns itself with drugs to be stocked by the hospital *pharmacy (2)* and

P

their correct use. It ordinarily has physician, pharmacist, and nurse members.

PHN: See *public health nurse.*

PHO: See *physician-hospital organization.*

physical: Having to do with physics, that is, mechanics, heat, radiation, sound, electricity, and similar phenomena. It is contrasted with *"chemical,"* which refers to the properties of substances.

physical examination: The portion of the examination of an individual which is carried out by the physician by the use of her own senses—looking, touching, and listening—with or without the aid of devices to assist these senses. It does not include examination of the blood or body fluids or the use of special procedures such as X-ray and electrocardiography.

physical medicine and rehabilitation: One of the medical specialties for which *residency* programs have been approved by the Accreditation Council for Graduate Medical Education (ACGME). See *specialty.*

Physical Rehabilitation Services (RH): The chapter giving the *standards* for this component of the hospital in the 1990 *Accreditation Manual for Hospitals (AMH)* of the *Joint Commission on the Accreditation of Healthcare Organizations (JCAHO).*

physical therapy (PT): The use of physical means such as exercise, massage, light, cold, heat, and electricity, and mechanical devices in the prevention, diagnosis, and treatment of diseases, injuries, and other physical disorders. Physical therapy does not include the use of X-rays or other types of radiation. Synonym(s): physiotherapy.

physician: A person qualified by a doctor's degree in *medicine (4)* (*allopathy, homeopathy,* or *osteopathy*). To practice, a physician must also be *licensed* by the state. Note that "physician" is the generic term; a surgeon is also a physician, but a physician is not neces-

P

sarily a surgeon. A number of modifying words are used to describe a physician's qualifications or duties:

admitting physician: The physician who orders the *admission* of a given patient to a hospital or other health care institution.

alternate physician: In a *long term care facility (LTCF)*, the physician assigned responsibility for medical care to patients in the absence of the *attending physician*.

attending physician: The physician legally responsible, at a given time, for the care of a given patient in an institution. May or may not be the *operating surgeon*.

board certified physician: A physician who has passed an examination by a *specialty board* and has been certified by that board as a specialist in the subject of expertise of the board. For a list of medical specialties, see *specialty*.

board eligible physician: A physician who has met or can meet the requirements of a *specialty board* for eligibility to take the examination required to become *board certified*.

contract physician: A physician who provides care under a contract. A hospital, for example, may contract with a physician (directly or through a corporation) to provide emergency care. The contract stipulates the duties to be performed as well as the hospital's obligations. The contract physician is an *independent contractor*, rather than an *employee* of the hospital.

critical care physician: A physician specializing in the care of critically ill patients, wherever they may be—in intensive care units (ICUs), under emergency situations outside the hospital, and during transportation.

emergency physician (EP): A physician who specializes in the immediate care of patients who are injured or ill, and in their disposition (release without treatment, immediate treatment at the site or in the emergency facility, hospitalization, transport to another facility, and the like). Ordinarily such services are performed in the emergency department (ED) (sometimes called emergency room or ER) of a hospital (where the physician is often called an "emergency department physician") or in a free-standing emergency center (FEC). The emergency physician, by definition, sees the patient only once; continuing care is provided elsewhere, such as in a private physician's office, the outpatient department, or in the hospital, as appropriate.

Synonym(s): emergency medicine physician, emergency care physician, emergency department physician.

first year resident physician: A physician who has already had formal training in medicine, who is now obtaining her first year of supervised practical training. The term "graduate year 1" (GY-1) is now being applied to any *residency* program for the individual in the first year out of medical school. The term "intern" was formerly given to this person, but "intern" is no longer restricted to physicians; the term is applied in many disciplines.

full-time physician: A physician who spends the major part of her time within one or more specific hospitals, as, for example, a pathologist, radiologist, or emergency department physician. Synonym(s): hospital-based physician.

geographic full-time physician: A physician whose primary income is derived from a salary for services to a hospital, but who also engages in private clinical practice at that hospital.

graduate physician: A physician who has completed the education leading to the *Doctor of Medicine (MD)* or *Doctor of Osteopathy (DO)* degree, and who has obtained that degree.

hospital-based physician: See *full-time physician*.

marginal physician: A physician whose performance is just at (or below) the standards of performance for such physicians, either in terms of quality of care or cost.

nonparticipating physician: Under Medicare, a physician who has not signed a contract agreeing to refrain from charging a Medicare patient the difference between the physician's usual charge and the Medicare payment allowance.

participating physician: Under Medicare, a physician who has signed a contract agreeing not to charge a Medicare patient for the balance between the physician's usual charge and the Medicare payment allowance for the *service (1)* rendered.

primary care physician: A physician who specializes in family practice, general internal medicine, general pediatrics, or obstetrics and gynecology. Provides the initial care for a patient, and refers the patient, when appropriate, for secondary (specialist) care.

referring physician: A physician who has asked another physician to give a *consultation* or to take over the care of a given patient, or who has sent a patient to another institution.

resident physician: A *graduate physician* who is in an approved hospital training program in graduate medical education (a *residency*). Upon successful completion of the program, the resident is granted a certificate of that fact. A resident physician may be called simply a "resident," a "medical resident," a "surgical resident," or something similar.

salaried physician: A physician employed on a salary. Ordinarily such a physician does not also bill for services on a *fee-for-service* basis.

secondary physician: A specialist; one who treats patients on *referral* from another physician, most often a *primary care physician*.

physician assistant (PA): One of the 26 *allied health professionals* for whom the American Medical Association's *Committee on Allied Health Education and Accreditation (CAHEA)* has accredited education programs.

physician executive: An executive in a health care organization who is a *physician*.

physician-hospital organization (PHO): A term, without precise definition, which refers to any one of a number of arrangements between physicians and hospitals created in order to achieve some purpose. "PHO" may be a synonym for a *joint venture*.

physician recruitment: Finding, soliciting, and attracting physicians to a particular hospital or area. Hospitals devote resources to the search, and provide incentives, for physicians in specialties which are needed by the hospital and community. Such incentives may include relocation reimbursement and either initial employment of the physician or provision of a loan (with favorable terms) to enable the physician to start and build a practice in the area. Physician recruitment sometimes raises issues of *inurement* (private gain to an individual from the profits of a nonprofit corporation). For example, if the hospital pays the physician a salary in excess of reasonable compensation, or provides an interest-free loan, these incentives may be considered by the Internal

Revenue Service (IRS) to be inurement and thus jeopardize the hospital's tax exempt status. The hospital must show that it (and the community) receive measurable value for the incentives provided.

physician's assistant (PA): A person who assists a physician by carrying out designated tasks, such as taking medical histories and performing certain examinations. May or may not be a trained *allied health professional*.

Physician's Payment Review Commission (PhysPRC): A federal advisory body set up to provide input to the *Health Care Financing Administration (HCFA)* regarding methods of saving money in the payment of physicians for *services (1)* to Medicare patients.

Physicians' Current Procedural Terminology (CPT, CPT-1991): A publication of the *American Medical Association (AMA)*, containing its *classification (1)* of *procedures* and *services (1)*, primarily those carried out by physicians. It is widely used for *coding* in billing and payment for physicians' services. Each "package" of physician services (for example, care for a fracture—including diagnosis, setting the fracture, and putting on and removing the splint) is given one code number and commands one fee for the package. In contrast to *CPT*, *ICD-9-CM*, the classification used for hospital coding of *diagnoses* and procedures, has separate codes for each of the four factors: diagnosis, setting the fracture, applying the cast, and removing the cast.

CPT is similar in theory to the *Diagnosis Related Groups (DRGs)* (which currently apply to hospital—not physician—care) in that both are built on the "one code, one fee" basis.

Although the fourth edition of *CPT* appeared in 1977 (at which time it was called "CPT-4"), it has been revised repeatedly since then, and now the volume is labelled annually, for example "*CPT-1991*."

Physicians' Desk Reference (PDR): An annual publication (the 1991 issue is the 45th) of the Medical Economics Company, which is a compendium of information on *prescription drugs* and *diagnostic products*. Sections include listings of drugs by manufacturer, type (action) of drug, and brand name. Detailed information as furnished by the manufacturer is the same as that found in the "package inserts" required by law. One section shows color photographs of products as an aid in identification in poison control, and for use with patients who are not sure of the prescriptions they are taking. Supplements are issued periodically throughout the year. The Medical Economics Company also publishes a companion volume, *PDR for Nonprescription Drugs*, which deals with *over-the-counter drugs*.

physiological: Normal. When the body is functioning normally, its processes and activities are said to be physiological; when the function is not normal, it is "pathological" (abnormal).

physiological chemist: See *biochemist*.

physiology: The science dealing with the life processes of living things, the chemical and physical activity of body *organs* and *tissues*. It is contrasted with "anatomy," which deals with the structures of the organs and tissues rather than their activities.

physiotherapy: See *physical therapy (PT)*.

PhysPRC: See *Physician's Payment Review Commission*.

PIP: See *periodic interim payment*.

PL standards: See *Plant, Technology, and Safety Management standards*.

plaintiff: The person (or organization) who brings a lawsuit against another person or entity, called the *defendant*. Commonly, the plaintiff in a lawsuit is someone who alleges she was injured by the acts of the defendant.

plan of correction: A term used by the *Joint Commission on the Accreditation of Healthcare Organizations (JCAHO)* referring to a written statement which it has approved as to how an institution will correct *Life Safety Code* deficiencies.

planner: A person whose profession is *planning*.

P

planning: The analysis of needs, demands, and resources, followed by the proposal of steps to meet the demands and needs by use of the current resources and obtaining other resources as necessary.

plant engineer: See *administrative engineer.*

Plant, Technology, and Safety Management (PTSM): A department of the *Joint Commission on Accreditation of Healthcare Organizations (JCAHO).*

Plant, Technology, and Safety Management (PL) Standards: Standards of the *Joint Commission on Accreditation of Healthcare Organizations (JCAHO)* in regard to the physical environment of the institution. These standards cover safety management, life safety, equipment management, and utilities management. "PL" is taken from the two-character abbreviations used in the *Accreditation Manual for Hospitals (AMH)* for each chapter.

plastic surgery: The branch of surgery dealing with modification of the shape and appearance of body structures. One of the medical specialties for which *residency* programs have been approved by the Accreditation Council for Graduate Medical Education (ACGME). See *specialty.*

pledging of accounts receivable: Short-term financing where *accounts receivable* are used to secure the financing. The lender does not buy the accounts receivable, but simply accepts them as collateral for the loan. It is also called "discounting of accounts receivable."

PLM: See *product line management.*

PM: See *post mortem, meaning "after death.*

PM-DRGs: Pediatric-Modified Diagnosis Related Groups. See *Diagnosis Related Group (DRG).*

PNP: Pediatric nurse practitioner. See *nurse practitioner.*

podiatry: The diagnosis and treatment of foot disorders, diseases, injuries, and anatomic defects. Medical, surgical, and physical means may be employed. The practitioner is a podiatrist, and is subject to licensure by the state. Used to be called chiropody.

point of sale (POS): An information system in which the details about a transaction are picked up electronically, coincidentally with the transaction, and are used as input to an integrated computer system which transmits the details of the transaction to the places in the organization where they are needed and automatically records them.

The supermarket provides an illustration. Items for sale often carry "bar codes" which tell exactly what the item is, the quantity being purchased, and the price. At the checkout counter, an optical reader scans the bar code and picks up this information, which is "simultaneously" shown to the customer on the cash register display, is used in producing the customer's adding machine tape (often showing the item and quantity as well as the charge made for it), adding the dollar amount to the day's sales total, and subtracting the amount of goods sold from the inventory for the item, so that reordering is systematized.

Similar applications are appearing in hospitals, which increase efficiency, decrease cost, and protect patients. For example, in the hospital pharmacy, as a prescription is dispensed for a given patient, the transaction is transmitted to an electronic medication file, where all drugs being given that patient are recorded. Here the newest prescription is checked (1) to see that the dosage is within the normal range for the drug (this is primarily a safeguard against clerical errors in the prescription) and (2) to see that the new drug is not incompatible with other drugs the patient is already receiving. A warning is issued automatically if there is a problem in either regard. At the same time, a charge for the prescription is made to the patient's bill, a notation is made for the medical record, the nursing station is informed, and the inventory of the pharmacy is adjusted.

point of service option (health care plan) (POS): A *health care plan* which allows the employee (*beneficiary*) to select a health provider each time she needs medical care, rather than once a year as in a "*triple-option*" health care plan.

POL: Physician office laboratory or physician-owned laboratory.

P

police power: The authority of government to restrict the rights of individuals to protect the health and welfare of the public. In the health care context, police power may be invoked by public health officials, for example, to quarantine infected individuals in order to control an epidemic, or to carry out an unannounced inspection of a restaurant, housing, or institution to ensure compliance with health and safety codes.

political action committee (PAC): An organization which receives contributions, usually from individuals, and disburses them to candidates for office. May also engage in lobbying activities.

POMR: Problem-oriented medical record. See *medical record*.

POR: Problem-oriented record. See *medical record*.

portfolio: The aggregate of the investments (stocks, real estate, and other assets) of an investor. Unless there is more than one kind of investment, a portfolio does not exist.

POS (1): See *point of sale*.

POS (2): See *point of service option (health care plan)*.

positioning: A term used in public relations (marketing) indicating the place occupied by an institution or product in the minds of its constituency. For example, IBM is "positioned" in the number one spot with respect to computers in most peoples' minds. Hertz has the same position in car rentals.

positron emission tomography (PET): A diagnostic *imaging* technique which records *biochemical* and *physiological* maps of the body created by emissions from radioactive compounds. Synonym(s): positron tomography.

positron tomography: See *positron emission tomography (PET)*.

post mortem (PM): After death. The term also is used as an abbreviation for a postmortem (after death) examination of a body. See *autopsy*.

postacute convalescence: The period of recovery which follows the *acute* portion of an illness.

postnatal: The period immediately after birth or delivery. The term refers to both mother and baby.

postoperative: Occurring after a surgical *operation*.

postoperative recovery room: See *recovery room*.

postpartum: Following *delivery*.

power of attorney: A written agreement under which one person (the "principal") authorizes another (the *"agent (2)"*) to act on her behalf.   The agent need not be a lawyer.   An ordinary power of attorney automatically terminates if the principal becomes incompetent.   The theory behind this is that the agent's power derives from the power of the principal herself, and that when she is no longer legally *competent* (able to make decisions), the agent correspondingly loses authority to act.   See *durable power of attorney*, below.

durable power of attorney: A power of attorney which remains (or becomes) effective when the principal becomes incompetent to act for herself.   It should be noted that in most states, even an agent with a durable power of attorney cannot make medical treatment decisions for an *incompetent* patient, unless state law provides that she can or a court has given her specific authority.

PPA: See *preferred provider arrangement*.

PPO (1):   See *preferred provider option*.

PPO (2):   See *preferred provider organization*.

PPS (1):   See *prospective payment system*.

PPS (2):   See *prospective pricing system*.

PR: See *Professional Library Services*.

P

practitioner: An individual entitled by training and experience to practice a profession. Often such practice requires licensure, and the boundaries of the practice are prescribed by law.

pre-AIDS: See *AIDS-related complex (ARC)*.

preadmission certification (PAC): A process by which *elective* care which is proposed for a patient is reviewed and approved before the patient is admitted to the hospital. When a PAC program is in effect, the care will not be paid for unless the certification is obtained.

preadmission process for admission: A formal *admission* process (namely, initiating the paperwork) carried out by a hospital prior to doing *preadmission testing (PAT)* for an *elective* admission patient.

preadmission screening (PAS): A program of evaluation of applicants for admission to nursing homes under Medicare. PAS was required in 29 states in 1986. Some states also require preadmission screening for private pay applicants.

preadmission testing (PAT): The carrying out of laboratory and other diagnostic work on an *outpatient* basis within a few days of hospital *admission* for the patient scheduled for *elective* hospitalization. It is less costly to have the tests performed in this manner and, in some instances, the test results will be such that hospitalization will be avoided or postponed. The hospital usually goes through a formal acceptance of the patient, called the "preadmission process for admission," prior to carrying out the tests.

preferred provider arrangement (PPA): A form of organization for physician *services (1)*, in a *health care plan*, in which the *third party payer* (the plan) establishes a roster of physicians who are believed to be *cost-effective*. All services covered by the plan, when furnished by these physicians, are without charge to the *beneficiary*. The beneficiary may elect care from physicians not on the roster, but if she does, at least part of those providers' fees must be paid by the beneficiary (or, in some forms of health insurance programs, by the physicians making up the roster of preferred providers).

preferred provider option (PPO): A form of *health care plan* in which certain physicians are designated by a *third party payer* as preferred *providers* whom the payer has concluded are the most *cost-effective*. When a *beneficiary* elects to receive care from these physicians, the physicians' charges are paid in full—there is no additional charge to the beneficiary. The beneficiary may elect to obtain care from other physicians, but if she does, there is a financial penalty to the beneficiary—she must pay part of the charges.

preferred provider organization (PPO): An *alternative (health care) delivery system (ADS (2))* designed to compete with *health maintenance organizations (HMOs)* and other delivery systems. A PPO is stated to be an arrangement involving a contract between health care *providers* (both professional and institutional), and organizations such as employers and *third-party administrators*, under which the PPO agrees to provide health care services to a defined population for predetermined fixed fees. PPOs are distinguished from HMOs and other similar organizations in that: (1) PPO physicians are paid on a *fee-for-service* basis, while in other delivery systems payment is usually by *capitation* or salary; and (2) PPO physicians are not at *risk (1)*—the purchaser of the service retains the risk—while HMOs are at risk. The term "contract provider organization (CPO)" is preferred by the American Medical Association (AMA) for the arrangements discussed here. The term "CPO" might be preferable as a method of distinguishing a preferred provider organization from the other "PPO"—the *preferred provider option*. See also *exclusive provider organization (EPO)*.

premature: Before it should happen. In the case of birth, "premature" means before the 37th week of pregnancy, regardless of the birth weight of the infant.

premium: A payment required for an insurance policy for a given period of time.

prenatal: A term that refers to the fetus (baby) before birth, and also to the period of pregnancy before delivery, as in "the prenatal period" or "prenatal care" of the mother.

preoperative: Preceding a surgical *operation*.

P

prepaid health plan: A *health care plan* in which the insurer agrees, for a fixed fee paid periodically in advance, to provide a specified array of *services (1)* to the *beneficiary*.

prepayment: Payment in advance. Under a prepayment system, a fee is paid to a *third party payer*, such as a *health maintenance organization (HMO)*, *Blue Cross/Blue Shield (BC/BS)*, or *commercial insurance*, and the third party agrees to pay for stipulated care when it is provided. The *voucher system* now being put in place for Medicare is a prepayment system.

prepayment plan: A contractual arrangement for health care in which a prenegotiated payment is made in advance, covering a certain time period, and the *provider* agrees, for this payment, to furnish certain *services (1)* to the *beneficiary*.

prescription: A written direction for the preparation and use of anything for the treatment of a patient. The term "prescription" is most often thought of in connection with a drug, but it is also used for eyeglasses, treatment such as physical therapy, and artificial limbs and other devices. For *controlled substances* (certain drugs), the prescription must be written by a *licensed* individual, and constitutes the pharmacist's authority to dispense the drugs.

president of the medical staff: The term used by some *medical staff organizations (MSOs)* to denote the "chief of staff." Some MSOs, however, have placed the administration and management functions done on behalf of the hospital under a "chief" (or similar title), while placing the "spokesperson" functions under a "president." This latter usage seems to clarify the distinctions between the two roles played by the MSO. See *chief of staff*.

prevailing: When used in conjunction with physicians' *fees*, "prevailing" refers to the charges made for the *service (1)* in question in the area, provided by physicians of similar specialty qualifications.

prevailing fee: See *customary, prevailing, reasonable charge (or fee) (CPR)*.

prevalence: The number of events or cases of disease present in a given population at a given time. "Prevalence" is often confused with "incidence," which is the number of new events taking place in a defined period of time in a specified area or population. Usually both incidence and prevalence refer to cases of disease or injury. Both are numerators in the calculation of an incidence rate or a prevalence rate, respectively, for the event in question. The denominator is, for both, the population at *risk (3)* (the given population).

preventive medicine: The branch of medicine which deals with the prevention of disease. One of the medical specialties for which *residency* programs have been approved by the Accreditation Council for Graduate Medical Education (ACGME). See *specialty*.

price: The amount of money to be paid for something. Each *Diagnosis Related Group (DRG)*, for example, carries a price, the amount of money to be paid for the hospital care of a patient classified to that DRG.

price blending: A method of adjusting a hospital's price for a given *Diagnosis Related Group (DRG)* under the *prospective payment system* (PPS) after comparing the hospital's cost per case for that DRG with the national average for the same DRG. Synonym(s): DRG-specific price blending.

price-fixing: Two or more competitors agreeing on prices (charges). Price-fixing is a "per se" violation of the *Sherman Act*, an antitrust law. "Per se" means that no proof of intent, effect on competition, and so forth are required to prove a violation of the law.

prima facie tort: See *tort*.

primary care: The care by a *primary care physician*. Care requiring more specialized knowledge or skill is obtained by *referral* from the primary care physician to the specialist (*secondary physician*) for consultation or continued care.

The term is also used to mean the care given at the initial contact of the patient with the health care system or with a health care provider. It usually takes place in an office or other *outpatient* setting.

P

primary care center (PCC): An institution for furnishing *primary care*. A PCC may be free-standing or part of another institution.

primary nursing: A system of nursing care in which one *professional nurse* is responsible around the clock for planning, supervising, and, when present, giving nursing care to an assigned individual or group of patients. This approach to nursing care is replacing *team nursing*, in which a group of individuals of different levels of skill rather than a given individual carries out these functions.

principal: A person (or entity, such as a corporation) who authorizes another to act on her behalf as her *agent (2)*.

Principles for Accreditation of Community Mental Health Service Programs (CMH Principles): A former publication of *standards* by the *Joint Commission on Accreditation of Healthcare Organizations (JCAHO)*, now merged into its *Consolidated Standards Manual for Child, Adolescent, and Adult Psychiatric, Alcoholism, and Drug Abuse Facilities and Facilities Serving the Mentally Retarded/Developmentally Disabled (CSM)*.

prion: A specific class of particles that can cause infection. Certain infections which were once thought to be caused by viruses are now recognized as caused by a different kind of infectious agent called a prion (from "small PROteinaceous INfectious particle").

privacy: See *invasion of privacy* and *right of privacy*.

private room: A hospital room for only one patient. A "semi-private room" has two to four patients. A patient care room with more than four patients is called a "ward."

privileged communication: Information which is legally protected from *discovery* in a lawsuit or use as evidence in a trial. Communications between a physician and patient are privileged communications, and cannot be revealed without the permission of the patient or a court order; most of the contents of a *medical record* are protected by this privilege. It should be noted that the privilege belongs to the person protected and can only be *waived* by that person; in this instance, the patient is the one whose rights are protected, so the privilege cannot be waived by the physician (or hospital), nor can the physician invoke the privilege if the patient waives it.

privileges: Rights granted by the *governing body* of the hospital to physicians and other health care professionals, who are members of the *medical staff*, giving them permission to carry out specified diagnostic and therapeutic procedures within the hospital and, in some cases, to admit patients. Privileges are granted upon recommendation of the *medical staff organization (MSO)*, usually working through its credentials committee, which reviews the person's *credentials* and *performance* in determining the privileges to be recommended. Privileges may be withheld, increased, diminished, or withdrawn by the governing body at its discretion (subject, of course, to *due process* requirements). See also *credentialing* and *recredentialing*.

admitting privileges: Authority, granted by the governing body, to admit patients to the hospital. Generally, admitting privileges are restricted to physicians (MD and DO) and to podiatrists and qualified oral surgeons who are members of the *active medical staff*. The privileges ordinarily are limited with respect, for example, to the "kinds" of patients a physician may admit; a specialist in obstetrics and gynecology would not likely be granted privileges to admit psychiatric patients.

clinical privileges (1): Rights granted by the governing body of the hospital to a physician or other health care professional, who is a member of the *medical staff*, designating the types of *diagnostic* and *therapeutic procedures* the individual is permitted to perform, and also the types of patients that person is permitted to treat. Privileges granted are based upon the professional's education, training, and licensure, i.e., credentials, and on performance. "Other health care professionals" may include dentists, podiatrists, clinical psychologists, nurse practitioners, speech pathologists, physical therapists, and others, depending upon hospital policy as to requirements for membership in the *medical staff organization (MSO)*.

Privileges are determined upon initial appointment to the medical staff, and are subject to formal review periodically (usually no less frequently than every two years, or more frequently if required by law), and also ad hoc upon the practitioner's request or on the basis of allegations of performance problems. Privileges are expanded as the physician (or other professional) acquires additional credentials and/or experience and demonstrates proficiency; they should be reduced if warranted by the physician's performance (subject, of course, to due process requirements).

Provisional privileges are granted initially, with performance being observed by peers (other physicians or peer professionals on the medical staff) and periodically reviewed with the assistance of hospital personnel who collect data and provide it to a review body (usually the medical staff member's clinical department) which makes recommendations to the credentials committee. Such periodic review continues for all medical staff members, even after the "provisional" requirements are dropped; it is a necessary part of *quality management* and of the process of reappointment of *medical staff* members.

clinical privileges (2): When used in the statement that a certain physician "has clinical privileges" in a given hospital, the term indicates that the physician has been granted membership in the *medical staff* of that hospital in a category which permits him to treat patients there.

prn: As (often as) or if necessary.

PRO: See *Peer Review Organization.*

problem: A *disease, injury,* or any other condition or situation which brings an individual into contact with the health care system. Certain conditions, such as alcoholism, are not admitted by all to be diseases, but they do bring individuals to health care, as do ill-defined symptoms, behavioral problems, the need for well-person examinations, and the like. This is the usage of the term "problem" in the *"problem-oriented medical record (POMR)."*

Chapter XXI of the *International Statistical Classification of Diseases and Related Health Problems (ICD-10),* entitled "Factors Influencing Health Status and Contact with Health Services," lists among others the following "factors": loss of love relationship (code number Z61), removal from home (Z61), failed exams in school (Z55), stressful work schedule (Z56), and extreme poverty (Z59.5).

problem-oriented medical record (POMR): See *medical record.*

problem-oriented record (POR): See *medical record.*

procedure: In medicine, something which is "done" or "carried out" for a patient by a physician or other person. A procedure is usually discrete, and a relatively short time is required for its execution. Procedures are generally either diagnostic or therapeutic (treatment). A diagnostic procedure would be the taking of an X-ray or blood pressure, while a therapeutic procedure might be anything from removing a splinter from a finger to an extensive operation such as repair of a hernia.

A given *operation*, which might be called a "procedure," is often actually several procedures, and the array of procedures which make up a given operation will vary from patient to patient. For example, cholecystectomy (gall bladder removal) for one patient may include "exploration of the common bile duct," while for another patient, this procedure may be omitted. For this reason, a proper description of an operation requires that its procedures be listed.

In the context of health care financing, there often appears to be a distinction between a "procedure" and a *"service (1)."* However, the terms "procedure" and "service" are often combined without distinction, as in the classification used for payment of physicians' services, *Physicians' Current Procedural Terminology (CPT)*. In the case of a hernia operation, for example, the preoperative care and postoperative care are listed as "services," while the operation itself is called a "procedure"; however, the surgeon includes the preoperative and postoperative care and the operation in one billing for a "procedure." For purposes of health care financing, a "procedure" (or "service") might more accurately be defined as the unit for which a charge is made. Thus, under the "financial" definition, the hernia repair "procedure" would include both preoperative and postoperative care. See also *operating room procedure.*

procedure capture: The mechanisms by which one given health care facility (a hospital, laboratory, or imaging service, for example) or specialist physician is selected in preference to another. Since such "procedure services" are the results of *referral*, primarily from physicians, "procedure capture" really is the sum of the efforts to persuade the referring person to make the referral to the institution or specialist seeking more business.

P

process: The things done (for a patient, for example). It is commonly stated in *quality management* that three things can be measured: structure (resources or organization), process, and outcome. "Structure" refers to resources and organization. "Outcome" is a somewhat vague term that presumably refers to the results of the process. There is a tendency on the part of some individuals to take an "either-or" position, to the effect that one need only be concerned with one of the three dimensions. This tendency is not logical; all three must be considered. Clearly, certain structure is needed; and equally clearly, there is no way to change outcome except through changing process, since "outcome 'tells on' process."

proctor: A person appointed to supervise, as, for example, the physician or surgeon appointed to observe the work of an individual applying for membership on a hospital *medical staff* or for certain clinical *privileges*.

product administration (PA): A type of administration of an organization in which the focus is on "products." In a hospital, PA would focus on "products" such as surgery and internal medicine. Other forms of organization are the traditional functional administration (FA), in which the units administered are functional components (in a hospital, for example, nursing and pathology), and market administration (MA), in which the administration is organized around the organization's markets (in a hospital, for example, the elderly, women, and specific payers).

product liability: See *liability (1)*.

product line: A term now being used in health care to denote the kinds of services offered by a health care institution, including, for example, the kinds of patients (defined by their diagnoses, procedures required, and age limitations accepted for care). For example, a hospital's product line might include three "products"—acute care, hospice care, and home health care—and might specifically exclude another product, obstetric care. See also *strategic business unit (SBU)*.

product line management (PLM): A type of management in which the organization is considered to be a cluster or assemblage of *strategic business units (SBU)*. Each SBU has a separate product with a distinct market. In a hospital, a specific operation or class of operations (for example, eye surgery) could be considered an SBU, as could an alcoholism rehabilitation service. Each SBU has its specific resource requirements, information system needs, and management demands. Hospitals try to determine which product lines are "saleable" in their service areas and for which they have appropriate resources, and which they feel put them in advantageous competitive positions, and concentrate on those product lines.

productivity: The relationship between the number of units of service provided or products produced per unit of labor (or other cost) required, per unit of time. Productivity is said to increase in a hospital, for example, when patient stay can be reduced for a given illness with no sacrifice in quality and no increase in labor. On a larger scale, a hospital is sometimes considered more productive than another when it uses fewer employees, or has a lower cost per day.

products of ambulatory care (PAC): A *classification (1)* developed by the New York State Ambulatory Care Reimbursement Demonstration Project in 1985 as a "sophisticated ambulatory care product definition." There are 24 PAC categories, into which patient visits are allocated by computer depending on "who the patient is" (type of problem presented) and what is done (resources received).

professional: A term which, when used as an adjective pertaining to health care workers, usually means an individual who is *licensed*, such as a physician, registered nurse (RN), or pharmacist. However, many health care workers—particularly those who fall under the heading of *"allied health professionals"*— call themselves or are called "professionals," even if they are not licensed.

Professional Activity Study (PAS): The prototype *hospital discharge abstract system*. PAS is a program offered to hospitals by the *Commission on Professional and Hospital Activities (CPHA)*. It uses abstracts of hospital *medical records* from enrolled hospitals as input to a *data base*, and provides hospitals with indexes of their medical records and statistics on hospital performance. The data base is also available for computer research on hospital activities, epidemiology, and health care studies. PAS offers *case-mix management information* and other services to member hospitals.

professional association (PA): See *professional corporation* under *corporation*.

Professional Library Services (PR): The chapter giving the *standards* for this component of the hospital in the 1990 *Accreditation Manual for Hospitals (AMH)* of the *Joint Commission on the Accreditation of Healthcare Organizations (JCAHO)*.

professional nursing: Nursing done by or under the supervision of a *professional nurse*.

professional service corporation (PSC): See *professional corporation*.

Professional Standards Review Organization (PSRO): An organization established under federal law to review medical necessity, appropriateness, and quality of *services (1)* provided to beneficiaries of the Medicare, Medicaid, and *Maternal and Child Health MCH)* programs. These organizations were physician-sponsored. They have now been replaced in function by *peer review organizations (PROs)* under the current federal program for the administration of Medicare.

profit: Excess of income over expense. Actually means an increase in *assets*. The word "gain" is often used in *nonprofit corporations* as a substitute for the word "profit."

profit and loss statement (P & L): See *income and expense statement*.

prognosis: The physician's forecast as to the patient's future course. The prognosis is based on the usual course of progression of or recovery from a given disease or injury, modified by the physician's estimation of the patient's condition and other factors and their effects. A patient will have several prognoses covering length of illness, survival, recovery of function, and so on.

program: A set of instructions to the computer (*software*) as to how to accomplish a given task (*application*), such as accounting or reporting laboratory results.

progressive patient care: A system of organizing patient care in the hospital in which the hospital establishes *patient care units* ready to provide different intensities of care (for example, intensive, inter-mediate, and self-care), and moves patients from unit to unit as they progress in their illnesses.

projection: In statistics, a calculated estimate for a whole calculated from data for a part of the whole, or an estimate of a future situation based on information currently available. The term "projection" is often used when *sampling* has given information from a part of a whole (for example, a population), and a projection is made as to the actual situation in the whole population. For example, a candidate's actual performance in opinion polls is "projected" from the response of a sample of voters.

prompt: The *Joint Commission on Accreditation of Healthcare Organizations (JCAHO)* equates "prompt" with "immediate."

ProPaC: See *Prospective Payment Assessment Commission*.

proportion: A specific type of *ratio* in which the numerator is a part of the denominator. (A ratio is a value obtained by dividing one number, the numerator, by another number, the denominator). Proportions are always between 0 and 1 (inclusive). They are often expressed as *rates* such as percentages.

proprietary: For-profit and privately owned and managed.

prospective: Pertaining to the future. When used to refer to prospectively collected *data* in a research study, "prospective" means that special care is taken that the desired data are obtained from all individuals starting as of a given date.

prospective payment: A term often used as a misnomer for *prospective pricing*. "Prospective pricing" is the term which more accurate-ly denotes the intent of the payment system currently being used

P

for Medicare, which is discussed under *prospective payment system (PPS)*.

Under some circumstances, prospective payment for goods or services is made in advance (*prepayment*), either in whole or in partial payments, with adjustments made to the total when the actual amount due is determined. Payment in advance provides cash flow for the payee.

Prospective Payment Assessment Commission (ProPaC): An advisory body established under Medicare to give advice and assistance to the *Health Care Financing Administration (HCFA)* on matters pertaining to the *prospective payment system (PPS)* under which Medicare operates. Advice from ProPaC is not binding on HCFA.

prospective payment system (PPS): The name given the system currently in use for paying for *services (1)* for Medicare patients (payment for patients "by *Diagnosis Related Groups (DRGs)*"). The idea is that patients are classified into categories (in this case, DRGs) for which prices are negotiated or imposed on the hospital in advance; thus it is actually "prospective pricing" rather than "prospective payment." At present PPS is only applied to hospital care, not physician care, although the idea is the same as a single fixed "package fee" which includes prenatal care, delivery, and postpartum care for a maternity patient, or the inclusion of preoperative care, operation, and postoperative care for an appendectomy patient within one fixed physician's fee. (In fact, the package fee concept is inherent in *Physicians' Current Procedural Terminology (CPT)*, published by the American Medical Association (AMA)). PPS, while not mandated by federal law for payers other than Medicare, is being applied to patients under other health care plans.

PPS is sometimes referred to as the "DRG system." (The letters "PPS" are sometimes translated, incorrectly, to mean a prospective "reimbursement" system.)

prospective pricing: Setting (or agreeing upon) prices in advance for the furnishing of a product or service. This is in direct contrast with the concept of reimbursement, in which the service or product is provided first, and then the provider is paid whatever it cost. The *prospective payment system (PPS)* adopted for Medicare, and applied also for other payers, is the most widespread example of prospective pricing.

The first step in prospective pricing is the definition of the product or service for which the price is to be set. Thus the *DRG* system of *classification (1)* of patients, used in the PPS, is the first step in that prospective pricing application. The definition of *procedures* in *Physicians' Current Procedural Terminology (CPT)* could be a first step toward prospective pricing for physician services. Prospective pricing facilitates budgeting on the part of payers, since only the units of service or product likely to be needed have to be estimated or predicted; the cost of each unit is fixed in advance. On the other hand, prospective pricing increases the budgeting problems of the provider, since the provider is now at *risk (1)* and must plan much more carefully or else lose on the prospectively priced "transaction" (of course, the provider may also gain on the transaction).

prospective pricing system (PPS): A sometimes translation of "PPS," which is generally translated to mean *"prospective payment system."* "Prospective pricing system" is, however, a more appropriate description of this payment system. See *prospective pricing.*

prospective reimbursement: A term sometimes used, incorrectly, instead of *prospective pricing* or *prospective payment.* See *prospective payment system (PPS).* Also, "prospective reimbursement" is sometimes used to describe the prospectively estimated amount to be paid a hospital on a current schedule so that it will have operating cash, with the understanding that adjustments will be made later in the light of actual operating cost data. The concept is similar to that of the *periodic interim payment (PIP).*

prosthesis: A manufactured substitute for a part of the body, such as an arm, a leg, a heart valve, or a tooth.

protected person: A person for whom a *guardian* has been appointed, or who is otherwise "protected" by the law; for example, a *minor* or a legally *incompetent* person.

protocol: A plan of treatment or management. As used currently in hospital finance and quality management, a "protocol" typically means that, for a patient with a given problem, certain diagnostic and treatment procedures and length of stay are expected. See *reverse protocol,* which pertains to the proposition that use of a given procedure implies certain problems in the patient.

provider: A hospital or other health care institution or health care professional which provides health care services to patients. A "provider" may be a single hospital, an individual, or a group or organization.

Provider Reimbursement Review Board (PRRB): A panel of five members appointed by the Secretary of the *Department of Health and Human Services (DHHS)*, to which a *provider* may appeal a decision of a *fiscal intermediary* denying reimbursement for *services (1)* under Medicare.

provider-driven system: An economic system in which *providers* (in health care, physicians, other professionals, and institutions), "prescribe" and furnish those *services (1)* which they consider to be the best care for the patients. Such a system is intended to meet the needs of the patients as determined by the providers rather than to meet the demands of the purchasers of care.

The contrast is with a *"market-driven system,"* in which the system responds to the demands of the market, that is, of the purchaser of care. The latter term is currently being applied in health care with the emergence of competitive health care delivery plans which seek to attract "customers" by offering (1) more of what the customers want (amenities as well as services) or (2) attractive prices (that is, price competition). Note that the "customer" is the person paying for the service, and is not necessarily the "consumer" (the patient).

proximate cause: A legal term describing the direct cause of an injury. The proximate cause is that which in a natural sequence, unbroken by intervening factors, produced the injury, and without which the injury would not have happened. A negligent person's *liability (1)* is usually limited to those injuries proximately caused by the negligence. See also *intervening cause*.

PRRB: See *Provider Reimbursement Review Board*.

PSC: Professional service corporation. See *professional corporation* under *corporation*.

PSRO: See *Professional Standards Review Organization.*

psychiatry: The branch of medicine which deals with mental, emotional, and behavioral disorders. One of the medical specialties for which *residency* programs have been approved by the Accreditation Council for Graduate Medical Education (ACGME). See *specialty.*

psychic: Referring to the mind.

psychographics: The analysis of populations on the basis of certain characteristics of individuals, specifically their attitudes, values, and lifestyles. The psychographic attributes of individuals are obtained by surveys or forms of *psychometric* testing. Such analyses are extensions of *demographics.* The attributes involved are not what are usually considered demographic; the analyses combine the psychographic data with demographic data. For example, it may be essential for some purposes to know the *social consciousness* (a psychographic item) of a population as it relates to various age and sex groups (demographic items).

psychology: The science pertaining to the mind and to behavior.

    clinical psychology: The application of psychology in the clinical setting, with especial emphasis on testing and counseling. The specialty is practiced by a clinical psychologist (a non-physician) who must, in some states, be *licensed.*

psychometric: The measurement of intelligence and of mental processes.

psychotherapy: The type of therapy which treats mental, behavioral, and emotional disorders by communication, nonverbal as well as verbal, rather than by chemical or other means.

psychotropic: A drug which acts on the patient's mental processes; a drug used in treating mental illness. Such drugs may also be used for recreation; some are *addictive.*

PT: See *physical therapy.*

P

PTCA: See *percutaneous transluminal coronary angioplasty*.

PTSM: See *Plant, Technology, and Safety Management*.

PTSM standards: See *Plant, Technology, and Safety Management (PL) standards*.

public accountant (PA): An individual who performs a variety of functions, such as *audit* of an organization's financial statements and design of financial systems. Use of the term and the designation as "PA" requires state licensure, and the PA is under state regulation. Most health care organizations employ a Certified Public Accountant (CPA) for these functions. This individual not only meets state requirements, but also meets the much higher standards set by the American Institute of Certified Public Accountants (AICPA), which controls the credential "CPA."

public health: The organized efforts on the part of society to reduce disease and premature death, and the disability and discomfort produced by disease and other factors, such as injury or environmental hazards.
   Public health is also a branch of *preventive medicine*, a *medical specialty*. Specialization in public health also occurs in engineering, nursing, nutrition, law, and other disciplines.

public health nursing: Nursing practice which synthesizes the body of knowledge from *public health* and *professional nursing* for use in improving the health of the entire community or population group. Public health nurses work with groups, families, and individuals. Primary prevention and *health promotion* are basic concerns. The term is sometimes confused with *community health nursing* which is *generic*, applying to any nurse practicing in the community setting.

public health nutritionist: See *nutritionist (2)*.

public relations: The efforts to communicate with the hospital's audiences and constituencies and to enhance the hospital's image.

pulmonary diseases: A branch of *internal medicine* which deals with diseases and disorders of the respiratory (breathing) system. One of the medical specialties for which *residency* programs have been approved by the Accreditation Council for Graduate Medical Education (ACGME). See *specialty*.

Q

QA (1): See *quality assessment.*

QA (2): See *quality assurance.*

QA (3): See *Quality Assurance.*

QALY: See *quality-adjusted life-year.*

QAM: See *Quality Assurance Monitor.*

QAP (1): See *quality assurance professional.*

QAP (2): See *Quality Assurance Program.*

QC: See *quality control.*

QI: See *quality improvement.*

QIP: See *quality improvement project.*

QM: See *quality management.*

QRB: See *Quality Review Bulletin.*

QRM: See *quality and resource management.*

qualified: A term which can only be understood in context. For example, the *Joint Commission on the Accreditation of Healthcare Organizations (JCAHO)* uses the term "qualified" frequently, and the glossary in the *Accreditation Manual for Hospitals (AMH)* defines its requirements for the use of the term "qualified" for a number of individuals. Usually, the definition includes documentation with reference to training, education, experience, continuing education, certification, registration, "or their equivalent."

quality-adjusted life-year (QALY): A measure proposed to be used in economic analyses of the benefits of various procedures and programs.

quality and resource management (QRM): A term being used in some hospitals to indicate that *quality management* and the conservation of resources are seen as a single topic, or at least, topics which are closely interrelated. Such hospitals may have, for example, quality management, *utilization review, risk management,* and *infection control* under the "QRM department" headed by the "QRM Director."

quality assessment (QA): The former name for the activity later called *quality assurance.* The name of the activity was changed to reflect that the intent was to maintain and improve the *quality of care (1)* rather than merely measure it (assess it). Current terminology has, in turn, replaced "quality assurance" with "*quality management.*"

quality assurance (QA): The efforts to determine the *quality of care* (find out the quality being provided), to develop and maintain programs to keep it an at acceptable level (quality control), and to institute improvements when the opportunity arises or the care does not meet the desired *standards of care (1)* (quality improvement).

The term "quality assurance" is being replaced by "*quality management.*" The advantages of the term "quality management" are: (1) there is no implication of a "guarantee," an idea which may be suggested by the use of the word "assurance," which is sometimes used as a synonym for "insurance"; and (2) "quality management" is more accurate, since the achievement of quality depends

Q

on people carrying out their responsibilities without error, and getting people to perform is the task of management.

Quality Assurance (QA): The chapter giving the *standards* for this component of the hospital in the 1990 *Accreditation Manual for Hospitals (AMH)* of the *Joint Commission on the Accreditation of Healthcare Organizations (JCAHO).*

quality assurance coordinator: A person given certain duties with respect to *quality assurance (QA)* activities. The duties may, for example, include data gathering, assisting QA committees in their work, maintenance of records of QA activities, and preparation of reports dealing with the QA program.

quality assurance function: See *quality function.*

Quality Assurance Monitor (QAM): A part of the *Professional Activity Study (PAS)* of the *Commission on Professional and Hospital Activities (CPHA).* The care of patients, as reflected in their computerized *case abstracts,* is compared with standards established by clinical *specialty societies,* and the findings are displayed for use in hospital *quality management.*

quality assurance professional (QAP): A person in a health care institution who carries out *quality assurance (QA)* activities. The term "QAP" has not been tightly defined; it includes administrators with QA duties, quality assurance coordinators, directors of quality assurance, utilization review coordinators, DRG coordinators, discharge planners, and risk managers. These and other individuals in quality assurance are eligible for membership in the *National Association of Quality Assurance Professionals (NAQAP).* NAQAP has instituted an examination procedure leading to a *credential,* namely, designation of the individual as a *Certified Professional in Quality Assurance (CPQA).*

Quality Assurance Program (QAP): A program promulgated by the *American Hospital Association (AHA)* in the 1970s.

quality circle: A group, formerly called a "quality control circle," which deals with concerns that relate to the quality of performance or quality of work life. There are six "non-negotiable" characteristics of a group which must be present if it is to be called a quality circle: (1) the group must be small; and (2) composed of individuals in the same work area (of a hospital, for example); (3) it must be voluntary; (4) it must consider problems (or opportunities for improvement) which the group itself selects; (5) the problems must affect the quality of work life or the quality of performance; and (6) the circle must propose solutions to management.

A quality circle is not to be confused with a *committee* or *task force*, both of which are appointed (not voluntary) and work on assigned tasks rather than self-selected tasks. Morale, productivity, and quality of performance are typically improved by the activities of quality circles. The groups often carry locally determined titles rather than being named "quality circles." Synonym(s): quality control circle.

quality control (QC): The sum of all the activities which prevent unwanted change in quality. In the health care setting, quality control requires a repeated series of feedback loops which monitor and evaluate the care of the individual patient (and other systems in the health care process). These feedback loops involve checking the care being delivered against *standards of care (1)*, the identification of any opportunities for improvement or problems, and prompt corrective action, so that the quality is maintained. The illustration on page 362 shows this feedback loop and also the effect of the entire quality control process (a great many ongoing feedback loops) in maintaining the "quality floor." See *quality improvement*, the other major process in *quality management*, which is the sum of all the activities which create desired change in quality. A proper quality management system must have both quality control and quality improvement.

quality control circle: See *quality circle*.

quality function: The sum of all the activities, wherever performed, through which the hospital achieves the *quality of care* it provides. This usage is comparable to speaking of the "fiscal function," which is the sum of the activities, wherever performed, through which the hospital achieves fiscal soundness. The term "quality function" is replacing "quality assurance function."

Quality Control
The Quality <u>Floor</u>: Preventing unwanted change for today's patient

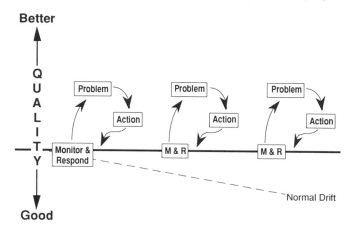

Quality Improvement
The Quality <u>Staircase</u>: Creating desired change for future patients

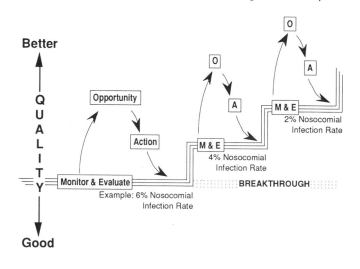

quality improvement (QI): The sum of all the activities which create desired change in quality. In the health care setting, quality improvement requires a feedback loop which involves the identification of patterns of the care of patients (or of the performance of other systems involved in care), the analysis of those patterns in order to identify opportunities for improvement (or instances of departure from *standards of care (1)*), and then action to improve the quality of care for future patients. An effective quality improvement system results in stepwise increases in quality of care. The illustration on page 362 shows both the feedback loop and the *"quality staircase."* *Quality control*, with which quality improvement is sometimes confused, is the sum of all the activities which prevent unwanted change in quality. A proper *quality management* system must have both quality control and quality improvement. See also *quality improvement project*.

continuous quality improvement (CQI): As used in health care today, CQI means the application of industrial quality management theory in the health care setting, based upon principles of quality "gurus" W. Edwards Deming and Joseph M. Juran. While traditional "quality control" theories seek out "fault" and attempt improvement by exhorting people to change their behavior, continuous improvement seeks to understand processes and revise them on the basis of data about the processes themselves. CQI sees "problems" as opportunities for improvement. The CQI process involves a project-by-project approach to systematically improve quality, not just to maintain the status quo. A major project in this area is the National Demonstration Project on Quality Improvement in Health Care, sponsored by a grant from the John A. Hartford Foundation, being conducted by Harvard Community Health Plan in Brookline, Massachusetts, in conjunction with the Juran Institute (a quality consulting and education firm in Wilton, Connecticut). See also *quality improvement project (QIP)* and *total quality management (TQM)*.

quality improvement project (QIP): One activity in the process of *continuous quality improvement (CQI)*. Each project involves a process which has been identified as deserving improvement, and which has been given priority (prioritizing of effort is critical in CQI). For each project, a team is assigned consisting of representatives from all departments involved in the process targeted for improvement, along with support from senior management. The team studies the process, comes up with theories for improve-

Q

ment, tests the theories, puts successful theories into place, and also puts into place measures to assure that the improved quality is maintained.

Examples of hospital QIPs conducted as part of the the National Demonstration Project on Quality Improvement in Health Care are reduction in medication errors; reduction of unbilled drugs (thereby increasing revenues); reduction of delays in surgery starting times (with a corresponding savings in hospital staff overtime expenses). See also *continuous quality improvement (CQI)* and *total quality management (TQM)*.

quality management (QM): A term replacing *"quality assurance."* Quality management includes the efforts to determine the *quality of care*, to develop and maintain programs to keep it at an acceptable level (*quality control*), to institute improvements when the opportunity arises or the care does not meet standards (*quality improvement*), and to provide, to all concerned, the evidence required to establish confidence that quality is being managed and maintained at the desired level. (These are the same elements that are inherent in industrial quality management.) The advantages of the term "quality management" over "quality assurance" are: (1) there is no implication of a "guarantee," an idea which may be suggested by the use of the word "assurance," which is sometimes used as a synonym for "insurance"; and (2) "quality management" is more accurate, since the achievement of quality depends on people carrying out their responsibilities without error, and getting people to perform is the task of management.

total quality management (TQM): Used to describe a philosphy (and actions) of an organization which is dedicated to *continuous quality improvement (CQI)* throughout the organization. A hospital with total quality management will, for example, set specific quality goals, choose a number of high priority *quality improvement projects (QIPs)*, make quality improvement part of job descriptions throughout the organization and legitimize time spent on quality improvement, provide necessary resources (financial and otherwise), provide essential training for staff involved, and formally recognize quality improvement efforts. Total quality management requires commitment and personal involvement of senior management. It should be emphasized that *quality control* (prevention of *unwanted change* in quality) must be maintained in parallel with quality improvement, and that quality control demands the same energy commitment as does quality improvement. See also *quality control* and *quality improvement*.

quality management audit: See *audit*.

quality of care: The degree of conformity with accepted principles and practices (standards), the degree of fitness for the patient's needs, and the degree of attainment of achievable outcomes (results), consonant with the appropriate allocation or use of resources. The phrase "quality of care" carries the concept that quality is not equivalent to "more" or "higher technology" or higher cost. The "degree of conformity" with standards focuses on the provider's performance, while the "degree of fitness" for the patient's needs indicates that the patient may present conditions which override strict conformity with otherwise prescribed procedures.

patient care quality: The *Joint Commission of the Accreditation of Healthcare Organizations (JCAHO)* in 1989 defined patient care quality as "the degree to which patient care services increase the probability of desired patient care outcomes and reduce the probability of undesired outcomes, given the current state of knowledge."

quality of life: A condition often given as one attribute or dimension of health. It is ill-defined, depending on the individual and his goals, the social setting and expectations (often of others), and other factors. The goal of much of health care is stated to be improved quality of life. One of the most challenging problems in health care is to measure quality of life so that (1) improvement can be identified, and (2) it can be used as a factor in *cost-benefit analysis*. There is a real danger that inability to express quality of life in numerical terms will mean that much valuable care will not be available because quality of life cannot be given a value and therefore cannot be used to justify the expenditure (to end up with a positive *cost-benefit ratio* rather than a negative ratio); consequently, mere survival could be the measure.

An illustration is the debate over the "value" of some coronary bypass operations; patients in some studies have not shown significantly greater life expectancies with the operation than without it, but the patients operated on regularly testify to their pleasure with their relief from pain. In some instances (intractable pain or

Q

helplessness, for example), life itself is of such low quality to the individual that he may prefer not to live.

Quality Review Bulletin (QRB): A monthly publication of the *Joint Commission on the Accreditation of Healthcare Organizations (JCAHO)* dealing with *quality of care* and its management.

quality staircase: A method of representing the results of quality improvement efforts. Joseph M. Juran in the industrial setting has represented quality improvement as an ever-rising spiral, an inclined plane. The processes involved in making the product or providing the service are constantly monitored and, as opportunities for improvement are identified, changes are made which result in breakthroughs to higher levels of quality. In certain respects, the concept of a staircase is more appropriate than that of a spiral, since breakthroughs actually improve quality in steps rather than in a continuous fashion. See the illustration on page 362.

quick ratio: See *ratio*.

Quinlan case: The landmark legal case concerning the right of an *incompetent (1)* person to refuse medical treatment, commonly referred to as the *"right to die."* In 1975 Karen Quinlan, a 22-year-old who had sustained severe brain damage, perhaps as a result of consuming alcohol and drugs, became comatose and remained in a chronic vegetative state. A mechanical respirator was used to aid her breathing. Her parents requested termination of the life support systems, but the hospital and physicians refused. Ms. Quinlan's father sought court approval to be appointed *guardian* of his daughter and to have the support systems discontinued. The New Jersey Supreme Court ruled in favor of the father, permitting him to decline treatment on his daughter's behalf. After Ms. Quinlan was removed from the respirator, she continued to receive antibiotics and was fed through a nasogastric tube. She continued to breath on her own until her death in 1985.

The legal basis for the decision was the patient's constitutional right of privacy, which gave Ms. Quinlan the right to determine her medical treatment. Since she was incompetent to exercise that right herself, her father as guardian could do so under the "doctrine of substituted judgment." That doctrine requires that the decision-maker determine, to the best of his ability, what the incompetent person herself would decide under the circumstances. *In re Quinlan*, 70 N.J. 10, 355 A.2d 647, *cert. denied*, 429 U.S. 922 (1976).

It should be noted that this was a state court case, and did not establish the law for other states. In fact, there is still much controversy surrounding the so-called "right to die." The United States Supreme Court recently considered some of the issues in *Cruzan v. Director, Missouri Dept. of Health*. See *Cruzan case*.

R

RA: See *Radiation Oncology Services.*

RAD: See *radiographer.*

radiant energy: The energy of electromagnetic waves, including visible light, X-rays, radio waves, and waves emitted by radioactive substances, such as radium.

radiation: *X-rays* and other forms of *radiant energy*. The term "radiation" excludes visible light and radiation in the frequencies near the spectrum of visible light.

Radiation Oncology Services (RA): The chapter giving the *standards* for this component of the hospital in the 1990 *Accreditation Manual for Hospitals (AMH)* of the *Joint Commission on the Accreditation of Healthcare Organizations (JCAHO)*.

radiation therapist: See *health physicist.*

radiation therapy: Treatment by the use of *X-rays* or other forms of *radiation.*

radiation therapy technologist (RADTT): One of the 26 *allied health professionals* for whom the American Medical Association's *Committee on Allied Health Education and Accreditation (CAHEA)* has accredited education programs.

radioactive: A term applied to chemical elements which give off (or are capable of giving off) particles of radiant energy, such as alpha, beta, and gamma rays. Some chemical elements, such as plutonium, radium, and uranium, are radioactive as they are found in nature, while others can be made radioactive by special physical processes. Both natural and "artificial" radioactive chemical elements are used in *nuclear medicine*. See also *nuclide*.

radioactive isotope: See *nuclide*.

radioactive nuclide: See *nuclide*.

radioactivity: See *nuclide*.

radiographer (RAD): One of the 26 *allied health professionals* for whom the American Medical Association's *Committee on Allied Health Education and Accreditation (CAHEA)* has accredited education programs.

radioisotope: A *radioactive* form of a chemical element. Some radioisotopes are used in medical care for diagnostic and therapeutic purposes; this use is called *nuclear medicine*. See also *nuclide*.

radiologic technologist: A person who operates radiologic equipment, ordinarily under the supervision of a *radiologist*, and who assists in radiologic procedures. See *radiology*.

radiologist: A physician specializing in *radiology*, the use of *X-rays* and other forms of *radiation* for diagnosis and treatment. See *radiology*.

radiologists, anesthesiologists, and pathologists (RAPs): Only the abbreviation is new. It came into use with efforts in the 1987 federal budget to include payment for these three specialists into the *Diagnosis Related Group (DRG)* (*prospective payment system (PPS)*) payments to hospitals rather than paying the physicians directly, as was previously done.

R

radiology: The use of *X-rays* and other forms of *radiation* for diagnosis and treatment. Diagnostic radiology is a kind of *imaging*. Several *medical specialties* concern radiology (for a list of all specialties, see *specialty*):

diagnostic nuclear radiology: The branch of radiology which deals with making diagnoses with the use of *radioactive* materials.

diagnostic radiology: The branch of radiology which deals with making diagnoses.

therapeutic radiology: The branch of radiology which uses *radiation* in the treatment of disease.

radionuclide: A *nuclide* which emits nuclear radiation.

radiopaque: Any material which blocks the passage of *X-rays*. Such materials are used in certain types of X-ray examinations; in bowel examinations, the *barium enema* is radiopaque, and will produce a contrast (shadow) on the film.

radium therapy: *Radiation therapy* through the use of radium.

RADTT: See *radiation therapy technologist*.

random: A statistical term used in *sampling* which means that every "element" or "event" in the whole "universe" being sampled has an equal chance of being "drawn." If a hospital wants to know how well patients like the food, for example, the universe could be all the patients who have been eating it; a random sample would mean that each eater had an equal likelihood of being questioned.

RAPs: See *radiologists, anesthesiologists, and pathologists*.

rate (1): A financial term referring to a hospital or other institution's *charges*. Typically rates are "fixed" in that they are for specified *services (1)*, and the same rate is charged to all individuals or to purchasers of a given class (such as Medicare patients). For example, a hotel could have different rates for senior citizens, commercial travellers, and the general public.

blended rate: A term used in the *prospective payment system (PPS)* of Medicare to designate a rate which is formed by combining the hospital-specific rate and the federal Medicare rate.

hospital-specific rate: A term used in the Medicare *prospective payment system (PPS)* in the computation of the hospital's payment. This rate is "blended" with the federal Medicare rate in certain circumstances.

inclusive rate: A prospectively established rate for a day of care which includes all hospital *services (1)* that may be required, regardless of their nature or cost.

interim rate: A temporary rate used in a reimbursement system which periodically makes payments to the hospital on the basis of an estimated figure. The rate is subsequently adjusted retrospectively to reflect actual expenses: additional payments are made to the hospital, or the hospital refunds part of the payment it received; and corrections are made to future rates as appropriate. Using an interim rate provides operating cash for the hospital in a "retrospective reimbursement" payment system, where payment is based on actual costs as determined at the end of the fiscal period.

per diem rate: A rate established by dividing total costs (plus a percentage for excess of income over expenses) by the total number of inpatient days of care for the same period. Thus the per diem rate is the same for each patient, regardless of the patient's illness, its severity, or the diagnostic or therapeutic measures required.

room rate: Same as "daily service charge": the dollar amount the hospital charges for one day of *inpatient* care for "room and board" and basic nursing and hospital care. The term is not used when, for example, an *inclusive rate* system is employed since, in that case, the daily rate includes more than these items.

rural rate: A type of rate computed by Medicare for hospitals Medicare classifies as rural.

urban rate: A type of rate computed by Medicare for hospitals Medicare classifies as urban.

rate (2): A *ratio* or *proportion*, often expressed as a percentage (per 100), but which may also be expressed per 1,000, per 10,000, per 100,000, or even per million. These "per" numbers are called the "base." Thus a rate expressed per 100,000 is said to have 100,000 as the base. The base chosen is usually large enough to insure that the rate will be expressed in whole numbers; the more rare the event, the larger the base chosen. A death rate of 7 per 10,000 is easier to understand than a rate of 0.07 percent (although both actually give the same information). Rates often used in health care include:

death rate: The number of deaths divided by the number of patients at risk. See the separate listing under *death rate*.

infection rate: The number of patients developing infections divided by the number of patients at *risk (3)*, usually expressed as a percentage (by multiplying by 100). Many different infection rates are used, depending on the group of patients at risk. For example, hospitals calculate *postoperative infection* rates, infection rates for various units of the hospital, and the like.

mortality rate: See *death rate*.

occupancy rate: The *ratio* between occupied and available beds, expressed as a percentage. The rate is calculated by dividing the average number of beds occupied for a given time period by the average number of beds available for that same time period (and multiplying by 100 to create the percentage). Sometimes the term "occupancy" alone is used.

readmission rate: A statistic showing the *proportion* of a hospital's patients (or of a given class of patients) who enter the hospital a second (or subsequent) time within a given interval after *discharge*. This statistic is sometimes used to give, for example, an estimate as to whether the initial hospitalizations were of sufficient duration, on the theory that patients discharged prematurely will be readmitted more frequently than those with an adequately long initial stay.

There is no standard formula for this statistic. Therefore, the compiler of the statistic should (1) give the interval from the prior discharge in which a subsequent admission is to be classed as a "readmission," (2) state whether the readmission was for a condition related to the previous admission (for the purpose of the example above, only related readmissions should be included), and (3) give the time period over which the initial discharges took place.

It usually is not feasible for one hospital to obtain information on *admissions* from other hospitals, so the readmission rate is likely to underestimate the frequency with which patients return to a hospital for further care.

rate setting: A process of regulation of hospital charges (*rates (1)*) by an external agency which sets the rates for the institution.

ratio: A value obtained by dividing one number (the numerator) by another (the denominator). A *proportion* is a special kind of ratio; in a proportion, the numerator is included in the denominator.

cost-to-charge ratio: A term used in finance, which shows whether a *charge* for a given product or service is set so that it covers the *cost*. A ratio of 1.0 means that the cost and charge are identical; a ratio greater than 1.0 means that the charge does not recover the cost; and a ratio less than 1.0 means that the charge exceeds the cost. See also *ratio of costs to charges*.

current ratio: A financial term used to express *liquidity*. It is the ratio of *current assets* to *current liabilities*. A ratio of 2:1 or higher is considered good.

debt ratio: Total *debt* divided by total *assets*.

quick ratio: The ratio of cash plus accounts receivable to current liabilities. This differs from the *current ratio* in that inventories are not included in the quick ratio (since they may not easily be convertible into cash in order to meet short term obligations). A good ratio would be 1:1.

ratio of costs to charges (RCC): A method of estimating costs in accounting. There is generally a desire that charges for health care reflect the costs of that care. This is fairly easy to achieve globally, that is, the total costs for a hospital, say, for a year can be ascertained and the charges or reimbursement can be matched to those costs. It is also easy to learn the total costs and the total charges for a revenue producing department, such as radiology. Typically, the total charges exceed the total costs, and the ratio between these two figures is easily obtained.

Since it may be virtually impossible (or far more costly than can be justified) to find the actual costs of specific *procedures* and *services (1)*, such as the cost of a chest X-ray, an approximation is made. Under the RCC approach, this is done by simply multiplying the charge for the procedure by the cost/charge ratio for the

R

department, and using the resulting dollar amount as (an estimate of) the cost of the procedure. For example, if the (total) costs for the department are $100,000 and the (total) charges are $200,000, the ratio, $100,000/$200,000, is 0.5. Applying the RCC method, then, all charges would be multiplied by this ratio, and a chest X-ray, say, for which there is a $50.00 charge would be considered to have a $25.00 cost.

RBRVS: Resource-based relative value scale. See *relative value scale.*

RCC: See *ratio of costs to charges.*

RCT: See *registered care technologist.*

RD: See *registered dietitian.*

RDS: See *respiratory distress syndrome.*

readmission: A second (or later) *admission* of a patient to a facility. Sometimes the term is used in a manner that implies that the readmission is for further treatment for the condition occasioning the previous admission, because of recurrence of the problem or failure of completion of care; however, this inference is not warranted. See *readmission rate* under *rate (2).*

reasonable costs: A term with a specific definition given by the federal government for use in Medicare. It is used only in connection with *services (1)* in institutions which are exempt from the *prospective payment system (PPS)* and for *beneficiaries* who are not *inpatients.*

receipt: A document acknowledging that money or goods have been received.

reciprocity: An agreement among specific states under which one state will grant a license to a physician or other health professional if that person produces evidence that she is *licensed* in any other state which is a party to the agreement. Usually the initial license must have been granted on the basis of an examination, either that of the National Board of Medical Examiners (NBME) or of the state of origin; in other words, a license granted itself on the basis of reciprocity cannot be used to gain another license by reciprocity.

recoding: Placing data (cases, for example) from one *classification (1)* into categories of a second classification (when there is one-to-one correspondence) or by concatenating one or more categories from the first classification into the second, a sort of "compound grouping." Where the groups of the second classification are more specific than or different from those of the first classification, recoding should not be attempted, because no exact recoding is possible; data once coded to a category cannot be "split" without going back to more detailed sources. See also *coding*.

recovery (1): Regaining of the condition of health or function which preceded the occurrence of a disease or disability. Used in the context of postoperative care, recovery refers to the period of time immediately following surgery, during which the patient is closely monitored in the *recovery room* until stabilized. Patients stay in the recovery room until they are ready to be returned to their hospital room (if inpatients) or to go home (if outpatients).

recovery (2): The money awarded by a court to the successful *plaintiff* in a lawsuit. The term can also mean the amount of money actually collected.

recovery room: A special *patient care unit* of the hospital used for the monitoring and care of *postoperative* patients until each patient's condition becomes stable after anesthesia. Synonym(s): postoperative recovery room.

recreation therapist: See *therapeutic recreation specialist*.

recredentialing: Determining and certifying as to the competency of a physician or other professional at some time after the initial determination of his or her qualification for licensure or hospital *privileges*. Recredentialing is required at periodic intervals in some hospitals and health care organizations. It is also under consideration by several states as a procedure to be followed at the time of renewal of licenses (most states simply require payment of a fee). As being discussed with regard to renewal of license, "recredentialling" does not rely on evidence of meeting continuing education requirements or written examination as to knowledge. The focus is on the physician's actual *performance*. Under consideration are computer-based "clinical" testing and the use of hospital quality review records. In the case of physicians whose practice is entirely in their offices, an *office audit system* (now used in Canada) is under consideration. See also *credentialing*.

referral: The sending of a patient by one physician (the referring physician) to another physician (or some other resource) either for *consultation (1)* or for care. Specialist care (*secondary care*) is ordinarily on referral from a *primary care physician* (or another specialist). Care of the patient is given back to the referring physician if the referral was for consultation or where the specialist has completed the care required; otherwise the patient is transferred to the specialist, who takes over responsibility for the patient.

For example, if a primary care physician refers a patient suspected of having appendicitis to a surgeon (and the surgeon also diagnoses appendicitis), the surgeon customarily performs the appendectomy and returns the patient to the referring physician afterward. However, if a general internist refers a problem diabetic patient to an endocrinologist (specialist in diabetes and other endocrine diseases), the referral might result in the permanent transfer of the patient.

referral center: A rural hospital classified as such by the federal government, for purposes of reimbursement under the Medicare *prospective payment system (PPS)*.

regimen: A planned course of treatment or therapy (including such components as diet, drugs, and exercise) designed to achieve a specific result. The more complete phrase would be "therapeutic regimen"—the plan laid out for treatment of the patient.

registered care technologist (RCT): A category of care giver proposed by the American Medical Association (AMA) in 1988 in an effort to alleviate the nursing shortage. RCTs would have been required to have little education before entering a brief training program, after which they would have been "registered under an arm of the state medical board" (not the state nursing board) and would have given "technical" bedside care under the supervision of the physician.

registered nurse (RN): See *nurse*.

registered record administrator (RRA): A *credential* provided by the *American Medical Record Association (AMRA)* to a *medical record administrator (MRA)* who has met AMRA's standards for sitting for its registration examination in *medical record* science, and who has passed the examination.

registered respiratory therapist (RRT): A *respiratory therapist* awarded the *credential* of *registration (1)* by the *National Board of Respiratory Therapy*.

registrar (1): A governmental official whose duty it is to keep official records. There are a number of kinds of registrars keeping, for example, vital statistics such as births, deaths, marriages, and divorces, and legal documents such as deeds.

registrar (2): See *admitting officer*.

registration (1): A process established by a governmental or non-governmental agency under which individuals meeting the agency's requirements can be recorded on an official roster ("registry") and can use "registered" ("registered nurse," for example) as a *credential* with the public and with their employment.

registration (2): The recording of an individual in a *registry (1)*, such as a cancer, trauma, or tuberculosis registry.

registration (3): The official recording of births, deaths, marriages, and divorces, with maintenance of permanent records.

registry (1): A central *agency (3)* where data from an institution or specific geographic area can be collected and made available for study and, in the health care field, sometimes made available for assisting in patient care management. An illustration of the latter use is in sending reminders to patients when follow-up examinations are scheduled (for example, in the case of tumors).

R

cancer registry: See *tumor registry*.

trauma registry: A repository of data on *trauma* patients, including such information as the external causes of the trauma, diagnoses, treatment, and outcome, and demographic information about the patients.

tumor registry: A repository of data on patients with *cancers* and other *tumors*. The tumor registry is used to: develop statistics on the *incidence* and *prevalence* of cancer; relate data on the tumors to the characteristics of patients (such as age, sex, racial background, or other diseases); study relationships with patients' environment; attempt to evaluate therapy; and, in some instances, help keep the patients under treatment. A tumor registry is also called a "cancer registry." The establishment and operation of tumor registries has been a special interest of the American College of Surgeons (ACS). Synonym(s): cancer registry.

registry (2): An official roster, maintained by a governmental or nongovernmental agency, of individuals who have met the requirements set up by the agency as to qualifications (both initial, and, in some cases, continuing) which permit *registration (1)*. A person may use her listing on the registry as a *credential* to display to the public as, for example, in "Registered Dietitian."

regression: A statistical method used to measure and express the effect one variable, the "independent variable," has on another variable, the "dependent variable." A physician may want to increase the concentration of a drug in a patient's blood. The question: if the physician doubles the dose of a given drug (the dosage of the drug is the independent variable, because it can be controlled), will it double the concentration of the drug (the dependent variable) in the patient's blood, or will it less than double, and will the effects vary from patient to patient? Regression is used to help answer this question. A collection of data on drug dosages (related to patients' weights, for example) and the same patients' blood concentrations of the drug are analyzed by an appropriate regression method. The analysis will tell the relationship between doses and blood levels—not only the probable increases (or decreases, which could happen) in proportion to dosage, but also the ranges of response which are likely to occur.

A common form of regression is a "linear regression," in which the "model" chosen for the analysis is a linear equation.

regularly maintained beds: The number of beds a hospital has set up for daily operation (in units of the hospital in use and staffed) on a regular basis. This number may change from time to time. It would ordinarily be a number smaller than the number of *licensed beds* or the number of *constructed beds*. The count is usually expressed in three segments: for adult inpatients, pediatric patients, and newborns. See *bed capacity* and *bed count.*

regulation: A rule or procedure made by a governmental *agency (1)*, and having the force of law, as contrasted with a *guideline*, which is merely advisory.

Another type of regulation is that adopted by a corporation or association as part of its internal *rules and regulations*. However, this latter type of regulation is seldom spoken of separate from the phrase, "rules and regulations" of the corporation.

rehabilitation: Efforts to assist the patient to achieve and maintain her optimal level of function, *self-care*, and independence, after or in correction of a disability. The disability may be physical, mental, or emotional.

rehabilitation counselor: A person who advises disabled individuals and assists them to achieve and maintain an optimal level of *self-care* and independence.

rehabilitation potential: Realistic goals for the individual patient with respect to (1) management of the patient's specific health problems and (2) achievement of self-care, independence, and emotional well-being. These goals are set and stated by the attending physician for each patient at the time of admission to a *rehabilitation hospital* or *long-term care facility (LTCF)*.

rehabilitative care: Coordinated *rehabilitation* care, provided under the supervision of a physician.

rehabilitative nursing care: A nursing care program directed at assisting each *long-term care* patient to achieve and maintain an optimal level of *self-care* and independence.

reimbursement: The payment to a hospital or other *provider*, after the fact, of an amount equal to the provider's expenses in provid-

R

ing a given service or product. The current trend is away from such a "blank check" approach and toward *prospective pricing*, that is, toward agreement in advance as to the amount which will be paid for the service or product in question. Several varieties of reimbursement are discussed in health care:

cost-based reimbursement: Payment of all *allowable costs* incurred in the provision of care. The term "allowable" refers to the terms of the contract under which care is furnished.

retroactive reimbursement: Additional payment to a provider for costs not considered at the time of original reimbursement.

retrospective reimbursement: Payment based on actual costs as determined at the end of the fiscal period.

third party reimbursement (TPR): Payment for health care services by a *third party* such as an insurance company. See *third party payer*.

reimbursement specialist (1): A person who prepares the statements and other materials needed to obtain reimbursement from *third-party payers* and insurers for *services (1)*, and who maintains the related records. Synonym(s): insurance clerk.

reimbursement specialist (2): A person who is involved with working out the terms and details of *reimbursement* systems with *third-party payers*.

relative value scale (RVS): A numerical system (scale) designed to permit comparisons of the resources needed (or appropriate prices) for various units of service. The RVS is the compiled table of the *relative value units (RVUs)* for all the objects in the class for which it is developed.

An RVS takes into account labor, skill, supplies, equipment, space, and other costs into an aggregate cost for each *procedure* or other unit of *service (1)*. The aggregate cost is converted into the *relative value unit (RVU)* of the procedure or service by relating it to the cost of a procedure or service selected as the "base unit." For example, the developer of the RVS for laboratory work might decide to use the cost of a red blood count as the base unit. Its actual cost might be $5.00, but, as the base, its RVU would arbitrarily be set at 1.0. If a blood sugar estimation, then, actually cost

$25.00, it would have an RVU value of 5.0 ($25.00 divided by $5.00) (the illustration is imaginary as to the prices given). If a urinalysis cost $3.00, it would have an RVU of 0.6.

resource-based relative value scale (RBRVS): A method of determining physicians' *fees* based on the time, training, skill, and other factors required to deliver various *services (1)*. The term came into use in 1988 upon release of the report of a study commissioned by the *Department of Health and Human Services (DHHS)* and carried out under the direction of Harvard economist William Hsiao, PhD. See *relative value scale*.

relative value unit (RVU): The numerical value given to each *procedure* or other unit of *service (1)* in a "relative value scale." See *relative value scale (RVS)*.

release: A giving up of a legal claim or right, to the person against whom the claim could have been asserted. For example, when a *malpractice* case is settled, the injured patient signs a release freeing the physician and hospital from any further *liability (1)* for the injury, in exchange for the money paid in the settlement.

relief: The thing sought by a *plaintiff* in a lawsuit; usually whatever it is that would make the plaintiff whole or at least compensate for the injury. For example, in a *malpractice* suit the plaintiff may ask for money; a physician suing a hospital for denial of *privileges* may ask that her privileges be reinstated. The term "relief" may also refer to that which has been granted by the court, or in general to the fact that the plaintiff won or lost the suit ("relief was denied").

remedy: In law, something which a court (or a statute) grants to redress a wrong or make an injured person whole. The most common remedy is money. Another, less common remedy is an *injunction* (ordering the defendant to do something or stop doing something). See also *relief*.

exclusive remedy: A remedy provided by law which precludes a person from trying to obtain any kind of compensation other than that provided by the law. An example is *workers' compensation*, which is the exclusive remedy for on-the-job injuries; an injured worker who is entitled to receive workers' compensation benefits may not sue his employer for damages.

R

renal dialysis: Removal by an artificial method of the waste materials which would be removed by the kidneys (renal) in a normally functioning individual. The techniques involve either (1) *hemodialysis,* in which the person's blood is passed through a machine where the process takes place before being returned to the body, or (2) *peritoneal dialysis,* in which a fluid is circulated through the person's abdomen (peritoneal cavity) where the waste materials pass from the body into the fluid, which is then removed. Peritoneal dialysis may be done either in an institution or on an ambulatory basis. Renal dialysis may be used for long periods of time, in the hospital, in dialysis centers, and in the home. It is often a temporary measure preceding a kidney transplant. Renal dialysis is one of the costliest elements of the *end-stage renal disease (ESRD) program,* a component of Medicare.

renal dialysis unit: See *hemodialysis unit.*

required request law: A law which requires hospitals to develop programs for asking families of deceased patients to donate the organs of the deceased for *transplantation.* Synonym(s): routine inquiry law.

res ipsa loquitur: "The thing speaks for itself." A legal doctrine which states that a *plaintiff* (person filing suit) does not have to prove *negligence* in a specific factual situation; rather, negligence may be presumed from the facts that are proved, and it is up to the defendant to prove that she was not negligent. Res ipsa loquitur is applied when it is obvious that there was negligence (the injury could not have been caused without someone's negligence), but the knowledge regarding the negligent act is solely within the control of the defendant(s). An example is the leaving of a sponge in a surgical patient: the unconscious patient could not possibly know who left it there, but there is no doubt that the act was negligent.

It should be noted that the doctrine of res ipsa loquitur varies a great deal among legal jurisdictions, and that not all courts will permit its application. For example, some courts hold that the doctrine does not apply if more than one person could have committed the negligent act.

reserve accounts: Earnings retained for a specific purpose.

residency: A program in a hospital or other health care institution or organization which has been approved for providing medical or other professional training by allowing the individual in training to perform actual duties under supervision. In medicine, a formal *Residency Review Committee* grants approval to *medical residencies* which meet established standards. *Administrative residencies* need only be acceptable to the institution in which the trainee (*administrative resident*) is enrolled.

administrative residency: A position in a health care organization or institution where a student in a *health care administration* education program may obtain a practical training phase of his education. Upon completion of the administrative residency training, the student returns to the educational institution for further training. The student may be enrolled in the educational institution at the undergraduate or graduate level.

medical residency: A generic term which may be used for a *residency* providing training for *graduate physicians* in any *medical specialty*. The term may also be used specifically for a residency in *internal medicine*. For a list of approved residency specialties, see *specialty*.

Residency Review Committee (RRC): A national committee of experts that reviews individual clinical training programs in medical specialties (such as internal medicine, surgery, or psychiatry) for determination of quality. RRCs submit recommendations for *accreditation* of the programs to the *Accreditation Council for Continuing Medical Education (ACCME)*. For a list of approved residency specialties, see *specialty*.

resident (1): An individual undergoing training by carrying out actual duties under supervision in a *residency* program in an institution or organization.

administrative resident: A student in an *administrative residency* program.

medical resident: A *resident physician* who is specializing in *internal medicine*.

medical specialty resident: A *resident physician* in training in a *medical* or *surgical specialty*.

R

resident (2):   A patient residing in a long-term care institution.

long-term resident: A term sometimes applied to a patient who is not *acutely* ill, but who needs hospital care.

Resource Utilization Groups (RUGs) II: A *case mix* payment system used in New York state for *long-term care* patients under Medicare and Medicaid.

resource-based relative value scale (RBRVS):   See *relative value scale*.

respirator: A machine which performs or assists in the function of breathing for a patient.

respiratory arrest: The cessation of breathing.

Respiratory Care Services (RP):   The chapter giving the *standards* for this component of the hospital in the 1990 *Accreditation Manual for Hospitals (AMH)* of the *Joint Commission on the Accreditation of Healthcare Organizations (JCAHO)*.

respiratory diseases unit: A *patient care unit* of the hospital set aside for the care of inpatients with respiratory (breathing) problems.

respiratory distress syndrome (RDS):   A sometimes fatal condition occurring in the newborn in which there is difficulty in breathing. Most frequently RDS is caused by *"hyaline membrane disease (HMD)"* (for which the term "RDS" is sometimes a synonym), although the *syndrome* occasionally occurs in the absence of HMD.

respiratory therapist (1):   A person who provides *respiratory therapy* services under the supervision of a physician.

respiratory therapist (2) (REST):   One of the 26 *allied health professionals* for whom the American Medical Association's *Committee on Allied Health Education and Accreditation (CAHEA)* has accredited education programs.

R

respiratory therapy (RT): Treatment of respiratory (breathing) problems by administration of gases, such as oxygen, and the use and teaching of breathing exercises.

respiratory therapy assistant: A person who helps a *respiratory therapist* by maintaining and transporting equipment, transporting patients, and otherwise assisting.

respiratory therapy technician (1): A person who provides certain *respiratory therapy* treatments under the supervision of a physician.

respiratory therapy technician (2) (RESTT): One of the 26 *allied health professionals* for whom the American Medical Association's *Committee on Allied Health Education and Accreditation (CAHEA)* has accredited education programs.

respite care: Short term care (usually a few days) for a *long-term care* patient in order to provide a respite (rest and change) for those who have been caring for the patient, usually the patient's family. Respite care may involve hospitalization of the patient, or provision of round-the-clock care at home or in a nursing home as needed.

respondeat superior: "Let the master answer." A legal doctrine which makes an employer liable for the negligent acts of its employees, even though the employer was itself not negligent. Similarly, a *principal* is liable for the acts of its *agent (2)*.

responsible party: The individual or organization responsible for placing a patient in a health care facility and ensuring that adequate care is given to that patient there. For example, a parent is usually the responsible party in the case of a child; the parent is not only responsible for the child receiving care, but also for the payment for that care. In less formal usage in the hospital, the term "responsible party" is used to mean simply "responsible for payment." Legally, there can be more than one "responsible party." For example, one person, such as a *guardian*, may be authorized to make treatment decisions, while another person may be responsible for payment.

REST: See *respiratory therapist (2)*.

R

rest home: A *free-standing facility (2)* set up to provide care for patients who are unable to live independently, that is, who need assistance with the *activities of daily living (ADL)*, and who may need occasional assistance from a *professional nurse*. Such professional nursing service is obtained from a visiting nurse. Regulations usually apply the designation of rest home to a facility with over, say, six beds, but as a practical matter it is usually not economical to operate a rest home with fewer than thirty or forty beds. A facility providing similar service to a smaller number of persons may be called (and licensed as) a "family care home" (FCH) or "adult foster home." Rest home was formerly called "custodial care home."

rest home care: Care for a patient who is unable to live independently, that is, who needs assistance with the *activities of daily living (ADL)*, and who may need occasional assistance from a *professional nurse*. Such professional nursing service is obtained from a visiting nurse. The setting for rest home care (formerly called custodial care) is, understandably, a rest home.

restructuring: Reorganization of a corporation (a hospital, for example) in order better to handle new functions and enterprises. The restructuring may involve the creation of several corporations where there was only one, *consolidation* or *merger* of corporations, establishment of foundations, and the like. Restructuring is often essential to achieve effective *diversification*.

RESTT: See *respiratory therapy technician*.

resuscitate: To restore vital functions after the person is apparently dead, for example, to restart the heart.

resuscitation: See *cardiopulmonary resuscitation (CPR)*.

retirement center: A facility which provides social activities to senior citizens, usually retired persons, who do not require health care. The provision of housing is not required for an institution or organization to be called a retirement center. A retirement center may furnish housing and may also have *acute hospital* and *long-term care facilities*, or it may arrange for acute and long term care through affiliated institutions.

retroactive date: The date stipulated in a *claims-made insurance* policy as the earliest date an event may occur and be covered under that particular claims-made policy. For example, a policy for calendar year 1990 with a retroactive date of January 1, 1985, would cover an event occurring anytime on or after January 1, 1985, if the *claim* based on that event is made during 1990.

retrospective: Dealing with events in the past.

retrovir: A drug used in the treatment of acquired immunodeficiency syndrome (AIDS). The drug was formerly called azidothymidine (AZT).

retrovirus: A type of virus with certain unique genetic properties. The best known of this class of virus is the human immunodeficiency virus (HIV) which causes acquired immunodeficiency syndrome (AIDS). (The family of viruses was named "retro" because they contain an enzyme called "reverse transcriptase.")

revenue: Increase in an organization's *assets* or a decrease in its *liabilities* during an *accounting period*. This is in contrast with *income*, which refers to money earned during an accounting period.

marginal revenue: The addition to or subtraction from total *revenue* resulting from the sale of one more or one less unit of service or product.

reverse protocol: A term coined for the proposition that a given diagnostic or therapeutic procedure implies that a certain kind of diagnosis or problem must have been presented by the patient. For example, administration of a certain drug should have been explained by a class of disease (or prophylaxis) for which the drug was an appropriate treatment. Failure to find such a disease in the record would indicate an error in documentation or inappropriate use of the drug. See *protocol*, which pertains to the proposition that a patient's problem dictates certain procedures.

review: There are many kinds of review carried out in health care. All are processes of evaluation. Some are defined here:

admissions review: An evaluation of the appropriateness of the *admission* of the patient to the hospital. The admissions review determines whether the patient in question was in a condition which warranted use of the hospital, or could (or should) have been treated in some other setting (for example, at home or as an outpatient, or in a hospital more suited to managing his problem). Typically, the admissions review is carried out at or shortly after admission.

capital expenditure review (CER): A process carried out by a state agency prior to granting permission to the hospital to incur a *capital expenditure*.

claims review: Retrospective review of hospital *claims (1)* by a *third party payer* in order to determine the: (1) *liability (2)* of the payer (whether the benefit was included in the contract); (2) eligibility of the *beneficiary* and the *provider*; (3) appropriateness of the *service (1)*; and (4) appropriateness of the amount claimed.

concurrent review: Evaluation of medical necessity for *admission* and *appropriateness* of *services (1)*, carried out while the patient is in the hospital (concurrent with the care). The advantage of concurrent review is that if any action (change in the care) is found to be necessary as a finding of the review, it can be taken while the patient is still in the hospital.

continued stay review: Concurrent review (review while the patient is in the hospital), conducted at a specified time after admission, for the purpose of determining the appropriateness of continuation of hospital care for the individual patient.

drug utilization review: Review of the use of drugs, either in the practice of a physician or in the hospital.

medical services review: *Retrospective review* of the use of *services (1)* (and failure to use services), for both *inpatients* and *outpatients*, with respect to the medical *appropriateness* of the services and, in some situations, review of whether the services are included in the patient's insurance *benefits*.

peer review: See the separate listing *peer review*.

preadmission review: Evaluation, prior to *admission*, of the necessity for *elective* hospitalization for the individual patient in question.

preprocedure review: A review of a *case (1)* prior to the performance of a given *procedure* in order to determine (1) if the procedure is medically indicated, and (2) if the procedure could equally well be performed in an alternate setting.

private review: *Utilization review* performed on patients whose care is paid for by private sources (sources other than government).

prospective review (1): A term sometimes used to refer to evaluation of a patient's need for hospitalization prior to admission. *"Preadmission review"* is a better term for this meaning.

prospective review (2): A misnomer when used for what should be called *concurrent review*, that is, the review of the *quality of care* during the patient's hospitalization, at a time when intervention could alter the care for the patient under review.

prospective review (3): A term now being applied to a review of the planning for a patient's future treatment, site of care (home, hospital, and so on) and other details.

rate review: Review by a regulatory *agency (1)* of a hospital's budget and financial picture in order to determine the reasonableness of the hospital's proposed rates and rate changes. Rate review is also applied to rates for certain *prepayment plans*, such as *Blue Cross/Blue Shield (BC/BS)*, depending on state laws.

retrospective review: Review after the fact. The term most often refers to a *patient care audit*.

utilization review (UR): The examination and evaluation of the *efficiency* and *appropriateness* of any health care service. Often the term applies to a concurrent process, one carried out during hospitalization, for determination of the individual patient's need for continued stay.

RH: See *Physical Rehabilitation Services*.

rheumatologist: A physician who specializes in the diagnosis and treatment of "rheumatism" or "rheumatic disorders," that is, disorders of the joints and related muscles and other structures.

rheumatology: The branch of *internal medicine* which deals with rheumatic conditions, that is, with pain and other disorders of the joints or other parts of the musculoskeletal system. One of the medical specialties for which *residency* programs have been approved by the Accreditation Council for Graduate Medical Education (ACGME). See *specialty*.

right of privacy: The right of the individual to be left alone, free from unwarranted intrusion. The United States Supreme Court has recognized this as a constitutional right, and used it as the basis upon which to restrict governmental intrusion in such matters as birth control, sterilization, abortion, and the right to refuse medical treatment (sometimes called the *"right to die"*).

right to die: The legal right to refuse life-saving or life-sustaining treatment. A *competent* adult has the legal right to refuse medical treatment, even if that treatment is essential to sustain life. Some refer to this right as the "right to die." The issue of the "right to die" arises in the situation where a person has a condition in which the *quality of life* is so intolerable that death, at least in the belief of that individual (or those responsible for that person), is preferable. If the person is conscious (and mentally competent), she may exercise the right to refuse treatment for herself; but if she is unconscious or otherwise *incompetent (1)*, others must make the decision for her. Serious legal and ethical issues are involved in the latter case. See *living will, natural death act, Quinlan case, Cruzan case*.

risk (1): *Health care plan* risk. A term which, when used in connection with organizations for providing patient care, refers to finances. For example, a *health maintenance organization (HMO)* which offers prepaid care for a given fee or premium is "at risk"; that is, it must provide the care within the premium funds available or find the money elsewhere (the individual assets of the partners, for example). See also *risk pool* and *risk sharing*.

risk (2): Chance of loss, the type of which can usually be covered by insurance. To a health care institution, the risk may arise through *general liability* (such as a visitor slipping and falling on hospital premises) or *professional liability* (harm to a patient from medical or hospital care). It may also arise because of other hospital liability (antitrust violations, for example) or physical property damage.

risk (3): The likelihood of disease, injury, or death among various groups of individuals and from different causes. Individuals are said to be "at risk" if they are in a group in which a given causal factor is present. Patients who smoke are at risk from smoking; patients undergoing appendectomy are at risk from this operation. This definition is that employed in public health.

risk adjustment: The use of *severity of illness* measures to estimate the *risk (3)* to which a patient is subject.

risk contract: A contract under which a *provider* agrees to furnish a given service for a prearranged fee, and thus assumes the *risk (1)* that the fee will cover its costs for providing the service. A *health maintenance organization (HMO)* which operates under a *capitation* method of payment is a risk contractor.

risk management: The process of minimizing *risk (2)* to an organization at a minimal cost in keeping with the organization's objectives. Risk management includes risk control and risk financing. Risk control involves: (1) developing systems to prevent accidents, injuries, and other adverse occurrences, and (2) attempting to handle events and incidents which do occur in such a manner that their cost is minimized. The latter might involve, for example, special attention to personal relations with the injured party, attempts to reach satisfactory settlement without lawsuit, and the like. Risk financing involves the procurement of adequate financial protection from loss, either through an outside insurance company or through some form of self- insurance.

risk manager: A hospital employee who coordinates the hospital's activities with respect to *risk management*; this is a *staff (2)* position, as contrasted with a *line* position.

risk pool: A fund set up as a reserve for unexpected expenses in a *prepaid health plan*. Organizations which provide prepaid health care for a fixed fee typically set up such pools to cover, for example, unusually large demands for hospital care or specialist services. See *risk (1)*.

risk sharing: The division of financial *risk (1)* among those furnishing the service. For example, if a hospital and group of physicians form a corporation to provide health care at a fixed price, they will ordinarily do it under an arrangement in which the hospital and

R

physicians are both liable if the expenses exceed the revenue; that is, they share the risk.

RN: Registered nurse. See *nurse*.

Robinson-Patman Act: A federal *antitrust* law which prohibits price discrimination. A seller cannot charge a buyer a discriminatory price and a buyer cannot knowingly benefit from such a price. The prohibition applies only to sales of goods. Discrimination may be justified in some cases if the seller can show a relationship between the discount and the cost of manufacture or delivery of the product (for example, in a volume discount), or if the discount is needed to meet the competition. The Robinson-Patman Act is an amendment to Section 2 of the Clayton Act. 15 U.S.C. secs. 13-13b.21(a) (1982).

An important exemption from the Robinson-Patman Act is that granted to *nonprofit hospitals* (and certain other organizations) which purchase supplies for their own use. For example, "own use" has been interpreted to prohibit a hospital from selling prescription drugs (which it obtains at favorable prices) to the general public and outpatients coming in for refills, but to allow the hospital to sell or furnish drugs to inpatients, outpatients seen at the hospital, and physicians and employees and their families.

Roe v. Wade: The landmark United States Supreme Court case which liberalized abortion law in 1973. The Court struck down restrictive state abortion laws as unconstitutional, ruling that those laws violated the individual's right of privacy to make her own decisions concerning her body. *Roe v. Wade* held that the state could regulate abortions only where necessary to serve a compelling state interest. Those state interests were recognized to be protection of the life and health of pregnant women, and protecting the "potentiality of human life."

In *Roe v. Wade* the Court balanced the state interests against those of the individual. It found that during the first trimester of pregnancy, the risk to a woman's health from an abortion was less than the risk of childbirth; therefore, the state's interest in maternal health did not outweigh the right of privacy. Thus the state could regulate abortions during the first trimester only as they might restrict other surgical procedures (for example, requiring that they be performed only by licensed physicians). During the second trimester, the risk accompanying abortion was greater, and therefore greater restrictions could be placed to protect maternal health,

R

as long as they did not unreasonably interfere with the woman's right to make her own abortion decision.

Once the *fetus* became viable, however (at about 28 weeks in 1973), the Court ruled that the state's interest in protecting potential life became compelling, and therefore the state could prohibit third trimester abortions altogether except where abortion was necessary to protect the life or health of the mother. The Court did not address nor did it decide the question of when life began or when the fetus became a "person" as far as the law of abortion was concerned. 410 U.S. 113 (1973), *reh'g denied*, 410 U.S. 959 (1973).

Roentgen ray: See *X-ray (1)*.

room rate: See *rate*.

rooming-in: An organization of the maternity and newborn services of a hospital which permits the newborn to share the room with the mother.

routine inquiry law: See *required request law*.

RP: See *Respiratory Care Services*.

RRA: See *registered record administrator*.

RRC: See *Residency Review Committee*.

RRT: See *registered respiratory therapist*.

RT: See *respiratory therapy*.

rubber: See *condom*.

rubric: The title or label given to a *category* in a *classification (1)*.

RUGs: See *Resource Utilization Groups II*.

Rule of Reason: A doctrine in *antitrust* law which states that only unreasonable restraints of trade are prohibited. Thus, in most cases of alleged anticompetitive behavior, the specific facts must be examined to decide whether an antitrust violation has occurred. For example, an *exclusive contract* between a hospital and a group of radiologists is anticompetitive on its face; that is, it precludes other radiologists from practicing in the hospital. However, courts have decided, by applying the Rule of Reason, that such arrangements may be upheld for reasons of quality of care, administrative efficiency, or other valid institutional goals. By contrast, if the *per se* standard were applied, the exclusive contract would be illegal regardless of its purpose. In health care cases, courts have been more likely to apply the Rule of Reason analysis than they have been in other industries.

rules and regulations: Official statements (statements authorized or commissioned by the *governing body*) as to the conduct of the hospital's affairs in specific areas. The term most often applies to statements which supplement the *medical staff bylaws*. Such rules and regulations have the force of the bylaws themselves, but contain more detail than would be appropriate in the bylaws; also, the process for their revision is less cumbersome than that for the revision of bylaws. For example, the bylaws could require the keeping of a *medical record* on each patient, while the rules and regulations could specify more detailed requirements concerning the content of medical records, promptness of completion, penalties for failure to comply, and so on.

RVS: See *relative value scale*.

RVU: See *relative value unit*.

Rx: Shorthand for *prescription*, or, more loosely, for treatment.

S

SA: See *Surgical and Anesthesia Services.*

safe harbor regulations: Regulations which describe certain acts or behaviors which will *not* be illegal under a specific law, even though they might overwise arguably be illegal. Recently, the term has been applied to proposed *Department of Health and Human Services (DHHS)* regulations which would provide a "safe harbor" for certain *joint ventures* and other arrangements between hospitals and physicians or among physicians, so that these activities would not violate federal Medicare *fraud and abuse* laws.

same-day surgery: Surgery performed on an *outpatient*, with arrival and departure on the same day. If the patient has to be kept over night, he is admitted and then discharged the next day. Same as ambulatory surgery and outpatient surgery.

sample: A part of a population, intended to be in some way representative of the population.

sampling: A technique used in statistics in which a part of a whole is examined with the intent that the results of the examination can be taken as representing the condition of the whole. A large body of theory and experience has been developed as to various sampling methods (methods of drawing samples), and their reliability, that is, the trustworthiness of the *projections* made from them. In general, the more *random* the sample, the better (i.e., the more likely the sample will accurately reflect the condition of the whole). One example of sampling involves coal, which is sometimes sold on the basis of its heating value. Small quantities thought to represent the

S

whole are analyzed, and payment is based on these analyses. The same principle is used in polls as to a political candidate's popularity: a sample of people are questioned and their responses are projected as representative of the whole population from which they were selected (for example, a city). Most skepticism about sampling revolves around whether the sample was a correct one for the purpose.

SAMS: See *Society for Advanced Medical Systems*.

sanction: A term used with two, opposite meanings: (1) a kind of permission or support; and (2) discipline, punishment, or prohibition. Only by the context can one determine which meaning is intended.

SBBT: See *specialist in blood bank technology*.

SBU: See *strategic business unit*.

SC: Service corporation. See *professional corporation* under *corporation*.

school nurse practitioner (SNP): A *registered nurse (RN)* with postgraduate training in school nursing.

school rule: A legal doctrine which states that the *standard of care (2)* in a *malpractice* lawsuit will be measured by the degree of care exercised by professionals within the same specialty or "school" of medicine. For example, under the school rule, osteopaths would be measured by the practices of other osteopaths (*DOs*), not those of medical physicians (*MDs*). Some states use this rule; others do not.

scintigraphy: An *imaging* technique in which a camera sensitive to emissions from *radioactive* substances is used to photograph the distribution in the body of a radioactive drug administered internally.

SCM: See *Society for Computer Medicine*.

screening (1): A method for separating some kinds of things or patients from others. The term is often employed in one method of assessing *quality of care,* in which medical records of patients are subjected to a "screen" which isolates for detailed review the records of those with unusually long stays, or those with complications of care, for example.

generic screening: Screening in which the criteria used to "screen" cases apply to patients regardless of their diagnoses and procedures employed; thus the criteria are *generic* rather than diagnosis- or procedure-specific. Examples of generic screening criteria include injuries, *incidents*, documentation failures (including *informed consent*), failure to respond to abnormal laboratory or X-ray findings, and nosocomial (hospital-acquired) infections. Many of the criteria which define *adverse patient occurrences (APOs)* are generic.

occurrence screening: The process of examining *medical records* and other data in the hospital (or other health care settings) in order to find cases in which there may have been *adverse patient occurrences (APOs)*, cases which meet predefined criteria. The cases detected by the screening are reviewed by experienced personnel who make judgments as to whether each case should enter the occurrence reporting process for further review. This is a step in the *Medical Management Analysis (MMA)* system employed by some hospitals in quality management.

screening (2): Giving *diagnostic* tests to "normal" individuals or a population in order to detect diseases. The tests employed include examinations of the blood and urine, X-rays, blood pressure measurements, height and weight, questionnaires, and vision and hearing testing. Screening may be employed for detection of a single problem, such as hypertension (high blood pressure) or drug usage, or it may be a "broad spectrum" screening for "anything abnormal" which can be suspected by using a battery of tests. The latter approach is called *multiphasic screening* (see below).

Increasing attention is being given to the *cost-benefit ratios* of various screening approaches. In a population with very little tuberculosis, for example, the cost of finding new cases by chest X-ray screening is far higher than finding cases by examining contacts of known cases; consequently, chest X-rays are rarely included today in community screening programs. On the other hand, automation of blood chemical determinations has made it often cheaper to perform the standard battery of tests provided by the analyzer than to single out specific tests (which are included in the battery). The laboratory work done in routine examinations on admission to the hospital is primarily a screening process. For example, even though the physician may be most interested in the patient's blood sugar, the whole array of tests—which screens for other disorders—is done simultaneously. Furthermore, such screening on admission to the hospital provides a clinical *data base (1)* on the patient which often helps in timing the onset of abnormalities.

multiphasic screening: Applying batteries of diagnostic tests, usually to persons "on the street" (primarily adults without symptoms) in such settings as shopping malls and county fairs. Often the tests include some blood chemistry determinations (such as for sugar and cholesterol levels), hearing, blood pressure, intra-eyeball pressure (for detection of glaucoma), and chest X-rays. The process has been criticized as to its value, on account of such problems as cost per case identified, *false positive* findings, *false negative* findings, and unnecessarily alarming the persons tested.

scrub: To prepare to carry out or assist in a surgical operation. The term "scrub" is taken from the routine of thorough hand washing (scrubbing) prior to putting on sterile rubber gloves and operating garments.

second opinion: A *consultation (1)* which involves the examination of a patient by a surgeon, and the rendering of an opinion by that surgeon, with respect to the need for *elective* (non-emergency) surgery which has been recommended by another surgeon.

second opinion program: A mandatory or voluntary program calling for *second opinions* for *elective* (non-emergency) surgery prior to authorization of the performance of the surgery.

secondary care: Specialized care provided by a physician or hospital, usually on *referral* from a *primary care physician*. See *physician*. Synonym(s): specialized care.

secretariat: The base office of an organization, including its professional and clerical staffs, along with the essential technological and other resources necessary for carrying out the work of the organization.

Section 1122: A section of the Social Security Act which denies payment for certain *capital expenditures* not approved by state planning agencies.

self-care: Those activities that individuals initiate and perform for themselves in connection with their health and well-being.

self-governance: A term commonly used in connection with the *medical staff organization (MSO)*, to which the hospital *governing body* delegates certain duties, for example, those connected with evaluation of care or the control of physician practices. It should be noted, however, that the governing body retains the ultimate responsibility for the care in the hospital, even where the MSO is described as "self-governing." See *accountability.*

self-insurance: See *insurance.*

self-pay patient: See *self-responsible patient.*

self-responsible patient: A patient who pays either all or part of his hospital bill from his own resources, as opposed to *third-party payment* (payment by an insurance company, Medicare, or Blue Cross/Blue Shield (BC/BS)), for example). Synonym(s): self-pay patient.

semi-private room: A hospital room set up to accommodate two to four patients. A "private room" has only one patient; a "ward" has more than four.

Senior Plan Network (SPN): An alliance of *health maintenance organizations (HMOs)* which offers enrollment in the SPN, and thus in its constituent HMOs. Medicare prepays part or all the cost of enrollment in an SPN as it does in an HMO under certain circumstances.

separate billing: Billing which clearly identifies hospital and physician *services (1)* and *charges* (and thus permits their separa-

S

tion). This may be accomplished on a properly designed single bill, or through the use of two bills, one for the hospital and one for the physician. See also *combined billing*.

separation: A term used in Canada to mean the same as patient *"discharge"* in the United States. It is the formal release of a patient from a hospital (or other care). Different types of *discharge* are discussed under that term.

serology: The study of serum. Serum is the liquid portion of a body fluid, for example, blood, that remains after clotting. Serum contains immune substances (antibodies) which represent the response of the body to exposure to certain disease causing *agents (1)*. For many diseases, these antibodies are highly specific (each disease tends to cause the production of a unique substance). Detection of the presence of disease-specific antibodies is helpful in making diagnoses and in keeping track of the progress of the diseases for which the antibodies develop.

Serology is also involved in preparation of serums used to protect persons against certain diseases. An example of such a serum is tetanus antitoxin, used to give *passive immunity* against tetanus (a bacterial disease).

serum hepatitis: See *hepatitis B*.

service (1): Something "done" for a patient by a physician or other person. The term often occurs in health care *financing (2)* in the phrase "procedures and services," and it is sometimes difficult if not impossible to distinguish the two; a specific act might equally well be called a "procedure" or a "service." Generally, procedures tend to be distinct actions, and are carried out in a brief time, as, for example, a surgical operation (a procedure or group of surgical procedures done at one time). On the other hand, services (such as the preoperative and postoperative care for the same operation) are less distinct and are carried out over longer (and variable) periods of time.

In the context of health care financing, the physician's "initial hospital care" of a patient is called a "service," although it is largely limited (in billing for care) to what is done upon admission of the patient; each subsequent day's care is defined as another "service." However, the "50-minute hour" in the psychiatrist's office for "medical psychotherapy" is listed in *Physician's Current Procedural Terminology, 4th Edition (CPT-4)*, as a "procedure."

For purposes of health care financing, a "service" (or procedure) might more accurately be defined as "the unit for which a *charge* is made." See also *procedure*.

revenue-producing service: A service of the institution for which charges are made directly on the patient's bill, such as use of the operating room.

support service: A service which is necessary for the operation of the institution, but for which direct charges are inappropriate. Heating, for example, is essential, but is not itemized on the patient's bill. The cost of support services is recovered by allocating the costs to the revenue-producing services, using an appropriate accounting method.

service (2): A title given in some hospitals to a division of the hospital organization, such a "the nursing service," or of its medical staff, such as "the oncology service."

clinical service: A division of the *medical staff organization (MSO)* according to clinical specialty, such as surgery, specialties of surgery, internal medicine, specialties of internal medicine, obstetrics and gynecology, pediatrics, neurology, and the like. In some hospitals, clinical services are called departments; for example, the "surgical service" may mean the same thing as the "surgical department." In other instances, a service may be a subdivision of a department; for example, the "orthopedics service" may be part of the larger "department of surgery."

hospital service: A term used interchangeably with "department" when referring to elements of the hospital organization, and which may refer to the hospital or its medical staff. The nursing department may be called the nursing service, the pharmacy the pharmacy service, the housekeeping department the housekeeping service, and so on. When used in the plural, "hospital services" more commonly refers to the *clinical services* or clinical departments of the medical staff than to the hospital's administrative units.

service (3): A term used in the *American Hospital Association (AMA)* classification of hospitals to describe hospitals themselves as general or specialized and, if specialized, the nature of the specialty. For example, a hospital's classification according to service could be "children's general hospital" or "alcoholism and other chemical dependency" hospital. A given hospital can be put in only one class according to service.

service (4): An activity in a hospital or other health care institution, such as food, supplies, medical records, or maintenance, which supports the activities of other departments. The service is typically under a specific individual who is responsible for its execution, but it may be provided from one central point ("centralized service") or from a number of points in the organization ("decentralized service").

service (5): The supplying or meeting of some public demand, as contrasted with producing goods. The health care industry is a "service" industry. "Service management" in health care attends to the demands and wishes of the patients, rather than simply the satisfaction of the provider.

service (6): A term used broadly to describe a variety of facilities, programs, and capabilities of hospitals (and other health care facilities), which provide for various needs of patients and the community. For example, a hospital may provide open heart surgery, genetic counseling, hemodialysis, organ transplants, psychiatric intensive care, weight loss programs, blood pressure screening, and so forth. Each of these might be described as a service.

The American Hospital Association (AHA) uses the term "facility" to describe a number of these various services provided by hospitals in its annual *Guide to the Health Care Field*. In the 1990 edition, some 77 categories of "facilities" are provided, which cover a mixture of physical facilities (for example, birthing room/LRDP room), equipment (for example, CT scanner), activities (for example, genetic counseling/screening services), types of care (for example, psychiatric inpatient unit), and other hospital attributes. See *facility (1)* for a list of the categories.

service (7): A "utility" necessary to care for patients in a hospital. Those services which are essential for any institution to be called a hospital include nursing, food service, pharmacy, medical records, laboratory, and diagnostic radiology. The *Joint Commis-*

sion on *Accreditation of Healthcare Organizations (JCAHO)* has *standards* for these services in its *Accreditation Manual for Hospitals (AMH)* and makes certain stipulations regarding hospital performance in 16 chapters which are entitled "[Name] Services" (for example, "Dietary Services" or "Radiology Services"). Some services are required of all hospitals; some must be available on site; some can be provided by suitable arrangements with other institutions (that is, they need not be provided on site); some are not required for hospitals offering only to care for psychiatric or substance abuse patients; some services (for example, home health care) need not be offered by all hospitals, but if they are offered, must meet the standards given. See *Accreditation Manual for Hospitals (AMH)* for a complete listing of "service" chapters.

service area: The geographic area served by a hospital or other *facility (2)*, or, perhaps more accurately, the area from which the institution or organization draws its patients or clients. A "service area" is sometimes referred to as a "catchment area." The catchment areas of organizations with like services may overlap.

service contract: A health care insurance contract in which the benefits are the actual *services (1)* rather than money (the latter would be *indemnity benefits*).

SET: See *surrogate embryo transfer*.

settlement: An agreement made by the parties to end a dispute or lawsuit before (or during) the hearing or trial, without a formal adjudication (decision by the arbitrator, judge, jury, or other decisionmaker) of the merits of the dispute. The term "settlement" is also sometimes used to refer to the specific terms of the agreement (such as the amount of money to be paid).

structured settlement: A settlement which provides for payment of money by the *defendant* to the *plaintiff* in other than one lump sum. A structured settlement often provides that the defendant may pay an agreed-upon amount in installments over a period of time. In some cases, a structured settlement might provide that the defendant will reimburse the plaintiff for medical and other expenses as they occur, rather than pay a fixed amount. Other variations are possible, since the terms of the structured settlement are negotiated by the parties.

S

severity of illness: The gravity of a patient's condition. Patients with the same diagnosis often vary from being mildly ill to being extremely ill, or even dying. Under the *prospective payment system (PPS)*, every patient with the same diagnosis (actually, every patient within a given *Diagnosis Related Group (DRG)*, of which there are only 468) is given the same "price tag." No allowance is made for the severity of his illness. Efforts are underway to persuade the federal government to make such an allowance, and other efforts are being made to develop practical methods for quantifying "severity of illness" so that it can be reliably incorporated in the mathematics of the pricing formula. Such quantification is referred to as developing a "severity index" or "score." The stimulus for severity measures is illustrated, for example, by the fact that a diabetic patient in coma (very severely ill) understandably should cost more to treat than one hospitalized simply to "fine-tune" the control of the diabetes. Note that a measure of severity on admission to the hospital, followed by another later measure, permits evaluation of the patient's progress under care, while a measure which can only show severity on discharge does not permit this interpretation.

Several systems are now in development or use in hospitals: *Apache II*, disease *staging, patient management categories (PMCs), computerized severity index (CSI), personal computer (PC)-stager*, and *MedisGroups*.

severity score: A mathematical score which expresses the *severity of illness* of a patient according to one of several severity measurement methods. The goal is to use such scores in a formula for determining payment for care, and in quantifying the quality of care.

sexual harrassment: A form of discrimination in the workplace which violates the Civil Rights Act of 1964 (a federal law; 42 U.S.C. secs. 2000 et seq.). "Sexual harrassment" can be of two forms: (1) "quid pro quo" (the employee must submit to sexual advances to obtain tangible job benefits, or be penalized for refusing); or (2) "hostile environment" (the workplace is offensive, and seriously affects the employee's well-being). Offensive conduct may include unwelcome advances, comments, touching, questions about marital status, and so forth. Both men and women may be victims. Employers are subject to legal liability for sexual harrassment of their employees whether or not they are aware of its existence.

sexually transmitted disease (STD):   A disease which may be transmitted by sexual contact. The "classical" sexually transmitted (venereal) diseases were syphilis and gonorrhea. Today, acquired immunodeficiency syndrome (AIDS), genital herpes, chlamydia, and hepatitis B are also included.

shared service organization: An organization, external to the hospital, set up to provide *shared services*, such as *group purchasing*. Such an organization may or may not have been set up by the organizations receiving the services, and may or may not be under their joint control.

shared services: Administrative, clinical, or other services provided by or for two or more institutions. The services are used jointly or under some arrangement which improves service, reduces cost, or both. A common type of shared service is *group purchasing*. Synonym(s): cooperative services.

shareholder: The owner of shares of stock in a corporation. Synonym(s): stockholder.

SHCC: See *statewide health coordinating council*.

Sherman Act: One of the primary federal *antitrust* laws. Section 1 of the Sherman Act prohibits contracts, combinations, and conspiracies in restraint of trade, and Section 2 prohibits monopolies and attempts to monopolize. The Sherman Act has been interpreted by the courts to apply only to unreasonable restraints of trade, since every contract restrains commerce to some extent. 15 U.S.C. secs. 1 & 2 (1982). See also *Rule of Reason*.

S/HMO: Social/Health Maintenance Organization. See *health maintenance organization*.

shock (1):   In relation to injury, "shock" refers to a sudden failure of circulation, with a drop in blood pressure, pale skin, drop in body temperature, and other signs. Shock may be caused by blood loss, but also by a general reaction of the body to the injury. Immediate treatment is essential to sustain life, and to reverse the process, that is, to restore blood pressure and normal circulation.

shock (2): A sudden disturbance of the emotions and the mind caused by an unexpected and major event.

SI units: See *Systeme International units.*

sign: In medicine, a departure from the normal appearance or function of the patient, of which the patient may be unaware, but which may be detected by the physician or another observer. This is to be distinguished from a "symptom," a disturbance of which the patient himself is or should be aware. Diagnoses are made on the basis of signs, symptoms, and findings, the latter meaning data about the patient detected by laboratory, X-ray, or other diagnostic procedures, or the response to therapy.

sign oneself out: The act of a patient to sign a document (release form) (1) refusing the recommendations of the physician and (2) releasing the physician and the hospital from *liability*—"signing himself out" (discharging himself) rather than being "signed out" (discharged) by the physician, which is the normal procedure— and leaving the hospital. The act of leaving the hospital without permission and not returning is tantamount to signing oneself out. Also called a "discharge against medical advice" or "AMA." See *discharge.*

sign out: See *discharge.*

signing out (the patient): Discharging the patient; the act of the *attending physician* which records his permission for the patient to leave the hospital. By this act, the physician in effect states that, in his opinion, the patient does not require further care in the institution. See *discharge.*

single-diagnosis category: See *category.*

single photon emission computer tomography (SPECT): A computer-enhanced *X-ray* technique in which patients are injected with a drug which emits a small amount of radiation. The chemical settles in tissues in direct proportion to the amount of blood flow in the area. Scanning which is coupled with a computer produces images which are useful in diagnosing various conditions. It has been most used to date in the brain, where it is helpful in detecting

Alzheimers disease and certain psychiatric disorders. The technique is invasive, in that an injection is required. The cost of an examination is said to be less than half that of a *computed tomography (CT)* scan or *magnetic resonance imaging (MRI)*.

skilled nursing care: The highest level of nursing care recognized outside the acute hospital setting: nursing care for a patient whose professional nursing needs are not so demanding as to require acute hospital nursing care, but are of a nature to need inpatient supervision by a *registered nurse (RN)*. Patients require skilled nursing care either because the procedures prescribed for them are those which must be given by a *professional nurse*, or the amount of professional nursing care necessary is considerable ("heavy care"), or both. The term "skilled nursing care" is not used for regular nursing care in an acute hospital, but rather for care given in a skilled nursing facility (SNF), in a skilled nursing unit (SNU) (a portion of another facility), or in a home health care (in-home care) program.

The payer (a government program such as Medicare and Medicaid, insurance, or other prepayment program) often has its own definition of the term, under which specific procedures and services are included as skilled nursing care, while others are excluded. While "skilled nursing care" has some general meaning, it is wise to consult the regulations governing the program, such as Medicare, or the terms of the insurance contract for specific inclusions and exclusions.

Formerly called "extended care." See also *intermediate care* (the immediately lower level of care).

skilled nursing facility (SNF): A *free-standing facility (2)* set up to provide *skilled nursing care*. To qualify as an SNF, the facility must have an *organized professional staff* including medical and nursing professionals, and meet the other social and health needs of patients who do not require acute hospital care, but who do need inpatient professional nursing care. An SNF typically must have on-site *registered nurse (RN)* supervision for at least two nursing shifts each day. Patients may be discharged from an acute hospital and then admitted to an SNF. A portion of an SNF may be organized so as to provide "intermediate care," and called the "intermediate care unit" of the SNF. Skilled nursing care may be provided in a portion of an acute hospital, in which case that portion is called a "skilled nursing unit" (SNU). Formerly called "extended care facility" (ECF).

skilled nursing services: A Medicare term referring to nursing and to other rehabilitation *services (1)* provided to Medicare beneficiaries under conditions set up by the Medicare program. See *skilled nursing care.*

skilled nursing unit (SNU): A portion of a hospital devoted to providing *skilled nursing care,* rather than acute care. To qualify as an SNU, the unit must have an *organized professional staff* including medical and nursing professionals, and meet the other social and health needs of patients who do not require acute hospital care, but who do need professional nursing care as inpatients. An SNU typically must have on-site *registered nurse (RN)* supervision for at least two nursing shifts each day. Patients may be discharged from an acute hospital and then admitted to its SNU. A free-standing facility offering the same care skilled nursing care is called a "skilled nursing facility" (SNF). Formerly called "extended care unit" (ECU).

skim: A term which, in hospital usage, usually means to select patients who will be financially profitable (for example, because they have an illness for which the *prospective payment system (PPS)* favors the hospital, or because they have insurance and are not charity patients).

slander: Spoken words which injure the reputation of another; oral *defamation.* Written defamation is called "libel." See *defamation.*

SM: See *surrogate mother.*

SNF: See *skilled nursing facility.*

SNP: See *school nurse practitioner.*

SNU: See *skilled nursing unit.*

SO: See *Social Work Services.*

SOAP: A common form of organization for a *problem-oriented medical record (POMR)*. "SOAP" stands for Subjective (complaints), Objective (observations, test results), Assessment, Plan.

social consciousness: The awareness of an individual of the needs of society and of the impact of events on society. It is contrasted with what might be called "personal consciousness," an awareness of the needs of the individual and the relationship of events to the individual.

Social/Health Maintenance Organization (S/HMO): See *health maintenance organization*.

Social Security Administration (SSA): The division of the federal government which administers Medicare, Medicaid (on the federal level), Social Security Insurance (SSI) pensions, and other programs.

social services: See *social work*.

social work: Assistance to patients and their families in handling social, environmental, and emotional problems (in health care usage, primarily such problems associated with illness or injury). Synonym(s): social services.

Social Work Services (SO): The chapter giving the *standards* for this component of the hospital in the 1990 *Accreditation Manual for Hospitals (AMH)* of the *Joint Commission on the Accreditation of Healthcare Organizations (JCAHO)*.

social worker: A person who does *social work* with patients and their families. Several specialized types are identified in health care:

hospital social worker: A person designated as a social worker by the hospital.

medical social worker: A person qualified by a master's degree to do social work in the hospital or health care setting.

psychiatric social worker: A person qualified by a master's degree to do social work in the psychiatric or mental health setting.

S

social worker designee: A member of the staff of a *long-term care facility (LTCF)* responsible for identification of the emotional and social needs of a patient and for the services to meet these needs. Note that this term pertains to the duties assigned the employee, rather than the employee's qualifications.

Society for Advanced Medical Systems (SAMS): A national organization which was merged with the *Society for Computer Medicine (SCM)*, forming the *American Association for Medical Systems and Informatics (AAMSI)*.

Society for Computer Medicine (SCM): A national organization which was merged with the *Society for Advanced Medical Systems (SAMS)*, forming the *American Association for Medical Systems and Informatics (AAMSI)*.

software: Computer programs and systems, as contrasted with "hardware," which refers to the physical (hard) components of the computer and its accessories.

solo practice: A practice in which the physician (or other professional) is alone, that is, not a member of a group or associated with other physicians. Solo practitioners may, however, arrange with others to provide care for their patients in cases of the practitioner's absence or illness.

somatic: Pertaining to the body as opposed to the mind.

SOP: See *standard operating procedure.*

SP: See *Special Care Units.*

special care unit: An area of the hospital for critically ill or injured patients. Special care units include intensive care, burn, neonatal (newborn) intensive care, and cardiac care units. *The Joint Commission on the Accreditation of Healthcare Organizations (JCAHO)* has *standards* which apply specifically to special care units.

Special Care Units (SP): The chapter giving the *standards* for certain components of the hospital in the 1990 *Accreditation Manual for*

Hospitals (AMH) of the *Joint Commission on the Accreditation of Healthcare Organizations (JCAHO)*. The units included are the burn unit, intensive care unit (cardiac, cardiovascular, or respiratory), intensive care unit (neonatal), and the renal unit.

special diet: See *modified diet*.

specialist: A person who has special experience and training in a portion of the field (discipline) of his major expertise. Although a person may simply claim to be a specialist, in most instances, there are specific *credentials*, such as *board certification* in medicine, which can be obtained by qualified individuals to back up the claim. For example, a physician may be a specialist in *internal medicine*, with board certification to prove it.

specialist in blood bank technology (SBBT): One of the 26 *allied health professionals* for whom the American Medical Association's *Committee on Allied Health Education and Accreditation (CAHEA)* has accredited education programs.

specialized care: See *secondary care*.

specialty: A particular branch of medicine, or a limited division of another profession, such as nursing. The practitioner of a specialty is a *specialist*, usually qualified by added training, plus added experience, within the branch of the discipline. See also *certified nurse* under *nurse*.

medical specialty: A branch of *medicine (4)* in which physicians specialize, such as general surgery, internal medicine, neurosurgery, family medicine, and public health. For such specialties, there is available special training and, often, special *credentials*, namely *certification* by *specialty boards* (bodies which examine qualified candidates). A certified specialist is commonly referred to as "board certified"; one who is eligible, but has not yet taken the examinations, is called "board eligible."

The term "medical specialty" is occasionally used to refer only to the "subspecialties" of internal medicine, such as gastroenterology and pulmonary diseases. Such usage can only be determined by reference to the context.

The Accreditation Council for Graduate Medical Education (ACGME) currently (1990) accredits the following 65 medical residency specialty programs (a 66th type of program called a *"transitional year"* program is also accredited by the ACGME; in addition, the ACGME accredits new specialty programs from time to time):

allergy and immunology
anesthesiology
> critical care

colon and rectal surgery
dermatology
dermatopathology
emergency medicine
family practice
> geriatrics

internal medicine
> cardiovascular disease
> critical care
> endocrinology and metabolism
> gastroenterology
> geriatrics
> hematology (medicine)
> infectious diseases
> medical oncology
> nephrology
> pulmonary diseases
> rheumatology

neurological surgery
neurology
> child neurology

nuclear medicine
obstetrics/gynecology
ophthalmology
orthopedic surgery
> hand surgery
> musculoskeletal oncology
> pediatric orthopedics
> sports medicine

otolaryngology
pathology
> blood banking
> chemical pathology
> forensic pathology
> hematology (pathology)

immunopathology
medical microbiology
neuropathology
pediatrics
    pediatric cardiology
    pediatric endocrinology
    pediatric hemato-oncology
    pediatric nephrology
    neonatal-perinatal medicine
physical medicine and rehabilitation
plastic surgery
preventive medicine, general
    aerospace medicine
    occupational medicine
    public health
    combined general preventive medicine/
        public health
psychiatry
    child psychiatry
radiology, diagnostic
radiology, diagnostic (nuclear)
radiation oncology
surgery
    critical care
    pediatric surgery
    vascular surgery
thoracic surgery
urology

surgical specialty: A branch of *surgery (2)* in which surgeons specialize, such as general surgery, neurosurgery, and plastic surgery. Surgical specialties are one classification of *medical specialties* (see above). "Medical specialties" is the term covering all types of accredited specialties in medicine, whether they are "subspecialties" of surgery or internal medicine or are independent, such as family medicine and public health.

specialty association: See *specialty society*.

specialty board: A nongovernmental, voluntary body which *certifies* a physician or dentist as a specialist when that person has met the specialty board's requirements. Examples of specialty boards in medicine are the American Board of Internal Medicine (ABIM) and the American Board of Surgery (ABS). When the term "specialty *boards*" (plural) is used, it refers to the examinations.

specialty boards: A short term for "specialty board examinations," examinations given by a voluntary *specialty board* to eligible professionals who wish to become *certified specialists*. A certified specialist is a person who has been given a statement by the *board* involved that he has met the qualifications for specialty "rating" in that specialty. Such a specialist is called "board certified." The term "specialty board" (singular) refers to the certifying body.

specialty society: A society whose membership is made up of *specialist* physicians, such as surgeons or internists. Conversely, a "medical society" is a term generally used with reference to an association of physicians of various specialties, geographically defined (for example, a city, county, state, or national medical society). The *medical staff organization (MSO)* of a hospital is not a medical society. Synonym(s): specialty association.

SPECT: See *single photon emission computer tomography*.

speech pathology: The science which concerns disorders of speech.

spell of illness: A term, used in determining Medicare benefits, which is defined as a period of time starting when the patient enters the hospital and ending at the conclusion of a 60-consecutive-day period during which the patient has not been an *inpatient* of any hospital or *skilled nursing facility (SNF)*. (The patient's actual illness ordinarily would have started prior to the hospitalization, and might or might not have concluded within the 60-day period outside the hospital.)

spin density: See *nuclear magnetic resonance imaging (NMRI)*.

SPN: See *Senior Plan Network*.

sports medicine: An emerging branch of medicine which started with specialized interest in sports injuries—first their treatment, then their prevention. Sports medicine has expanded to include all aspects of health related to sports and other similar physical activities, such as *fitness programs, nutrition,* and psychology.

squeal rule: A law requiring a *family planning* agency to report to parents when family planning advice or services are provided to a *minor.*

SSA: See *Social Security Administration.*

ST: See *surgical technologist.*

staff (1): A term which means either the body, or the individual members, of either of two hospital groups:

> **hospital staff:** The body of hospital employees. This term may easily be misused when the intent is to designate the *medical staff.* One must deduce the meaning of "hospital staff" from the context.

> **medical staff:** Physicians, dentists, and other professionals who are officially members of the organized medical staff of the hospital. Members of this group are often referred to as "hospital staff" or merely "staff"; however, in better usage, "hospital staff" refers to hospital employees, while "staff" alone is ambiguous unless taken in context. See the separate listing for *medical staff.*

staff (2): A term which, in the context of *"line and staff,"* refers to positions (persons) in an organization who assist those with line authority. Those with line authority have responsibility, in an organizational hierarchy, to require those beneath them to perform tasks, and to set the standards for that performance. Staff persons have such authority only within the confines of the staff department in which they work.

staff development: The *inservice training* of hospital employees.

stage (of disease): A point or period in the course of an illness. For example, many illnesses have first an *acute* stage which is followed by a *chronic* stage. For some diseases, such as *cancers*, the stages are specifically identified and named by processes called *staging*, with the stages important in both *treatment* and *prognosis*.

S

staging (1): One of the methods developed for taking into account a patient's *severity of illness*, in addition to simply the diagnosis and surgical procedures, in predicting and analyzing the length of stay, cost, and outcome. For a number of diagnoses, objective factors have been identified by which the patient's condition can be classified into several "stages" representing degrees of severity. For example, a diabetic person whose diabetes is under control could be in "Stage 1," and not require hospitalization, while one in diabetic coma (a life-threatening condition) could be in "Stage 4," and require intensive care in the hospital. In this system, the severity score is specific to the disease. As currently applied, using discharge abstract data, only the severity on discharge from the hospital can be estimated. Synonym(s): disease staging.

staging (2): A term applied to various systems devised for describing the extent of *tumors*, both as to the tumor itself and its spread through the body, and with consequent implications as to the patient's likelihood of survival. Some of the staging systems for bowel cancer are, for example, the Dukes system, the Kirklin system, the Astler-Coller system, and the TNM (tumor, node, metastases) system. Synonym(s): tumor staging.

stakeholder: An individual who has an interest in the activities of an organization and the ability to influence it. A hospital's stakeholders, for example, include its patients, employees, medical staff, government, insurers, industry, and the community.

standard (JCAHO): A statement, developed by the *Joint Commission on the Accreditation of Healthcare Organizations (JCAHO)*, of the requirements which must be met by the institution in question (such as a hospital, mental health facility, or ambulatory care program) if the institution is to meet JCAHO's requirements for *accreditation*. Each annual *Accreditation Manual for Hospitals (AMH)* gives the standards, and for each of them spells out a number of "required characteristics," which in total number into the thousands. Some of the items are designated as "key factors in accreditation." The standards from the 1990 *AMH* are under 24 chapter headings (see *Accreditation Manual for Hospitals*) and each standard has a number, preceded by the abbreviation for the relevant *AMH* chapter. For example, a standard concerning Infection Control (IC) might be specified as IC2.10.11.

standard of care (1): The principles and practices which have been accepted by a health care profession as expected to be applied for a patient under ordinary circumstances. Standards of care are developed from a consensus of experts, based on specific research (where such is available) and expert experience. "Under ordinary circumstances" refers to the fact that a given patient may have individual conditions which are overriding; absent such considerations, a medical staff or nursing staff quality review committee will expect the generally accepted principles and practices to be carried out.

For example, the standard of care for a bedfast patient requires the nursing service to carry out certain procedures to minimize the patient's chances of developing bedsores. The standard of care for a patient with a suspected fracture is to X-ray the area; however, severe bleeding may override (for an extended period of time) the standard calling for the X-ray. In other words, the *first* standard of care is that the individual patient's needs come before the "general" standard. See also *parameter*.

standard of care (2): The measure to be applied, in a *malpractice* suit, to the actions of the health care professional in order to determine if the professional was *negligent*. The rule for determining the standard varies from state to state, but it can be generally stated that the standard of care for health care professionals is to exercise that degree of care and skill practiced by other professionals of similar skill and training (and, in some states, in the same geographic locality) under similar circumstances (see *school rule* and *locality rule*).

The legal "standard of care" may or may not be the same as the "general" *standard of care (1)* in a particular case. The jury (or, in some cases, the judge) in a malpractice case decides what the appropriate "degree of care and skill" is in *that* case, based on the facts and upon the expert testimony offered by both the *plaintiff* and the *defendant*. Differences in juries' opinions on the relevant standard of care is one reason why two malpractice cases with similar facts can have different results.

On rare occasions, the legal standard of care may be higher than that of the health care profession. For example, a 32 year old woman developed glaucoma and suffered permanent eye damage, after her physicians failed to detect the condition while treating her from 1959 until 1968. Medical experts for both plaintiff (the woman) and defendant ophthalmologists testified that the stand-

S

ards of the ophthalmology profession did not require routine glaucoma testing for patients under 40. However, the court concluded that since the test was simple, inexpensive, and painless, the standard itself was negligent. *Helling v. Carey*, 83 Wash.2d 514, 519 P.2d 981 (1974).

standard operating procedure (SOP): An action (or series of actions) to be carried out in a given situation. SOP may or may not be written. For example, it is "SOP" in most households to lock the doors at night.

standardization: A statistical procedure for permitting valid comparisons among several populations. The procedure involves *adjustments* so that the rates of occurrence of some variable (a disease, for example, by age and sex) are applied to a "standard" distribution of persons by age and sex. Standardization is basically an application of weighting of averages.

standards compliance summary report: A prose version of the *accreditation decision grid*, which is a numerical summary of the institution's *Joint Commission on Accreditation of Healthcare Organizations (JCAHO) survey* scores and findings. Both the accreditation decision grid and the standards compliance summary report are available only on request from JCAHO.

standards manuals: Manuals published periodically by the *Joint Commission on the Accreditation of Healthcare Organizations (JCAHO)* giving the *standards* which must be met by a given type of institution if that institution is to be *accredited*. The number and type of manuals changes from time to time; examples are manuals for acute care hospitals (*Accreditation Manual for Hospitals (AMH)*), psychiatric and substance abuse facilities, long-term care facilities, nonhospital ambulatory health care facilities, home health care programs, and community mental health service programs.

standing orders: Orders for the care of a patient under prescribed circumstances, for example, in preparation for specific diagnostic procedures or surgical operation. Standing orders are to be followed for all such patients unless the physician or surgeon directs otherwise. Establishment of such standing orders is done under formal procedures established by the hospital and its medical staff.

S

Stark bill: A proposed federal law which would prohibit, among other things, physicians from referring Medicare patients to facilities or services in which the physician has an ownership interest, or from which the physician receives compensation. The law is intended to save Medicare dollars by discouraging overuse of health services. The bill, originally called the "Ethics in Patient Referrals Act of 1988," was introduced by Representative Pete Stark (D-California) to amend Title XVIII (reintroduced in 1989 as H.R. 939; not yet passed into law as of the printing of this book). See also *fraud and abuse* and *safe harbor regulations*.

stat: "Do at once."

state approved: A term which comes up especially in nursing with regard to nursing education programs. To be eligible for registration (to be able to become a *registered nurse (RN)*), a nurse must be a graduate of a program approved by the State Board of Nursing. The program, however, may or may not have been *accredited* by the *National League of Nursing (NLN)*, the voluntary body which accredits professional and vocational schools of nursing, since state approval may not require meeting the standards set by NLN.

state board of medical examiners: A body, established by the laws of a state, which oversees the practice of medicine within the state. In particular, the board of medical examiners reviews the *credentials* of physicians applying for licensure to practice within the state, administers examinations if required, investigates the background of applicants, and approves or denies licensure. These medical examiners are to be distinguished from the "medical examiner" who acts as coroner, performing autopsies and investigating suspicious deaths.

state health plan: A statement issued by the *statewide health coordinating council (SHCC)* covering goals and priorities for the health systems within the state and the desired health status of the residents. The state health plan describes the health systems which would result in high quality health services, available and accessible to all residents, and providing continuity of care at reasonable cost.

S

state health planning and development agency: A state government *agency (1)* required under federal law as a unit in the official planning process. Among its duties are the development of a *state health plan* and the administration of the state's *certificate of need (CON)* program.

state medical board: The *agency (1)* in a state which is authorized by that state's legislature to license physicians to practice within the state.

statewide health coordinating council (SHCC): An organization of health care *providers* and *planners* required under federal law as a unit in the official planning process. An SHCC concerns itself with where, how large, and what kind of health care facilities are needed and will be permitted.

statistic: A number calculated from *data.*

statute: A law enacted (passed) by a legislative body.

Statute of Frauds: A law specifying which kinds of *contracts* must be evidenced by a writing to be enforceable. Examples are contracts concerning real estate (except short term leases), sales of goods with a price of more than $500, and contracts which by their terms cannot be performed within a year. The entire agreement does not have to be written to satisfy the Statute of Frauds; all the law requires is a memorandum signed by the party against whom enforcement is sought.

statute of limitations: A law requiring that certain types of lawsuits be initiated within a specific length of time. For example, if a patient wishes to sue for *malpractice,* state law may require that the suit be started within two years after the date of the alleged act of malpractice (the length of time varies from state to state). In some states, the time period begins when the patient discovers (or should have discovered) the injury, rather than on the date of the alleged act of malpractice; this is called the "discovery rule."

In certain circumstances, the law allows the statute of limitations to be suspended ("tolled"). For example, a *minor* is not legally competent to file suit. Therefore, the law allows that minor to reach majority before the time period begins to run. Thus, even though a statute of limitations for malpractice may be only two years, a suit could be initiated as long as 20 years after the birth of an injured infant (18 years to reach majority, plus the two-year limitations period).

STD: See *sexually transmitted disease*.

steering committee: A generic term for a committee set up to provide broad guidance for a program, project, or activity.

sterile: Free from all living bacteria, viruses, and other living organisms and their spores (resistant forms of such life). Synonym(s): aseptic.

sterilization (1): The process of treating an object in such a manner that all living microorganisms are destroyed. Surgical instruments and dressings, for example, must be sterilized so that they do not transmit infections. Sterilization may be accomplished by heat, certain chemicals, radiation, ultraviolet light, or other means.

sterilization (2): Making a person unable to reproduce. Sterilization may be undertaken simply to prevent conception ("contraceptive sterilization"), to prevent inheritance of a mental or physical disability or disease ("eugenic sterilization"), or because bearing children would be harmful to the individual ("therapeutic sterilization"). To prevent inappropriate sterilizations, especially of those unable to give voluntary consent, there are often special laws concerning consent for sterilization. For example, federal regulations govern all sterilizations performed under federally financed programs. Those regulations require, among other things, that the person to be sterilized be at least 21 years old, not institutionalized, and fully informed about the procedure, and that he wait for 30 days after giving consent except in an emergency.

stock: Evidence of ownership of a corporation, and of a claim against the company's assets and earnings. Stocks are of two kinds:

common stock: Evidence of ownership of a corporation, but with claims on assets and earnings having lower priority than *preferred*

S

stock. Common stockholders have voting rights and dividend rights.

preferred stock: A class of stock which has preference over *common stock* in the distribution of earnings or in the case of liquidation of the corporation. Preferred stockholders do not ordinarily have voting rights.

stockholder: See *shareholder.*

stone center: A *lithotripsy* facility, that is, a facility which treats kidney stone patients by use of equipment which shatters the stones rather than by their surgical removal.

strategic business unit (SBU): A term applied to each "product line" of an organization employing *product line management (PLM).* An SBU is a more or less distinct line of business (for example, in a hospital, knee replacement surgery or alcoholism rehabilitation) which has a specific market, resource requirements, and management demands. The hospital operating under PLM acts as though it were managing an array of more or less independent SBUs, rather than thinking of itself as a hospital. Thus it would, for example, advertise each product line separately, staff it more or less independently, and expect each product line to be profitable. Synonym(s): product line.

strategic planning: A term derived from "strategy" in the military sense; *planning* which is long-range, and which is intended to lay out the nature and sequence of the steps to be taken to achieve the large goals of the organization. In traditional thinking, strategic planning should precede the development of the *tactics* with which it is implemented. A current insight is that a successful strategy can only be developed after the available tactics are assessed and used to their maximum.

strategy: A term derived from the military, and which concerns the long-range, large goals of the organization. In traditional thinking, strategy should precede the development of the *tactics* with which it is implemented. A current insight is that a successful strategy can only be developed after the available tactics are assessed and used to their maximum.

structure: In *quality management,* a term referring to the resources and organization of the health care institution. It is commonly stated that three things can be measured in relation to quality: structure, process, and outcome. "Process" refers to the things done. "Outcome" is a somewhat vague term that presumably refers to the results of the process. In various usages "outcome" may refer to survival, *quality of life,* or the outcomes of tests or procedures; it must be defined in a given usage. The Joint Commission on the Accreditation of Healthcare Organizations (JCAHO) originally considered only structure on the theory that "given a good nest, good birds will result." More recently, while affirming that it is now "outcome-oriented," JCAHO has also given attention to process in its surveying of health care organizations.

subcutaneous: Beneath the skin, but outside the muscle (within the muscle is "intramuscular"). "Subcutaneous" refers to the administration of medication or nourishment.

subjective: A term used to describe "reality" as it is perceived by an individual. Pain is subjective in that only the person experiencing it can describe it. "Subjective" is used in contrast with "objective," which refers to observations which do not depend on the perception of the observer. A broken arm is objective in that it can be observed by others.

subpoena: "Under penalty." An order to appear in court (or at a *deposition*) to give testimony.

subpoena duces tecum: "Under penalty" plus "bring with you." An order to appear in court (or at a *deposition*), and to bring specific documents within the possession or control of the person being subpoenaed. The hospital does not ordinarily permit medical records out of its custody; thus a medical record administrator (MRA) (or other responsible person) sometimes receives a subpoena duces tecum commanding him to appear in court, and to bring specific medical records for which he is the custodian.

subscriber: A person enrolled in a *prepayment* plan.

subspecialist: A term often applied to a physician, nurse, or dentist whose field of special training, experience, and, usually, practice is a subdivision of a broader specialty. For example, a cardiologist is a physician who has narrowed his field from the specialty of all of *internal medicine* to the subspecialty concerned with just the diseases of the heart and circulatory system (cardiology). This development might perhaps more accurately have been termed "superspecialization" rather than "subspecialization."

substance: Matter or material. A generic word used for simplicity, as in "dangerous substance," to be inclusive of all chemicals, drugs, biological *agents (1)*, and other materials which are dangerous.

substance abuse facility: A hospital or other *facility (2)* specializing in the treatment of patients suffering from alcoholism or chemical dependency.

substituted judgment doctrine: A legal rule, applied by some courts, which requires a *guardian* or other person making treatment decisions on behalf of an *incompetent (1)* person to base that decision on what the incompetent person himself would want under the circumstances, as distinguished from what the decision-maker believes would be in the best interests of the incompetent patient.

supermed: A term applied to giant, vertically integrated health care firms which some have predicted will appear in the United States. Such firms are envisioned as national in scope, *market-driven*, capitalizing on their "brand names," and specializing in contractual services to large nationwide industries. See also *integration*.

support group: A group of individuals with the same or similar problems who meet periodically to share experiences, problems, and solutions, in order to support each other. For example, group members may themselves have, or have a family member or friend suffering from, a disease such as cancer, Alzheimer's, or alcoholism. The group may be sponsored by the individual members, a health care institution, a church, or other body.

surgeon: A physician specializing in *surgery (2)*.

operating surgeon: The surgeon responsible for a given surgical operation and the care directly associated with that operation. He may have other surgeons assisting, but the one surgeon has the prime responsiblity. If the operating surgeon admits the patient himself, he is also the *attending physician*. But often a patient is admitted by another physician, who does not operate. If an operation is deemed necessary, this is performed by a surgeon (the operating surgeon) and, unless the patient is transferred to the surgeon's care, the first physician remains the attending physician.

surgery (1): The treatment of disease, injury, or deformity by means of operation, which usually involves the use of instruments, and the removal of body tissues or the rearrangement, rebuilding, or replacement of body structures. Treatment by manipulation is also included under the term "surgery." A number of modifying terms are applied to surgery:

ambulatory surgery: Surgery performed on an *outpatient*, with arrival and departure on the same day. If the patient has to be kept over night, he is admitted and then discharged the next day. Same as outpatient surgery and same-day surgery.

elective surgery: Surgery which does not have to be done immediately in order to prevent death or serious disability. If surgery can be scheduled at some future date it is, by definition, elective. Thus there is time for a *second opinion* to be obtained without hazard to the patient because of delay. Elective surgery may be performed for correction of medical problems, such as the repair of a hernia or the removal of a uterus, or it may be performed because of the wishes of the patient, as in the case of cosmetic surgery, face lifts, or hair transplants.

emergency surgery: Surgery which the physician has determined should be performed without delay in order to prevent death or serious disability. Such surgery is not subject to *second opinion* programs.

major surgery: A term no longer in repute, which referred to surgery that was extensive or hazardous, in contrast with "minor surgery," which was neither extensive nor hazardous. However, both terms defied precise definition, and various tongue-in-cheek definitions were used (one definition, offered by a surgeon, was "surgery which I do or which is done on me is major surgery"; another definition considered surgery with a price tag above a certain point as "major," and surgery with one below that as "minor"). In light of the failure to develop an acceptable definition, the terms "major" and "minor" were dropped, and specific operations were studied and reviewed.

Nevertheless, there clearly remains a wide range of complexity to the procedures carried out as surgery. Currently the problem of such a distinction arises in the *prospective payment system (PPS)*, where it is the general policy that care for a patient in a given *Diagnosis Related Group (DRG)* should have a higher price if the patient has "major" surgery than if he does not. The solution has been to devise the *operating room procedure* as a surrogate for "major." Any procedure which the PPS has declared to be an "operating room procedure" as defined by its *ICD-9-CM code*—whether or not it was done in an operating room—is "major surgery."

minor surgery: A term no longer in repute, which referred to surgery which was neither extensive nor hazardous, in contrast with "major surgery," which was considered either extensive or dangerous; however, both terms defied precise definition. See *major surgery*.

operating room surgery: Literally, surgery which should be or ordinarily is done in an operating room, in contrast with surgery which may be done in the patient's bed or a treatment room. At present, a more specific definition is used in the *prospective payment system (PPS)*. PPS uses an arbitrary list of *operating room procedures* published by the federal government. A patient undergoing one of these procedures is placed in a *Diagnosis Related Group (DRG)* with a different price than a similar patient not undergoing such a procedure.

outpatient surgery: See *ambulatory surgery*.

same-day surgery: See *ambulatory surgery*.

unjustified surgery: Surgery which was, in the judgment of the surgeon's peers, not "justified" by the evidence presented by the patient prior to operation—his history, physical examination, laboratory, or other data available. Surgery may be "justified," that is to say, the surgeon's peers would have operated under the circumstances, but it may prove (in retrospect) to have been *unnecessary surgery*. Sometimes the added evidence provided by the operation itself reveals that the case could have been treated without operation (or by a different operation).

unnecessary surgery: Surgery which, at least in retrospect, was not required as treatment for the patient's condition. A distinction is made between unnecessary surgery and *unjustified surgery*. Unnecessary surgery could have been justified, but the condition proved (often with the added information provided by the surgery itself) to be one which, in hindsight, could have been managed without the operation (or by some other operation). Some surgery is both unjustified and unnecessary.

surgery (2): The branch of the practice of medicine which treats diseases, injuries, and deformities by means of operation, which usually involves the use of instruments, and the removal of body tissue or the rearrangement, rebuilding, or replacement of body structures. Treatment by manipulation also falls into this branch of medicine. One of the medical specialties for which *residency* programs have been approved by the Accreditation Council for Graduate Medical Education (ACGME). See *specialty*.

general surgery: That branch of surgery which is often defined as dealing with surgical problems of all kinds. However, general surgery does not include the more complex procedures of the surgical specialties such as orthopedic surgery, hand surgery, and vascular surgery. For a list of all surgical specialties, see *medical specialty* under *specialty*.

surgery (3): A term sometimes given to an operating room or a treatment room.

surgical: When used in reference to therapy (*treatment*), "surgical" means "by the use of surgical methods, operation and manipulation." It is contrasted with "medical," which means non-surgical, the avoidance of surgical methods.

Surgical and Anesthesia Services (SA): The chapter giving the *standards* for this component of the hospital in the 1990 *Accreditation Manual for Hospitals (AMH)* of the *Joint Commission on the Accreditation of Healthcare Organizations (JCAHO)*.

surgical resident: A *resident physician* who is undergoing training in *surgery (2)*.

S

surgical technologist (ST): One of the 26 *allied health professionals* for whom the American Medical Association's *Committee on Allied Health Education and Accreditation (CAHEA)* has accredited education programs.

surrogate: A person designated to act in place of or substitute for another. See *surrogate mother.*

surrogate embryo transfer (SET): The nonsurgical recovery (by uterine lavage (washing)) of an *embryo* from a woman (the *surrogate*) in whom the egg (ovum) has been artificially fertilized by the sperm from an *infertile* woman's husband, and the subsequent transfer of that embryo into the uterus of the infertile woman. This is a technique of *noncoital reproduction.*

surrogate mother (SM): A *fertile* woman who agrees to bear a child for an *infertile* couple, conceiving the child after *artificial insemination* by the sperm of the husband of an infertile woman, and then (presumably) turning the child over to the infertile couple after it is born. The famous "Baby M" legal case involved a surrogate arrangement where the surrogate mother changed her mind after the child was born and decided to keep her. A very unusual custody battle followed; custody was eventually awarded to the biological father. Many legal and ethical issues have been raised relating to surrogate motherhood. A number of states have outlawed surrogacy for hire.

survey: An on-site inspection of a health care facility by the *Joint Commission on the Accreditation of Healthcare Organizations (JCAHO).*

accreditation survey: The survey of an institution for the purpose of determining its compliance with the relevant JCAHO *standards* and its eligibility for *accreditation.*

focused survey: A survey which examines only the institution's progress with respect to action on *Type I recommendations* (contingencies). Type I recommendations, given in the institution's survey report, are so urgent that the institution must take appropriate action on or before the dates specified by JCAHO or risk loss of *accreditation.*

S

tailored survey: A single *accreditation survey* for an institution that carries out services which fall under more than one of the JCAHO *standards manuals*. For example, an acute care hospital may also provide home health care services, for which there is a separate JCAHO manual.

surveyor: The title given an individual from the *Joint Commission on the Accreditation of Healthcare Organizations (JCAHO)* who performs on-site inspection and examination of hospitals and other institutions as a part of the *accreditation* process.

symptom: A disturbance of appearance or function or sensation of which the patient is or could be aware. If the disturbance can only be detected by the physician or other observer, it is called a "sign." Those disturbances which must be elicited by laboratory, X-ray, or other diagnostic procedures, or by response to therapy, are called "findings."

symptom complex: A group of *symptoms* which occur together, and which may or may not be characteristic of a specific disease.

syndrome: A pattern of *signs* and *symptoms* which occur together and form a picture of a given disease.

system (1): One of the functional components of the body, for example, the respiratory (breathing) system or the circulatory (heart and blood vessels) system.

system (2): A process by which a complex of people and machines (and other essential resources) work together in an orderly fashion to accomplish a given task.

Systeme International (SI) units: The international measurement system, commonly referred to as the "metric system." The SI is used by most of the world, and a transition from the "English system" to SI is underway in the United States. The system is based on seven base units, from which all other measurements are derived:

length:	meter
mass:	kilogram
time:	second
amount of substance:	mole
thermodynamic temperature:	kelvin
electric current:	ampere
luminous intensity:	candela

Examples of three derived units are:

area:	square meters
volume:	cubic meters
density:	kilograms per cubic meter

The change to SI units will ultimately improve the quality of medical care by providing direct correlation between laboratory values and dosages of drugs, for example. In addition, it will facilitate communication between sciences and between nations.

The effort to change the thinking of physicians and others will require years of work and must be carefully done so that errors do not result (for example, misunderstanding of drug dosages or laboratory results reported in SI units). Extensive educational efforts are underway to make the transition safe and effective. A first step, for example, is the use of SI units in the *Journal of the American Medical Association (JAMA)* and the other clinical journals published by the *American Medical Association (AMA)*, effective in July 1986. The SI units for clinical laboratory data are shown in parentheses following the English system units throughout the journals.

S

systemic: A term which, in referring to a disease, means a disease that affects the body as a whole.

systems analysis: An analysis of the resources (personnel, facilities, equipment, materials, funds, and other elements), organization, administration, procedures, and policies needed to carry out a given task. The analysis typically addresses alternatives in each category, and their relative *efficiency* and *effectiveness*.

systems review: The traditional method of organizing the *medical record* under headings such as "respiratory," "past illnesses," or "cardiac." A newer method, the *problem oriented medical record (POMR)*, instead traces each of the patient's *problems* separately.

T

tactics: A term derived from the military usage concerning actions which, while directed toward the large goal, are smaller in scale or scope than strategic actions. Tactics are those actions through which a "strategy" is carried out. Strategy is long-range, and lays out the nature and sequence of the steps to be taken to achieve the large goals of the organization. In traditional thinking, strategy should precede the development of the tactics with which it is implemented. A current insight is that a successful strategy can only be developed after the available tactics are assessed and used to their maximum.

tail coverage: See *insurance coverage*.

tailgate pricing: A pejorative term used to describe pricing which the commentator feels simply responds to the demand of the market (competition) at the moment, that is, pricing which is not based on costs or a consistent pricing policy.

task force: A group of persons established to carry out a specific task. Its assignment is usually fact-finding or advisory. A time limit is typically given by the appointing authority for completion of the task, and upon its completion the task force is automatically disbanded. A task force is not to be confused with a committee, which is a standing body, or a *quality circle*, which selects its own tasks.

Tax Equity and Fiscal Responsibility Act (TEFRA): A 1982 federal act which, in its provisions pertaining to Medicare and Medicaid, contained provisions limiting hospital costs.

taxonomy: An orderly classification of entities according to their logical relationships with respect to a particular viewpoint, e.g., diagnoses would have different relationships if the point of view were their etiology (cause) or their physiological manifestations (symptoms, for example).

TB unit: See *tuberculosis unit*.

team nursing: A type of organization of *nursing services* in which a team headed by a *registered nurse (RN)*, and with other registered nurses and ancillary personnel, cares for an assigned group of patients in a *patient care unit*. A team of four to six members gives care to from 15 to 25 patients. Each duty shift has its own team, with a team leader who assigns patients to team members for care according to the complexity of need and the team members' capability. See also *primary nursing*.

technician: A specialist in the technical details of a subject or process. A *technologist* is skilled in the application of knowledge for practical purposes. The distinction between the terms "technician" and "technologist" is not clear, particularly when they are used in the health care field.

technologist: A person skilled in the application of knowledge for practical purposes. A *technician* is a specialist in the technical details of a process or subject. The distinction between the terms "technician" and "technologist" is not clear, particularly when they are used in the health care field.

technology assessment: The process of describing and analyzing specific technologies from various viewpoints: their effectiveness, cost, safety, dissemination, training required for their use, effects on public policy and financing, relative merits of various technologies used for the same purpose, disciplines involved, impact on human resources, effects on organizations, interactions between people and technologies, ethical implications, and the like.

TEFRA: See *Tax Equity and Fiscal Responsibility Act*.

telecommunications department: The hospital department responsible for the technical aspects of telephone, computer wiring (intra-

T

and inter-building), intercommunication, radio, paging, and other communications systems and networks (excluding computer networks).

telecommunications manager: A person who is in charge of the technical aspects of telephone, computer wiring (intra- and inter-building), radio, paging, and other communications systems and networks (excluding computer networks).

teleconference: A conference held via telecommunication equipment among individuals who are physically separated (perhaps by thousands of miles). Ordinarily the individuals all participate in the "conversation" interactively, that is, each in response to the input of the others. Telecommunication equipment includes computers (or computer terminals), telephones, and television. In the health care field, one of the earliest applications of teleconferencing was in continuing medical (and other professional) education, usually with the educator at an education center, and the students in their hospitals or other settings. Teleconferencing may also be used, for example, for official meetings, such as governing body meetings (provided the institution's bylaws and relevant statutes permit).

telepathology: A technique for sending the image seen through a microscope over a distance to a television monitor. A television camera records the image, which is then transmitted by wire or radio to a remote site where the pathologist can examine the image as though she were looking directly through the viewing microscope. The microscope must be a special, robotically controlled device, so that the pathologist at the remote location can move the slide about and examine various areas, vary the magnification, change the brightness, introduce optical filters, and focus, just as though she were actually seated at an optical microscope.

This new technique makes possible a number of advances in the quality of care, including providing pathology services to isolated areas, *consultations*, and instant *second opinions*. Further possibilities include the use of the technique in the examination of entire organs as well as microscopic sections.

term: A word or phrase used for naming an entity (item) in a universe.

terminal care: Care for a patient in the terminal stages of her illness; care for a dying patient.

terminal care document: See *living will*.

tertiary care: Care of a highly technical and specialized nature, provided in a medical center (usually one affiliated with a university), for patients with unusually severe, complex, or uncommon problems. Tertiary care is the highest level of care.

test: A term without specific definition which generally refers to a laboratory procedure.

therapeutic: Pertaining to therapy (*treatment*).

therapeutic recreation specialist: A person who works either with individual patients or with patient populations in order to provide recreation for therapeutic (*treatment*) purposes. Synonym(s): activities therapist, recreation therapist.

therapy: *Treatment*.   A term which, when used alone, as in "the patient is undergoing therapy," means that the patient is being treated. When used with a modifier, as in "speech therapy," the term means a specific treatment method or technique.

thermogram: An *image* made by *thermography*, a process for recording differences in the temperatures of body tissues.

thermography: A diagnostic technique which detects and records heat in tissues. Tissues in different states of chemical activity have different temperatures, and mapping the pattern of temperatures is used, for example, in efforts to find tumors in breasts.

third party: A term used in connection with health care *financing (2)*. The first and second parties are the patient and the provider. The third party is a *payer* who is neither of these. Examples are Blue Cross and Blue Shield, commercial insurance, and government.

third-party administrator (TPA):   An organization which administers health care *benefits* (and other employee benefits), primarily for corporations which are self-insured. The third-party administrator's services include *claims review* and *claims processing*, primarily of medical claims but also dental, disability, workers' compensation, life insurance, and pension claims.

third party payer: A *payer* who neither receives nor gives the care (the patient and the provider are the first two parties). The third party payer is usually an insurance company, a *prepayment plan*, or a government *agency (1)*. Organizations which are self-insured are also considered third parties.

thoracic surgery: The branch of surgery dealing with surgery of and in the chest. One of the medical specialties for which *residency* programs have been approved by the Accreditation Council for Graduate Medical Education (ACGME). See *specialty*.

tie-in sale: See *tying arrangement*.

tissue: A collection of *cells* of the same type, along with the materials between them, which have a similar function. Muscle, bone, and blood are examples of tissues. An *organ* may be made up of several kinds of tissues.

tissue bank: A facility for collecting, cataloging, storing, and distributing body *tissues* for use in surgery. Bone, for example, is a commonly stored tissue. While the term "tissue" may cover entire *organs*, organs ordinarily are immediately transplanted rather than banked. The tissues stored in a tissue bank are primarily human. As implantation and transplantation technology advance, an increasing variety of tissues may be expected to be banked, rather than being available only by immediate transfer from donor to recipient. A concomitant development in health care has been the establishment of regional (and national and international) communications networks which help bring together available tissues (and organs) and people who need them.

tissue committee: A committee of the *medical staff* whose purpose is to review the appropriateness of the surgery performed in the hospital. The "tissue committee" got its name because many surgical procedures result in the removal of *tissue*, which is then examined by a pathologist, who formally reports on her findings.

These findings provide hindsight for the surgeon. The tissue committee does not confine itself to operations involving tissue removal, but rather considers the appropriateness of all surgery. See also *unjustified* and *unnecessary surgery* under *surgery (1)*.

Title XIX: See *Medicaid*.

Title XVIII: See *Medicare*.

TLC: Tender, loving care.

TNM system: See *tumor, node, metastases system*.

tort: A wrong for which the law provides a civil remedy, and which is not a breach of contract (contracts are covered by a separate body of laws). A person who commits an act which is a tort is legally liable (responsible) to anyone injured by the act. "Civil remedy" means that the person doing the legal "wrong" must pay the victim money to make good her losses. (A few other civil remedies exist, which are less often used; for example, if A publishes a defamatory statement about B, A may be required to print a retraction.)

An act which is a tort may also be a crime. For example, if someone steals a car, she can be prosecuted by the state (the public) for the crime of theft, and possibly pay a fine or go to jail. She can also, however, be sued by the car's owner for the tort of "conversion" (taking another's property without his permission).

There are three basic kinds of torts: intentional torts, negligence, and strict liability. Torts which are significant in health care include negligence (which includes malpractice), defamation, invasion of privacy, false imprisonment, abuse of process, and fraud.

prima facie tort: A tort "on the face of it." A legal term which describes a tort which has no legal classification, but which the law will recognize on the facts of a case because there should be a remedy. This is a *cause of action* which has been defined by Justice Holmes as "the intentional infliction of harm, resulting in damage, without excuse or justification, by an act or series of acts which would otherwise be lawful, and which acts do not fall within the categories of traditional tort." *Aikens v. Wisconsin*, 195 U.S. 194 (1904).

T

tortfeasor: A person who commits a *tort*.

tortious interference with business relationship: A *tort* in which someone wrongfully interferes with a business relationship and causes someone else an economic loss, such as a broken contract, loss of job or position, or suspension from the medical staff.

total quality management (TQM): See *quality management*.

toxicology: The study of poisons, their effects, their detection, and the treatment of poisoned individuals.

TPA: See *third-party administrator*.

TPR (1): See *third party reimbursement*.

TPR (2): Hospital jargon meaning "temperature (reading), pulse (rate), and respiration (rate)."

TQM: Total quality management. See *quality management*.

training coordinator: An individual in an institution who has responsibility for coordinating *inservice* training programs.

transfer: The formal shifting of responsibility for the care of a patient from one physician to another, from one institution to another, or from one unit of the hospital to another. There are specific Medicare payment implications depending on the type of transfer. In general, the following types of institutional transfer are recognized:

discharge transfer: A transfer from one institution to another; the patient is discharged from one and admitted to the other.

intrahospital transfer: A transfer within the same hospital (1) from one patient care unit to another, (2) from one clinical service to another, or (3) from the care of one physician to another.

transfer in: A term used in Medicare for a patient admitted to the hospital by transfer from another *short-term hospital* (or "*nonexempt distinct part unit*" of the same hospital) for whose care the hospital is to receive a portion of the *Diagnosis Related Group (DRG)* "price" under the formula prescribed by the *prospective payment system.*

transfer out: A term used in Medicare for a patient transferred from the hospital (or from a *"nonexempt distinct part unit"* of the same hospital) directly to another *short-term hospital* (or to another "nonexempt distinct part unit" of the same hospital) and for whose care the recipient hospital or unit is to receive a portion of the *Diagnosis Related Group (DRG)* "price" under the formula prescribed by the *prospective payment system (PPS).*

transfer agreement: A formal agreement between two institutions regarding the conditions under which there can be *transfer* of patients between them and the exchange of clinical information on the patients.

transfusion hepatitis: See *hepatitis B.*

transitional care: A term covering care which is not *acute care* and not *long-term care.* "Transitional care" includes care in postacute convalescence, rehabilitation, and psychiatric care, whether given within acute or long-term care facilities, or in separate programs or facilities.

transitional year: A type of medical *residency* with the purpose of providing a balanced experience in a variety of (two or more) clinical disciplines. The name is somewhat misleading because, rather than being used by physicians seeking to change from one specialty to another, most of the transitional year positions are occupied by physicians in their first year of graduate medical education. In addition to the 65 (1990) medical specialty programs approved by the Accreditation Council for Graduate Medical Education (ACGME), ACGME also approves transitional year programs. For a list of all medical specialties, see *specialty.*

transplant: To move one living part of the body to another, or from one individual (the "donor") to another. The organ or tissue transplanted is called an "allograft" if from a donor, and an "autograft" (or "homograft") if from the same individual. The term "transplant" may also be used as a noun to indicate the tissue or organ which is transplanted. Synonym(s): graft. See also *implant.*

trauma: A wound or injury. Although one can speak, properly, of psychic trauma, the term in health care usage ordinarily refers to physical injury. Thus "trauma centers" are set up to care for victims of accidents and other violence.

trauma center: A center for the *emergency* and specialized care of patients who are injured. A trauma center may also be used for patients who are critically ill. It may be within a hospital, where it may be called either a "trauma center" or a "trauma unit," or it may be *free-standing*.

treatment: A term which, when used in "treatment of the patient," means any or all elements of the care of the patient for the correction or relief of the patient's problem. When used in a phrase such as "antibiotic treatment," the term means a specific method or technique. Also called therapy.

extraordinary treatment: Medical treatment or care which does not offer a reasonable hope of benefit to the patient, or which cannot be accomplished without excessive pain, expense, or other great burden. The decision whether to provide extraordinary treatment is basically an ethical determination; also, whether treatment is "extraordinary" can only be determined in relation to the condition of the patient and the *prognosis*.

treble damages: See *damages*.

tree structure: A term used by the United States National Library of Medicine (NLM) in its annual *Medical Subject Headings (MeSH)* publication. Each document in the biomedical literature in the library has been classified to *all the subjects* to which it pertains according to a hierarchical list of subjects reviewed and revised annually by NLM. The list is published in two forms, an alphabetical list of the subjects along with their reference code numbers (MeSH numbers), and a "tabular list," called the tree structure, in which the subjects are categorized and subdivided, often to several levels, according to the hierarchical arrangement of the classification. It is this branching structure of the hierarchies which gives the tree structure its name.

The tree structure is the basis of searching for a given subject in the literature, because it groups together the documents pertaining to each subject. Each tree structure is itself a *classification (1)* of the subjects within its purview. Note that a given document usually will be found in more than one branch of the tree, that is, under more than one heading, having been classified to as many subjects as logically necessary.

triage: Sorting or classification of patients according to the nature and urgency of their illnesses or injuries, and assigning priorities for treatment.

Tringa: A genus in the sandpiper bird family. Tringa includes the Greater and Lesser Yellowlegs.

triple option: An insurance "package" offered to employers. The three portions are an *indemnity* program, a *health maintenance organization (HMO)*, and a *preferred provider option (PPO)*.

trustee: A member of the *governing body* when that body is called a board of trustees. When the governing body is called the board of directors, then each member is called a "director."

tuberculosis unit (TB unit): A *patient care unit* for the care of patients with tuberculosis.

tumor: An abnormal growth of tissue which is not a temporary response to inflammation or injury, and which stems from tissue which is already in place. Certain kinds of tumors possess the potential for unlimited growth, and are called "malignant," or "cancers." Other kinds do not have this potential, and are called "benign."

tumor staging: See *staging (2)*.

tumor, node, metastases (TNM) system: A method of *staging tumors*.

tying arrangement: Requiring a buyer to purchase a second product or service in order to get the first product. Tying arrangements may violate the federal *antitrust* laws. Synonym(s): tie-in sale.

U

UBIT: See *unrelated business income tax.*

UCC: See *Uniform Commercial Code.*

UGME: Undergraduate medical education. See *medical education.*

UHDDS: See *Uniform Hospital Discharge Data Set.*

ultra vires: "Outside the powers." A legal term referring to activities of a *corporation* which it is not authorized to do either by its charter or the laws of the state in which it is incorporated.

ultrasound: Sound with a pitch above human hearing (above 20,000 Hz). Ultrasound is used in an *imaging* technique to visualize internal structures by recording the reflection of the sound waves by the tissues. Ultrasound is also used in some forms of therapy, such as the liquidizing of cataracts and their removal by suction, a process called "phacoemulsufication."

ultrasound images: Images (pictures) of internal body structures, produced by recording (via computer) the sounds wave reflected from the body structures. *Ultrasound* waves are sound waves higher in frequency than the range of human hearing.

umbrella coverage: See *insurance coverage.*

unbundling: Selling individual components of a service or product separately rather than as a package. Sometimes unbundling is

442

done for the convenience of the customer, but often it is done in order to sell the same components for a greater total price than if they were packaged together (bundled). For example, a complete automobile can be purchased for far less than its parts. In health care, the care of a fracture, for example, may be priced to include the diagnosis, treatment, and aftercare as single package (bundled); alternatively, diagnosis, setting of the fracture, applying the cast, removing the cast, and other services may be priced individually (unbundled).

uncompensated care: Care for which no payment is expected or no charge is made.

undergraduate: A student in an academic institution who has not achieved a given degree. The term most often refers to an individual before the bachelor's degree, but in medicine, the degree in question is the *Doctor of Medicine (MD)* or *Doctor of Osteopathy (DO)* degree.

Uniform Commercial Code (UCC): A compilation of laws governing commercial transactions including sales of goods, banking transactions, and secured transactions for personal property. The Code has been adopted, with minor modifications, by all 50 states (Louisiana did not adopt the UCC in its entirety), the District of Columbia, Guam, and the Virgin Islands. The UCC has greatly facilitated interstate commerce.

Uniform Hospital Discharge Data Set (UHDDS): The items of *medical record* information (*data set*) required by the federal government as the medical content of the patient's bill under Medicare. Assignment to a *Diagnosis Related Group (DRG)* is made from this data set by the *fiscal intermediary*. UHDDS contains, among other data, patient age, sex, and up to five diagnoses and four procedures. Both diagnoses and procedures are expressed not in words but in the numerical *category codes* of *International Classification of Disease, Ninth Revision, Clinical Modification (ICD-9-CM)*.

uniform reporting: Reporting of patient care information, financial information, or both under uniform definitions (and sometimes formats) in order to permit comparisons among hospitals or physicians.

U

unit: See *patient care unit (PCU)*.

unit clerk: A person who performs clerical duties in a *patient care unit*. Synonym(s): ward clerk, unit secretary.

unit manager: The person in charge of a *patient care unit*. Synonym(s): ward manager.

unit record: A *medical record* (file) in which are kept the records of all hospitalizations of the individual. This is the preferred method of filing of medical records.

unit record system: The system for filing *medical records* in which a separate file is kept for each individual patient, and the medical records of all hospitalizations of that individual are placed in the one file.

unit secretary: See *unit clerk*.

United Network for Organ Sharing (UNOS): A national organ *transplant* network. This network is under contract to the Health Care Financing Administration (HCFA) to coordinate United States organ procurement activities.

United States Pharmacopeia (USP): The *Pharmacopeia of the United States of America* (also called the *United States Pharmacopeia (USP)*), a publication of the United States Pharmacopeia Convention (USPC), originally (1820) issued every ten years, now every five years. The volume, which was made a legal standard in 1907, contains authoritative discussion on various drugs and other agents, directions for their preparation, and requirements as to their potency and purity.

UNOS: See *United Network for Organ Sharing*.

unrelated business income tax (UBIT): Tax paid by a *nonprofit corporation* on the profits of activities which are not related to the nonprofit purpose of the corporation. A nonprofit corporation is normally exempt from taxation, but may engage in profit-making activities and pay taxes on those, while preserving its tax-exempt status, by complying with specific federal tax law requirements regarding unrelated business income.

upcoding: Changing the *coding* of a patient's diagnoses (and perhaps operations) in order to obtain a higher payment for the *services (1)* rendered.

UR (1): See *utilization review*.

UR (2): See *Utilization Review*.

UR committee: See *utilization review committee*.

UR coordinator: See *utilization review coordinator*.

urgent: A term that, in regard to a patient's condition, refers to a degree of illness which is less severe than an *emergency*, but which requires care within a reasonably short time (more quickly than *elective* care).

urgent care center: A sort of competitor of an *emergency department*, but presumably for less "emergent" problems. The term has no legal (or regulatory) definition as yet. Sometimes it is stated that a *facility (2)*, to be called an "urgent care center," must have certain laboratory and X-ray services, but must not hold itself out as ready for emergencies such as those brought by ambulance or to provide continuity of care. An urgent care center may be free-standing or a part of another facility.

urology: The branch of medicine dealing with diseases and disorders of the genitourinary tract in males and females, and with the reproductive system in males. One of the medical specialties for which *residency* programs have been approved by the Accreditation Council for Graduate Medical Education (ACGME). See *specialty*.

use effectiveness: When a treatment fails to achieve its intended results, the failure may be due to the method employed or its use. For example, a contraceptive failure may occur because the method was inadequate or because it really was not employed or

U

was employed improperly. Thus the "method effectiveness" or the "use effectiveness" may have been at fault, and the failure may have been a "method failure" or a "use failure."

use failure: When a treatment fails to achieve its intended results, the failure may be due to the method employed or its use. For example, a contraceptive failure may occur because the method was inadequate or because it really was not employed or was employed improperly. Thus the "method effectiveness" or the "use effectiveness" may have been at fault, and the failure may have been a "method failure" or a "use failure."

USFMG: United States foreign medical graduate. See *foreign medical graduate (FMG)*.

USP: See *United States Pharmacopeia*.

USPC: United States Pharmacopeia Convention. See *United States Pharmacopeia*.

Utilization Review (UR): The chapter giving the *standards* for this component of the hospital in the 1990 *Accreditation Manual for Hospitals (AMH)* of the *Joint Commission on the Accreditation of Healthcare Organizations (JCAHO)*.

utilization review committee (UR committee): A committee, made up primarily of *medical staff* members, designated to carry out the utilization review function, that is, reviewing the *appropriateness* of hospitalizations and of the *services (1)* used, and the *lengths of stay (LOSs)* of patients subject to such review.

utilization review coordinator (UR coordinator): A hospital employee, typically a *medical record professional* or a *nurse*, who coordinates the hospital's *utilization review* activities, gathers data from medical records and elsewhere for the use of the *utilization review committee* and others, and otherwise assists in utilization review. The UR coordinator may also have duties involving liaison with other community agencies regarding transfer of patients to other facilities or services, including home care.

V

vaccine: A preparation which, when introduced into a human or other animal, stimulates the development of *active immunity* against specific infections. Most vaccines are either (1) killed bacteria or viruses of strains which, when alive, are able to cause the disease in question, or (2) live bacteria or viruses of attenuated (weakened) strains of the disease-causing organism (closely related bacteria or viruses which are not able to cause the disease but are able to stimulate the production of immunity). Vaccines do not produce *passive immunity*; passive immunity is the result of introduction into the body of prefabricated immune serum against the disease in question.

VAD: See *ventricular assist device*.

vascular surgery: The branch of surgery dealing with the heart and blood vessels. One of the medical specialties for which *residency* programs have been approved by the Accreditation Council for Graduate Medical Education (ACGME). See *specialty*.

venereal disease: A *sexually transmitted disease*.

ventricular assist device (VAD): A mechanical device used to perform the pumping tasks of the heart during surgery or in an emergency while waiting for a heart transplant. This device does not replace the entire heart as does an artificial heart.

viable (1): Capable of living, as a baby born above a certain birth weight.

V

viable (2): Capable of being carried out or of succeeding, for example, "viable plans."

visit: In ordinary use a "visit" means, for example, the appearance of a patient in the emergency department or the appearance of a physician at the bedside. In health care, however, very specific definitions of "visit" are employed in calculation of statistics and in payment. Nevertheless, the use of the term "visit" is not uniform: the "visit" of a patient to an outpatient department in which a physician sees the patient, and then the patient goes to the laboratory and X-ray departments, may be considered one visit or three. Such definitions are often unique to the hospital, the departments involved, and the payment system; one must inquire as to exactly what is meant locally.

office visit: All *services (1)* provided a patient in the course of a single appearance for care at a physician's office.

outpatient visit (OP visit): All *services (1)* provided an *outpatient* in the course of a single appearance for care.

visiting nurse association (VNA): A private nonprofit organization with the purpose of providing *skilled nursing* and other health care *services (1)*, primarily in the home, on an hourly basis. Most VNAs are classified as *home health agencies*.

vital signs: A medical term referring to the patient's evidence of heart beat, breathing, and blood pressure. Synonym(s): life signs.

vital statistics: Statistics dealing with births, deaths, marriages, and divorces, compiled from official *registrations (3)* of these events.

VNA: See *visiting nurse association*.

vocational rehabilitation counselor: A person who counsels disabled individuals with respect to vocations and vocational training in order best to fit together the individual and a vocation suitable to her physical, mental, and emotional abilities.

voluntary hospital system: The national aggregate of *nonprofit* and *investor-owned hospitals* in the United States. As in the case of the

448

term *"American Hospital System,"* the voluntary hospital system is not a formal system, but a de facto one.

volunteer: A person who performs services without pay. In the hospital, *governing board* members are often volunteers, as are persons who provide *patient assistance services,* as well as amenities and revenue-producing services such as the library and gift shop.

inservice volunteer: A volunteer who performs services in the hospital which augment, but do not replace, those of paid personnel and professional staff.

volunteer services: Services provided by *volunteers.*

volunteer services department: A hospital department which coordinates *volunteer* services to the hospital.

voucher: A certificate which may be exchanged for a contract for care for a given period of time under a *prepayment* plan.

voucher system: A system in which Medicare *beneficiaries* use *vouchers* issued by the federal government to enroll in *health care plans* of their choice. Early in 1985 Congress enacted legislation permitting this approach to the provision of care for Medicare beneficiaries in an effort to introduce competition into the provision of health care. Under the voucher system, the beneficiary enrolls in a federally qualified health care plan, and payment is made directly to the care-providing organization in a predetermined, fixed amount in exchange for the beneficiary's voucher. Thus, the beneficiary decides which competing health care provider she believes will give the best *services (1)* (best quality, cheapest, most accessible, or with the most desirable amenities, for example) in exchange for the voucher. The beneficiary receives the services by enrolling in a health care plan, which might be a *health care organization (HCO),* a *health maintenance organization (HMO),* or some other organization set up to provide all the care benefits (outpatient, hospital, home care, and so on) required of a qualified program.

W

wage index: A component used by the *Health Care Financing Administration (HCFA)* in adjusting payments (prices) under the Medicare *prospective payment system (PPS)*. The wage index is derived by HCFA starting with data supplied by hospitals in response to a questionnaire; it takes into account normal work hours, as well as part-time and overtime work hours.

rural area wage index: A wage index computed by Medicare for hospitals it classifies as *rural hospitals*.

waiver (1): A voluntary giving up of a known right or benefit. To be legally effective, a waiver must be made intentionally by someone who understands what he is relinquishing.

waiver (2): A term used currently in connection with the exemption of a state from participating in the Medicare program under the *prospective payment system (PPS)*.

ward (1): A patient care room for more than four patients. A room for only one patient is a "private room"; a "semi-private room" holds two to four patients.

ward (2): A term sometimes applied to a *patient care unit* of a hospital.

ward (3): A person for whom a *guardian* or *conservator* has been appointed by a court, to care for and make decisions concerning the ward's person, property, or both. The ward is legally *incom-*

W

petent (1) to act on his own behalf, usually because of immaturity or lack of mental capacity.

ward clerk: See *unit clerk.*

ward manager: See *unit manager.*

waste: See *hazardous waste.*

WC: See *workers' compensation.*

Webster case: The first major United States Supreme Court abortion decision since *Roe v. Wade.* While *Webster* neither reexamined nor expressly overruled *Roe v. Wade,* the Court's opinion was divided (this means that the Justices did not all agree with one another), and showed a willingness to reexamine *Roe v. Wade* in an appropriate case. It is believed that states will now test the limits of *Roe v. Wade* with increasingly strict legislation on abortion.

In 1986, Missouri enacted a law which included: (1) a preamble declaring that life begins at conception and that unborn children have protectable interests; (2) a prohibition on the use of public facilities and employees to perform abortions not necessary to save the life of the mother; (3) a prohibition on the use of public funds for "encouraging or counseling" a woman to have an abortion not necessary to save her life; and (4) a requirement that the physician perform a test to determine *viability* of the *fetus* prior to performing an abortion after 20 weeks of gestation.

The United States Supreme Court upheld items (2) and (4) of the statute as constitutional (items (1) and (3) were not addressed by the Court for technical legal reasons). The Court ruled that the prohibition on public facilities and employees did not interfere with a woman's right to choose abortion, because she had the same choice she would have if the state had opted not to operate any health facilities. The Court also ruled that the requirement of testing for viability was valid because it furthered Missouri's interest in protecting potential human life, and Missouri had decided that viability was the point at which potential life must be safeguarded. Some Justices disagreed with the reasoning for the validity of the testing for viability requirement, and others disagreed that the requirement was constitutional. *Webster v. Reproductive Services,* 492 U.S. , 109 S.Ct. 3040 (1989).

W

wellness program: See *health promotion.*

wet location: An area of a building so designated because it often has standing water or because the floor is regularly drenched to a greater degree than with ordinary floor cleaning.

WHO: See *World Health Organization.*

wholistic health: A view of health as consisting of the health of the "whole" person—body, mind, and spirit. That view requires the coordinated attention to all three components by the several disciplines involved, and places major responsibility for health on the individual. Synonym(s): holistic health.

WIC: See *Women, Infants, and Children's Program.*

Women, Infants, and Children's Program (WIC): A federally funded program which provides specific food vouchers and nutrition education to "at risk" pregnant women and children five years old and under.

workers' compensation (WC): A system of compensating workers for on-the-job injuries, developed as an alternative to lawsuits by injured employees. The typical workers' compensation law compensates workers who suffer work-related injuries (regardless of fault), and provides that workers' compensation benefits are the "exclusive remedy," the only means of receiving compensation for work-related injuries and illnesses. Workers may therefore not sue their employers. Workers' compensation was formerly called workmen's compensation.

   In some states, workers' compensation also covers injuries or illnesses resulting from negligent treatment (by the employer) of work-related injuries or illness; in that case, workers' compensation is usually the exclusive remedy for the negligent treatment, and the worker-patient cannot sue the employer for *malpractice.* However, in some cases exceptions have been made to the exclusive remedy rule by application of the *dual capacity doctrine* and the *dual injury doctrine.* The dual capacity doctrine states that the employer who negligently provides health care wears two "hats"—employer and health care provider—and may be sued as health care provider. The dual injury doctrine allows a worker injured on the job and further injured by the employer's concealment of the workers' injury or illness (asbestos poisoning, for example) to sue the employer for the aggravated injuries. This doctrine recognizes two injuries: the first injury (the poisoning) which is governed by workers' compensation; and the second injury (the intentional concealment which aggravated the worker's illness), which is not governed by workers' compensation and could provide the basis for a lawsuit.

workmen's compensation: An obsolete term for *workers' compensation*.

World Health Organization (WHO): The division of the United Nations (UN) which is concerned with health.

WPR: See *written progress report*.

written progress report (WPR): A term used by the *Joint Commission on Accreditation of Healthcare Organizations (JCAHO)* for the documentation it requires of a facility which is attempting to "clear" a *Type I recommendation*. JCAHO gives general directions for organization of the WPR.

wrongful birth: A type of lawsuit concerning a baby who would not have been born but for the existence of professional *negligence*. A wrongful birth action is brought by the parents on their own behalf, as opposed to a *wrongful life* action, which is brought by or on behalf of the child. Wrongful birth cases, which involve the birth of both healthy and unhealthy children, may allege contraceptive failure or unsuccessful sterilization, the failure to diagnose pregnancy, unsuccessful abortion, the failure to warn the parents of genetic risks, or the failure to timely diagnose (or inform the parents about) a birth defect or disease of the fetus. Not all states permit wrongful birth suits.

wrongful death: A death for which there is legal *liability (1)*; for example, one caused by *professional negligence*. Deaths are treated differently than injuries in the legal system. For example, a different *statute of limitations* may apply to a wrongful death action than to a *negligence* action, even though negligence may have been the cause of the wrongful death. Also, some states limit the amount of recovery to a specific dollar amount (for example, $50,000) in a wrongful death action.

wrongful discharge: Termination of employment of an individual "employed at will" (an employee without a personal or union contract) when the discharge was against public policy, violated an implied contract, or was not carried out in "good faith and fair dealing." For example, firing an employee who reasonably refuses to do something dangerous may be against public policy.

wrongful life: A type of lawsuit concerning a baby who would not have been born but for the existence of *professional negligence*. A wrongful life action is brought by (or on behalf of) the baby, where the child is suffering from a birth defect or genetic or other disease, as opposed to a *wrongful birth* action, which is brought by the parents and where the child may be healthy. Wrongful life cases may involve the failure to warn the parents of genetic risks, failure of contraception or sterilization, unsuccessful abortion, or the failure to timely diagnose (or inform the parents about) a birth defect or disease of the fetus. Not all states permit wrongful life suits.

X

X-ray (1): Electromagnetic radiation in a certain portion of the electromagnetic spectrum, used for diagnostic and treatment purposes. Synonym(s): Roentgen ray.

X-ray (2): The process of exposing a person or object to *X-rays (1)* for the purpose of making an *image* on a sensitized surface of the transmission of the rays through the object.

X-ray (3): An *image* on a sensitized surface of the pattern of transmission of *X-rays (1)* through a person or object.

xenograft: An *organ* or *tissue implanted* (grafted) from one species to another. The Baby Fae case, in which the heart of a baboon was transplanted into a human baby, was a case in which a xenograft was used. Synonym(s): heterograft.

Z

ZEBRA: See *Zero Balanced Reimbursement Account.*

Zero Balanced Reimbursement Account (ZEBRA): A type of health care benefit plan provided by employers who are self-insured and pay for the care as it is given. The ceiling under such a plan is typically "unlimited." The Internal Revenue Service (IRS) has ruled that funds spent for a beneficiary (here an employee) under such a plan are taxable to the beneficiary, and that the employer is liable for withholding income tax on benefits, except for those benefits which are nontaxable under federal statutes. Synonym(s): cafeteria plan.

zeumatography: See *nuclear magnetic resonance imaging (NMRI).*

Production Notes

This second edition of *Health Care Terms* relied even more heavily on the use of microcomputers than did the first edition, which was published in 1986. Most of the work done on this book was done on IBM compatible computers, including an XT, an AT, and a 386.

In the first edition, the text was written and manipulated by the use of WordPerfect (versions 4.x) and Notebook II, a text oriented database program. The database software has been helpful since a certain amount of "housekeeping" data is kept with each term, in addition to the definition itself. When it came time to produce the book, the terms and their definitions were extracted from the database, typesetting codes were inserted using "macros," and the results were placed on standard 9-track computer tape. This tape was then sent to the book manufacturer whose typesetting machinery read the tape to set the type, and then manufactured the book itself.

The second edition proceeded in much the same way, except that the software involved has been updated on several occasions since 1986. In an effort to gain more control over the format and appearance of the book, as well as to keep costs down, the book's producers decided to extend the use of microcomputers to do the actual design, layout, and typesetting as well. The finished book is the product of commonly available tools in today's office. Ventura Publisher was used, running on an "ancient" but highly efficient XT compatible (built right here in Minnesota by PC Tech of Lake City) to combine, format, and print the text on a Hewlett Packard LaserJet III, using the optional PostScript cartridge. The pages were printed oversized and then reduced to 69 percent of their original size, raising the effective resolution of the type from 300 dpi (dots per inch) to over 400 dpi.

The cover was designed by Debora Slee using Ventura Publisher, and was then output by a service bureau on its PostScript compatible imagesetter to get a higher resolution (although the resolution was surprisingly good even at the lower 300 dpi). She also produced the *ICD* table using Ventura Publisher.

The "Quality Control/Quality Improvement" graphic was done by Roey Kirk (President, Roey Kirk Associates, Miami, FL) using MacDraw on an Apple Macintosh computer. Ms. Kirk adapted the graphic from artwork that had originally been manually produced according to Dr. Vergil Slee's specifications. She furnished the book's producers with a Macintosh disk containing an encapsulated PostScript (EPS) file which could be directly loaded into Ventura Publisher. A special disk controller card made by Central Point and installed in the XT was used to read the otherwise incompatible Macintosh disk format.

The various "Tringa bird" (sandpiper) graphics appearing in this book as the logo of Tringa Press were "scanned," using Logitech's hand held scanner, from artwork done manually years ago. The scanned images were then printed by Ventura Publisher either as "bit map" (paint) files, or converted into PostScript (draw) files via the "auto trace" feature of CorelDraw, a software program used to produce original designs and drawings.

The publisher is currently exploring the possibility of offering an electronic version of *Health Care Terms*, distributed on a computer disk. To make this a truly useful tool, a specific type of computer software known as "hypertext" would be used. This type of software allows the reader, with the aid of the computer, to see a defined term in a more meaningful context. The reader can easily and quickly explore related terms and concepts to gain a better understanding of the term initially looked up. Readers interested in such a possibility are encouraged to contact Tringa Press, P.O. Box 8181, St. Paul, Minnesota 55108.

Tringa Press
P.O. Box 8181, St. Paul, MN 55108

Order Form

Additional copies of *Health Care Terms* are available by mail from Tringa Press directly. The single copy price is $25.00. Quantity discounts are available at 20% for 2–4 copies; 40% for 5–19 copies; 50% for 20 or more copies. Prepaid orders are shipped free, either by U.S. Postal Service book rate, or by UPS ground, depending on weight and distance. While most orders are shipped within 48 hours after receipt of the order, please allow three to four weeks for delivery. Special shipping requests can be accommodated if sufficient details are included with your order.

Name:		
Title:		
Institution:		
Address:		
City, State, Zip:		
Quantity ordered:	books.	
@ $25.00 per copy =		
Discount for	2–4 copies:	-20%
	5–19 copies:	-40%
	20 or more copies:	-50%
Less quantity discount from above schedule: (		)
Minnesota non-exempt residents add 6% sales tax:		
Tax exempt number, if applicable:		
Total amount of order:		
☐ My check is enclosed. ☐ Please bill me; add postage & handling.		